Francis John Curtis

An Investigation of the Rimes and Phonology of the Middle-Scotch Romance Clariodus

A Contribution to the History of the English Language in Scotland

Francis John Curtis

An Investigation of the Rimes and Phonology of the Middle-Scotch Romance Clariodus
A Contribution to the History of the English Language in Scotland

ISBN/EAN: 9783337412463

Printed in Europe, USA, Canada, Australia, Japan

Cover: Foto ©Thomas Meinert / pixelio.de

More available books at www.hansebooks.com

AN INVESTIGATION OF THE RIMES
AND
PHONOLOGY OF THE MIDDLE-SCOTCH ROMANCE
CLARIODUS.

A CONTRIBUTION TO THE HISTORY OF THE
ENGLISH LANGUAGE IN SCOTLAND.

DISSERTATION

PRESENTED TO THE PHILOSOPHICAL FACULTY

OF THE

UNIVERSITY OF HEIDELBERG

FOR THE ACQUISITION OF THE

DEGREE OF DOCTOR OF PHILOSOPHY

BY

FRANCIS JOHN CURTIS

OF BLANDFORD, ENGLAND.

HALLE,
EHRHARDT KARRAS, PRINTER.
1894.

REPRINTED FROM "ANGLIA" VOLS. 4 AND 5 N F

AN INVESTIGATION OF THE RIMES AND PHONOLOGY OF THE MIDDLE-SCOTCH ROMANCE CLARIODUS.

A CONTRIBUTION TO THE HISTORY OF THE ENGLISH LANGUAGE IN SCOTLAND.

Texts and Works consulted and referred to in the following treatise.

(The abbreviations under which they are referred to are given in brackets.)

Scotch.
A. Texts.

Morte Arthure, ed. Brock, EETS. 8 (**Morte A.**). Bruce, ed. Skeat, EETS. Ext. Ser. 11, 21, 29, 55 — (quoted by number of book and line) (**Bruce**). — Scotch Legends, ed. by Horstmann as, 'Barbour's des schottischen Nationaldichters Legendensammlung', 2 vols. Heilbronn 1881. (only the 1st vol. is quoted by *page & line*) (**Sc. Leg.**). Trojan War — in vol. 2 of the foregoing (**Troj. W.**). Wyntown, Orygynale Cronykil of Scotland. (Unfortunately no complete edit. of this work was at my disposal) (**Wynt**). James I, The Kingis Quair, ed. Skeat, Sc. T. Soc. (**K. Q.**). Henry the Minstrel, Schir William Wallace, ed. Moir, Sc. T. Soc. (**Wall.**). The knightly tale of golagros and gawane, ed. Trautmann in Anglia, II, 395 ff. (**Gol.**). Lancelot of the Laik, ed. Skeat, EETS. 6 (**Lanc.**). Ratis Raving and other Moral & Religious Pieces, &c., ed. Lumby, EETS. 43 (**Rat. Rav.**). William Dunbar, Poems, ed. Small, Sc. T. Soc. (quoted by number of poem and line in Small's edit.) (**Dunb.**). Douglas, The Poetical Works of Gavin Douglas, ed. Small, 4 vols. Edinburgh, 1874 (quoted by vol., page & line) (**Dougl.**). The Complaynt of Scotlande, ed. Murray, EETS. Ext. Ser. 17, 18 (**Compl. Sc.**). John Gau, The Richt Vay to the Kingdom of Heuine, ed. Law, Sc. T. Soc. (**Gau**). Sir David Lyndesay's Works, EETS. 11, 19, 35, 37, 47 (**Lynd.**): Johne Rolland, The Court of Venus, ed. Gregor, Sc. T. Soc. (**Roll. C. V.**). Satirical Poems of the Time of the Reformation, ed. Cranstoun. (**Satir. P.**). Winzet, Certain Tractates, &c., ed. Hewitson, Sc. T. Soc. (**Winz.**). Leslie's Historie of Scotland, transl. by James Dalrymple, ed. Cody, Sc. T. Soc. (**Lesl.**) Alexander Montgomerie, Poems, ed. Cranstoun, Sc. T. Soc. (**Montg.**) Roswall and Lillian, ed. Lengert, Engl. Stud. vol. 16 (**Rosw.**). Irving, History of Scotish Poetry, Edinburgh, 1861 (containing numerous extracts which are sometimes quoted) (**Irving**).

1

B. Treatises on Grammar, Phonology, &c.

Murray, The Dialect of the Southern Counties of Scotland. London, 1873. **(Murray, DSS.)** Wackerzapp, Geschichte der Ablaute der starken Zeitwörter innerhalb des Nordenglischen. Münster, 1890. **(Wackerzapp).** Buss, Sind die von Horstmann herausgegebenen schottischen Legenden ein Werk Barbere's? Halle, 1886, also in Anglia 9, p. 490 ff. **(Buss).** Wischmann, Untersuchungen über das Kingis Quair. Wismar, 1887. **(Wischmann).** Noltemeier, Ueber die Sprache des Gedichtes 'The knightly tale of golagros and gawane'. Marburg, 1889. **(Noltemeier).** Kaufmann, Traité de la langue du poète écossais William Dunbar. Bonn, 1873. **(Kaufmann).** Collin, An Essay on the Scoto-English Dialect. Lund, 1862. **(Collin).** Regel, An inquiry into the Phonetic peculiarities of Barbour's Bruce. Gera, 1877. **(Regel).** Gregor, Glossary of words in the Banffshire Dialect. — Dialect Society. Also the grammatical introductions or closing words to some of the above text-editions: e. g. Bruce **(Skeat, Bruce).** Kingis Quair **(Skeat, K. Q.).** Lancelot **(Skeat, Lanc.).** Ratis Raving **(Lumby, Rat. Rav.).** Complaynt of Scotlande **(Murray, Compl. Sc.).**

Northern English.

A. Texts.

Sir Tristrem, ed. Kölbing. Heilbronn, 1883. ed. McNeill, Sc. T. Soc. **(Sir Tr.).** Cursor Mundi, ed. Morris, EETS. 57, 59, 62, 66, 68 **(Curs. M.).** Northern Legends, ed. Horstmann, Altengl. Legenden, Neue Folge **(Northⁿ Leg.).** York Mystery Plays, ed. L. Toulmin Smith. Oxford, 1885 **(York P.).** Hampole, Pricke of Conscience, ed. Morris, Philolog. Soc. 1863 **(Hamp., P. C.).** Octavian, ed. Sarrazin, Altengl. Bibliothek, III. Heilbronn, 1885 **(Octav.).** Rauf Coilzear, Roland, Otuell, &c., ed. Herrtage, EETS, Ext. Ser. 39 **(Rauf C., Rol., Ot.).** Sege off Melayne, ed. Herrtage, EETS. Ext. Ser. 35 **(Mel.).** Thomas of Erceldonne, ed. Brandl. Berlin, 1880 **(Th. Erc.).** Regula beati benedicti, ed. Büddeker, Engl. Stud. II, 61 **(Bened.).** Lay Folks' Mass Book, ed. Simmons, EETS, 71 **(Mass B.)** Religious Pieces in Prose & Verse, ed. Perry, EETS, 26 **(Relig. P.).** Henry Bradshawe's Life of St. Werburghe, ed. Horstmann, EETS. 88. **(St. Werb.).** The Wars of Alexander, ed. Skeat, EETS, Ext. Ser. 47 **(Wars Alex.).** Guy of Warwick, ed. Zupitza, EETS. Ext. Ser. 25, 26, 29 **(Guy W.).** The Gospels in Anglosaxon & Northumbrian Versions, &c., ed. Skeat. Cambridge, 1878, &c. Die vier Evangelien in alt-nordhumbrischer Sprache, ed. Bouterwek. Gütersloh, 1857.

B. Treatises on Phonology, &c.

Caro, Horn Childe & Maiden Rimnhild. Breslau, 1886 **(Caro, Horn Ch.).** Schlüter, Sprache und Metrik der mittelenglischen weltlichen u. geistlichen lyrischen Lieder des MS. Harl. 2253. Braunschweig, 1884 **(Schlüter, Lyric. P.).** Wende, Ueberlieferung und Sprache der mittelenglischen Version des Psalters, &c. Breslau, 1884 **(Wende, Surt. Ps).** Perrin, Ueber Thomas Castelford's Chronik von England. Boston, 1890 **(Perrin, Th. Castelf.).** Kamann, Ueber Quellen und Sprache der York Plays. Halle, 1887 **(Kamann).** Schleich, Ywain und Gawain. 1887 **(Schleich, Yw. Gaw.).** Ullmann, Studien zu Richard Rolle de Hampole. Heilbronn, 1883 **(Ullmann, Hamp.).** M. Adler und M. Ka-

Iuza, Studien zu Richard Rolle de Hampole, Engl. Stud. X, 215 (**Adler & Kal.**). Dannenberg, Metrik und Sprache der mittelenglischen Romanze The Sege off Melayne. Göttingen, 1890 (**Dannenberg**). Zielke, Untersuchungen zu Sir Eglamour of Artois. Kiel, 1889 (**Zielke, Sir Egl.**). Böddeker, Ueber die Sprache der Benedictinerregel, Engl. Stud. II, 344 (**Böddeker**). Ellinger, Ueber die sprachlichen und metrischen Eigentümlichkeiten in 'The Romance of Sir Perceval of Galles'. Troppau, 1889 (**Ellinger, Sir Perc.**). Wilda, Ueber die örtliche Verbreitung d. zwölfzeiligen Schweifreimstrophe in England. Breslau, 1887 (**Wilda**). Hilmer, Zur altnordhumbrischen Laut- und Flexionslehre. Goslar, 1880 (**Hilmer**). Also the introductions to some of the above mentioned texts, e. g. Sir Tristrem (**Kölbing, Sir Tr.**). York Plays (**Smith, Y. P.**). Hampole, P. C. (**Morris, Hamp.**). Octavian (**Sarrazin**). Thomas of Erceldoune (**Brandl**).

NW Midland.

Ipomedon, ed. Kölbing, with introduction (**Kölbing, Ipom.**) Fick, Zum mittelenglischen Gedicht von der Perle. Kiel, 1885 (**Fick**). Knigge, Die Sprache des Dichters von Sir Gawain and the Green Knight, &c. Marburg, 1885 (**Knigge**).

NE Midland.

Brate, Nordische Lehnwörter im Ormulum. Halle, 1884 (**Brate**). Heesch Debate of the Body and the Soul. Kiel, 1884 (**Heesch, Deb. Body & S.**). Kölbing, Amis & Amiloun, Altengl. Bibliothek II. Heilbronn, 1884 (**Kölbing, Am.**). Brandl, Review of the preceding in the Anzeiger für deutsches Altertum, 13, 92 ff. Scholle, Laurence Minots Lieder. Strassburg, 1884 (**Scholle**). Schipper, Englische Alexiuslegenden, in Quellen und Forschungen, 20 (**Schipper, Alex.**) Lüdtke, Erl of Tolous, Sammlung englischer Denkmäler III. (**Lüdtke, Erl. Tol.**). Adam, Ueber Sir Torrent of Portyngale. Görlitz, 1887 (**Adam, Sir Torr.**). Kirschten, Ueberlieferung und Sprache der mittelenglischen Romanze 'The lyfe of Ipomydon'. Marburg, 1885 (**Kirschten**).

SE Midland.

ten Brink, Chaucers Sprache und Verskunst. Leipzig, 1884 (**t. Br.**). Morsbach, Ueber den Ursprung der neuenglischen Schriftsprache. Heilbronn, 1888 (**Morsb.**). Menze, Der ostmittelländische Dialekt. Cöthen, 1889 (**Menze**). Münster, Untersuchungen zu Thomas Chestre's Launfal. Kiel, 1886 (**Münster, Launf.**). Hoofe, Lautuntersuchungen zu Osbern Bokenham's Legenden. Altenburg, 1885 (**Hoofe, Bokenh.**). Hattendorf, Sprache und Dialekt der spätmittelenglischen Romans of Partenay. Hildesheim, 1887 (**Hattendorf, Partenay**). Hausknecht, The Sowdone of Babylone. EETS. Ext. Ser. 38 (**Hausknecht, Sowd. Bab.**). Hilmer, Ueber die Sprache der altenglischen Story of Genesis and Exodus. Sondershausen, 1876 (**Hilmer, Gen. Ex.**).

Southern dialects.

Bülbring, Geschichte der Ablaute der starken Zeitwörter innerhalb des Südenglischen, Quellen und Forschungen 63 (**Bülbring**). Pabst, Die Sprache der mittelenglischen Reimchronik des Robert von Gloucester. Berlin, 1889 (**Pabst, Rob. Gl.**). Mohr, Sprachliche Untersuchungen zu den

1*

mittelenglischen Legenden aus Gloucestershire. Bonn, 1888 (**Mohr, South**ⁿ **Leg.**). Zietsch, Ueber Quellen und Sprache des mittelenglischen Gedichts, Seege oder Batayle of Troy (**Zietsch, Bat. Troy.**). Carstens, Zur Dialektbestimmung des mittelenglischen Sir Ferumbras. Kiel, 1884 (**Carstens, Sir Fer.**). Danker, Laut- und Flexionslehre der mittelkentischen Denkmäler. Strassburg, 1879 (**Danker**). Elworthy, The Dialect of West Somerset. English Dialect Society. London, 1875 (**Elworthy**).

General and Miscellaneous.

Sweet, History of English Sounds. Oxford, 1888 (**Sweet or HoES.**). Paul's Grundriss der germanischen Philologie. Strassburg, 1891 (**P. G.**). The following sections are referred to: Kluge, Geschichte der englischen Sprache, pp. 780—930 (**Kluge, P. G.**); Behrens, Französische Elemente im Englischen, pp. 799—836 (**Behrens, P. G.**). Sievers, Angelsächsische Grammatik. Halle, 1886 (**Sievers**). Mayhew, Synopsis of Old English Phonology. Oxford, 1891 (**Mayhew**). Ellis, On Early English Pronunciation, 5 vols (**Ellis or EEP**). Behrens, Beiträge zur Geschichte der französischen Sprache in England, in Französ. Studien 5 (**Behrens**). Sturmfels, Der altfranzösische Vocalismus im Mittelenglischen, in Anglia VIII, pp. 201 ff. (**Sturmfels**). Skeat, Principles of English Etymology. Oxford, 1887 & 1891 (**Skeat Princ.**). Holthaus, Beiträge zur Geschichte der englischen Vokale, in Anglia VIII, pp. 86 ff. (**Holthaus**). Köllmann, Die englischen *a* - Laute. Marburg, 1889 (**Köllmann**). Lloyd, Vowel Sound. Liverpool, 1890 (**Lloyd**). Murray, New English Dictionary (**NED**). Skeat, Etymological Dictionary (**Skeat Dict.**). Jamieson, Etymological Dictionary of the Scottish Language, 4 vols. and supplement by Donaldson (**Jam. Dict.**). Stratmann-Bradley, Middle English Dictionary (**Stratm.-Bradl**). Bosworth-Toller, Anglosaxon Dictionary (**B.-T.**). Kluge, Deutsches Etymologisches Wörterbuch (**Kluge, Wörterb.**).

Other abbreviations.

AFr. = Anglo-French
Angl. = Anglian
AnzfdA. = Anzeiger für deutsches
cons. = consonant   [Altertum
dial., diall. = dialect, dialects
EMidl. = East Midland, NEMidl. = North East Midland, &c.
Engl. St. = Englische Studien
Frz. St. = Französische Studien
Gmc. = Germanic
Germ. = German.
Kt. = Kent, or Kentish
Litt.-Bl. = Litteratur-Blatt für german. und roman. Philologie
ME., MSc., MHG. = Middle English Middle Scotch, Middle High German

Midl. = Midland
N = North
NE., NSc., NHG. = New English, New Scotch, New High German.
Nthmb. = Northumbrian
OE., ON., OHG. = Old English, Old Norse, Old High German.
OFr. = Old French
pronunc. = pronunciation
Q & F = Quellen und Forschungen
rec. sp. = received speech (Ellis)
S. = South
ZtsfdA. = Zeitschrift für deutsches Altertum
Ztsfdph. = Zeitschrift für deutsche Philologie

Indroduction.

The following treatise was originally intended to be only an investigation of the rimes of the Scotch metrical Romance 'Clariodus', and, based on this, an attempt to arrive at some particulars as to the pronunciation of the author. But it was found impossible to confine the investigation to this one poem; although it is a work of no mean proportions, 11849 lines in Piper's edition, in many cases the evidence given by the rimes was still too scanty to allow any decided conclusions without a comparison with other Sc. texts, in others it seemed advisable to seek a corroboration of what the rimes of Clar. alone appeared to prove, and the writer had to make a large use of such texts as lay within his reach, as will be seen from the numerous quotations and references made. In the present primitive state of the study of the Scotch language, there is not much help to be had from the few treatises which exist on the phonology of MSc. texts; they can easily be counted on one's fingers and are by no means of an exhaustive nature, so that it was often necessary to examine personally such texts as have already been the subjects of dissertations, as well as those which have not yet been subjected to examination at all. Here the editions of the Scottish Text Society and of the Early English Text Society formed a rich store. Beyond this an extensive use has been made of the word-lists of the mod. Sc. diall. given by Ellis in Vol. 5 of his splendid work 'On Early English Pronunciation'. The evidence afforded by these has often given the hint for observations made with regard to MSc. rimes which might otherwise have been missed, and there is no doubt that there is urgent need for a completion and extension of these lists; for a more certain knowledge of the central and northern Sc. diall. would throw much valuable light on the history of the Sc. language. We want a few Scotchmen of philological training to do for other diall. what Dr. Murray has done for his in his excellent work on the 'Dialect of the Southern

Counties of Scotl.', which has also been of invaluable assistance in the present investigation. I was able to supplement these works in one or two cases by the kind information of my friends Mr. David Anderson, M. A., L. L. B., Advocate, Edinburgh, and Mr. J. Webster Low, B. A.; of the former by means of letter, of the latter, who was fortunately residing in Heidelberg, by word of mouth. To both I here tender my best thanks for their assistance. Failing more complete materials for the mod. diall., it is often impossible to come to any decided conclusions, and some that have been ventured upon in the following pages are only given with some hesitation until confirmed by further research. In a few cases, e. g. words in -*ind*, -*und*, the ONthmb. Gospels have also been turned to account. A good and cómplete phonology of the Oldest Nthmbr. texts is necessary for any satisfactory treatment of the Sc. diall., and the want of this makes itself at present sadly felt.

The writer is very conscious of the many short-comings of this dissertation, and is well aware that much more might have been made of the materials at his disposal; but it was necessary to draw a limit somewhere, and time did not allow of an attempt to exhaust the matter. As it is, he has gone far beyond the limits of the original plan; occasionally excursions have been made across the border far into English territory, where it seemed impracticable to confine the investigation to Scotl. alone, and a comparison with the northern diall. of Engl. suggested itself as being specially instructive. Doubtless a native Scotchman with a thorough personal knowledge of at least one of the mod. diall. would have treated the matter more ably and have been less liable to err than a Southerner studying in a foreign Country.

Clar. is always the starting-point in our investigation; its rimes are given at the head of each section, quoted by number of Book and line, reference always being made to the second line of a couplet. When the same rime occurs twice, reference is made to both passages in which it occurs; when it is found three or more times, its first occurrence only is quoted followed by (&c.) in brackets, e. g. 1. 246 (&c.) means that the rime occurs first in 1. 246 and then at least twice more. The rime lists are complete except where the contrary is distinctly intimated by the words, 'and many more', or similar words;

this is only done when the rimes are very numerous and nothing would be gained by a complete register. Where a rime-word is only conjecture, printed by Piper in brackets, but failing in the MS., or where a transposition of the words of the MS. is necessary, the rime is only registered in the lists when it can be accepted with comparative certainty. A final -(e) in brackets, e. g. *fair(e)*, means that the word in question appears both with and without the *e*, e. g. *fair* and *faire*; the *e* has no meaning and there is no consistency in its use in the MS., the separation of the two forms, with & without the *e*, would be, therefore, of no practical use.

As so large a use has been made of Ellis's work, it was found almost unavoidable to employ his palaeographic transcriptions, which are always given in brackets, in accordance with the custom of Sweet and Ellis himself. Otherwise the usual phonetic symbols are used. Vowels in *open* and *closed* syllables are distinguished in the same way as in Ellis, EEP.: thus $A-$ means short $ă$ in open syll., A: Short $ă$ in closed syll., $A'-$ long $ā$ in open syll., &c.

As Clar. stands upon the borders of, or in, the mod. period of NSc., most of the changes from MSc. to NSc. have already taken place; but when we compare with earlier MSc. & ME. texts, it would be confusing if we always in referring to Clar. gave the new forms of the vowels, e. g. if we called the vowel in *steid* an $ī$-vowel instead of an $ē$-vowel, and that in *maid* an $ē$ instead of an $ā$; therefore in treating of the rimes in comparison with other texts we have often retained the nomenclature *e*-rime or *a*-vowel, &c., when we mean for Clar. the $ī$ and the $ē$ which have arisen out of previous $ē$ and $ā$.

Norse vowels are taken together with OE. vowels, as far as possible, i. e. wherever they are of the same nature and undergo the same treatment. Norse Æ' is treated in §§ 244—246, EI in §§ 247, 248, JU' in § 358, Œ' and ØY in §§ 497—499.

Sometimes it is necessary to distinguish between Old French (OFr.) and Anglo-French (AFr.); by the letter is meant the Norman dial. as it developed on English soil; cf. Skeat Princ. 2. 5, Behrens, PG. 1. 808.

The Text of Clariodus. 'Clariodus; a Scotish Metrical Romance. Printed from a Manuscript of the sixteenth Century.

Edinburgh 1830.' Such is the title of the edition 'presented to the Members of the Maitland Club by Edward Piper.' It is shortly to be re-edited for the Early English Text Society by Prof. Bülbring,*) to whose kindness I am greatly indebted for the loan of his copy of Piper's edition, now a rare book, with his careful collation with the unique MS., in the Advocates' Library, Edinburgh. I have, therefore, the advantage of knowing the exact text of the MS., which was not always correctly rendered in Piper's edition. The MS. lacks seven leaves at the beginning and one or two at the and. The 5th Book had a Prologue, of which, however, only 5 lines, exist.

The Maitland Club edition has a preface by David Irving, (author of the 'History of Scotish Poetry'), from which the following extracts are taken. 'It is printed from a folio manuscript, which .... seems to have been written about the year 1550 or somewhat later; but the composition is evidently of a much earlier date than the transcript, and may at least be referred to the close of the preceding century. The author's phraseology is more antiquated than that of Sir David Lindsay and makes a nearer approach to the phraseology of Henry the Minstrel.' Of the poet 'we can scarcely hope to retrieve the name; it was not to be expected in a MS. curtailed of its title and colophon; nor am I aware that the author of the romance is mentioned in any existing record of our literary history. To the work itself we find an apparent allusion in Stewarts abridgement of the Orlando Furioso ... Clariodus, like many of the English romances, is derived from a French original .... In the French language there is a prose romance of Cleriadus and Meliadice, which was printed apparently before the close of the 15th century'..... The author 'not only refers to the French original, but likewise to a translation, probably into the English tongue ... We learn that he followed, not a metrical, but a prose original and a prose version.' .... 'The poet's phraseology is not without its peculiarities. He occasionally introduces Latin and French words which retain a very extraneous appearance.'... 'The manuscript of Clariodus

---

*) I must here express my deepest obligation and sincerest thanks to Prof. Bülbring, not only for the first suggestion of this treatise, but also for much most valuable advice and assistance in the preparation of it.

appears to have been transcribed with less than ordinary care and attention.'

Date. With regard to the original date of composition, Irving's conjecture seems to me to place it somewhat too early; his remarks about the phraseology are open to question. I should consider it to agree more with that of Lyndes. than with that of Henry the Minstrel. The very quantity of Latin & French words noticed by Irving connects it more with the 16th than with the 15th century. Trautmann assigns to Gol. a date somewhere about 1500, and the language of Clar. certainly has a more modern stamp than Gol.; it is less thoroughly Scotch and contains more French and Latin words. It might very well be placed by the side of Douglas' and Dunbar's poems, with the former of which it shows great resemblance in the number of Anglicisms in pronunciation. Reasons will be found in the course of the following pages for dating not earlier than 1500. But the question of date must be left doubtful, until we have more exact criteria for deciding it. We must allow some time perhaps to have elapsed since the original composition before the date of the MS., by which time the poem has evidently gone through several hands; it shows far too many corruptions for the assumption that one copyist is responsible for them, and besides we shall see below that there are orthographical differences which show that in one stage at least two hands were employed in the copying of different parts of it. Prof. Bülbring tells me that the present MS. is all by one hand. Assuming Irving's date of the MS. to be correct, I would set the date of original composition about the middle of the first half of the 16th century; this agrees fairly well with the few criteria we have as yet to go upon.

The Dialect. Before anything definite can be asserted about dial., it is necessary that more MSc. texts, and especially such whose locality and date are known, should be investigated; and we require, too, a thorough examination of the mod. diall. with much fuller materials than are given in Ellis's EEP. Failing this we cannot pronounce with certainty on the dial. of the author of Clar., although we are from the very first naturally inclined to suppose that it must have been the literary dial. of Central Scotl., and as a rule the rimes offer no contradiction to this. In the course of the following treatise attention will be drawn to various pieces of evidence which preclude the possibility of the author hailing from the dial. designated by Ellis as D. 33 = Murray's 'Southern Counties', also to various traces of the influence of standard English, which, we know, characterised the later works of the literary period of the Sc. language, and produced an artificial literary dial. which did not coincide with any actual spoken dial., or, at the most, only with the fashionable language of Court at Edinburgh, which was also subject to the Anglicising influence, and possibly may have been as varied and confused in character as the language of Douglas and Clariodus with their numerous two-fold pronunciations. It is very possible that in the following we have sometimes allowed the mod. diall. to have too much weight in our estimate of the author's pronunc. and that his language was much more Anglicised than we have allowed; in the absence of decided evidence to prove this we have generally taken for granted that he remained true to his native dial.

References to the story of Clariodus. Besides the allusion by Stewart mentioned by Irving, the romance of Clariodus & Meliades, in some form or other is referred to in other Sc. works, e. g. Compl. Sc., p. 63, where it is mentioned among a long list of 'storeis' and 'flet taylis', 'sum in proce and sum in verse', as 'claryades and maliades'; (if our poem be referred to here we have a date ante quem, 1549, the date of Compl. Sc.); also Rosw., 'Nor the gentle Clariadus' (: Achilles), 19, 'For blyther was not Meledas, When as she married Claudias', 801, 802.

Sir W. Scott, in his notes to Sir Tristrem, quotes a passage descriptive of the equipment for a tournament; which might be supposed to be from the missing portion at the beginning of Clar., as Scott gives it as being from 'Clariodes, MS.' But the quotation is really from Lydgate's Troy Book, and either Scott's 'Clariodes' must be a mistake, or there was another MS. known to him, perhaps containing a similar story to ours, but with a passage copied from Lydgate. The name Clariodes as well as the vocabulary and style show that it cannot have been a part of our poem.

Part I.
Vowels.
Chap. 1.
Germanic Vowels (Old English & Norse).

A -

§ 1. Not followed by g, rimes with.

a) itself.
crave : have 1.100, 4.1998 (*have to be explained, not from OE. habban*, but from inflectional forms, with *a* in open syll., e. g. 2 & 3 sg. *hafast, hafað*).
take : make (for MS. *be make* read *to make*) 1.114.
name : schame 2.1074, 5.1142: eschame (vb.) 5.2038.
gaming : samyne (adj. = same) 4.2086, gamjng : samming (OE. *samen*, adv.?) 5.1386.

b) OE. æ : or a-? (see §§ 3—10).
take : blake (OE. *blæc*) 1.1230, 1486 : spake 4.1924.
make : spak 1.218.
crake (sb.) : brake (prt.) 1.50.
hate (sb. from vb. *hatian*) : sate, prt. 2.134.
fair (sb. OE. *faru*) : baire (prt.) 4.1075.
crave : gave (prt.) 3.684.

c) OE. æ + g.
fair (OE. *faran*) : fair (OE. *fæger*) 3.820.
nichtingall : haill (*hægl*) 3.516.
caire (OE. *caru*) : fair 3.514.
maine (OE. *manu*) : againe 4.250.

d) OE. ā.
take : waike (OE. *wāc* = N. *veik*) 4.68.
saike : strake (prt.) 1.516 : stryke (read *strake*, MS. *did stryke*; the alteration was probably made by the scribe for the sake of the metre) 4.2134: aike (OE. *āc*) 5.1480.

make : straike (sb.) 2.1530.
name : hame 3.706.
mone (read *maine* = OE. *manu*) : scheine (read *schaine* = OE. *scān* prt.) 4.246.
taill (OE. *tālu*) : haill (OE. *hāl*) 1.1138.
brydell (OE. *brȳd-alu*) : haill 4.2832.
have : draue (OE. *drāf*, prt.) 3.1656 : leave (sb. OE. *lāf* = remains) 1.1548 (&c).
skaith (OE. *scaða*) : baith (N. *báþir*) 2.496.
heat (= hate, sb.) : wait (3. sg. *wāt*) 3.2196.
fair (OE. *faru*) : more 3.1354.
cair (OE. *caru*) : mair 3.1742.
ar (OE. *arun*. 3. pl.) : mair 3,618.
Also in the following, where the rime words had in W. S. *ǣ* but in ONorthmb. *ā, þār, þāra*, cf. § 195 (f.).
weilfair : thair 2.608, 3.1340.
fair(e), vb. : thair 2, 422. 3.948;
feire (= faire, OE. *faru*) : thair 5.1176.
cair : thair 3,598.

e) OFr. a or Lat. a.
lait(e) (OE. *læt*, infl. *latu*, &c.) : stait 2.250 : estait 2.1220: debait 3.322 : dulcorate 4.1832.
gate (N. *gata*) : estaite 4.2572.
weilfair : declaire 1.238.
aip (OE. *apa*) : jape 4.254.
name : defame 2.286 : fame 2.62, 1184 : blame 3.1886 : proclame 5.1314.

f) Fr. al.
  have : save (*salver*) : 1. 196 (&c.),
  heave (= have) : sane 4. 646.
g) Fr. ai.
  weilfair : air 5. 2602.
  fayre (sb.) : chyre (Fr. *chaiere*) 5. 1530.
  waill (vb. = choose, see § 18) : prevaill 4. 1426.

h) Fr. ei.
  knaue : deceave 4. 1452.
  have : resave 1. 680 (&c.) : ressave : 1. 816, 4. 2776 : persaue 3. 1920.
  having : persaving 5. 840.
i) ?
  game : drame (see § 14) 2. 1658.
  wndertake : lake (sb. see § 15) 1. 206.

§ 2. OE. *a*- was lengthened probably in the 2nd half of the 13th century, but could not, in Midl. and South" England, coincide with OE. $\bar{a}$, as this had shortly before become $\bar{q}$. But in Scotl. OE. $\bar{a}$ has not been rounded in the vernacular even up to the present day, and hence th new-lengthened $\bar{a}$ is to be found in rime with it in all Scotch texts, see the rimes in (d), as well as with $\bar{a}$ from all other sources, see (e). In mod. Sc. all of these $\bar{a}$'s (just as in mod. Engl. with the exception of OE. $\bar{a}$ which became ME. $\bar{q}$), have been fronted to an $\bar{e}$-vowel. This change, like many others, was completed earlier in Scotl. than in Midl. and S. England, and reasons will be found below in §§ 148 ff. to show why we are led to conclude that for the author of Clar. $\bar{a}$ had already become $\bar{e}$; we must accept this sound for the earlier diphthongs *ai*, *ei* arising out of $æ + g$, $e + g$, Fr. *ai*, *ei*, &c., and we must therefore accept it for earlier $\bar{a}$ as well; see the rimes in (c), (g) & (h); those in (h) are particularly instructive, cf. § 155. That it was certainly so pronounced by one or more of the scribes is shown by the preponderance of the spelling with *ai*, of which there is no doubt that it meant $\bar{e}$ in Scotl. in the 16th cent.; cf. below § 319; the spelling with *a* is, however, rather frequent in words of this class, and may in some of them really denote vowel-shortness, as we shall shortly see; but *ai* is written almost always before *r*.

The change $\bar{a} > \bar{e}$ is generally dated for Engld. in the 16th cent., see Köllmann, p. 50. Kluge dates it from the 2nd half of the 15th cent., see PG. 1. 877 and says it may have taken place even earlier in Scotl. Putting Clar. even at the early date which Irving assigns to it, it is from the very first natural to suppose that the author already had the new pronunciation, and everything tends to confirm this.

§ 3. The rimes in (b) cause some difficulty; we should expect them also to contain a long vowel, and, judged by themselves, the rimes all admit of this; for, although OE. *æ*: cannot regularly produce ME. or MSc. $\bar{a}$, yet sometimes there were in OE. inflected forms of the words in question containing *a*-, which would sufficiently explain a MSc. $\bar{a}$, e. g. OE. *blæc*, but infl. *blacu*, &c.; in other cases there were external influences at work, e. g. Norse influence in *gave* (N. *gáfu*), or analogy and transference, as in *baire*, *sate*. But at the same time every one of the rime words in (b) except *baire* admits of a short vowel and is to be found with one in other Sc. texts, and also in the modern diall. So that the above rimes, e. g. *take*: *blake*, can be interpreted in two ways, viz, either that *take* has a short vowel, or that *blake* has a long one, &c.

§ 4. We will take the rimes in order. *take* and *make* both have a short vowel in all the mod. Sc. diall. except D. 33. We shall see later on that the dial. of the author was certainly *not* D. 33, and therefore we should expect him to be using *măk* and *tăk*, unless we suppose that in these words he abandoned his native dial. altogether, or that the shortening belongs to a later period than the author's, and this is disproved by the frequent rimes in other texts, cf. § 7; the long vowel of D. 33 may, however, be of later origin, and in MSc. all the diall. may have had *măk*, *tăk*. *black* is only given once by Ellis, in D. 39, and then with short vowel as in rec. sp. (it appears with *ĕ* in Dunb. *blek* : *neck* : *effek* 34. 34); *spake* has *ă*, too, in D. 41 & 42, and in most MSc. texts it has a short vowel. The second rime in (i) points to a short vowel too, for the word *lak* or *lake* rimes in almost all MSc. texts with *ă*, cf. § 17. On the other hand, *blake* is found with a long vowel in ME. texts (? and in MSc.), which it is not even necessary to explain from a ME. lengthening of *a*- in the inflected forms, for the word appears already in OE. with *ā* and was often confounded with another word *blāc* = shining, white, cf. NED. s. v. *black*; further, *take* and *make* certainly have a long vowel in the rimes in (d). Clar. gives us no further rimes to fix the vowel in *blake* and *spake*; but other texts prove a short vowel by rimes, e. g. Satir P. *spak*: *back* 45. 248, cf. § 7.

§ 5. Although we are thus not compelled by the rimes to accept a short vowel in *make* and *take*, the probability is that the author knew this pronunc. as well, in fact, that he used two forms; *măk* & *tăk* were the forms of his dial., *māk*, *tāk* or *mẹk*, *tẹk* were forms borrowed from Engl. We have to accept double forms in other words in Sc. texts, e. g. *hăd*, *stĕd*, see Buss. p. 20. The short vowel in *măk* & *tăk* is found also in the N. of Engl. except D. 32 (Northumb. and Durh.) and most of the Midlands; the long vowel is confined to the Eastern Counties, the whole of the S. and one district in the N., comprising D. 32 in Engl. and D. 33 in Scotl.

§ 6. ˙ Considering the wide extension of these forms it is most likely that in *măk* & *tăk* the vowel has never been lengthened in Sc.; words exactly similar, *bake*, *sake*, &c., have *ē* quite regularly in the mod. Sc. diall. as well as Engl. The difference of treatment, which is apparently of long standing, still requires a satisfactory explanation. But before *k* short vowels in open syllable seem often to have remained short in Sc. cf. Montg. *brek*: *infek* (= infect), C. 273. We have the same in rec. sp. *crack* (OE. *cracian*), cf. also *suck* (OE. *sūcan*) which shows that even long vowels may be shortened before *k*.

§ 7. The consistent spelling in the MS. with *a*, not *ai*, is conspicuous, when we compare the other words *faire*, *saike* (the latter nearly always has *ai*), &c. From this it would seem that the scribe only knew the pronunc. *măk*, *tăk*, and therefore did not belong to D. 32 or 33, unless the long vowel there is only of recent date. The same doubleness is apparent in Douglas who writes *taik* and *tak*, *maik* & *mak*, cf. Kaufmann p. 48; his imes prove *ă*, e. g. mak : contrak 4. 105. 8 : abak 4. 124. 2. Other Sc. texts prove by rimes & spelling the shortness of vowel, e. g. Dunb., *takkis* (3. sg.): *lakkis* (= maligns, 3. sg.) 44. 6, *tak*: *lak* (= disgrace)

44. 11; John Knox, *mack* (see DSS., p. 66), Roll. C. V., *wndertak*: *bak*: *slak*: *stupefact* 3. 148, *tak*: *wraik*: *knax*: *lak*: *staik* (of wood) 4. 383; Satir. P. *vndertak it*: *detractit* 12, 109, *tak it*: *bakit*: *mak it*: *spak it* 12. 195, *make*: *contrake* 17. 72, *mak*: *sacke* 25. 121, *mak*: *tak*: *ak* (= act): *bak* 39. 376, &c., Montg. *tak*: *bak*: *slak*: *spak* MP. 1. 2, *maks* (3. sg.): *actis*: *crakis*: *laks*: *contracts*: *taks*: *waxe*: *wraks*: *paks*. ME. 43, 6, &c.

§ 8. **crake: brake.** Here again the vowel may be short or long, but the former is more probable, for *brake* generally has a short vowel in MSc. texts (for instances see Wackerzapp p. 69 &c.); it rimes elsewhere in Clar. with short-vowel (: *abake*, see § 80, a) and *brăk* still exists at the present day in Sc. Although OE. *cracian* should produce ME. *krāk*, and perhaps does so in Sir Tr. *crake*: *take*: *sake*: *schake*, 887, it generally has *ă* in MSc., and of course the vowel is short in rec. sp. Perhaps we should assume for the sb. an OE. form **crœc*, but this is not necessary when we find in mod. Sc. *shăk* for rec. sp. *shake*. Bruce also has the sb. *crakkis*, 19. 399. & Dunbar, *crak*: *blak*, 38. 3, *thwndir crak*: *wrak* (OE. *wrœc*): *frak* (= rush), 21. 79.

§ 9. **hate: sate.** *Sate* rimes besides only with *at*, which proves a short vowel, but I can find no instance of the sb. *hate* (= hatred) being pronounced *ă*; we must therefore accept two pronunciations for the word *sate*, unless *hate* stands for rec. sp. *hat*, OE. *hœt*; the passage '*And syne anone dispuilʒeit of his hate, Before thir prissoneris on kneis sate*' might admit of this, but *hate* = hatred is far more suitable, and the other would be rather comical; the knight otherwise generally has a *helm* and the one in question is the '*felloun but pitie*', whose bitter hatred had, up till the time referred to in the text, been so conspicuous.

§ 10. **faire: baire, crave: gave.** Here the vowel is long, as is shown by the other rimes of *baire* and *gave*, which are discussed in their proper places below.

§ 11. A following *n* or *m* makes no difference to the vowel sound, but a scribe seems in one place to have changed *a* to *o* wrongfully, viz. in *mone* for *mane* or *maine*, see above in (d), a mistake due to carelessness and the habit of changing *a* to *o* in words containing OE. *ā*, in Anglicising Scotch texts, e. g. *gane* to *gone*. In the other line of the couplet he seems to have missed the sense altogether, and destroyed the rime, so that we have only conjecture to go upon, but there is no doubt as to the meaning *mane*, and *schane* or *schaine* saves the rime.

§ 12. It remains to give a glance at the mod. Sc. diall. for other words of this class. We should expect to find (*i'*) in D. 33, but a long *ē* in the other diall., for so MSc. *ā* is reflected to-day. This is generally the case, too, e. g. in *bake*, *cake*, *sake*, *behave*, *knave*, *tale*, *lame*, *name*, *tame*, *same*, *shame*, *mane*, *wane*, *late*; *have* has (ææ) in D. 33, but regularly *ē* in most of the other diall. in contrast to rec. sp. (hæv), cf. the rimes in (a), (d), (f), (h). But we also find a short *ă* or *ǟ* in other words besides *make* & *take*, e. g. *grave* (vb.), in D. 35, *quake*, *wade* in 41, *shake* in 42, *same* in 41 & 42 (these are the only quotations of these words that Ellis gives; perhaps fuller material would show this non-lengthening of *a*-, or subsequent reshortening, to be more extensive).

§ 13. gaming, samyne, samming, see (a): The two passages run as follows: 'The hall was all arayit with the samyne [= the same] Thair was grit joy of menstrallie and gaming', 4.2686; 'Thairwith he lewch and maid grit gamjng. Thir Lordis to meit the King ar gone in samming', 5.1386. In the former *samyne* is an adj. & comes from the infl. forms of OE. *sama*. In the text we frequently find *samyn(e)*, *samin(e)*, (once *sameine* 5.2533), particularly in the phrase 'in the samin wayis', especially in the 4th & 5th books, rarely, if at all, in the 1st & 2nd; cf. Dunb. on the samyn wyse, 1.100. The form is usual in all Sc. texts, but often *same* appears as well. In Wall. the monosyllabic form would sometimes suit the metre better, where *samyn* is written, e. g. 'In this samyn time to him approchit new', 6.17, 'Lo, Schyr, thai said, forsuth ʒon sammyn is he', 5.885. The dissyllabic form was till quite recently still in existence in Banffshire, cf. Gregor's note to Roll. C. V. 1.28. The rime-word *gaming* must either be changed to *gamin* (= OE. *gamen*), for which compare Sc. Leg. *sammyne* : *gammyne* 6/112, Gen. Ex. *gamen*: *samen* 411, 2015 : *namen* 3498 : *unframen* = be hurtful, 1214, or else be derived from an OE. verbal noun *gamung*, *gaming* (the latter is given in BT.) and the rime be accounted for by the usual Sc. loss of *g* in final -*ng*; or there may have been a confusion of suffixes on the part of scribe or author, the *g* having no meaning at all, cf. Murray DSS. pp.124,125. The second rime may be understood in the same way, although *samming* appears to be a verbal noun, the phrase *in samming* being substituted for the more usual *samyn* (without *in*) which is frequently found in Bruce, and = OE. *samen*, adv. It is possible that we should alter to *game* and *same* in 4.2686; cf. *game* : *drame* 2.1658, also Dougl. *sam* (adverb. = together) : *ram* 3. 92. 22, *gam* : *am* : *gram* : *dram* 2. 169. 23. These rimes show that, even in the monosyll. form, the vowel may be short. As already hinted, the rule of secondary lengthening in open syll. seems to be subject to many exceptions in Sc.; perhaps here the vowel of *game*, *gam*, is affected by that of *gamin*, which would be kept short by the *n* of the following syll.; so also with *sam* & *samin*.

§ 14. brydell: haill, see (d). The *e* points to the change $\bar{a} > \bar{e}$ having already taken place for the scribe, unless it is merely the result of the unstressedness of the syll.

§ 15. heat (= hate), see (d). The *ea* (Engl. orthography) in this word and in *heave* (= have, with long vowel), see (f), is also evidence of the $\bar{e}$- sound in the pronunc. of the scribe. The long vowel in *have* corresponds to the $\bar{e}$ of the mod. diall., cf. § 12, and the pronunc. in rec. sp. of *behave*.

§ 16. game: drame, see (i). 'And then luich all and maid grit game, He could not mirrie be that thair was drame.' The last word evidently means *sad*; Jam. Dict. says it is 'North Scotch = sullen, melancholy, same as *drum* = Kelt. *drwm*, moestus. Rudd. refers to Icel. *dramb*, pride, Icel. *draums* = melancholy.' (!) It is difficult to see how Jamieson's *drum* (with which compare *drummoolich* = melancholy, in Gregor's Banffshire Glossary) can have anything to do with *dram* or *drame*. We have the same word with short *ă*, in Dougl. *dram* : *gam* : *am*: *gram* (OE.

gram), 2. 169. 23, Dunb. *dram*: *Lam* (= lamb) 52. 23, Satir. P. *dram*, 10, 16, Rosw. *dram*, D. 50.

§ 17. lake, sb. = reproach, disgrace, see (i), can scarcely, on account of its universal appearance with a short vowel, be derived from OE. *lāc*, for, although shortening does seem sometimes possible in long vowel + k, the regular form for this word in MSc. is *laik*, with long vowel and corresponding meaning to OE. *lāc*, viz. stake, play, &c., c. g. Montg. *laik*: *waik* (= weak) C. 1109, and the meaning, reproach, disgrace, would not be satisfactorily explained by this derivation. Perhaps we must go to some Norse word for the origin. Morris, Hamp. P. C., compares Swed. *lak*, fault, Jam. in his Dict., s. v. *lake*, OSwed. *lack-a*, Icel. *hlacka*. Skeat's derivation from OE. *lēahan*, to scorn, abuse, is quite impossible. The verb *lack* = despise, is still, acc. to Gregor in his notes to Roll. C. V., to be heard in Scotl., and the following examples may be given in proof of the short vowel: Barbour, Good Wife, *lak*: *tak*, 230; Gol. *lak*: *abak*: *rak*, 919; Ratis R. *lak*, 3092; Roll. C. V. *schame and lak*, 1. 455: *bak*: *s!ak*: *wndertak*: *stupefact* 3. 149, : *wraik* (= wreck): *knax*: *tak*: *staik* (of wood) 4. 387; Satir. P. *lakit* (disgraced, mocked): *vndertak it*: *bakit*: *detractit* 12. 109, *lak*: *mak* 42. 68, *lack*: *contrack*: *aback*: *frack* 47. 98, *lak*: *fact*: *abak*: *mak* 28. 146; Rosw. *shame and lack*: *take* A. 784; also Destr. Troy. *lak*, 7617, 12106.

§ 18. waill, vb. = to choose, see (g), cannot be derived from N. *velja*, (= Goth. *waljan*), which, on the analogy of *dwell* < OE. *dwellan* < N. *dvelja*, should produce *well*; the corresponding OE. verb would be *wellan*. It must be a new-formed verb from the sb. *waill* (see Stratm.-Bradl. s. v. *wāle*) = N. *val*, whose long vowel would be quite regularly developed from the oblique forms with *a* in open syll. Both vb. and sb. are frequent in Sc. — Wall. *men of waill*, 11. 273, : *haill* (OE. *hāl*) 6. 334, *quhat was his grettest waill*: *daill* (= dale) 6. 606; Dougl. *waill* (vb.): *trauaill*: *deuaill* (vb. = lower): *vaill* (= valley) 1. 48. 2, *waill* (sb.): *faill* 3. 99. 26; Dunb. *wale* (vb.) 1. 186; Roll. C. V. *cled in waill Morigerate* 1. 153. The vb. occurs again in Clar.: 'and twa with ʒow the best ʒe can waill', 3. 1712, but the second line of this couplet is wanting in the MS. so that we have no rime-word. The by-forms *wyle*, *wile*, given by Jam. Dict. are difficult of explanation. For quotations from ME. see further Stratm.-Bradl., where also the form *welen*, vb. is given, and *wale*, adj., corresponding to Goth. *walis*.

§ 19. Words in which an intervocal consonant has been lost. 1) OE. *latost* appears only as *last* and rimes with a) OE. æ : *fast* 1. 60 (&c.). b) N. a : *cast* 4. 1788. c) Fr. a : *past* (prt. & ptc.) 2. 582, 4. 1388. These rimes are perfectly regular; the vowel is short, as is shown by the *ă* or *ĕ* of the mod. diall. and the spelling with *a*, not *ai*. Cf. Morsb. p. 28.

§ 20. 2) OE. *macode*, prt. and *macod*, ptc., appear only as *maid* and rime with a) OE. ā : braid (*brād*, adj.) 5. 2648, 2, 1334 : *abaid* (sb.) 2. 506, 3. 2366 : raid(e) (prt. OE. *rād*) 3. 38 (&c.). b) OE. æ: or a-? : glaid (OE. *glœd*) 3. 888 : hade (prt.) 2. 1728, 5. 256. c) OE. æ + g : said 3. 1638 (&c).

§ 21. Here there is everywhere a long vowel, indicated also by the spelling with *ai*; the rime words in (b) contain a long vowel occasionally, especially in Sc., and are therefore no contradiction to the others, cf. §§ 90, 91. It is immaterial to us whether the long vowel is to be explained according to ten Brink or to Morsbach, whether first the vowel between *k* and *d* was lost, *makede* > *makde*, and then *k* disappeared with compensatory lengthening of the *a*, *māde*, or first *a* was lengthened in open syllable, *makede* > *mākede*, & then *mākede* > *māde* by contraction; the vowel is always long, and there is no difference between pret. & ptc. Cf. further Kluge PG. 1. 875, ten Brink p. 15, Morsbach p. 22.

§ 22. 3) OE. *taken* generally appears as *taine*, once *tone* & once *toine*; the rime words contain — a) OE. ā. taine : gaine (OE. *gān*, ptc.) 3. 1262 (&c.) (read *gaine* for *went* 5. 468) : ane 4. 2020 : anone 5. 164. 2318, tone : anone 4. 2754, toine : gone 5. 2804. — b) OE. æ + g. taine : againe 1. 856, 2. 280. — c) OE. ō. taine : sonne 5. 1408. — d) Fr. ai. taine : remaine 5. 644 : soverane 5. 2698.

§ 23. tane or taine is the usual form in Northern & Scotch texts, and its regularly developed form (teen) still exists in Sc. diall. The rimes above prove the long vowel $\bar{e}$ from previous $\bar{a}$, except the one rime in (c), which, however, is not altogether free from suspicion, for *soune* may very well be a scribe's mistake; it is preceded by another *soune* in the same line, 'thay passit soune and him vnarmit soune', and this repetition is scarcely likely to be genuine. In Piper's edition the second *soune* is emended to *then*, which is also unsatisfactory; it would be better to change the first *soune* to *then* and leave the second as it is; then we have a parallel rime to *ton* : *don* in Sir Tr., cf. Kölbing's introduction p. 73, and NB *tone* : *Demophoon* : *anone* : *one*, in Dougl. 1. 32. 17. But we need not accept *tōn* as a real form existing in any dial. of living speech in ME. It would be quite a solitary instance of the rounding of the $\bar{a}$ which arose by secondary lengthening, and if it were a genuine dialectal form we should expect to find it oftener in rime and also to find some trace of it in mod. diall.; and further, the very fact of its only being as yet proved by rime in Northern texts casts a doubt upon its genuineness, for the Northern dial. is, as we know, altogether averse to the change $\bar{a} > \bar{\varrho}$. The form *tōn* could not be of natural growth anywhere. The contracted form is not confined to the North; (teen) is found to-day in D. 20 & 22 (Linc. & S. Lancs.) and (tiin), the corresponding form, in D. 25 (Cheshire), where ME. $\bar{a} < a$- has always become (ii). *Tone* must be an erroneously invented form, the Northern author, not the scribe alone, going too far in his substitution of the Southern *o* for the Northern *a*, just in the same way as in *mone*, see above, § 11. It is true that from this point of view we have to suppose that the author of Sir Tr. at that early date was already addicted to the copying of Southern forms, and such an early beginning of the normalising tendency has not as yet been accepted, although there is no reason against its being possible.

§ 24. If we suppose, with Brandl, that (toon) was invented by a Midl. man, we must then assume that he was addicted to copying Northern forms, which is very improbable; the form (toon) could not arise organically in his Midl. dial., but (taan) or (teen) could, and if this were known to him he would certainly have used it in its correct form, or if it were strange to his dial., and he used (toon), he must have consciously adopted a North^n form and falsely changed its vowel to suit his dial., as he thought. But we have no evidence that there was ever a tendency to normalising in this direction, and we know there was in the other; the question is, how early it began.

§ 25. It should be remarked that Brandl, AnzfdA. 10. 333, argues from the occurrence of the above-mentioned rime in Sir Tr. against the North for the dial. of the poem, because the form *tōn* has 'hitherto been only found in Midl. copies of Northern texts'. But with our rime in Clar., and the one in Dougl., which is beyond all doubt, this argument falls to the ground. In any case Sir Tr. cannot be located further South than the very extreme North of the Midl. district, if not in the Northern district itself. The form *tone* is more likely to be the mistake of a Northerner trying to write Southern, than of a Midl. man trying to introduce Northern forms, and Dougl. with his altogether mixed, artificial dial. is just the very man from whom we might expect such a form.

2. Followed by g.

§ 26. a + g produces *au* (written *aw*) and rimes with. — a) OE. ǽh aw (N. *agi*): saw (Angl. *sœh*) 1. 996. draw (*dragan*): saw 3. 762. — b) ū + w aw(e): know 1. 626, 4. 1310. law (OE. *lagu*): know 2. 932. saw (OE. *sagu*): know 2. 224. 4. 202. schaw (OE. *scaga*) : raw (OE. *rāw*) 4. 1770 : snaw 1. 740: know 1. 1298 (&c.).

§ 27. In these words there is no difference between ME. and MSc.; in both, *œh* produces the diphthong *au*; the *o* of the rime words in (b) is merely due to the scribe who uses an English orthography. In Midl. and Southern Engl. *ău* and *āu* did not ever coincide, as the *ā* in *āu*, like every other *ā*, became *ǭ* & produced the diphthong, ME. *ǭu* > *ǫu* and later *ō*, cf. below, § 53. The rimes in (b) would, then, be impossible in a Midl. or Southern text. In Scotl. *ău*, from *œh* and *ag*, became lengthened to *āu*, as shown by the rimes in (b), and then, of course, followed the same fortunes as *āu* from OE. *āw*, i. e. the *ā* remained unrounded, as usual in Sc., and later, the *u* disappeared, just as it did in ME. *āu* and *ǭu* (see Sweet § 855), on account of the length of the preceding vowel, and hence the mod. Sc. diall. show quite regularly (AA), like rec. sp., or (aa), in the words *awe, law, dawn, draw, gnaw, saw, maw, haw*, &c.

A:

1. Followed by nasals.

§ 28. α) before nd, rimes with — a) itself. hand: brand 1. 872 : understand 1. 1052, &c., &c., in numberless examples; also many rimes with the Sc. partic. form in -*and*, which will be found below in § 429. — b) Fr. a. land: command 1. 1344, 5. 2358 : ordand (prt.) 1. 700. fand (prt.): demand 2. 1918. hand: command 2. 1844. Ingland: ordande (pte.) 5. 46. — and many more. Further also many rimes with Fr. participial forms in -*ant*, which have adopted the native form -*and*, for which see § 428.

THE MIDDLE-SCOTCH ROMANCE CLARIODUS. 19

§ 29. β) before nt, rimes with — Fr. a. scantit (N. *skamta*): plantit 4. 958. wante (N. *vanta*): instante 4. 2492.

§ 30. γ) before ng, rimes only with — OE. or N. a. long : strong 1. 1354, 4. 562. lang : wrang (N.) 3. 558. thrang (prt.) : fang (vb.) 2. 1548 : fong (sb.) 2. 1762 : among 3. 2318. among : fange (vb.) 3. 1888 : song (sb.) 4. 1834 : dang (prt.) 5. 1170. song (sb.): sprang (prt.) 4. 1638 : rang(e) (prt.) 4. 2416, 5. 2086. swang (prt.): strong 5, 2348.

§ 31. δ) before n or nn rimes only with — itself. ran(e): begane 1. 722 (&c.): wan (adj. OE. *wann*) 3. 568 : mane (homo) 1. 764. man(e) (homo) : than (e) (tum) 2. 192 (&c.) : begane 2. 1878 (&c.) : cane (vb. posse) 4. 2518 — and many others. There are no examples in rime of *a* followed by nc, nk, nor of *a* + *m*.

§ 32. In the above we only have rimes with *a* (OE., N. or Fr.), none to prove an o- pronunciation. An examination of the orthography in the text of the 1st Book, 1576 lines, gives the following results as to the treatment of *a* before *nasals* by the scribes.

Before nd, only *a* is written — *and*, *stand*, *land*, *hand*, *fand(e)*, prt., *husband*, *sand*, *band*, *brand*.

Before nt, only *a* — *scant*.

Before final n, we have a and o in *mon*, *mone* (each once) = must, and *man*, *mane* (each once). Otherwise only a — *man. woman*, *can* (= did, auxiliary), *can* (posse), *begane*, *ran(e)*, *wan* (prt.), *wan* (adj.), *than(e)* (19 times), *quhan* (twice). The forms *then* (15 times) & *quhen* or *when* (33 times) are to be explained from OE. *þænne*, *hwænne*.

Before nk, only a — *thank* (15 times).

Before ng, both o and a, but oftener o — *strong* (only *o*), *long* (15 times), *lang* (15 times), *longer* (twice), *among* (1), *amongs* (2), *amongis* (2), *song*, prt. (once), *sang*, prt. (once), *song*, sb. (twice), *hang*, prt. (once), *langing* = belonging (once).

Before m + cons, both a and o — *wompill*, *ramping* (each twice).

Before final m; here again o is somewhat in the majority — *from* (9 times), *fro*, prep. after the sb. (4), *fro*, adv. (1), (but the *o* in *fro* is probably from *ā*, cf. rimes in § 38); a in *am* (9) and *fra*, prep. (6). The prt. of the verb *come* appears as *come* (6), *com* (4), & *came* (4), *cam* (2). Omitting this, and also *fro*, *fra*, we have only *from* (9 times) against *am* (9 times).

So our final result is, that there is only a preference for *o* before *ng*, as in mod. rec. sp., and that before *m* the evidence in equally divided.

§ 33. In the mod. Sc. diall. it is only very seldom that *o* is found in any of the words in the above classes, and where it does appear, it cannot be genuine dial., but must be a borrowing from rec. sp. Ellis gives *o* only in *wan* adj. in D. 39, *want* in 36, *among* in 38, 39, *strong* in 35, 39, 42, *throng* in 39 & *thong* in 39; but all of these appear with an *a* in other diall., and in all other words, except those to be immediately mentioned, we only find *a* on *æ*, with an occasional (E), (ə) or (e), i. e. where the vowel has remained short. Before *mb* it has been lengthened as in rec. sp., for we find (ee) in *comb*, (*i*') of course in D. 33, and in *womb*, correctly representing an *ā* in MSc.; *lamb* has (aa) in D. 34, a later length-

2*

ening. Before *nd* there has been a lengthening of recent date; we find (aa) or (ᴀᴀ) in *hand, land, band, stand*. Before *ng* there are occasional traces of lengthening, both early and recent, e. g. *tongs* has (i') in D. 33, pointing to a MSc. *ā*, in D. 32 (Northumberland) it also has (ɪᴇ), the corresponding form, and *sang*, prt. has (aa) in D. 33. Otherwise we find *a* or *æ* in all of the following words — *thank, hang* (sometimes with *e*), *man, can* (sb.), *lamb, long, among, strong, throng, wrong, song*.

In all probability the *o* 's in the MS. of Clar. are only due to the copyists.

§ 34. The form *fand*, prt. of *find*, see § 28 (b), appears as (fan) in 34 & 36 & (fand) in 33 & 37; similarly (wan) = prt. of *wind*, in 35. Instead of *from* we nearly always find (fee) or (free), the descendant of MSc. *frā*.

§ 35. We have seen above that before *m* & *n* in open syllable, *a* is the only usual form, cf. § 11, but we must add here that *o* is found in the words *mony* or *monie* (6 times in Bk. 1) and *ony* (5 times). These are the usual forms in Sc. texts, and in them we find a reversion of the usual rule; here *o* appears in Sc., where the South has *a*. It is so also in NSc., see DSS. p. 144.

2. Followed by other consonants,

§ 36. rimes with — a) OE. a. cast (N. kasta): last (superl.) 4. 1788.
— b) OE. æ. cast: fast 3. 202. — c) Fr. a. ass (OE. *ascian*): trespas 1. 528.

§ 37. The vowel sound is *a*, not lengthened, for the mod. diall. show (*a*). The form *ass* for *ask* is still the usual form in Scotl., & is to be found in almost all MSc. texts, e. g. Wall. *ass* : *was* 7. 912 (&c.), *ast* (prt.) : *cast* 5. 740 : *past* 8. 534; Satir. P. *ast* (= asked) : *past* 45. 620, 793; Wedderburn, *assis* (3 sg.): *lassis* (see Irving, p. 390).

A

1. Final ā

§ 38. is almost always written *o* in the MS. It rimes exceedingly often with itself, especially the following words often riming with each other: *so, also, wo* (also spelt *woe* and once *woo*), *go, mo, two, fro*, adv. & prep, *tho*, adv.. A few rimes of the latter forms may be interesting. — mo : fro 1. 402 (&c.) : two 1. 1266 (&c.) : go 1. 1562 (&c.) : also 2. 520 : wo 3. 552, 5. 878 : so 3. 1518, 5. 1650, moe : go 3. 692. — two : go 1. 1270 (&c.) : fro 3. 2136 (&c.) : so 3. 1082, 5. 1162 : also 3. 1770 (&c) : wo 3. 1488, 4. 1496. — fro : go 1. 844 (&c.) : so 4. 1418 : also 1. 1346 (&c.) : wo 1. 434 (&c.) : woo 3. 190. — tho (adv.) : so 5. 280 : also 1. 108 (&c.); tho (pron. OE. *þā*) : also 3. 1694.

§ 39. Here follow rimes with other vowels & combinations: — a) OE. ā + w. so : know 5. 1742. — b) OE. æ + g. tway : day 2. 1250. — c) OE. ō. so : to 1. 1438 : ho (sb.) 5. 1232. two : ho (sb.) 1. 498, 2. 1018 : ho (vb.) 4. 1036. fro : to 2. 1286 : ho (vb.) 2. 1534, 3. 1530. go : ho (vb. imperat.) 1. 778, (inf.) 3. 1666 : ho (sb.) 3. 1154, 4. 650.

§ 40. The spelling with *a* is also found, e. g. sa : sla 3. 460, fa : fra 2. 1072, twa : so 5. 2192 &c. cf. also *tway* in § 39 (b). The following rime is also worthy of note: ha (interj.) : sa (inf. OE. *secgan*) 3. 1526.

Cf. Satir. P. ha : say 29. 22, sua : gea (= go, *ea* is Engl. orthography pronounce *gĕ*) 45. 630, sea : gea 45. 899; Montg. fra : pray C. 727.

§ 41. The rimes in § 39 (c) prove abundantly that the *o*'s of the MS. are not merely due to the copyists; at the same time the rime in (b) shows that the author also used his native form with ē, and it may be that many of the self-rimes in which *o* is written should have the spelling altered to *a* or *ay*; the few that are found with *a*, *ay*, may be unaltered forms of the original which the copyist has forgotten to alter, but the two forms *two* & *tway*, both proved by rime, clearly demonstrate a two-fold pronunciation on the part of the author. We have here a good instance of his artificial mixture of language. Like Douglas, he introduces numerous Engl. forms, but retains the native Sc. forms by their side, using whichever suit his rimes best.

§ 42. In the mod. diall. we generally find (*i'*) in D. 33 and (ee) in the others. Some have in addition occasionally (aa) or (AA), e. g. *toe* in 38; *who* in 34, 35, 41, 42, especially in the form (faa) in 38, 39, 40, [this word has (ee) only in 35 & 36]; *two* has (*i'*) in 33, (ee) in 34, 35, 36, (aa) or (AA) in 34, 35, 36 & all the others. Sometimes (oo) is found too, e. g. in *so* in many of the diall., but (ee) is much more general & mostly given side by side with (oo), where the latter is given. *No* has (aa) in 38, 39, it is not given in the other diall. It should be added that the *w* is always pronounced in the forms of *two*, except in the solitary (tiu) of 36. The (oo) forms are evidently borrowed from Engl., the (aa) & (AA) of *who* & *two* are probably due to the preceding *w*.

2. Before n rimes with

§ 43. a) itself. Self-rimes are very numerous. Both *a* & *o* are written in the MS. but *o* is much more frequent than *a*. We also occasionally find *ai*, *ea* and once *y*, see (c), evidently a mistake for *a* or *ai*.

The following words rime exceedingly often together: *gone, one, alone, allone. anone* (the final *e* is frequently omitted).

Here follows a complete list of other spellings than *o* in self-rimes: aleane : anone 2. 348. grane (sb. = groan) : staine (OE. *stān*) 2. 1132. gaine (ptc.) : anone 4. 2824 : ane 5. 1078. goŭne (ptc.) : anone 2. 796. Further worth noticing are: onis (OE. *ānes*) : bonis 3. 1732 : gronis (sb.) 5. 2028. ons : bonis 5. 1166. fone (= foes, pl.) : anone 3. 1048. anone : fro (prep.) 4. 496 (faulty rime, cf. § 554). — b) OE. a-, see §§ 1 (d), 41 (a), 43 (a). — — c) OE. ǣ + g. schyne (OE. *scān*, prt.) : again 2. 686. ane : againe 3. 258. — d) OE. ǣ or ā in mone (rec. sp. *moan*) see § 226 (h). — e) OE. ā:, ō:. gone (ptc.) : þairon 3. 928. anon : on (prep.) 5. 2362. — f) OE. ō. gone : soune (OE. *sōna*) 4. 1156. — g) Fr. ai. alleane : plane (MS. place) 2. 252. gang (inf., for *gane*) : certain 3. 1912. — h) Fr. or Lat. a. gane (inf.): chirurgiane 5. 1494. — i) Fr. or Lat. o. anone : dispone 4. 172, 5. 1370 : Tutabon(e) 2. 774, 844 : Philippon 4. 2436, 5. 170   gone (inf.): dispone 4. 1306. gone (ptc.) : Philipon 5. 1750 : dispone 3. 1056 : guthrone (?) 5. 990. one : Tutabon 2. 736 : Philipon 5. 806. none : dispone 3. 2044. naine : dispone 3. 1132. ons (OE. *ānes*) : disponis (ind. pl.) 5. 2088. — k) AFr. u ? schone : comparisoun 5. 1788. — l) OE. u - allone : owercum, ptc. 3. 780, cf. §§ 500 (d), 501.

§ 44. Here again there is plain proof of two pronunciations. The rimes in (b), (c), (g), (h) prove $\bar{\varrho}$ and those in (e), (f), (i) and perhaps (d), prove o, short or long. In (c) we have evidence of the occasional shortening of the $\bar{o}$ in *gone* & *anon*, which has been carried out in rec. sp. The rime in (k) should perhaps have been placed in (i), for the vowel sound in *schone* cannot possibly be $\bar{u}$, the usual representation of AFr. u in the ending -*un*, as indicated by the spelling *ou*; the sound is $\bar{o}$ and we must explain the use of this in *comparison* by the influence of later Central French, with o for AFr. u.

§ 45. The varied orthography is here proof that the poem has been, either as a whole or in parts, through the hands of more than one copyist. We have the Scotch *a* & *ai*, the Southern English *o*, which must have often been also written, as the rimes show, by the *author*, and occasionally the English *ea*, for the open $\bar{\varrho}$-sound. The *oŭ* in *goŭne* = gone (with the curve over the *ŭ* to distinguish it from *n*) is very remarkable. One of the scribes must have been more Scottish than the author, for, although we notice on the whole rather a more Anglicising tendency in the copying than the author shows in his rimes, the reverse must have been the case in *naine* : *dispone*; the author must have written *none* as in the other rime in (i).

§ 46. The mod. Sc. diall. show in these words generally the correct continuation of MSc. $\bar{a}$, i. e. (*i'*) in D. 33, (*ee*) in the other diall., except sometimes (ii) in the NE. and N., where the $\bar{\varrho} < \bar{a}$ has been further raised to a high front vowel, e. g. in *bone*, *stone* in 38, 39, 41, *none* in 38, 39, 40, 41, *one* in 39, 41, 42. There is no trace of *o* in the words just mentioned, but *only* is given by Ellis always with an *o*-vowel and *lone* with (oo) in 33 & 36, but (ee) in 35, 38, 39 & *alone* has *e*-vowel in 35 & 37. The $\bar{o}$'s are plainly invasions from English.

§ 47. **The verb NE. slay = WS. slēan**, North. slā or slǣ, cf. Sievers § 374, n. 1. The rime-words contain — a) OE. ā. slo : go 1. 86 (&c.) : so 3. 632, 4. 1412 : also 3. 1510 : goe 3. 666 : wo 3. 2012, 4. 2278. sla : sa (*swā*) 3. 460. — b) OE. e + g. slay : say 2. 292. Here there is positive proof of an $\bar{e}$-pronunc., none of $\bar{o}$. Perhaps the rimes in (a) should be altered in spelling from *o* to *a*, but the rimes in the preceding paragraphs make this doubtful.

§ 48. The forms of the pte. = NE. *slain*, (WS. *slægen*, but perhaps in the N. new-formed **slān* from *slā*) are in perfect agreement; there is no proof of an *o*-pronunc. The rime-words contain — a) OE. œ + g. slaine : againe 2. 694 (&c.) (in 4. 1790 read *againe* for *againis*). — b) OE. e + g. slaine : saine (inf. *secgan*) 3. 1356, 4. 1784. — c) Fr. or Lat. a. slaine : Philistiane 5. 86 (*a* perhaps direct from Latin suffix -*anus*, cf. t. Br. p. 54, Behrens, Frz. St. 5. 2. 85 &c., Sturmfels, Angl. 8. 234). — d) Fr. ei. slaine : pain(e) 1. 916 (&c.).

§ 49. In the mod. Sc. diall. Ellis only gives (*ee*) for *slay* in 35 (also in 32), and an *e*-vowel for *slain* in 33, 35, 39 (also in 32); this can be from *slægen* or *slān*, both of which would produce NSc. $\bar{e}$, except in D. 33, which agrees with D. 32 (Northumberland) in having a fractured *i* sound for OE. $\bar{a}$, but an $\bar{e}$-vowel for OE. *æg*, *eg* &c. The occurrence of *slēn* in

D. 32, is therefore, if genuine, a proof of descent from *slægen* not *slān, but perhaps the forms are influenced by rec. sp.

3. Before m — rimes with

§ 50. — a) OE. a-. hame : name 3. 706. — b) OE. u- or a? home : come (ptc.) 3. 822. The first rime proves $\bar{e}$ and the second perhaps $\bar{o}$. The line: 'Wnto the sea strandis whill thay come', is evidently too short; Piper supplied *be* before *come*, making this into a ptc. instead of a prt., which was more probably the meaning of the author. In NSc. *home* has (i') in 33, (ii) in 41, and everywhere else an $\bar{e}$-vowel, the continuation of MSc. $\bar{a}$; the ptc. of the verb *come* is everywhere (kam) and the prt. generally (kam). We could perhaps alter to *hame* : *came* (prt.), but it is quite possible that the Anglicising tendency of the author permitted him to write *home* : *come* (ptc.), if we allow the development $u - > \bar{o}$, cf. §§ 43 (l), 377, 501.

4. $\bar{a} + g$ rimes with

§ 51. — a) OE. $\bar{a} + w$ ($\overline{ea} + w$ after palatal cons.). throw (sb. OE. *prāg*, time) : schow, inf. 3. 1028 : schew, inf. 3. 1346. — b) OE. æ + h. throw : saw, prt. 4. 1076. The *o* in *throw* is probably only due to the scribes; the sound was *au*, as in *saw*, &c. The word is only used in the sense of a 'short space of time', often preceded by little, so in 4. 1076 'within a litill throw', but 3. 1348 'Now ceise I of Clariodus ane throw', & 3. 1028 'Now of this Ladar leave I will ane throw'. Cf. K. Q. *a lytill thrawe* (: *alawe*) 35, (: *snawe*) 67.

5. $\bar{a} + w$ rimes with

§ 52. — a) OE. $\bar{a} + w$ ($\overline{ea} + w$ after palatal cons.) vnknawin (MS. *vnschawin*) : schawin 3. 1410. — b) OE. or N. a + g, see § 26 (b). — c) OE. æ + h, see § 98 (c). — d) OE. $\bar{a}$. know : so, 5. 1742.

§ 53. OE. $\bar{a} + w$ produced in most ME. diall. ǫu, the $\bar{a}$ here being rounded as usual to $\bar{o}$, and this ǫu afterwards became ǭu and later $\bar{o}$. In the 16th cent. ǫu represented no less than six different combinations in OE., $\bar{o}w$, $\bar{a}w$, *ow*. $\bar{o}g$, $\bar{a}g$, *og*, see Kluge P. G. 1. 887. But in Scotl. the $\bar{a}$ remained unrounded in $\bar{a}u$, just as it did in all other positions, and hence the rimes with $\bar{a}u$ from earlier $\check{a}u$, from OE. *ag*, *œh*, &c., and the further development to NSc. (aa) or (AA) instead of the (oo) or (ou) of mod. Southern English; cf. § 27. That is, in Scotland it is so:

earlier ău } > MSc. āu > NSc. (AA), (aa)
.... āu }

while in England it is thus:

earlier ău > ME. āu > NE. (AA)
.... āu > ǫu > (oo), (ou).

§ 54. The disappearance of the *u* in $\bar{a}u$ must, of course, have taken place after the change $\bar{a} > \bar{\varrho}$ was complete, otherwise the $\bar{a}$ from $\bar{a}u$ would have gone with original $\bar{a}$ and become NSc. $\bar{e}$ and we should expect to find rimes in MSc. with OE. *æg*, *eg*, Fr. *ai*, *ei*, &c.; but such are not to be found and the mod. diall. have nearly always (aa) or (AA), never (ee), e. g. in *blow*, *mow*, *snow*, *crow*, *throw* (vb.), *sow*, &c. Occasionally, but only rarely, *o* is found, which must be explained as due to the influence of rec. sp. We find (au) in *mow* in 35 & 38, (ou) in 39, otherwise it has (aa) or (ΑΛ). D. 39 has also the strange development of (īaav) in *blow, mow, sow*. We find the same sound (īaav) in *gnaw*, OE. *gnagan, saw* (vb. to saw timber), *awe*, from the same intermediate stage *au*.

§ 55. In spite of the spelling with *o* in the text (always so in *know* & *throw*) there is no evidence to prove an *o*-pronunc. beyond the one rime *know* : *so* see (d). How is this rime to be interpreted? We have two rimes to prove the *o* in *so*, see § 39 (c), and none which decisively prove $\bar{a}$ or $\bar{\varrho}$, although such was undoubtedly the native pronunc, and the *sa* which occurs once in the MS. was probably often used by the author. It is possible that *know* may in this case have been written by him too. But all the rimes of (b) & (c) demand an *a*, not *o*, which would induce us to change to *knaw* : *sa*. But then, again, if the rime is pure, it proves the loss of the second element of the diphthong, i. e. *knaw* is equivalent to *knā*, and then *sa* must have here the older $\bar{a}$ and not $\bar{\varrho}$, contrary to the preceding §. Although final $\bar{a}$ has in some cases remained in Sc., yet *so* is only found with $\bar{e}$ or $\bar{o}$ in Ellis's lists, and the two words *know* & *so* could not rime together in any of the mod. Sc. diall., where these have remained unaffected by rec. sp. We must consider this a purely English rime, with $\bar{o}$ in each word, and loss of *u* in *know*. This latter feature is a reason for not dating before 1500, for as yet no proof of the change $\bar{o}u > \bar{o}$ has been brought forward for the 15th cent. We have a similar rime later in Montg. *go* : *kno* MP. 38. 2.

6. Before r rimes with

§ 56. — a) OE. $\bar{a}$. more : sore 1. 1014 (&c.) : sair 3. 1536. moire : sore 1. 172, mair : sair 2. 86, see also § 195 (g). — b) OE. a-. more : fair (OE. *faru*) 3. 1354. mair(e) : ar (ind. pl. OE. *arun*) 3. 618 : fair 3. 634 (&c.) : cair 3. 1742. — c) OE. æ + g. sair : fair (*fæger*) 3. 114. — d) OE. o. more : before 2. 100 (&c.) : thairfore 2. 498 : befor 5. 1686 : Windieschore (= Windsor, OE. *Windles-ora*) 2. 1936, moir : thairfore 2. 472. sore : befor(e) 1. 10 (&c.). — e) Fr. a. mair : declair 2. 1640. saire : declaire 4. 2078. — f) Fr. ai. rare (OE. *rārian*) : air 1. 724, 2. 1128. rair (sb.) : air 5. 2322. — g) Fr. or Lat. o. more : restore 3. 596 : glore 3. 1312, 4. 2032 : decore 5. 1874. sorie : glorie 3. 968. — h) ? sore : schore 3. 498 ('with awful cheir & schore').

§ 57. The rimes in (b), (c), (e), (f), prove $\bar{e}$, those in (d), (g), (h), prove $\bar{o}$. For *more* & *sore* we have therefore a twofold pronunc., one native, the other an Anglicism. The mod. Sc. diall. have every where $\bar{e}$, even in D. 33, where we generally find (*i'*) for OE. $\bar{a}$; probably the retention of the $\bar{e}$ is due to the following *r*, cf. § 310. Ellis gives $\bar{o}$ in D. 38, as well as $\bar{e}$; (we notice in his list for this dial. many suspicious agreements with rec. sp., contrary to the speech of the surrounding diall.).

7. $\bar{a}$ + ht.

§ 58. *a)* OE. *āwiht, nāwiht*. The rime words contain — a) OE. $\breve{o}$ + ht. nocht : wrocht 1. 242 (&c.) : bocht 1. 1178, 3. 1832 : foght (ptc.) 5. 1698 : micht (for *mocht*, prt., perhaps from a form **mohte*) 4. 1378. nought : wrought 4. 2634. — b) OE. $\bar{o}$ + ht (i. e. original $\bar{o}$, which according to Sweet, § 403, became shortened in OE. in the words *brohte, sohte, gepoht*, &c.). nocht : brocht 1. 766, 1468 : brought 5. 774 : bethocht 1. 1008 : thocht (sb.) 3. 1826, 4. 1432. nought : sought 4. 712. ocht : brocht 2. 1608 :

thocht (sb.) 3. 1468. — c) OE. ā + t. not : wote (OE. wāt, 1. sg.) 3. 1868.
β) OE. āhte, prt. rimes only with Fr. a + ch. awcht (= owed) : caucht
2. 1202.

§ 59. The ME. forms *ought, nought*, are usually explained from forms with *ō* instead of *ā*, which are found already in OE., *ōwiht, ōht, nōwiht, nōht*, instead of *āwiht*, &c.; see Sievers § 344 & t. Br. § 45, note. In the combination *ōht* the *ō* was shortened at an early date, and this and original *ŏht* produced ME. *ouχt*. It seems that we must accept these *ō*-forms even in the extreme N., since *oght, ocht, noght, nocht*, are found in quite early texts and proved by rime, e. g. Curs. M. *noght : wroght*, Early Sc. Laws, *ocht, nocht* (see Murray DSS. p. 32).

§ 60. In Clar., too, we have rimes with OE. *ŏht, ōht*, see above, § 58 (a) & (b). Cf. further Bruce, *nocht : thoucht* 7. 557, *ocht : nocht* 3. 282; Sc. Leg. *nocht : brouchte* 6/84, *ocht : thocht* 11/450; *nocht : socht* 11/454; K. Q. *noght : rought* (= cared) 27, *ought : thoght : ybought* 36; Wall. *nocht : thocht* 1. 252 : *socht* 2. 136, &c., innumerable rimes (always spelt *nocht* and *only* in rime with OE. *ŏht, ōht*), *ocht : thocht* 9. 1678 : *socht* 11. 664; Craft of Deyng, *nocht*; Dunb. *nought : bocht* 6. 51, *nocht : wrocht : thocht* 15. 1, *ocht : thocht : brocht : nocht* 42. 61; Dougl. *nocht is : bocht is* 4. 5. 5, *nocht : brocht* 4. 27. 24 : *thocht* 4. 94. 10: Roll. C. V. *ocht*; Satir. P. *nocht : thocht* 31. 224 : *bocht* 36. 152, &c. &c.; Montg. *ocht, oght : wroght : thoght : moght* MP. 20. 29, *nocht : bocht* C. 149 : *socht* MP. 22. 16, *ought : wroght : brought : sought* F. 328, &c.; Sir Tr. *ouχt : brouχt : wrouχt : nouχt*, Surt. Ps. *oght : noght : broghte* (see Wende, p. 18), Lyric. P. Ms. Harl. 2253, *noht : boht : wroht : soht* (see Schlüter p. 8), &c., &c.

§ 61. But it is questionable whether in the extreme N. a parasitic *u* was developed between *o* & *ht*, as in the Midl. & S.; for *ou* is rarely found in Sc. MSS., & where found, it is generally far less frequent than simple *o*. Clar. has -*ocht* in the first three books, & *ought* sometimes (but also -*oght*) in the 4th & 5th. (We notice also here, by the way, the same difference as we shall find below with regard to the *icht*-words; -*cht* prevails in the first three books, and -*ght* in the last two, in which Engl. influence is more strongly marked in the orthography). Zielke, p. 17, understands the -*oght*, -*ocht* of Northern texts as = the -*ought* of Midl. & Southern, and would pronounce everywhere with the diphthong *ou*. But the words which appear in rime above, e. g. *wrought, bought, thought, brought*, &c., are pronounced with (okht) in *all* the mod. Sc. diall., *nought* is also given by Ellis as (nokht) in D. 41, (otherwise he only gives the shortened forms *not, no*, &c., and *ought*, sb., he does not mention at all). The *u*, as well as the -*ght*, where they appear in the MSS., may be Anglicisms introduced by the scribes, and -*ocht* should be pronounced, at any rate in MSc. texts, as it is spelt, and not as Zielke suggests. We might perhaps suppose that the *ŏ* of NSc. is of quite recent origin, due to a simplification of MSc. *ou* to *ŏ*, in *ouχt*, just as in Engl. but with retention of the gutt. and shortening of the vowel; but the consistent spelling with *o*, not *ou*, in MSc. texts, is against this.

§ 62. It might be suggested that the abbreviation, ‘ above the line, which is so frequent in Sc. texts, means *ucht* or *ught* after *o*, i. e. that *tho'* means *thoucht* or *thought*; but this can hardly be so, for whenever these words are written in full, they nearly always appear without *u*, whereas the words of the other class, containing OE. *-äht*, generally have *-aucht, -awcht,* &c.; (the latter seem to be always written in full, according to the few published texts which correctly represent the MSS. e. g. Skeat's Bruce, & Horstmann's Sc. Leg.; unfortunately, the texts of the Scottish Text Soc. do not always mark contractions).

§ 63. Noltemeier's mere suggestion (p. 20), without any attempt at proof, that *o* in *broght* &c., is equivalent to *ñ* (!), is one of many remarks in his very superficial treatise which it is scarcely necessary to take seriously.

§ 64. The OE. forms being *-ŏht, -ōht*, the regular forms in MSc. texts being *-ocht, -oght,* & there being no trace of an *u* in the mod. Sc. diall., it is much simpler to suppose that there never was a diphthong in these words; though, of course, the other development would be possible, $ōht > ŏht > ouχt > ōuχt > ōχt > ŏχt$, and would have an exact parallel in that of OE. *-ăht, -äht,* see § 68.

§ 65. However this may be, it is certain that in Sc. original *-äht, -āht* and *-ŏht, -ōht* never coincided as they have done in Engl., for in the mod. Sc. diall. they are generally kept quite distinct (with the exception to be immediately mentioned). This difference is also shown in our text, cf. the rime in § 58, β.

§ 66. The rime in § 58 (c) gives us the contracted form of *nocht,* spelt *not,* with loss of the gutt.. We have here evidently an imitation of Engl. in the case of *wote;* for, although OE. *wāt* elsewhere in Clar., cf. § 72, only rimes with OE. or Fr. *ā*, yet *nāt* or *nęt* is impossible, and we must therefore read, with Engl. pronunc., *wǫt,* or *wǭt*, with shortened vowel as in the *wot* of the Bible, (we also find a short vowel in this word in Satir. P. wat : that, 17. 173), and consequently, if the rime is good, *nǫt* *nǭt*, probably the latter, which may also be an Anglicism.

§ 67. The treatment of OE. *āhte* is very different, see § 58, β), although, strange to say, the mod. Sc. diall. acc. to Ellis have everywhere (okht) for the verb *ought,* and are thus at variance with all MSc. texts, which generally show *aucht, awcht,* i. e. they have no sign of a change from *a* to *o*, and also have the diphthong with *u*. Can Ellis's lists be here misleading, the form of the sb. *ought* being meant, or has MSc. *auχt* really become *oχt*? This would be a striking anomaly, for in other words with MSc. *auχt* the mod. Sc. diall. have (akht) or (aakht), e. g. in *taught, draught, eight* [the latter also occasionally (eekht) and (ækht)], and even in *haughty*; cf. Murray DSS. p. 88, note. And if we can draw any conclusion from the MSc. orthography, we must allow that *-aht* has developed the parasitic *u* and produced MSc. *auχt,* for we nearly always find *-aucht, -awcht*, and only in a few of the earlier texts *-acht, -aght,* which probably mean that the *u* was not yet developed in their time. In texts which have always *-ocht* without variation, we find *-aucht* written with the same consistency, never *-acht*.

§ 68. It is difficult to see why there should be a difference in development of -oht and -aht, especially as they present a similar appearance in mod. Sc., viz. (okht) and (akht). The latter is apparently to be explained thus -āht > ăht > auχt > āuχt > āχt > ăχt, the āu losing its u here in the same way as simple āu, see § 53, and the parallelism -ōht > ŏht > ouχt > ōuχt > ōχt > ŏχt suggests itself at once. But the striking difference in the orthography of MSc. texts must surely have a meaning; for it is hardly likely that in the one combination there should be a general following of Engl. orthography and not in the other. Cf. the following examples:

§ 69. Bruce, has -awcht, -aucht, and occasionally -owcht, but the latter not in rime, e. g. maucht (OE. maht) : raucht (= reached) 2. 420, 15. 490, 19. 587, raucht : straucht (= stretched) 8. 298, faucht, fawcht, passim, aucht (= eight); Sc. Leg. acht : tacht 240/836, aucht 21/445, awcht : tawcht 20/428, taucht : mawcht 7/200, 11/504, tawcht (= given) : lacht (= seized) 17/202, maucht : fyreslacht 192/16, &c., &c.; (the spelling in the Sc. Leg. is altogether very irregular, we find broucht 5/39, 7/140, browcht 7/139, nocht : brouchte 6/84, but brocht : thocht, nocht : wrocht, p. 21); K. Q. aught (OE. āhten) 120, straught 151, straucht 158, oure-straught 164; Gol. aught, laught (= taken) : vnsaught : raught : straught 460; Lanc. oucht 2995 (of course, Engl. spelling); Dunb. aucht, (but nocht, e. g. 'to put handis on Him that aucht the nocht'); Dougl. auchtin, prt. pl., 4. 1. 5, aucht (= eight), aucht (= possession, OE. ǣht) : taucht 2. 127. 2, caucht 4. 13. 12, betaucht : vpstraucht 4. 63. 22 : straucht 4. 110. 26, onsaucht (adj. OE. onsǣht) : claucht (= seized) 4. 116. 4, (but always nocht &c., without u); Bellenden's Livy (DSS. p. 62) slauchter, faucht; Compl. Sc. aucht; Satir. P. faucht : saucht (OE. saht?) 13. 177; and so on in all texts, while nocht, brocht, thocht, &c., nearly always appear without u. (Montg. has ocht MP. 42. 6 instead of aucht; is this a later form, or merely a false spelling? we also find ou instead of au in some of the later writers, e. g. Satir. P. foucht 26. 22, Douchter 33. 102).

§ 70. English examples — Sir Tr. fauʒt : mauʒt : tauʒt : drauʒt : sauʒt, mouʒt : pouʒt : nouʒt : wrouʒt : souʒt, fauʒt : wrouʒt : brouʒt : pouʒt : nouʒt, auʒt and ouʒt, prt. (see Kölbing p. 62 & glossary; these are very different from the Sc. rimes & spelling); Lyric P. ahte (OE. ǣht) : tahte : lahte (lǣccan) : sahte (saht) : raht (ptc. of rǣcan), see Schlüter, p. 8; Horn Ch. auʒt (OE. eahta) : bitouʒt, mouʒt (prt.) : brouʒt, mauʒt (meaht) : auʒt : bitauʒt : fauʒt, see Caro, p. 19; Hamp. aght; Rol. & Ot. aughte, 406; Sir Eglam. aught, raght (reahte), see Zielke, p. 21.

§ 71. But for the general au, aw in MSc. we might suppose that OE. āht had remained undiphthonged all through the MSc. period to the present day, in the same way as ōht; but the au, aw, and especially the mod. Sc. (akht) in haughty as in taught, are strong enough evidence of MSc. auχt. But the mod. Sc. (okht) for the prt. āhte, if correct, is difficult to explain. It should be noticed that fought has also (okht) in D. 35, 38, 39, but this may be due to the ptc. OE. fohten; D. 41 has (faakht). In D. 33, the gutt. has completely disappeared in the ptc. aucht, (aad), see Murray DSS. p. 128, probably new-formed from pres. (aa).

§ 72. Before other consonants — rimes with — a) itself.
wait (OE. wāt, pres. indic.) : heicht (pres. ind. hātan) 3. 1838 : heat (sb.,
but to be derived here from OE. hāt, n., not hǣtu, f.) 3. 2196 : note (OE.
ne wāt) 4. 1024. raise (OE. rās, prt.) : gais (3 sg.) 1. 1168, rose : gois 2. 172.
strake : aike (OE. āc) 4. 1094 — and many others. — b) OE. a-, see § 1 (d).
— c) OE. ǣ, see § 80 (d). — d) OE. æ + g. raid (prt.) : said 2. 244 (&c.).
abaid(e), sb. : said 5. 438, 4. 1678 : abraid (OE. ābrægd, prt.) 3. 482. abaid,
prt. : said 5. 234, baid (prt. bād) : said 5. 1564. — e) OE. e + g. abaid, sb. :
abraid (ābregdan) 4. 1774 : laid, prt. 5. 1270. abaid, prt. : laid 4. 974. raise,
prt. : wayis ('upon this wayis') 4. 2478, (cf. §§ 440, 441). — f) OE. e. haill
(OE. hāl or ON. heil?) : tell 3. 912. — g) OE. c̄a. drave, drane : clave (clēaf,
prt.) 1. 48, 730, (cf. § 282). — h) Fr. or Lat. a. haill : royall 5. 2886. leave
(OE. lāf) : saue (with loss of l, salver) 4. 220, lave : save 4. 1912. raid,
prt. : avoide (for evaid) 4. 1072. wait (wāt) : estait 2. 226, 4. 138. — i) Fr. al.
haill : batell 1. 142 : travell 1. 606 : trawell 2. 1260 : awaill 2. 1206. — k) Fr.ai.
leave (lāf) : resaue 4. 738 (&c.). — l) Fr. e. wraite (prt. wrāt) : regrate
(= regret) 3. 1722. — m) Fr. o. gois (3 sg.) : repose 5. 596.

§ 73. The rime in (m) is the only one which proves an o-pronunc.,
and this is naturally explained from the uninflected form, which, as we
have seen, appears as go. All the others prove an ē-pronunc. Especially
the rimes in (f) and (l) are worthy of notice as proof of the change ā > ē;
we have a similar rime in 3. 712, grace : wilderness, cf. D u n b. place :
space : rekless 15. 34; D o u g l. soles (= solace) : maistres : craftines : in-
cres : expres 3. 16; they are, it is true, quantitatively inexact, but qualita-
tively they are correct, and in one case, regrate, even a is written for the
original vowel e. The rimes in (i) may be further similar evidence of
ā > ē; the spelling -ell shows that, for the scribe, the vowel of the final
syll. in travel & battle had already been shortened into ĕ.

§ 74. As we have already seen, the mod. diall. should have ē everywhere, with the exception of (i') in D. 33. But in Ellis's lists we find ō
preponderating in stroke, oar, goat, boat [only one exception (biit) in 42],
road (only once ē by the side of ō in 39; rode, prt. is regular), and only
ō in mole. Occasionally o is found also in wrote, oath, cloth, oak, loaf,
whole, ghost; but as ē is much more frequent, and the o-forms are not
confined to one dial. or set of diall., but scattered about singly amongst
them all, these are plainly recent borrowings from rec. sp.; and probably
all the other o-forms are of the same origin.

§ 75. It has been noticed by Brandl (AnzfdA. 13. 95 &c.), as peculiar
to many ME. texts, that ā has become ō only in one or more particular
positions, before r, or n, or finally; it will be seen from the foregoing
paragraphs that it is similar in Clar., we have proofs of the change in each
of the positions just mentioned, and in addition, before m. It is strange
that although the mod. diall. do sometimes show o, according to Ellis's
lists, it is not in those positions in which o is proved by rime in MSc.
texts, and therefore we shall probably be right in ascribing all the modern
ō's, as well as those of MSc. texts, to the influence of rec. sp. Brandl,
AnzfdA. 10. 333, &c., accepts those of the earlier texts as of genuine
growth in the local diall. of their respective authors. He even assumes

that in Scotl. the later introduction of *o* for *a* was helped by an occasional tendency in the same direction already previously existent in the vernacular. But the mod. diall. cannot be said to bear this out. Brandl, l. c. p. 337, allows for the later period that 'the *o*'s which gradually in increasing numbers invade the Scotch literary language, from the middle of the 15th century onwards, made their way into the language of learning, the Reformation & courtly poetry without affecting the vernacular diall.; they found their way into Scotland, but not into Scotch'. We must probably extend this Anglicising influence also to the earlier period, and account for the earlier *o*'s in the same way, rather than consider them as of actual native growth.

§ 76. The suffix -ledge in *knowledge*. No satisfactory etymology has yet been found for this suffix. ON. *-leikr* and OE. *-læcan*, (*-*lācian*) are insufficient (see Skeat, Princ. p. 219, Brate, p. 49). Possibly it is an instance of exchange of suffix, but the verbal form ME. *lēchen* cannot explain the MSc. form, which always rimes with *ā*; it also has a *g*, not *ch*, which, however, can be explained through unstressedness. In Clar. it is spelt with *e*, but rimes with Fr. a — *knowlege* : *courage* 4. 1768, *knowleg* : *age* 3. 74. Cf. Bruce *knawlage* 1. 337; Wall. *knawlage* : *passage* 9. 328 : *langage* 10. 602; Lanc. *knawlag* : *ag* (= age) 1658; Ratis R. *knawleg* : *outrage* 436, *mysknawleg* : *rage* 1421, *misknawlege* : *rage* 1631, *knawleg* : *age* 2. 20, *knawlage* : *Cusingage* 2. 330, *knawleg* : *ȝouthage* 3. 2, *knawlege* : *wysage* 3. 402, *knawlage* : *ȝouthage* (Thewis of good women) 222; so also St. Werb. *knowlege* : *rage* 1. 932, i. e. it is mostly spelt with *e* and rimes always with Fr. *-age*; perhaps it has merely adopted this suffix in Scotl. from the French. We find *a* in Destr. Troy. *knawlache* 1083, *knowlage* 1865. The verb appears with *e* in Lyfe of Joseph *knowlege*, Gau *knowledge*, Roll. C. V. *knawleging*, but Relig. P. (EETS. 26) *knaweliggynge* 57/6.

ÆE -

§ 77. Not followed by g — rimes with — a) OE. œ : quhidder (*hwæper*) : togidder (*togædre*) 2. 1162. — b) OE. ō : quhidder : vther (*ōper*) 3. 1730.

§ 78. The rime in (a) gives of itself no certain information as to the vowel sound, but the spelling with *i* is found in most MSc. texts, and is often proved by rime: e. g. Satir. P. *togidder* : *slidder* : *fidder* : *considder* 6. 53 : *considder* : *hidder* (= hither) 12. 105, *altogidder* : *widder* (= whither) 15. 22, &c.; Dougl. *togiddyr* : *quhiddyr* 4. 87. 4; Roll. C. V. *quhidder* 2. 147. Similar forms with *i* are found also in Chauc. and London documents, cf. t. Br. p. 35, Morsb. p. 30. The rime in (b), though at first sight strange, is not to be ranked among the imperfect rimes, for we find similar ones in other texts, e. g. Satir. P. *togidder* : *mother* 10. 28 : *vther* 10. 106 (&c.); (in the same poem we find *togidder* : *considder* 10. 178). The mod. diall. show that in each case the vowel *i* is to be understood, cf. below, § 491.

§ 79. It may be remarked, in passing, that the above rimes and the mod. diall. prove two possible forms of the conson. in the middle of the above words. *whether* appears with (dh) in D. 32, and (d) in 39, *together* has (d) in 32 & 42, and (dh) in 39 & 41, while *other, mother*, &c. generally have (dh), but also (d) in the N. of Scotland. Our two rimes leave it doubtful whether we are to pronounce with (d) or (dh). Completer knowledge of the mod. diall. would perhaps be valuable for localising MSc. texts according to the treatment of OE. vowel + *þer* & vowel + *der*. For æ + g see § 94.

Æ:

§ 80. Not followed by gutturals — rimes with — a) itself. was : hes (3. sg.) 3. 902. bade, prt. : glaid, adj. 4. 480. sate, prt. : at 4. 1384. had(e), prt. : sad 1. 1240 : glaid(e) 4. 2446, 5. 970. brake, prt. : bake (sb. OE. *bæc*) 3. 1066 : abake (*on bæc*) 4. 658. — b) OE. or ON. a : see § 36 (b) and § 264 (c). — c) OE. or ON. a - see §§ 1 (b), 19 (b), 20 (b). — d) OE. ā. glaid : abade (sb.) 5. 826. had(e) : abaid, prt. 3. 556 : baid 4. 560 : abaid, sb. 5. 1634. gaue : leave (*lāf*) 4. 1668, 2842. baire, prt. : thair (cf. below § 198) 4. 156, 856, büire : thair 1. 78. — e) OE. æ + g. bade : said 1. 1286. glaid : maid 2 248 : said 3. 248. had : said 3. 1910. — f) OE. e + g. glaid : laid, prt. 4. 310. — g) OE. e. fret (ptc. of OE. *frætwan*) : sete, ptc. 2. 1724 (&c.). was : humbilnes 2. 318 : bissines 3. 1980, 2. 356 : nobilnes 4. 2424, 5. 516 : blythnes 3. 2420. — h) OE. or ON. ō. bad(e) : led, prt. 3. 504 : rade (ON. *hræddr*) 4. 116. sade (*sæd*) : mad (*gemædd*) 3. 2126. hade, prt. : adred, ptc. 3. 1456. glaid : led (ptc. *lādan*) 2. 1034. was : les (OE. *læssa*) 2. 956, 3. 894. — i) OE. eo. carts (OE. *cræt*) : hearts 3. 1644 (cf. below §§ 303 ff.). — k) Fr. a. fast : past, prt. 3. 2084. was : cace 1. 1088 : space 2. 1190 (&c.). hes, 3. sg. : place 2. 114 : lace, vb. 2. 1518 : cace 5. 488 : grace 4. 2382, 5. 976. brase (*bræs*) : pas (vb.) 5. 2084. small : victoriall 5. 2246. — l) Fr. au. was : caus 1. 860. — m) OFr. & AFr. ai. bair, prt. : air 2. 24. — n) OFr. ai = AFr. ei, e. was : displease 3. 2050 : palice 3. 1768. — o) Fr. al. gane : saue 3. 798, 4. 356. — p) Fr. ͡ . was : princes 3. 2376 : duches 5. 454, 760 : lairges 5. 1624 : maistres 3. 852, 866. wes : dres, vb. 5. 736. — q) OFr. ei = AFr. e. gave, gaue : resave, resaue 2. 84 (&c.). — r) Fr. i. was : Palexis 1. 1540 (&c.). — s) Fr. u. was : Clariodus 1. 134. buire, prt. : indure 5. 2222.

§ 81. The usual ME. form of OE. æ is *a*, but *e* is also found in almost all diall, particularly before the dentals, *d, þ, t, n* and especially *s*; cf. Menze, p. 19, Zielke, p. 10, &c.; the latter gives abundant examples of the representation of OE. æ in different diall. & observes that the farther north we go, the less frequent *e* becomes. Clar. only gives us two examples of *ĕ*, viz in *fret* and *wes*; see the rimes in (g) & (p); *fret* is one of the few words which have short *ĕ* for OE. æ in rec. sp.

§ 82. OE. *wæs* appears in Clar. in a variety of forms. It is well known that in many texts both *was* and *wes* are found, and further that the *ĕ* or *ă* from OE. æ is sometimes lengthened before *s*; see t. Br. p. 27, Schlüter p. 16; cf. Bruce, *was* : *gais* : *tais* : *mais*, &c., (see Buss, p. 17); Sc. Leg. *wes* : *grace* 7/185 : *place* 10/386, *wess* : *place* 6/98, *wase* : *place* 8/248, Gol. *vves* : *des* (= dais) 1154, Rosw. *was* : *grace* 818. So in Clar., the rimes with *cace*, *space*, see (k), have the long vowel *ę̄* from previous *ă*. The rime with *caus*, see (l), is a solitary instance of the rounding influence of the preceding *w*, which we see in rec. sp. (woz), unless we are to suppose must be sought in the nature of the conson. r. The form *buire*, which is wrongly written by a scribe for *baire* in 1.78, see (d), was also known to the author, as is evident from the rime in (s); it appears in many other Sc. texts, (cf. Satir. P. *buir* : *iniure* : *huir* : *suir*, 39. 175, *bure* : *sure* 40. 115 : *cure* 41. 36, and see Wackerzapp), so also *schuir*, and both forms are reflected in the mod. diall., see Murray, DSS., p. 203, &c., Buss p. 30; the *u* is to be explained from the analogy of verbs of Class VI.

§ 88. The $\bar{e} < \bar{a}$ in *gave* is not to be considered as organic, but rather due to Norse influence, i. e. in the N. & in Scotl.; in the S. perhaps the $\bar{a}$ wrose in the same way as in *spāk*. There is no case of $\breve{a}$, $g\breve{a}f$, in Clar. and the mod. diall. also reflect a long $\bar{a}$. Sweet explains the long vowel from the long vowel of the infin., whence also *gave* got its *v*. This may also have helped; there may have been several influences at work, all tending in the same direction.

§ 89. The other preterites have regularly only a short vowel in MSc. texts & mod. Sc. diall.; where $\bar{a}$ or the later $\bar{\varrho}$ is found, (as in Clar.) it is due to Engl. influence. *brake* and *spake* have only short $\breve{a}$, see (a) & (c), for the rime-words *take* and *crake* have a short vowel, see §§ 4—8, and cf. Satir. P. *spak* : *crak* 42. 30; Sir Perc. *spake* : *sakke* : *blakke*, (see Ellinger, p. 5); cf. also NED. s. v. *brake*, prt. *Sate* appears to have two pronunciations, see (a) & (c) & cf. § 9. *bade* has a long vowel in rime with *glaid*, *said*, but probably a short one in rime with *rade*, *led*, see (a), (e), (h).

§ 90. *glaid* appears mostly with a long vowel, as the spelling *ai* implies, and the rimes in (e) & (f) prove. So in most Sc. texts; cf. also Sir Tr. *glade* : *brade* : *rade* : *made*, (Kölbing p. 61). The long $\bar{a}$, later $\bar{e}$, in MSc. *glaid* and other similar words, is to be explained from inflected OE. forms which contained *a*- instead of *œ* : . The passage in which the rime in (f) occurs was misunderstood by Piper, who took *glaid* to be a verb, (although no verb is necessary) and inserted an *it*, 'as ony lampe with blissfull beames [it] glaid'; the metre, too, is quite perfect without *it*, if we give *beames* two syllables. The same rime *glaid* : *laid* occurs in Montg. F. 37. As an instance of the confusion in pronunciation of *glad*, cf. Rosw. *glad* : *said* 386 : *made* 434,764 : *bed* 830 : *dead* 878.

§ 91. *had*, OE. *hæfde* is another word which appears in Clar. as well as in other texts with both long and short vowel; cf. Buss p. 20, Sc. Leg. *had* : *mad* (= made) 4/78, Satir. P. *had* : *maid* (= made) 42. 206, 402; Rosw. *had* : *laid* (prt.) 68. But in our text the long vowel is more frequent; we have $\bar{\varrho}$ in (c) and (d) and partly in (a), for *glaid*, as we have just seen, has a long vowel; *sad* has probably a short one, cf. *sade* : *mad* in (h), though, according to the analogy of *glaid*, a long vowel would be possible also here; but it lacks a rime of proof. The rime *hade* : *adred* also perhaps contains $\breve{a}$, for the rimes in (h) are not all capable of explanation from pure Sc.; we must accept Engl. influence somewhere; if we allow $\breve{a}$, the correct Sc. form, in *led*, *adred*, then the first rime *bad* : *led* can only be approximately correct with $\bar{\varrho}$ instead of $\breve{a}$ in *bad*, which is, of course, an Anglicism; the rimes *hade* : *adred* & *glaid* : *led* would then be $\bar{\varrho}$: $\breve{e}$ rimes in a similar way; if we accept $\breve{a}$ in *bad*, then the necessary $\breve{a}$ in *led* and *adred* is an Anglicism. It is true *glaid* otherwise only has that *caus* is a mistake for *cace*, which *could* suit the passage, but not quite so well as *cause*: 'The Earle demandit quhy he sorie was, My Lord, he said, this is the werie caus.' The rimes with *Palexis* and *Clariodus*, see (r) and (s), are probably merely the result of the unstressedness both of the verb *was* and of the final syllables of the rime-words, and should perhaps be placed among the imperfect, though it is possible that that with *Clariodus* may be approximately correct, if we interpret it as a sign of the rounding influence of the *w*.

§ 83. The rime with *displease*, see (n), does not mean that the vowel is the $\bar{i}$, arising from previous $\bar{e}$, for in Scotl. the words which in rec. sp. have $\bar{i} <$ ME. $\bar{e} <$ AFr. $\bar{e} <$ OFr. *ei*, *ai*, have nearly always $\bar{e}$ (riming in MSc. with previous $\bar{a}$, &c,) which is to be explained directly from Central French *ei*, *ai*. The spelling *ei* which sometimes appears in these words in Sc. texts, is a Sc. spelling for an English pronunc.; the *ea* in *displease* is an English spelling more correctly representing a pure Sc. pronunc., but cf. *pleis* : *malice*, 3. 488 : *appease*, 3. 2182, *displese* : *vneise* 4. 1410, in which we have all kinds of spelling for all kinds of pronunc.; the author pronounced $\bar{e}$ in all the words. The rime *was* : *palice* is similar; the Sc. pronunc. was $w\bar{e}s$: $pal\bar{e}s$; the *i* in *palice* is the result of an Engl. pronunc. with unstressedness of the final syll.

Both forms *was* and *wes* were known to the scribes, the last of whom was no more careful to preserve good eye-rimes with this word than he was with others.

§ 84. The mod. Sc. diall. show the same variety; Ellis gives (*a*, a, *e*, e, ᴂ, ʉ, *i*, y); in D. 35 alone he gives no less than three forms, (waz, wez, waz). In Clar. and other MSc. texts there is no sign of the voicing of the *s*, which we have in rec. sp. and NSc. We may accept as *proved* by rime in Clar. only *wĕs* and *wę̄s* ($<$ *wās*) and must consider the other forms doubtful, which only appear in solitary rimes; there is no rime to prove *was*.

§ 85. Most of the other rimes prove a MSc. *a*-vowel, but there is so much irregularity with regard to the vowel quantity, that it will be well to discuss the words singly or in single groups.

It is noticeable that *fast*, which has *e* in so many ME. texts, only appears here with *a*; in NSc. it has *a* in 33, 35, 36, and an *e*-vowel in 38, 39, 41.

§ 86. The group of preterites of Classes 4 & 5 of the strong conjug. show nearly all two forms, of which the one seems to be pure Sc., and the other a borrowing from Engl. The words in question are OE. *bær*, *scær*, *bræc*, *spæc*, *bæd*, *gæf*. We should expect an $\bar{a}$ everywhere where the development is regular, and this is the usual form in Sc. right down to the present day, except in words ending in *r* and in *gave*, in which the same lengthening seems to have taken place as in Engl.; for an explanation of this long $\bar{a}$ in ME. see Bülbring, p. 61, & cf. Sweet, § 624.

§ 87. *schare* and *baire* only have a long vowel, $\bar{e} < \bar{a}$. It will be seen from Wackerzapp's lists that this $\bar{a}$ in *bār*, *schār*, is found in all Northern English & Sc. texts of the ME. period; the cause of lengthening in these words and the non-lengthening in the others of the same class ę and *hade* mostly so, so that we might be inclined to accept ę in the doubtful cases, but the simplest way out of the difficulty is to assume a twofold pronunc. of these words on the part of the author, for which we have analoga in abundance, and to understand an ă in all the rimes in (h) (except in *was* : *les*).

Murray's dial., D. 33, has (æ) in *had* and (ææ) in *glad*, while D. 37, 41, 42 have an e-vowel in the latter word.

§ 92. *blake* : *take* is discussed in § 4; the vowel is ă. *was* : *hes*, see (a); the vowel here is probably ę, not ă, cf. Gol. *haise* : *grace*, 794. *small*, see (b) & (k), appears in Clar. only with a short vowel, but we apparently have a long vowel in Dunb. *small* : *travall* : *awaill* : *nychtingaill* 46. 114.

§ 93. We see that the author was particularly prone in the words we have just discussed to stray fnom his own dial. and to make use of duplicate forms.

§ 94. 2. œ + g rimes with — a) OE. œ + g. day : may, vb. 2. 1402, 3. 1682 : lay, prt. 5. 1924. said : maid(e) (OE. *mægden*) 1. 1474 (&c.) : madine (for *maid*) 2. 1734 (&c.) : braid (prt. OE. *brægd*) 4. 2644. — b) OE. e + g. madine (for *maid*) : laid, ptc. 3. 860. day : away 1. 330 (&c.) : play 1. 846 (&c.) : say 1. 1012 (&c.) : way 2. 1452, 5. 2606. again : saine (inf. *secgan*) 2. 150, 4. 1068. said : braid (inf. *bregdan*) 3. 206. lay, prt. : say 2. 396 : alway 2. 1380 : way 3. 441. may, vb. : say 1. 234 (&c.) : way 3. 1906, — c) OE. œ (not followed by *g*); see § 80 (e). — d) OE. a-; see §§ 1 (c), 20 (c), 22 (b). — e) OE. ā. see §§ 38 (b), 43 (c), 48 (a), 56 (c), 72 (d). — f) OE. ǣ or ā before *r*; cf. §§ 196 ff. fair(e) (*fæger*) : thair(e) 1, 818 (&c.) : war (*wǣron*) 4. 2290 : aire (*ǣr*) 5. 746. — g) OE. e. faire : godlier (compar.) 4. 524. — h) OE. ī. faire : wyre (OE. *wīr*) 4. 1008, (see §§ 164 ff.). — i) N. ei. day : thay 3. 384 (&c.) : ay 3. 1224, 1882. may, vb. : thay 3. 1632, 5, 1138 : ay 9. 2328, 5. 144. lay, prt. : thay 4. 2316. — k) ON. i + g. day : quyetlie 3. 1642 (see § 164). — l) Fr. or Lat. a. faire : declaire 5. 722, 1746. said : degraid 2. 1060 : evaid 3. 1622. haill (*hægl*) : vaile (= valley) 4. 1612. — m) Fr. ai. fair(e) : preclair(e), 1. 686 (&c.) : repair(e) (= go, proceed) 1. 848 (&c.) : debonar(e) 4. 782 (&c.), debonair 5. 2164 : aire 4. 258, 2750 : compaire (sb. = equal) 5. 1706. mone (for *mane*, or *main*, OE. *mægen*) : plaine, sb. 2. 1146. day : aray, array 2. 690 (&c.) : delay 2. 1294 (&c.) : assay 3. 42 (&c.). again(e) : remaine 1. 652 (&c.) : demaine (? ms. *demand*) 3. 90 : plaine, adj. 4. 2100 : soverane 1. 366. said : apayed 1. 1534. haill (*hægl*) : assaill 3. 1092. wainis (pl. of OE. *wægn*) : remains, vb. 3. 1626. may, vb. : assay 2. 1218 (&c.) : array 5. 2486, 2790. — n) Fr. ei. fair : aire (*heres*) 3. 1762. faine (*fægen*) : paine 5. 1482. day : perfay 2. 578 (&c.) : pray, vb. 4. 28 : tornay 1. 376 (&c.). againe : paine 3. 518, 4. 2074. taill (*tægl*) : apparrell 4. 456. abraid (prt. *abrægd*) : affrayit 3. 1546. may, vb. : perfey 4. 902 : pray 2. 230. — o) OFr. e, AFr. ei. may, vb. : jurnay 3. 270.

§ 95. The rimes in (a), (b), (c), (d), (e), (g), (i), (l), (m), (n), (o), are all discussed below in §§ 135 ff., where also the representation in the mod. diall. is given. The rimes in (f) might have been included in (e), for there is no doubt that we must accept double forms in ME. for the words *there*, *where*, &c., with ā & ē, from OE. ā & ǣ, cf. §§ 196 ff.

§ 96. *maid*. It is noticeable that a scribe has often completely destroyed the rime by replacing *maid* by *madine*, see (a) & (b). The same substitution is often made inside the verse to the detriment of the metre, e. g. 'Ane lustie madine with giltine traces bright', 4. 1007.

§ 97. *mone* for *main*, (OE. *mægen*) is another instance, similar to that mentioned in § 11, of the wrongful changing of *a* to *o* on the part of a scribe addicted to southernising the spelling.

§ 98. 3. æ + h. Only the word *saw*, prt. = Angl. *sœh* (cf. Bülbring p. 67, &c.) comes in rime. The rime-words contain — a) OE. or ON. a + g. : aw 1. 996 : drāw 3. 762. — b) OE. ā + g. : throw (OE. *þrāg*, sb.) 4. 1076. — c) OE. ā + w. : raw (OE. *rāw*) 4. 1102 : know 3. 1452. i. e. the vowel-sound is *au* or the later (AA); cf. the corresponding §§ for the rime-words. The mod. Sc. diall., as usual, have lost the *u* and we have everywhere (aa) or (AA). D. 42 shows also (EE) !

§ 99. 4. æ + ht. — Northmb. *œht* for W.S. *eaht*. Only the word *faught*, which rimes with — a) OE. ǣ + h : taught, 5. 618, cf. §§ 67—71. — b) ? : fyrflanght (= lightning) 5. 2326. The vowel sound is (au) or (aa), (AA).

Ē-sounds in ME. and MSc.

§ 100. The ME. *ē*-vowels have been divided by ten Brink (Anglia, I, 526, Chauc. Spr. §§ 23—25, 67, 68), into three classes, according to their different origins and their use in rime in ME. texts. For a clear exposition of these see Kluge P. G. 1. 878, &c. They may be briefly tabulated, with the addition of words of French origin, (see Behrens, P. G. 1. 815, &c., & t. Br. Chauc. §§ 67, 68), as follows: —

§ 101. *a*) 1. OE. ēa. e. g. *rēad*, NE. red. — 2. OE. e-, lengthened in ME., e. g. *etan* (to eat). — 3. N. ǣ. e. g. *sǣte* (seat) — 4. OFr. e = (I) Lat. *a* in open syll. before *l* and *n*, e. g. naturel. (II) Lat. *ě*, *ĭ*, ae, or Gmc. *e* in position, e. g. *requerre*, *net*, *Grece*, *werre*. — 5. AFr. e = (I) OFr. ei, ai, e. g. *pais* (N. B. only some of these produced AFr. *e*, see P. G. 822. 823). (II) Older eë, eia, &c., e. g. *veël*, *leál*.

§ 102. *β*) 1. W. S. ǣ, Angl. ē = Gmc. ǣ, Westgmc. ā, e. g. *dǣd*, Angl. *dēd*, (deed). — 2. OE. ū (*i*-mutation of ā = Gmc. ai) e. g. *mǣnan* (to mean). — 3. AFr. e = OFr. ee, when followed by *ch*, e. g. *preechier* (to preach), see Behrens, Franz. St. 5. 88. — 4. Lat. e, Gr. η, in proper names in *-ete*, e. g. *Crete*.

§ 103. *γ*) 1. WGmc. ē (including *ě* final, which was lengthened) e. g. *slēp* (prt. = slept), *hē*, (prn.). — 2. OE. ě before lengthening conson. groups, e. g. *feld* (field). — 3. OE ē, Northmb. ōē (*i*-mut. of ō), e. g. *swēte*, (sweet). — 4. Angl. ē = WS. īe, y (*i*-mut. of *ea*, *ēo*), e. g. *hēran*, *hīeran*, *hȳran* (to hear). — 5. OE. ēo = (I) Gmc. eu, e. g. *dēop* (deep). (II) Contracted from *ě*, *ĭ*, *ȳ* + a, u, e. g. *sēon* (to see) < *sehan*. (III) ēo (Gmc. *e* or *i*) before lengthening conson. groups, e. g. *leornian* (to learn). — 6. OFr. e = (I) Lat. a (exc. *α*. 4. I) e. g. *cler* (clear). (II) Lat. ē or Gr. η, Lat. ae or Gr. *αι*, Lat. oe or Gr. *οι*, & Lat. ě in open syll., in learned words, e. g. ME. *procede*, *hyene*, *tragedie*, *repete*. — 7. AFr. e = (I) OFr. ie, e. g. *grief*. (II) OFr. ue = Lat. *o* in open syll., e. g. *buef* (beef).

§ 104. Of these three groups, α produces in Chaucer's language an open $\bar{e}$, and γ a closed $\bar{e}$, while β produces a variable vowel, which is sometimes closed & sometimes open, and consequently rimes both with the vowel resulting from α & that resulting from γ. This is due to the position of Chauc.'s dial. between the Southern and Midland, for the rules generally observed with regard to these groups, in rime, are:

§ 105. 1. β & α rime together in the S. (exc. in Kt.), 2. β & γ rime together in the Midl. and N. (and Kt.). (Zielke, p. 25, distinguishes between WMidl. and EMidl., saying that the former goes more with the N. and the latter more with the S., but Menze shows that the EMidl. has also $\beta : \gamma$ rimes.) And we often find it stated that 3. α & γ do not rime together anywhere.

§ 106. This latter statement must be modified, for we find that in Scotl. α & γ *do* rime together, at any rate to a large extent; there may have been limits, which have yet to be definitely fixed. The occasional non-validity of t. Br.'s rule has been recognised by more than one investigator, e. g. Schlüter, pp. 11, 12, and, to a much larger extent, Zielke, pp. 24, &c.; the latter rightly questions whether the distinction is to be accepted at all for northern texts; it is not observed in the Psalt., Sir Tr., Yw. Gaw., Hamp., Th. Erc., Sir Egl., and Lyric P. We shall find that the rimes in Sc. texts are even more conclusive. In this coincidence of all three classes of *e*-sounds we have another instance of Scotch going ahead of English, cf· § 110.

§ 107. The rules must rather be stated thus: — 1. In the South (exc. Kt.) only γ produces $\bar{e}$ in ME. 2. In the Midl. & perhaps part of Northern England, only β & γ produce $\bar{e}$. 3. In the extreme North all three, α, β and γ produce $\bar{e}$, **NB.** with the exception of α. 3 (ON. $\bar{æ}$) and α. 5. (1) (OFr. *ei, ai*), with regard to which Scotl. has remained *behind* Engl. up to the present day, the mod. diall. still having an $\bar{e}$-vowel, not $\bar{\imath}$.

§ 108. In MSc. these latter vowels rime with $\bar{e}$ from previous $\bar{a}$. In Engl. rec. sp. it is only some of the words containing OFr. *ei, ai*, that have produced $\bar{\imath}$ through AFr. *e*, ME. $\bar{e}$, early NE. $\bar{e}$. In Scotl. it seems that none of them ever produced a closed $\bar{e}$ from which a mod. $\bar{\imath}$ could arise. The reason for this is to be sought in the difference of date of borrowing, or the later strong influence of Central French on the language of Scotl. during the period in which the relations between the two countries, France & Scotl., were so intimate; i. e. OFr. *ei, ai*, did not go through the AFr. stage *e*, but came direct as *ei, ai* into Scotch English, or the words containing an $\bar{e}$ from AFr. *e* (if they were first known in Sc. in this form) were afterwards adapted to the later Central Fr. forms with *ei, ai*, or perhaps the later $\bar{e}$, after all other $\bar{e}$'s had already become $\bar{e}$ or $\bar{\imath}$.

(In all the following remarks it is to be understood that the vowels just mentioned are always to be excepted from class α, when we refer to Scotl.; perhaps also some words of class β. 2 must be excepted, cf. § 230.)

§ 109. Or we can state the rules thus —

$$\begin{array}{ccc} \text{South} & \text{Midl.} & \text{Scotl.} \\ \left.\begin{array}{c}\alpha\\ \beta\\ \gamma\end{array}\right\} \bar{e} \quad \bar{\varrho} & \begin{array}{c}\alpha\\ \beta\\ \gamma\end{array}\left.\begin{array}{c}\bar{\varrho}\\ \end{array}\right\} \bar{e} & \left.\begin{array}{c}\alpha\\ \beta\\ \gamma\end{array}\right\} \bar{e} \end{array}$$

Or —

Sc. $\bar{e} < \alpha, \beta, \gamma$
Midl. $\bar{e} < \beta, \gamma \quad \bar{\varrho} < \alpha$
South $\bar{e} < \gamma \quad \bar{\varrho} < \alpha, \beta$.

§ 110. Or, from a chronological point of view, we may state difference of the diall. thus: 1. In the extreme N., α, β & γ coincided at any rate as early as the 16th cent., and perhaps earlier. 2. In rec. sp. and the Midl. dial. the three sounds coincided about 1750, in the form ī, for ME. $\bar{e}$ became ī in the 16th cent., while $\bar{\varrho}$ became $\bar{e}$, which then in the 18th cent. followed the course of ME. $\bar{e}$ to ī. 3. In the southern diall. they have not yet altogether coincided, although there is much confusion between the different groups.

§ 111. The last statement in based on a cursory examination of the lists in EEP. 5, in which the words, given in § 113, which in rec. sp. have ī, are found with an *e*-vowel. The numbers in brackets show in which of Ellis's districts the *e*-vowel is found; where the same number is repeated, we have more than one independent testimony for the same dial. It may be that any one examining the lists more fully will find even more; my list makes no pretence of being complete; only D. 1—12 were examined, and the specimens, which Ellis did not take into account in making his lists, were not always looked into, so that the numbers of examples may be taken as a minimum. With regard to the quality of the *e*-vowel, it is much oftener closed than open, so that the S. and SW. may be said to be following in the course of the Midl. and N. Group γ is generally represented as in rec. sp., though for some words *e* is in rare instances found, but the *e* is then of a very close nature, approaching very nearly to ī. There seems to be no distinction between α und β. Many words are found with both open and closed *e* in the same dial. district, and very often an ī is found by the side of the *e*.

§ 112. This uncertainty is to be expected, when one considers how rapidly the genuine diall. are disappearing before the inroads of rec. sp. The variety of the evidence shows that in many cases either the witnesses were allowing themselves to be influenced by rec. sp., or that they were truly representing a dial., which was no longer pure, but strongly tinged by rec. sp. It is noticeable that the farther west we go, the oftener *e* is found, and the nearer to London the place is, the less is the difference of the pronunc. from that usual in rec. sp. The *e* is most prominent in D. 4. 5. 6. 7. 10. 11, but, some of these being represented much more fully than others, (12 is scarcely represented at all), it is difficult to draw exact lines. That words of exactly similar form and origin should in the same dial. appear, now with $\bar{e}$ & now with ī, must show that the dial. is not pure, but has been subject to some outside influence, viz. that of rec. sp., and where *e* appears it is, of course, to be considered as the older form.

§ 113. In the following lists only those words are given which in rec. sp. have *ī*. The following appear in dial. with *ē*. *Class α.* 1. *sheaf* (4. 7. 11), *leaf* (4. 7. 11), *team* (5), *bean* (4. 4. 5. 5. 6. 6. 6. 7. 11. 11), *cheap* (5. 6. 7. 11. 11), *east* (6. 7), *beam* (7), and even *raw* & *straw* (11). — 2. *eat* (6. 10. 11; *jet* in 4), *speak* (2. 3. 3. 4. 4. 4. 5. 5. 6. 6. 6. 6. 7. 10. 11. 11), *lease* = *glean* (5. 7), *meat* (1. 4. 5. 6. 6. 6. 9. 10. 11. 11. 12), to *wean* (11), *weave* (5. 10. 11), *fever* (4. 4. 5. 5. 6. 10. 11), *knead* (5), *meal* (1), *beaver* (7). — 3. *seat* (6. 10), *heathen* (4). — 4. *neat* (10), *cream* (7. 10), *cease* (6), *beast* (1. 4. 4. 5. 6. 9. 11), *feast* (4. 5. 6. 10). — 5. *easy* (6. 7), *deceive* (4. 4. 6. 11), *receive* (4. 4. 6. 10. 11. 12), *veal* (4. 5. 6), *eagle* (5), *eager* (1. 4. 5. 10), *reason* (4. 4. 4. 6. 7. 10. 11), *season* (4. 4. 6. 10. 11), *leash* (6), to *treat* (4), *please* (5. 6. 6.).

§ 114. *Class β.* 1. *read* (4. 11), *cheese* (5), *bleat* (4. 4. 11), *speech* (5. 11), *deed* (5), *sheep* (5. 11), *sleep* (4. 11), *evening* (11), a *meal* (1), *leech* = doctor (1). — 2. *sea* (4. 4. 5. 11. 12), *teach* (4. 4. 4. 5. 7. 11. 11. 11), *lead*, vb. (11), to *leave* (1. 7), to *mean* (4. 5. 6. 11), *clean* (4. 4. 4. 11. 12), *wheat* (4. 4. 5. 6. 7. 11), *heat* (7. 11), *deal*, sb. (5. 6. 11), *each* (4. 5. 11), *least* (4. 4. 11), *reach* (7). — 3. *preach* (6). The word *tea* also nearly always with *ē* (4. 4. 4. 4. 5. 5. 6. 6. 6. 7. 9. 10. 11. 11. 12).

§ 115. *Class γ.* It is perhaps somewhat surprising that even some words of this class show an *e*-vowel, but this is of rare occurrence & chiefly in D. 5, var. III, where the vowel (EEæ) is found (as expressed by Prof. Schroer, EEP. 5. 98) in the following words — *ye, me, we, feed, believe, green, keep, meet, sweet*; (yyæ) is often found, however, in the same words. Of the above *we, keep, meet* & *sweet* are also found in D. 11, var. II, with an *e* vowel, which also appears in *here* (9), *believe* (1. 5. 9. 10. 12), *bee* (5. 6), *three* (11), *see* (6), *beat*, prt. (6. 11. 11), also in the very common form *beant, baint* (= are not) in the South West. In these words the *e* is generally very close, approaching to *ī*; the last mentioned, containing OE. *ēo*, have *only* this very close *e*, when they have not the *ī* of rec. sp.

§ 116. Strange to say, in a few instances *ī* is found where rec. sp. has *ĕ*, shortened from *ē*, which in these diall. was not shortened; so in *bread* (1. 5), *red* (1), *lead*, sb. (1), *dead* (1), *deaf* (2. 3), *breast* (5), also in *break* (5). This is chiefly in the Celtic districts and perhaps a special explanation is to be found in this circumstance. The *ī* found in D. 1 in *spīn* = spend, *īn* = end, is to be explained from ME. *spēnd, ēnd*, with lengthening before *nd*.

§ 117. As already stated, open *ę̄* is not so frequent as closed *ẹ̄* in these words; but still it is found, e. g. in D. 4. 10. 11. 12, occasionally in the following — *speak, fever, meat, weave, feast, tea, neat*, adj., *sea, bleat, sleep, reach, leech*, to *lead, read, mean, clean, wheat, speech, each, believe heat*; but generally the *ẹ̄*-form is more frequent, by the side of *ę̄* in the same diall.

§ 118. We thus see that the union of all three classes, *α, β* & *γ*, in the sound *ī*, which has been effected in rec. sp., is yet far from complete in the diall. of the South. The relationships in the Midl. & Northⁿ districts in ME. will be found stated by Schlüter, Zielke & Menze. We will now return to the consideration of MSc. For the sake of clearness, the *α : β* and α : γ rimes of Clar. are given here collectively, as well as in their respective places below, and will be followed by a selection of similar rimes from other Sc. texts.

§ 119. α : β rimes — α 1 : β 1 — eare : feare, 1. 1370, leaue (sb.) : evine (for *eve*) 3. 102. — α 1 : β 2 — reid : leid (*lǣdan*) 1. 1128, streimis : gleimis (sb. pl.) 4. 1188, reid : feid (OE. *fǣhð*) 5. 84, 1190. — α 2 : β 1 — speir : feir 1. 578, weir it : afeirit 2. 654, beir (vb.) : feare 3. 760. — α 4 : β 1 — conqueir : heir, vb. 1. 1306. — α 4 : β 2 — reveill : deill 3. 2148, feist : leist (superl.) 2. 1804 (&c.), feast : least 5. 52. — α 5 : β 2 — leill : dealle 3. 832.

§ 120. α : γ rimes — α 1 : γ 6 — reid, adj. : remeid 1. 442, 3. 1590, deid (mors) : remeid, 3. 1696, dead : remeid 3. 2270, deid (mortuus) : remeid 4.¡122 (&c.), eare : cleire 5. 814, great : repeit 1. 1146, 5. 2568 : quyet 2. 330, grite (= great) : repeit 5. 1360. — α 1 : γ 7 — leave, sb. : greiue, vb. 1. 878 : mischeve 1. 1258. — α 2 : γ 3 — eate : sweit 3. 796. — α 2 : γ 7 — weill (sb. *wela*) : quheill 3. 524. — The rimes *leaue*, sb. : *give* 3. 1014, *leave* : *geiue* 4. 146, are also worthy of notice as proof of a closed *ę̄* in *leave*.

§ 121. α : γ rimes (and others), from other Sc. texts. — Wynt. (see Murray DSS. p. 28) *dede* (mortuus) : *brede* (panis) : *lede* (plumbum) : *remede*; later MS., *deid* : *bread* : *leid* : *remeid*. Wall. *steid* (= place) : *rameid* 11. 876, *ded* (mortuus) : *pleid* (= plead, sb.) : *steid* (= place) : *ramede* : *reid*, sb. = advice, 2. 259, *ded* : *rameid* 11, 518, *breid* (= bread) : *rameid* 11. 442. Gol. *bere* : *weir* : *maneir* 1200, *steid* (place) : *leid* (*lēode*) : *deid* (*dǣd*) : *dreid* 184, *heill* (*helan*) : *steill* 890, *here* (here) : *cleir* : *lyere* (*hlēor*) : *suppere* 1143, &c. (see Noltemeier, p. 15, 16). Dougl. Vol 1. — *heid* (= head) : *reid* (*rēad*) : *deid* (*dēad*) : *gudliheid* 2. 16, *deid* : *reid*, sb. : *pleid*, sb. : *remeid* 8. 28, *speir*, sb. : *ʒeir* : *cleir* : *appeir* : *heir*, vb. 3. 2, *deiris* (3. sg. *derian*) : *eiris*, sb. : *steirs* (= stirs) : *heiris*, vb. 16. 7, *steid* (*stede*) : *ʒeid* (*ēode*) : *pleid* : *heid* (*hēafod*) : *meid* (*medu*) 45. 8, *speir* : *deir* (*dēore*) : *deir* (*derian*) : *feir* 46. 21. *leill* : *conceill* : *feill* (= many) : *steill*, vb. 28. 18. Vol. 2. — *weir* (= war) : *seir* (ON. *sēr*) 23. 6, 52. 20, *weir* : *deir* 23. 22, *teris* (= tears, 3. sg.) : *steris* (= guides, vb.) 35. 4, *speir*, sb. : *yfeir* 39. 16, *deid* (*dēad*) : *womanheid* 171. 7, 176. 4; *sweir* : *messingeir* 197. 10, *eir* (*ēare*) : *heir*, vb. 199. 12. Lyndesay (quoted by page only of EETS. edit.) *deid* (*dēad*) : *remeid*, Sq. M. 343, 348, *weir* (= war) : *seveir*, Sat. 436, *eit*, vb. : *leit* (= language) Sat. 475. Roll. C. V. *reid* (*rēad*) : *remeid* : *deid* (mors) : *feid*, sb. 1. 99, *forbeir* : *cheir* 1. 332, *speir*, sb. : *weir* (= war) : *cleir* : *geir* : *austeir* 2. 289, *beir* : *cheir* : *feir* : *hier* (= higher) 2. 804, *deir* (*derian*) : *heir*, adv. : *steir* : *feir* 2. 921. Satir. P. *deid* (mors) : *bleid* : *feid* : *dreid*, 4. 96, *beir*, vb. : *deir* 11. 45 (&c.), *teir*, vb. : *deir* 11. 60 (cf. *deir* : *reteir* 11. 80), *speir*, sb. : *heir*, adv. 12. 164, *eit*, vb. : *sweit*, adj. 20. 139, *speik* : *seik* 33. 276, *stremis* : *beymis* : *repremis* 37. 23, *meit*, sb. : *sweit* : *infenit* (= infinite) : *benefeit* 44. 303, *heid* (*hēafod*) : *homiceid* 20. 171, *commonweill* : *teill* (= till, vb.) 33. 372. Montg. *deues* (3. sg. *dēafian*) : *greuis* (3. sg.) C. 671, *neive* (ON. *hnefi*) : *preive* C. 1552, MP. 17. 93, *eist* : *breist* MP. 44. 22, *heep* : *weep* : *sleep* : *deep* S. 34. 5, *bemes* : *semes* S. 52. 14, *eit*, vb. : *feit*, (*fēt*, pl.) C. 640, *speikis* : *seikis* C. 669, *sweir* : *heir*, adv. C. 719, *beirs*, 3. sg. : *appeiris* C. 1162, *leip*, vb. : *deip* C. 1531, *eiris*, pl. : *appeiris* S. 7. 14, *deif* (= deaf) : *grief* : *relief* : *chief* S. 15. 5, *bereivis* : *givis* :

revivis, MP. 35. 80. — Rosw. *dead* : *heed* B. 70. — Cf. further Curs. M. Edinb. *bere*, vb. : *mistere* (= want) 19397, *beres*, 3. sg. : *afers* (= comrades) 19966, Curs. M. Cott. *bere* (vb.) : *sere* (ON. *sēr*) 386 : *caiser* 2687 : *morter* 5523, *ber* : *her*, adv. 904, *stele* (*stelan*) : *fele* (= many) 28022. The suffix-*heid* belongs, according to our etymology in § 240, properly to Class β; but it rimes in Sc. texts so frequently with γ-vowels, that we may be allowed to use this as proof of an $\bar{e}$, (we could make the same use of many other words in Sc. containing β-vowels).

§ 122. That the rules were not without exceptions was recognised by their author, ten Brink; for instance, he excepts the word *leave*, sb. from Class α, see Angl. 1. 544. Other exceptions have been made for the N., e. g. by Buss, p. 502, the words *well*, adv., *eke*, *ee* (= eye), *neir*, &c. The last mentioned have been omitted in the above lists, and mostly only such words have been given as have not yet been generally recognised as exceptions to t. Br.'s rules. But should not these so called exceptions be rather looked upon as perfectly regular for the northern dial. and as merely the forerunners of a general tendency there to change $\bar{e}$ to $\bar{e}$? It is probable that the change began in isolated instances, and was not at first general; besides the 'exceptions' already noticed, it seems at first to be most frequently found before *d* & *r*, and the later Sc. poets seem to rime α, β & γ promiscuously to a much larger extent than the earlier. For an exact chronology a careful investigation of all the Sc. poets is necessary; our object here is only to show that the distinction between $\bar{e}$ & $\bar{e}$ disappeared in Scotland, at any rate to a large extent, at an early date (with the exception of α. 3 & α. 5 (1)).

§ 123. The α : γ rimes taken in conjunction with the later development of the pronunc., show that $\bar{e}$ has become $\bar{e}$, and not, as Menze, p. 64, Noltemeier, p. 15, and others wrongly argue, that OE. *ǣ* did not always produce ME. $\bar{e}$, but sometimes $\bar{e}$. Such rimes are comparatively rare in S. Midl. texts, but appear with greater frequency the further north we go. Probably there are none to be found in texts of the S. W. diall., or only in such rare instances that they must be considered imperfect rimes or due to some external influence.

§ 124. Many rimes with such words as *need*, *near*, &c., which had in OE. different forms in different diall., and consequently two forms in ME., with $\bar{e}$ or $\bar{e}$ according to diall., have been so explained as to agree with t. Br.'s rules, by the assumption of the existence of both forms of these words in one and the same dial. This may be correct for the literary dial. of a poet like Chauc. who used forms from various surrounding diall., but it is doubtful whether any actual spoken dial. had such twofold forms, and whether a Sc. poet had second forms within reach, in any living dial. near his own; he may have borrowed, of course, artificially from English poetry, but the genuine northern forms were only *nēd*, *nēr*, *ēk*, &c., i. e. the vowel in these words was from the first only $\bar{e}$, (the OAngl. form was already *nēr*, &c.) and when found in Sc. texts riming with an *ē* of the α class, gives evidence that this latter has become $\bar{e}$, not that the Sc. poet occasionally made use of a form *nēr* from OE. *nēar*, &c.

§ 125. The occasional rimes with Fr. *i*, which sometimes retained its pronunc. as (ii) instead of becoming (əi), (ei), are especially instructive; they prove not only the change $\bar{e} > \bar{e}$, but further also $\bar{e} > \bar{\imath}$. We find such rimes in Clar. between Fr. *i* and ME. $\bar{e}$ of all three classes, (they will be found in their respective places below) also in Wall. *se* : *multiplye* 11.14, Dunb. *me* : *supple* (vb. = supply) 4.41, *sweit* : *compleit* : *feit* : *contreit* (= contrite) 9.4, *deming* : *redeming* : *blaspheming* : *expreming* 9.108; Dougl. *sweit* : *heit* : *compleit* : *repleit* : *spreit* 1.3.11; Lyndes. *queenes* : *concubeines*, Sat. p. 410; Roll. C. V. *supple* : *be* : *crueltie*, &c., 1.801, *me* : *veritie* : *se* : *authoritie* : *specifie* 3.323; Satir. P. *discreit* : *spirite* : *contreit* : *treit* : *sweit* : *compleit* 4.63, *heir* : *cheir* : *weir* : *feir* : *asteir* : *empire* 4.159, *aggreit* (= agreed) : *satisfeit* 10.214, *feit* (= foet) : *spreit* 24.88, *feit* (= feed, paid) : *glorifeit* : *notifeit* : *justifeit* 10.400, *sinceir* : *enteir* 27.11, *deceist* : *resist* 28.128, *greit* (= weep) : *hypocreit* : *contreit* 45.959; Montg. *me* : *magnifie* C.1589, *greit* (= weep) : *spweit* F.23, *deit* (= died) : *suppleit* S. 41.14, *sinceere* : *cleare* : *enteere* (= entire) MM. 19.39, and many others; (some with α-vowels are given in § 121).

§ 126. Similarly, the rimes with OE. and ON. $i + g$ in the suffixes, *-y*, *-ie*, and *-ly*, *-lie*, must be explained in the same way, and are not to be explained in Clar., as Buss & Brandl explain for earlier texts, (Buss seems to have misunderstood Brandl, but really looks upon the rimes in the same light as the latter), as imperfect rimes and due to the unstressedness of the final syllable *-y*, *-ly*. These rimes are abundant in all later Sc. texts.

§ 127. The predominant spelling with *ei* proves an $\bar{\imath}$ pronunc. for the copyist. This is evident from the occasional use of *ei* (1) for Fr. *i*, in words in which the original pronunc. $\bar{\imath}$ has been kept, (2) for short $\breve{\imath}$ in stressed and unstressed syllables, containing Fr. or Engl. $\breve{\imath}$, & (3) for OE. $\bar{\imath}$; e. g. *preike* (= prick) 1.46, *spreits* (= spirits) 1.177 (&c.), *spereit* 4.1064, *mediceine* 1.183, *chereis* (= cherish) 1.189, 653, *sweith* (: *kyth*) 1.532, *alsweith* 1.1019, *skeill* (= skill) 1.549, *seitie* (= city) 1.1079, *profeitable* 1.1152, *armeine* (= ermine), *chereist* (= cherished) 4.1596, *leoneinc* (: *fyne*) 4.1660, *promeis* (sb.) 4.2264, *ʒeing* (for *ʒing* = young), 4.2391, *vulpeine* (: *leonyne*) 5.68, *baneist* (= banished) 5.98, *Apolleine* 4.960, *Galeice* 5.448, 702, but *Galice* 5.480, *laseire* 4.410, *discipleine* 3.868, *seir* (= sire) 3.1960, *volateill* (: *will*) 5.2244, &c. &c.

The proper name *Meliades* is always spelt with *e*, but the original Fr. form was *Meliadice* (cf. Irving's introd. to Piper's edit. p. IV). It only rimes with previous $\bar{\imath}$, it is true, so that the author probably pronounced with a diphthong (əi) or (ei). The *e* of the scribe must prove that *e* was pronounced $\bar{\imath}$ by him, for we cannot assume that Fr. $\bar{\imath}$ had become $\bar{e}$. The use of both *ei* and *i* as equivalent in rime proves the same, e. g. *contine* : *susteine*, *leive* (= live) : *grive* 1.306; similarly the use of *i* in *frindly* 1.568, although we generally find *freind* with *ei*. Other examples of the same uses of *ei* will be found occasionally in the rime-lists. These peculiarities in the orthography of the MS. are in perfect agreement with that of the Satir. P. in which such spellings as *chereist*, *puneist*, *baneist*, *homiceid*, *practeiss*, *perreiss* (= perish) : *berreis* (= berries) 27.120, *keill* (= kill) : *weill* : *reill* 18.36, &c., are frequent.

§ 128. It seems certain, however, that *one* of the scribes did not yet know this pronunc. with $\bar{\imath}$, but still retained in some words an $\bar{e}$-sound, for which he employed an Engl. orthography *ea*; e. g. in Bk. 1, *creatour* 200, *realme* 205, *eardlie* 247, 1208, *speach* 284, *great* 314, *greattumlie* 1180, *heallit* 329, *eare* 335, *feare* 1370, *rehearsing* 369, *leave* (= permission) : *greiue* 878, *reasoun* 401, *please* : *ease* 594 (elsewhere *pleis*, *vneis*, &c.), *receave* 1485, *receavit* 1387, (in the words containing OFr. *ei*, *ai*, the author probably pronounced $\bar{e}$ too, cf. above § 108), *sweare* 529, *readie* 587, (*reddie* in other places), *feastit* 682, *feast* : *beist* 920 (cf. *baist* 951, *beist* 960), *heavinis* 945, *measoure* 1036, *adread* 1379 (elsewhere *dreid*), *heat*, and many others. In conjunction with this it is noticeable that *ea* is also sometimes used for the $\bar{e}$ arising out of previous $\bar{a}$, e. g. *alleane* 575, *eagit* (= aged) 718 (cf. *aigit* 783), *speace* : *face* 754.

§ 129. Our conclusion then is, that for the author and most of the scribes all $\bar{e}$'s have already become $\bar{\imath}$, as in mod. rec. sp. and the mod. Sc. diall., (except. the $\bar{e}$ from ON. $\bar{æ}$ and OFr. *ei*, *ai*, and perhaps from OE. $\bar{æ}$, β. 2).

E -

§ 130. 1. Not followed by g — rimes with — a) itself. speir : beir (*beran*) 1. 1156, 2. 1384 : weir, vb. 2, 174, 4. 886 : deire (sb. = injury, from vb. *derian*) 1. 974, speiris : bairis (sb. pl. OE. *beras*) 5. 2016. sweir : deir (vb. *derian*) 1. 530. weir : beir (vb.) 2. 904. speike : breke 3. 168, 1478. eit : meit (*mete*) 3. 746, 768. — b) OE. ea, see § 262 (a). — c) OE. $\overline{eu}$. steid(e) : reid (*rēad*) 2. 636 : deid (sb. *dēap*) 3. 610. eit : grite (*grēat*) 3. 1602. neives (pl. ON. *hnefi* = fist) : dives (= deafens, OE. *dēaflan*) 3. 602. — d) Angl. $\bar{e}$ = WS. $\bar{æ}$. speir : feir 1. 578. weir it : afeirit 2. 654. beir, vb. : feare 3. 760. In *weir it* : *afeirit* we seem to have a case of feminine rime, but it may be that the pronoun *it* is run closely on to the word *weir*, just as the partic. ending -*it* may be to the verbal stem, without making an extra syll. — e) OE. $\bar{e}$ (Angl. $\bar{æ}$ mut. of o). eate : sweit 3. 796. — f) OE. $\overline{eo}$. weill (sb. OE. *wela*) : quheill (OE. *hwēol*) 3. 524. — g) OE. $\bar{e}$: . get : let (vb. = hinder) 4. 2202. — h) OFr. e. beir, vb. : weire (*werre*) 2. 646.

§ 131. This belongs to t. Br.'s Class α. We have α : α rimes in (a), (b), (c) & (h), α : β rimes in (d), and α : γ rimes in (e) & (f).

In (d) the vowel is in each word followed by *r*, and in that case the $\bar{e}$ of the Midl. & South might become $\bar{e}$ in ME., (see Kluge PG. 1. 880), so that even a γ-vowel might rime with an α-vowel; but for Scotl. such a rime is to be interpreted in another way, viz. that the α-vowel has become $\bar{e}$, not that the γ-vowel has become $\bar{e}$. In the mod. Sc. diall. an $\bar{\imath}$ is often found even before *r* in words in which the vowel has been in rec. sp. kept open by the *r*, e. g. in *wear*, vb. (33. 35. 36. 39), *swear* (35. 36. 39), *bear*, vb. (33), *pear* (33), *tear*, vb. (33). And, again, we often find a short $\check{\imath}$ representing OE. *e*-, and this *i* is probably to be explained from a shortening of the $\bar{\imath}$ which was produced by early MSc. $\bar{e}$, especially as in some of the words $\bar{\imath}$ exists in other diall.; we find $\check{\imath}$ in *break* (34), *speak* (33. 34. 35. 38), *wear* (33), *swear* (33), *meat* (33), *meal* (33), *eat* (33. 41). Words with $\bar{\imath}$, as in rec. sp., are — *speak* (35. 38), *meat* (35. 36. 38), *weave* (33. 34. 35). It is true that on the contrary an *e* - vowel is sometimes found, where rec. sp. has ī, so in *speak* (40. 41), *meat* (42), *weave* (33. 42), with ē, and *speak* (42), *meat* (39), *eat* (35. 42), *break* (33. 35) with ĕ. Some special explanation must be found for these forms; it is to be noticed that *all* the words are found with ī or ĭ, or sometimes both, even when a form with *e* may exist as well.

§ 132. *weill*, sb. Buss says, p. 502, that OE. *wela* only appears in Bruce with open ę̄; in Clar. we have only one instance of it in rime, and then it rimes with ę̄. It might be supposed that the adv. which always rimes with ę̄ (so also in Bruce) may have influenced the noun, but this is altogether unnecessary, seeing that this α : γ rimes stands by no means alone; cf. also Satir. P. *commonweill* : *teill* (vb. = till) 33. 72, : *keill* (= kill) 33. 46.

§ 133. *yet* has here, as everywhere else, a short ĕ. The forms *brek* & *spek* mentioned in § 131 as appearing in NSc. may owe their short vowel to the same cause as *tăk* & *măk* do their short ă. Cf. Satir. P. *brek it* : *checkit* (= checked) : *suspectit* : *deckit* 37. 55, *brecking* (= breaking) 45. 25.

2. **E + G**

§ 134. rimes with — a) itself. say : way 1. 14 (&c.) : play 2. 350, 5. 2828 : away 3. 132 : alwayis (for *alway*) 3. 1620. — b) OE. ǣ + g, see § 94 (b). — c) OE. ǣ or a -, see §§ 80 (f), 90. — d) OE. ā, see §§ 40, 47, 48, 72 (e). — e) ON. ei. way : thay 2. 8 (&c.) : they 4. 566. say : ay 3. 1382 (&c.) : thay 5. 2152. play : thay 4. 440. — f) Fr. ai. way : say (= assay) 2. 18 : delay 2. 1230 (&c.) : assay 2. 1212 : array 3. 876, 5. 2364. away : assay 4. 2124. say : aray 2. 906 (&c.). saine : remaine 2. 322 : plaine 2. 840 : Spaine 1. 906. play : say (= assay) 4. 1368 : assay 2. 986, 2. 1744 : aray 2, 960 : afray 5. 1290 : delay 5. 1522. playit : arayit 2. 1664. saill (vb.) : travell 3. 844, 1966. — g) Fr. cl. say : pray, vb. 2. 110 : perfay 3. 2094 (&c.). sayis, 3. sg. : praise 4. 1130. lay (vb. trans.) : tornay 5. 2098. way : pray 4. 1962, 2848 : perfay 4. 2284. — h) Fr. a. laid : evaid 3. 2054. — i) Fr. i. alwayis : suppryse 3. 1218. — (This rime is due to the confusion between the two forms *ways* and *wise* = OE. *wīse*, manner, cf. §§ 440, 441; we should read *alwyse* for *alwayis*.)

§ 135. The rimes in (a), (b), (e), (f), (g) prove alone nothing for the pronunc.; (cf. above in § 94 (a), (b), (i), (m), (n)) for all the rimewords had *ai* or *ei* in early ME. and these two diphthongs soon coincided. The single resulting diphthong is generally held to have been *ai* (not *ei*), which in Scotl. at an early date underwent a special development, viz. the second element of the diphthong disappeared and a monophthong, *ä*, was the result, so that there was no distinction between previous *ā* and *ai*; *ai* was afterwards written in words in which the ā-sound represented an original *ā* and not a diphthong *ai*, and vice versâ, *a* was written in words which had formerly contained a diphthong. This interchanging of symbols is one of the most striking features of the MSS. of the middle period of Sc. literature, in which the same word often appears on the same page with four on five different spellings; e. g. *mad, made, maid, mayd, maide, mayde* may all express rec. sp. *maid* or *made*. Murray (DSS. pp. 52, 53) shows that this is limited to Central & NE. Scotl. and ascribes the monophthonging to Celtic influence; the two sounds 'are still distinct in the dial. of Southern Scotl. and Northern Engl.', where there is no confusion between such words as *maid* and *made*, or *tail* and *tale*. This is confirmed by Ellis's lists for these diall.

§ 136. The statement of Zielke (p. 13) and Brandl (p. 53) that the monophthonging of *ai* began in Northern Engl. almost at the same time as in Scotl. seems, therefore, at first sight somewhat questionable, for it would be strange if two sounds which were originally distinct and are still distinct in the dial. of the present day should have coincided during the ME. period. Z. expresses doubt as to whether the *author* of Sir Egl. pronounced $\bar{a}$ for earlier *ai* and there is no direct evidence that he did, but he accepts this pronunc. at the time of the copyist, about 1400, on the strength of such rimes as *slayn* : *tan* (= taken). As he suggests, the author may have written *slan*, a ptc. formed from the Nthmb. infin. *slā*, for there were two forms *slān* and *slain* in ME. (cf. Kölbing, *Am.* p. 25, Buss p. 507, Zupitza, *Guy W.*, note to l. 1126, & above § 48), and the above rime may mean that the author used the former and the scribe was a man to whom *ay* meant the same sound as *a*, (as it would to a Scotchman from the central counties or to men from some parts of England). But it may also mean that in the scribe's dial. only the form *slain* (with diphthong) was known and that he, in his copying, wrote what was for him an imperfect rime. But anyhow we cannot argue from this rime that *ai* had become *a* in the author's dial., even at the later time of the copyist, for, according to Z. p. 5, the diall. of author & copyist were not the same.

§ 137. But a further inspection of Ellis's dial. lists makes it clear that this pronunc. *was* possible, and that the statements of Brandl and Zielke may be true, with certain restrictions, i. e. if we may be allowed to draw any conclusions from the evidence of the mod. diall., to which probably no one will object. It all depends upon what part of the northern district we refer to. Zielke sets the home of the author of Sir Egl. on the southern border of the northern dial., in the neighbourhood of the WMidl. district; Brandl, p. 53, quotes a number of rimes from the Towneley Mysteries, which were acted at Wakefield in Yorks., and Zupitza gives some from Guy W., p. 13.

§ 138. Now in the mod. diall. we find the following relationships. As we have seen, *a* & *ai* coincided in Central & NE. Scotl., but have been kept distinct, down to the present day, in Southern Scotl. and in some of the northern Engl. diall.; not in all of them, for we find to day the same coincidence between ME. $\bar{a}$ (i. e. here only the $\bar{a}$ from OE. *a-*, &c., not from OE. $\bar{a}$, see further below) and ME. *ai, ei*; e. g. *made* and *maid* are pronounced alike, so also *tale* & *tail*. We know further that in the extreme south (cf. Fick, p. 27) the two sounds have been kept distinct. It thus appears that the coincidence of the two sounds took place in patches, with others between and beyond in which there was no coincidence, and we have the strange fact that the dial. of SW. Yorks. in this respect resembles that of Central Sc. more closely than that of Southern Sc.

§ 139. An exact examination of the mod. diall. is required to fix the limits of these various districts. The following particulars enable us to determine roughly the line of division between that part of N. Engl. in which the sounds are kept distinct and the more southern portion of it which, with the Midl. districts, has now only one sound for both the older ones.

In Ellis's D. 20, 21, 22, 23 (including Lincs., NW. Derbyshire, & South and Mid. Lancs.) both are pronounced alike with an *e*-vowel (small shades of difference are not taken into account, in each division the two sounds are pronounced with the *same e*-sound), and also in D. 24, SW. Yorks. including Wakefield where the Towneley Mysteries were performed.

§ 140. In D. 30 the coincidence is only partly complete; in many instances Ellis gives double forms as existing side by side, especially is this the case in Mid. Yorks., where both are represented by (eeɐ) and (iɐ), though the former is more frequent for both, and consequently connects this subdivision more closely with the districts further South, as far as OE. *æg, eg,* &c. are concerned; on the other hand (iɐ) would be quite regular for OE. *a-* further North. The two sounds seem to have influenced each other, or else Ellis's informants were acquainted with more diall. than the one they were desiring to represent. In NE. Yorks., too, the two sounds coincide oftener than not, but in the form (iiɐ), which connects this with the more northern districts, and (eeɐ) is also found for OE. *æg*, &c., but not for OE. *a-*; the examples given are few, but we shall probably be right in reckoning this to the northern division; so also the Wolds district, where the two sounds are usually kept distinct as (iɐ) and (eeɐ). In the Holderness division there is much confusion, but oftener than not we find the two sounds kept distinct as (iiɐ) and (eeɐ), so that this too belongs to the northern division. In the district of Goole and the Marshes, in the majority of cases the two sounds coincide in the form (eeɐ); this clearly belongs, then, to the more southern division.

§ 141. In the whole of D. 31 (which includes the NW. of Yorks., extreme N. of Lancs., whole of Westm. and most of Cumb.) there is no coincidence except in a part of Lancs., viz. Lonsdale South of the Sands, which thus agrees with the rest of Lancs. to the S.

D. 32, as may be expected, agrees with 31 & 33, i. e. there is no coincidence.

§ 142. We may, then, roughly speaking, say that a straight line drawn from Hull to the NE. corner of Morecambe Bay, where the Ken empties itself, is the boundary line, to the N. of which, as far as to the Northern limits of Ellis's D. 33, ME. *ā* & *ai* do not coincide, while to the S. of it they do. A small part of Yorks. would be on the wrong side of the line, S. instead of N., and perhaps more of central Yorks. ought to be to the S. of the boundary line.

§ 143. It seems, then, that these sounds give us a new criterion for fixing the locality of works written in the northern dial. (Of course, the question of date has yet to be settled; the following remarks can only apply for the time subsequent to the date of coincidence; thus for Sir Tr. perhaps the date is too early for this test; and it is, of course, possible that the boundary line may have shifted, but this has yet to be proved.) If rimes are found between early ME. *ai* and *ā*, the author probably lived to the S. of our boundary line, i. e. if his dial. was Northern Engl. at all, and not central Scotch, for which there would be, of course, plenty of other sure criteria, which are not far to seek. One criterion alone, closely connected with these sounds, would be sufficient. In Central Sc. the older diphthong *ai* can rime both with OE. *a-* and OE. *ā*; this would be impossible to the S. of our line, for there OE. *ā* has become (oo𝑣) or (uu𝑣), and the previous *ai* or *ei* can only rime with OE. *a-*, both of these having an *e*-vowel in the mod. diall. of these districts. (NB. Fr. *a*, which was treated in the same way as ME. *ā*, lengthened from OE. *a-*, is included in the same category as the latter).

§ 144. To the N. of the line, again, OE. *a-* and OE. *ā* have coincided, as in Central Sc. So if we call Central Scotl., A., the S. of Scotl. and the part of N. Engl. defined above, B, and the North[n] & Midl. country S. of our line, C, and if we designate early ME. *ai* by *α*, OE. *a-* by *β*, & OE. *ā* by *γ*, we can tabulate as follows:

in A *α* ⎫
 β ⎬ > an *ē*-vowel,
 γ ⎭

in B *α* > an *ē*-vowel,
 β ⎫
 γ ⎬ > an *i*-fracture, (i') or (i𝑣) or (ii𝑣),

in C *α* ⎫
 β ⎬ > an *ē*-vowel, also ī in D. 25. 26. 28. 29,
 γ > an *ō* or *ū* vowel, (oo𝑣) (uu𝑣). &c.

§ 145. Thus we see that *α* has in all three districts become *ē* (exc. in a part of C). Here is a great difference from the diall. of the S. of Engl. in which *α*, *β* & *γ* are all three kept distinct —

α has produced *ai* (still diphthong).

β .... an *i*-fracture or an *e*-fracture.

γ .... an *ū* or *ō* vowel.

(NB. Here only the most general pronunciations are given; there is by no means uniformity, as can at once be seen by a glance at Ellis's lists for D. 4, Dorset, Wilts & Somerset).

§ 146. Brandl's rimes from the Townl. Myst. agree perfectly with our observations with regard to district C, see §§ 143, 144; he gives none in which OE. *ā* appears in rime with *ai*, and probably such are nowhere to be found in any author whose home was S. of the Sc. border, or in fact, further S. than the Northern limits of Ellis's D. 33, and probably further investigations will show that no rimes at all between OE. *ā* or *ă*- and early ME. *ai*, *ei* are to be found between D. 34 and the boundary line which has been fixed above.

§ 147. The rime *slayn* : *tane* in Sir Egl. may, then, have been written by the author, if he lived to the S. of this boundary line, for, in that case, older *slain* (with diphthong) would have been pronounced by him with a monophthong, and *ay* may have been to him of the same value as *a*, in the same way as the two spellings were confused in Central Sc. But without further confirmation it is not necessarily so, for he may have lived to the N. of the line and used the form *slān*.

§ 148. The rimes in § 134 (c), (d), (h), are evidence of the monophthongal pronunc. in Clar. of earlier *ai*, *ei*, cf. also the rimes of *œ* + *g* in § 94. But the monophthong was most probably by this time *ē*; in fact, it is open to question whether it was ever *ā* and not of an *ē*-nature from the beginning of the monophthonging process.

§ 149. In rec. sp. the two sounds ME. *ai* and *ā* are pronounced alike as *ēi*, but here the coincidence must have been brought about by a process different from that accepted by Murray for Central & Northern Sc., for there can hardly be any possibility of Celtic influence here. It is, indeed, not at all necessary to explain by any external influence; the change might quite well have taken place by an independent internal process. We have exact parallels in mod. Fr. & mod. Greek, in which older *ai* has become *ē*, and we can compare Old Saxon, in which Gmc. *ai* always became *ē*, a change which also partly took place in OHG. (cf. Braune, Ahd. Gram. § 43, Gallee, Alts. Gram. § 41), also Sanskrit, which has *é* for Indog. *ai*, further Anglo-French. where *ai* & *ei* in the 12th cent. often became *ẹ̄* (cf. Behrens P. G. 1. 822), and we may suppose that the same change took place in the same way in the dial. of rec. sp. as in Anglo-French, (but, of course, at a later time, or the resulting vowel would have coincided with that arising from OFr. *ai*, *ei*, through AFr. *ẹ̄*, and we should have had i in mod. Engl. rec. sp. This result has actually taken place in some diall.; cf. Murray DSS. p. 107, where he says that *way* & *day* are almost (wii) & (dii) in parts of Central & Northern Sc.; we also find a long i quite regularly in *lay*, *way*, *say*, in Cheshire, Staffs. and Derbyshire.). The same explanation might be possible for *ai*, *ei*, in Central Sc., though, of course, Celtic influence may have helped as well.

§ 150. As already stated, it is generally supposed that the resulting monophthong from the coincidence of older *ei* and *ai* was *ā*; this then at a later time must, like genuine *ā*, have become *ẹ̄* and *ẹ̄*, which latter form exists in the present diall.; so that for the diphthong *ei* we must assume the following process, ei > ai > ā > ẹ̄, i. e. the front vowel *e* was first backed and then fronted again, a reversion of processes, which, although not impossible, is still not very probable, when we consider that the whole change must have taken place in a comparatively short space of time. Is it not better to suppose that *ai* first became *ẹ̄i*, a very natural change, and that so the two diphthongs coincided, and then, either in the same way as in AFr., or through Celtic influence, or both, became monophthonged to *ẹ̄*, not *ā*? Or, that first *ai* became *ā*, while *ẹ̄i* became *ẹ̄*, and then the former, *ā*, became *ẹ̄*, in the same way as orig. *ā*, and that it was in this way that finally *ā*, *ai* & *ei* all coincided? However the changes may have been brought about, the resulting monophthong is more likely to have been *ẹ̄* than *ā*; then all the changes are represented as having taken place in the same direction, and ceteris paribus such an explanation is surely to be preferred to any other. The rimes do not force us to the conclusion that *eg*, *œg*, &c. have produced *ā*.

§ 151. Ellis, EEP. 1, 410, note 3, says 'Mr. Murray thinks that *ai, ay* had in Scotl. the sound (ee) at the beginning of the 16th cent., at least a century before it was recognised in the S., although we learn from Hart that it was well known in 1551.' This opinion is based on the consistent orthography *ai, ay* in Dougl. and *a : ai* rimes. But this may have begun long before the consistent orthography was established. Ellis, p. 1085, says that there was an approach to a systematic orthography in Scotl. at the end of the 15th cent. We see this confirmed with respect to ī or its outcome əi, *ei*, cf. below §§ 433 ff., and, as there shown, the beginnings were probably of much earlier date.

§ 152. Of course the change *ei* > *ai* is possible, we have it in the S. of Engl. where *way* (OE. *weg*) is pronounced with *ai*; and the change *ai* > *ā* is just as possible, cf. the *waass* (= weiss), *haam* (= heim) of some Germ. diall. (in the Heidelberg district we have both *ā* & *ē*, *haam* and *heem*, existing side by side a very little distance from each other); it is the reversion of processes ei > ai > ā > ō which is difficult.

§ 153. As Fick, p. 26, says, the spelling has often little identity with the real sound, and the *a* & *ay* may well have simply meant *ē* for the copyist of the Pearl and so also in the case of MSc. texts; and in this way the *a : ai* rimes can be explained which are found above.

Further *a : ai* rimes will be found given by Buss, p. 506, from Bruce, Sc. Leg., Wall., Rat. Rav., Dunb. & Lanc. B. calls attention to the fact that Wyntown has no such rimes. Can this be taken as evidence that his home was in the S. of Scotl. while Clar. and the other works containing *a : ai* rimes belong to various diall. of Central & NE. Scotl.? We have direct historical evidence of the birthplaces and homes of many of the authors, but according to Irving, (Sc. Poetry p. 112) nothing is known as to Wyntown's birth; we know that he was afterwards Canon of St. Andrews.

§ 154. It is certain that at the end of the 16th cent. the pronunc. was *ē* in Engl., cf. Kluge, P.G. 1. 888. The pedantic and arbitrary rules laid down by many of the grammarians of the 16th cent. are often to be taken cum grano salis, for these men were to a large extent the slaves of the orthography, from the trammels of which they found it very difficult to free themselves. We can well imagine what rules might be laid down by a man of the present day, a man of education, say a schoolmaster or a clergyman, who had, however, no more real knowledge of phonetics than the grammarians of the 16th cent. had, but who made a hobby of the subject, and flattered himself that his pronunc. was really the most correct and refined, and that where it differed from that of other people, other people must be wrong and too ignorant to know better. How often would he, (for such people could easily be found), contrary to general usage, insist on a word being pronounced as it is spelt! In numberless instances he would give an antiquated or an artificial pedantic pronunc. In the same way evidence of the orthoepists of the 16th cent. must be very cautiously treated, and Gill's vituperations of Hart's 'vulgar' pronunc. of *ai* as *e* are shown by the later history of the sound to have been merely a piece of arbitrariness on his part.

§ 155. If then the monophthongal pronunc. was established at this date in Engl., it was probably firmly rooted in Scotl. long before Clar. was written. That there are few rimes between older *ai* and *ē* is very easily explained by the fact that *ē* had generally already become *ī*, or very near it, under ordinary circumstances. Such rimes would not, as a rule, prove that *ai* had become *ē*. If all three classes of *e*-sounds, t. Br.'s α, β, & γ, produced a closed *ẹ̄* in Sc., then a rime between the *ẹ̄* that arose from older *ai* or *ā* and one of these *ẹ̄*'s is not to be at all expected. We can only have rimes with α. 3, α. 5 (1), and perhaps β. 2 (see § 84), and such are found, cf. § 1 (h), and may be looked upon as indisputable proof of the *ẹ̄*-pronunc. On the other hand at a later time when in the rec. sp. of Engl. *ai* had become *ẹ̄*, as it did towards the end of the 16th cent., we do find rimes between this and *ē* from other sources, t. Br.'s α, e. g. claim : dream, &c.; such rimes are then of no rare occurrence.

§ 156. The rime in § 94 (g), *faire* : *gudlier*, may however be taken as a support of this *e*-pronunc. in Clar.; for although it is a case of an unstressed syll. becoming stressed in rime, this very fact gives it a different meaning to that which a rime with stressed *ē* would have. In this compar. suffix *-er*, the vowel, being unstressed, never underwent the usual change of *ē* to *ī*, especially as in its unstressedness it was not long *ē* at all; and when stressed in rime its quality would still be of an *e*-nature, certainly not *a*. Such rimes are, of course, to be treated with caution, but they often give us a hint, even though they may not be perfectly faultless rimes.

§ 157. We find an exactly similar rime in 3. 1418, *repaire* (Fr. *ai*) : *gudlier*. Importance must also be attached to the rimes *counsall* : *tell*, 4. 2222, *plet* (ptc. = plaited) : *set*, prt. 4. 1314, in which Fr. *ei* in unstressed syll. rimes with OE. *ĕ*, indicating that the stressed unshortened form of the vowel must have been of an *e*-nature; cf. Roll. C. V. *plet* : *met* : *set* : *get*, 4. 364, Montg. *plet* : *set*, S. 8. 10, *plets* : *violets* MP. 19.. 5. Further, a rime in the Prol. to the Sc. Leg. Horstmann. Vol. 1. *gest* (= ghost, 'þe haly gest') : *chaste*, 3/50, is of importance as evidence of the early date of the fronting of *ā*; if we derive *gest* from the OE. form *gǣst*, the rime proves an *ē* in *chaste* in the pronunc. of the author; if we derive from OE. *gāst*, then the spelling proves an *e*-vowel for the scribe; cf. Dunb. *gaist* : *chaist* 25. 30, where *ai* certainly means *ē*. Such rimes as those referred to in § 73, in which *ā* rimes with *ĕ* are also strong evidence, cf. Kluge, PG. 1. 877.

§ 158. In § 94 (o) we have apparently a rime with Fr. *e*, *may*, vb. : *jurnay*. If this were so, it would stand quite alone, there being no other example in Clar. of Fr. *e* riming with OE. *æg* or *eg*. The explanation is to be found in Behrens' excellent treatise on 'the Hist. of the French lang. in Engl.', Engl. Stud. 5, p. 82. *journeie* is given there as one of the words which in AFr. Mss. show a parasitic *i* between the two *e*'s of the suffix, *-ee*, *jurneie* for *jurnee*; hence the spelling in such words as *chimney*, *valley*, *attorney*, in which, however, in mod. rec. sp. the *ey* means now no more than the *-y* in *country*, *entry*, &c.; it is only a historic spelling, giving evidence of a former diphthongal pronunc.

§ 159. Fick's view of the whole question of the pronunc. of earlier *ai* & *ā* in the northern Engl. and Sc. diall. of the ME. period seems to be not so unfounded as has been maintained by some. Whether the change was complete at such an early date as he would set it, may perhaps be still left open to question, but there are no arguments to compel the acceptance of the *ei, ai* > *ā* theory, and there are no convincing reasons to reject the possibility of an earlier date of the *e*-sound in the N.

§ 160. In Clar. we do not find *e* in alternation with *a*, &c. as we do in older texts, cf. Fick, p. 21, *a* being the historical & *e* the phonetic spelling. The reason is that here *e* has gone further and represents an *ī* sound as in mod. Engl. But we do occasionally find *ea* (English orthography for open $\bar{e}$) instead of *ai*, e. g. *heat* (= hate) 3. 2196, *leave* (OE. *lāf*) 4. 738, &c.

Buss grants that *a* sometimes means *ē* in the MS. of Bruce; he says, p. 501, 'words with open *èè* before *r* are spelt, according to the later pronunc., with *a*.'

§ 161. Wischmann remarks that in the K. Q. native *ai* rimes with Fr. *ai*, but never with simple *ā*. This must be looked upon as another sign of the strong Engl. influence to which King James was subject, for, at the time at which he wrote, *ā* & *ai* were still distinct in Midl. & Southern Engl. The scribe, however, knew no difference between the two.

§ 162. With reference to Fr. words with *ai*, which shared the same fortunes as ME. *ai* from *æg*, &c., Fick says, on p. 29, that they must have been received into the language at an earlier date than those which have in ME. $\bar{e}$, e. g. NE. *peace, release, receive,* &c. Is this necessarily so? Could it not be possibly just the reverse, that the words with ME. *ai* were adopted later than those with $\bar{e}$, and from another dial., not Norman? Or even if both sets came from the Norman, as was often the case, they might have been adopted together, for the differentiation into $\bar{e}$ & *ai* seems to have taken place in Anglonorman, i. e. the Norman dial. as it developed on Engl. soil; cf. Behrens, Engl. St. 5. pp.130, &c. In MSc. all, or nearly all, such Fr. words have an $\bar{e}$ (so also in NSc.) e. g. also in *peace, receive,* &c., where NE. has *ī* < ME. $\bar{e}$, and this indicates a different dial. as origin, viz. Central Fr. instead of Norman.

§ 163. The representation of OE. *æg, eg,* &c. in the mod. Sc. diall. has already been referred to; an $\bar{e}$-vowel of some sort or other is found almost everywhere. It remains to be remarked that occasionally an *i*-vowel is found, e. g. (here OE. *eg, æg, ǣg,* & ON. *ei,* are taken all together) *again* (*ī*) in 33 & 35, *said* (*i*) in 35, to *weigh* (ii) in 34, 35, *key* (i) in 33, (ii) in 35, *clay* (i) in 33, *raise* (i) in 33, *steak* (i') in 33; but each of these words is found with an $\bar{e}$-vowel as well.

Sometimes a diphthong *ei* or *ai* is found: — *day* (éi) in 37, to *weigh* (éi) in 33, 38, (ái) in 39, *key* (éi) in 38, *clay* (éi) in 33, 35, *whey* (éi) in 35, 36, 38, (áai) in 38, (ái) in 39, *lain* (éi) in 35, 36, to *say* (êi) & (ái) in 37, *way* (éi) in 33, 34, 36, (êi) in 37, (ái) in 39, (áai) in 38, *aye* has a diphthong everywhere, *raise* (éi) in 35, *play* (ái) in 39. It should, however, be observed

4

that the sound designated by (éi) is only slightly diphthongal, and may be considered almost as an e-vowel, (it does not coincide with the sound representing OE. í) and the (ai) diphthong appears chiefly after w; both forms are probably of modern development.

There is one striking anomaly: while way, sb., generally has an e-vowel in EEP. 5, away, adv., always has an ā. Scott assigns an ā-vowel to the sb. way: 'let Rob come his wa's up the glen,' Rob Roy (ch. 32.).

§ 164. Here is perhaps the best place to mention a few rimes which at first sight seem really to belong to the imperfect, but which also admit of another interpretation. In all of them we have rimes between earlier ai, ei and í, or later ē and əi. They are —
1. say : I 4. 2242. — 2. faire : wyre (OE. wīr) 4. 1008. — 3. perfay : by 2. 1408. — 4. Per mon fay : leargly 2. 1710. — 5. day : quietlie 3. 1642.

It is on such rimes as these that Sarrazin bases his arguments for the diphthonging of í in early texts, e. g. in Octav. *pray : why : lye : bye*, see Sarrazin's introd. p. 37. But such rimes can only be considered approximately good for a certain limited period; later on, when the diphthong ai had become monophthonged, as it did in Scotl. at an early date, they would be again quite imperfect. And we know that the vowel sound in *day, say, perfay, faire*, was a monophthong long before Clar. was written. *faire : wire* never was, and is not now, an exact rime in any dial. of Scotl., and for the date and dial. of Clar., the vowel of *faire* could rime neither with (ii) nor with (əi). (Ellis gives an e-vowel for *wire* in one of the mod. diall. D. 35; but this is quite an isolated case, it is not supported by any other evidence and is probably due to some error). It is the same with the other rimes. But still they may perhaps be interpreted as evidence of a diphthongal pronunc., if we allow the author to have occasionally employed an antiquated pronunc. in words containing earlier ai; scarcely an antiquated Scotch pronunc. perhaps, for the monophthonging of ai was of too old a date to allow us to suppose that a survival of the diphthong in Sc. itself was possible, but rather a borrowing from English. If this cannot be allowed, then the rimes are imperfect. Zietsch, p. 77, gives a number of such rimes, ten, from the Seege of Troy, almost too large a number of one character to class among the faulty, although he says the number of faulty rimes is very considerable for the shortness of the poem, and he would therefore explain from carelessness of the scribe. Perhaps these too are examples of the use of antiquated forms in rime, cf. Kluge, PG. 1. 873, and the rime in Clar. *greine : syne*, see § 432. In Rosw. we find *cry : day*, 452. For the late date of this poem (printed 1663) a similar explanation is the only possible one, if the rime is pure. Bülbring, p. 70, interprets similar rimes in the S. as evidence that $ei < eg$ &c. has become í, which he considers to be a peculiarity of Kentish; if this be correct, it is remarkable if no confirmation should be found in the mod. diall. At any rate this explanation cannot be applied to a Scotch text.

§ 165. The two last rimes of the five given above admit of another explanation, viz. that, as the syll. *-ly* was generally unstressed, it might assume, on becoming stressed in rime, an uncertain sound, which would enable a poor versifier to associate it with more than one kind of vowel, and hence the variety in the treatment of such words, which, strictly speaking, are not fitted to be used in rime at all; according to this view, the uncertain sound rimes with an ẹ̈.

E:

1. = W. S. ie after palatals

§ 166. rimes with — a) OE. e. ӡeild : feild 1. 1332, 638. scheild : feild 1. 12 (&c.) — b) OE. ĭ. ӡit (= yet, OE. *get, giet*) : wite (*witan*) 1. 1348. chill (for *schill*, adj. = NE. shrill, OE. *scell, scyll*, see Stratm.-Bradl.) : still 2. 880. — c) Lat. ĭ. ӡit : promit, vb. (= promise) 4. 1456.

§ 167. In ӡ*eild*, W. S. *gieldan*, Angl. *geldan*, we have quite regularly an ĭ < ẹ̈, cf. below, § 172; the *g* became palatised and produced *y*, but the *e* was developed in the same way as any other *e*. (In Roll. C. V. we have a strange form with *a*: ӡ*ald* : *bald* : *tald* &c. 2. 250, *vpӡald* : *hald* : *tald* : *cald* 4. 742, *wpӡeild* : *tald* : *bald* : *fald* : *wald* 3. 737.) This palatisation of *g* was quite usual in Sc., just as in Engl., except where there was Norse influence. In Gol. the palatal is expressed by *y* or *yh*, cf. Noltemeier p. 26; *ӡh* is found in Craft of Deyng and other Sc. works; in most texts we find *ӡ* as here in Clar. Cf. further Fick, p. 40, Zielke, p. 36. With the word *scheild* it is exactly similar; the *sc* has become regularly *sh, sch*, and *e* is developed as any other *e*.

The mod. diall. of the N. nearly always show ĭ in the word *yield*, but without the initial *y*; we find (iild) in 32, 33, 35, 38, but also occasionally short ĭ, (il) in 35, (ild) in 39. This disappearance of the *y* is striking; it is confined to D. 32 in Engl. and the diall. of Scotl.

§ 168. In ӡ*it, chill*, (b) & (c), we have an *i* produced by this *e* = W. S. *ie*. This may be due to the palatal ӡ, *sc*, or merely another instance of the frequent concurrence of *e* & *i*. In the mod. Sc. diall. *yet* appears both with ĕ (33, 35, 39) and with ĭ (32, 38, 42), but nowhere has the *y* disappeared as in *yield*. We might expect *e* in the northern diall. (Angl. *get*) and ĭ in the S. (W. S. *giet, git*), and in the latter we do actually only find *i*, (jit), and occasionally with loss of the spirant, (it), (4, 7, 10, 14). Morsb., p. 155, explains the *i* in *yit* from unstressedness, just as the prefix *ge-* becomes *yi-, y-*, and says *yet* is either the Angl. or the stressed form. But ӡ*it* seems to have been a favourite form in MSc.; so in K. Q. st. 63, Compl. Sc. p. 3. l. 16, Montg. C. 148, ӡ*hit* Craft of Deyng, 168, 195. Dunb. has *yitt* & *yett* (Kaufmann, p. 66), Gau, ӡ*eit* 62/29, 104/29; so also in Bruce ӡ*eit* & ӡ*eyt*; these last would seem to indicate a long vowel ẽ or ĩ, for which cf. the rime *gete* : *mete* (= meat) Gen. & Ex. 1488. See also Sweet §§ 387, 628, where we learn that in OE. the *e* was already lengthened, so that there were two forms *gĕt* and *gët*, and cf. Academy, Dec. 19. 1891, Hempl & Mayhew; but there is no trace of the long vowel in the mod. Sc. diall. Cf. further for northern diall., Dannenberg, p. 25, ӡ*itt* (Sege of Mel. 649, 1372), Curs. M. *giet (yeit), giete : itte*, Hamp. P. C. *yhitte*, T. M. *yit*. Buss, to avoid *i* : *e* rimes, would change ӡ*it* into ӡ*ete* in the Sc. Leg., but seeing that ӡ*it* is found so often in other texts, and *i* : *e* rimes are no rarity, this change is unnecessary and probably incorrect.

4*

§ 169. ȝit was, then, the prevalent form in MSc.; the rime in (c) proves it also for Clar. and probably that in (b), although wite does not appear again in rime and in other texts often rimes with e. ȝit is scarcely likely to be a southern form which has forced its way into the far N. Therefore the ĭ in the N. must be due to the influence of the preceding ȝ (we have the same appearance in ȝis (= yes) and ȝisterday, in which Morsb.'s suggestion of unstressedness cannot hold and which are common in MSc. texts); i. e. the preceding ȝ was a strong support to a tendency which existed in many other words to change e to i, or į, and helped this latter to gain the upper hand over e, (in rec. sp. we have ĭ for OE. e without the help of any such palatal in the words grin, rid, nib); so that at a later period, in some words the N. followed the S. in the raising of e to i after g & sc, and the contrast was removed which existed in OE. in these words, ȝeldan, ȝet, sceld being the regular northern forms for WS. ȝieldan, ȝiet, scield, and later ȝyldan, ȝyt, scyld; cf. Sievers § 157. 2.

§ 170. Carstens, p. 12, remarks on the tendency of ȝe- to become ȝi-, and quotes exactly similar rimes, underȝyte : wyte (witan), forȝit : discoumfit. He adds that very frequently e appears after ȝ, and that no rule can be made as to when e and when i appears in such cases; perhaps this uncertainty in Sir Fer. is due to the mixed dial. in which it was written, and the double forms given by the orthoepists of the 16th & 17th centuries were probably forms from different diall. Clar., as far as the rimes go, only warrants us in accepting an ĭ in closed syll., and $i < \bar{v}$ before a lengthening group.

2. Before ld

§ 171. rimes with — a) itself — feild : scheild 1. 12 (&c.) : ȝield 1. 638 (&c.) — b) OE. ēo. — feild : beheld, prt. 1. 216 (&c.).

§ 172. The vowel was already long $\bar{e}$ in OE. f$\dot{e}$ld, and remained so through the ME. period, finally producing NE. ī; see Kluge P.G. 1. 877, Sweet § 635, t. Br. p. 18, Morsb. p. 18. 19. &c. It was so also in Scotl.; the rime in (b) with OE. ēo is rather proof of this than of shortening in beheld, and the mod. diall. have either the same form as rec. sp. fīld, or, with shortening, fĭld.

§ 173. The rime feild : behald 1. 40, cannot be correct as the passage stands in the MS., but a slight emendation easily puts it right. Place only a comma at fyre, l. 38, and a full stop at feild, l. 39, and alter can behald in l. 40 to than beheld, and then we have, 'In thrist of knichtheid birnand lyk a fyre, As furious lyounis eiger to the feild. Anone quhen ather vther than beheld (or beheild?)'. Generally the infin. appears as behald, behauld or behold, and the prt. as beheld. The consistent spelling beheld with e instead of ei is a sign that in the dial. of the scribe the vowel was already shortened as it is in rec. sp.; the rime with feild shows that it was not so in the dial. of the author, for there is no trace anywhere of a short ĕ in field in Scotl.

3. Before n + cons.

§ 174. rimes with — a) OE. or ON. e. send : kend, prt. 1. 1074 (&c.) : end 4. 1990 : wend 5. 676 (&c.). went : sent 4. 2844. wend(e) : end(e) 2. 1194,

1850 : sent 5. 12 : send, prt. 5. 676 (&c). strenth : lenth 4. 1042. ende : kende 4. 2796. kend, ptc. : send, prt. 4. 1398. — b) OE ē (shortened). ken : ten 2. 854. — c) OE eo, see § 298. — d) OE i, see 387 (c). — e) OE y, see § 544 (d). — f) Fr. or Lat. e. send : attend 1. 124, 2. 830 : commend 1. 538 (&c). went(e) : intend 1. 386 (&c) : jent 3. 1244 (&c) : convenient 1. 148, 900. wend(e) : commend 1. 608 (&c) : intent 1. 770 : decend 4. 1706. neme (vb. *nemnan*) : conteme 1. 224. schent : innocent 3. 1720 : content 4. 148 — and many more.

§ 175. Before *nd*, *e* was lengthened to $\bar{e}$ in the OE period, also in Northumb.; in the Lind. Gospels we find such forms as the following, marked with an accent over the *e*, *énde* Matt. 13. 40, Joh. 13. 1, *wénde* Joh. 20. 15, &c. Cf. Sweet § 395, Sievers § 124. This vowel-length was to a large extent retained in ME (cf. Morsb. pp. 18, 19, Kluge PG 1. 866), but not always (Morsb. p. 19, t. Br. § 16), and in mod. rec. sp. we always have a short ĕ. The same is the case in the mod. Sc. diall., and we shall probably be right in assigning a short ĕ to the pronunc. of the author of Clar.; there are no rimes with OE *ēo*, &c, which could prove a long vowel, such as Carstens, p. 12, quotes from Sir Fer., e. g. *wendes* : *freendes* (cf. Zielke p. 14). The universal use of *e* instead of *ei* is conclusive for the pronunc. of the scribe.

For the *e* : *i* rimes in (d) and (e) see below §§ 388 &c.

§ 176. *ding* = beat, strike (? ON. *dengja*), only rimes with OE *y*, *i* in *king*, 3. 624.

4. Before other consonants

§ 177. — rimes with — a) itself. rest, sb. : west (occidens) 1. 944. fell, adj. : hell 2. 54 : ʒell, vb. 2. 1130 : quell 3. 654 : weill (= well, sb.) 1. 750. tell : sell (= self) 2. 628 (&c) : well, sb. 3. 1240 &c. set : let, sb. 2. 772. best : seimliest, superl. 2. 968, &c. well, sb. : hell 5. 96. cousingis : tendernes 3. 864. — b) ON. e. tell : dwell (*dvelja*) 3. 1270 (&c). sell (= self) : dwell 4. 2764. let, vb. (= hinder) : get 4. 2202. — c) OE æ, see § 80 (g). — d) OE ea, cf. §§ 255, 261. sete, ptc. : ʒeat (*geàt*) 1. 570. sarke (ON. *serkr*) : marke, vb. (OE *mearcian*) 3. 484. — e) OE eo, cf. §§ 302 (d). sarke : warke (*weorc*) 2. 1404. start, prt. (ON. *sterta*) : heart 1. 160. — f) OE i, see § 387 (c). — g) OE y, see § 544 (d). — h) ON. ȳ, see § 550 (d). — i) OE ēa, see § 274 (g). — k) ON w̄, see § 244 (d). — l) Angl. ē = WS. w̄, see § 212 (f). — m) OE w̄, mut. of ā, see § 226 (i). — n) OE ē, mut. of ō, see § 185 (p). — o) OE ēo, see § 330 (l). — p) OE ā, see § 72 (f). — q) OE æ + g, see § 94 (g). — r) Fr. or Lat. e. rest : drest 1. 460 (&c) : devest 1. 1064, dewaist (= *divest*) 2. 850 : oprest 3. 904 : opprest 3. 1042 : prest 5. 2714 : adrest 4. 452 : manifest 4. 1888, reist : preist, prt. 2. 1124, 5. 1154. gaist (OE *gest*) : possest 4. 500. met : debt 2. 1210. tell : expell 1. 202 : excell 4. 1688 (&c) : damosell 2. 1876, 5. 1752 : jewell 3. 1406. selfis : damosellis 3. 2332. mirrines : ches 3. 1162 : distres 3. 1566 : dres 5. 2460. lustines : adrese 2. 1424 : maistres 2. 1318. and many others. — s) Fr. a. wildernes : grace 3. 712, cf. § 97. — t) Fr. i. With *Palexis* rime nobilnes 1. 1290 (&c), bissines 2. 502, and many other nouns in -nes. With *Meliades* (Fr. Meliadice) lustines 2. 824 : bissiness 2. 828 : lustines 2. 1312. — u) Fr. ei. tell : counsall 4. 2222. set, prt. : plet, ptc. (= plaited) 4. 1314. cf. § 157. — v) Fr. ai. gudlier, comp. : repaire, vb. 3. 1418, cf. § 157. — w) ? sell : kell 3. 956.

§ 178. The rimes in (a) (b) (r) are self-rimes and prove nothing; those in (f) (g) (h) (t) are e : i rimes and are discussed below in §§ 388 ff. Those referred to in (i) (k) (l) (m) (n) (o) are quite regular; the rime-words contain a ME $\bar{e}$ or $\check{e}$ which has been shortened to $\check{e}$ in closed syll.; cf. Menze p. 27, t. Br. § 11, Kluge P. G. 1. 878, Sweet § 652 and p. 377, Mayhew p. 220.

§ 179. After *w* there was a tendency in some diall. to change *e* to *a*, cf. Zielke, p. 14, Panning p. 33, &c, and in the mod. Sc. diall. we sometimes find *a* instead of *e* in *wedge*, *well*, sb., *wretch*, *web*, *wed*, *wedding*, *twelve*, *whelp*, *whetstone*, &c. Clar. gives us no proof of this in rime, but one of the scribes at any rate seems to have known it, for he has written *a* after *w* in *wade*, and *wate*, (k); inside the verse we also find *wadding*, 4. 2810, 5. 13, &c.

§ 180. The effect of a following *r* + *cons.* was often to change *e* to *a*, as in rec. sp. in the words *barn*, *mar*, *marsh*, &c; of this we have no decided proof in the above rimes, although the orthography sometimes shows it, see (d) and (e), for we shall see below in §§ 303 ff., that although *er* + *cons* has in some diall. become *ar* + *cons*, the tendency in Central and Northern Scotl. has been in the other direction, viz., to change *ar* to *er*, and we have there accepted this change as general for our author; but as all the mod. Sc. diall. show the form *wark*, and *a* is so frequently found in both words, *wark* and *sark*, (rec. sp. has also *sark*), we may doubtless look upon the spelling in (d) and (e) as not being merely due to the scribe, but as correctly representing the pronunciation of the author in these two particular words. Cf. further §§ 318, 323 below.

§ 181. *well*, sb., rimes always with a short vowel; the spelling *weill*, see (a), must therefore be a mistake of the scribe, who, without thinking of the sense, probably took it for the adv. *well*, which always had a long vowel in Clar. Ocasionally *ei* is written for *e* in other words, e. g. *reist*, *preist* (= pressed) see (r); the rime and spelling in other places plainly show that this is the result of carelessness of the scribe.

§ 182. *cousingis* : *tendernes*, 3. 884. It is very rare for the suffix -*is* (plur.) to be pronounced as a separate syll. in rime in Clar., although the metre sometimes demands a full syllable inside the verse, e. g. "Lyke Gód of ármis Márs armipoténť", 1. 4, "Behólding ón the stáirris bý and bý", 1. 15. But this was a matter of option with the poet, he could treat the suffix as a full syll. or not, just as it suited him. In older Sc. works the use of this and other suffixes as full syllables forms a strong contrast to the use of them in later works. The vowel is always written *i* on *y* in the plur. suffix, so that we can look upon the above as an *i* : *e* rime.

§ 183. *gaist*, see (r), = rec. sp. *guest*. The *ai* may mean that in the pronunc. of the scribe the vowel was long; so also in *dewaist* by the side of *devest*. Cf. §§ 2 ff., 319.

§ 184. *brist*, although only appearing as prt. or ptc., see (h), must be included here, for these forms are irregular and merely the pres. form used as prt. and ptc., all three being thus alike in the same way as in such weak verbs as *list*, *hit*, &c. Earlier Northern ME forms were *bresten*, *brast*, *brosten*. The present *bresten*, or *brist* in Clar. and other Sc. works,

THE MIDDLE-SCOTCH ROMANCE CLARIODUS. 55

with *i* instead of *e*, is to be derived from ON. *bresta*, or perhaps from an ONthmb. form *bresta = WS. *berstan*. It generally kept its strong pret. *brast* in Scotl. and the N. of Engl.; cf. Wackerzapp, whose lists give *brast* (generally proved by rime) in Curs. M., York P., Hamp., Yw. Gaw., Bruce, Townl. M., Alex., M. Arth. & Dougl.; it has also survived in dial. till the present time, cf. DSS. p. 203, where it is given as an *older* form in D. 33. But at the same time a weak prt. was in use as well in MSc.; Wackerz. gives *brest*, Bruce, Alex., *brist*, Bruce, Dougl., Lynd., *bryste*, Sc. Leg.; cf. also Dunb. *brist*: *vnblist*: *resist*: *list* 27. 102, Montg. *brist*: *thrist* (= thirst) MP. 11. 14. The weak form of the ptc. seems to have been rarer; Wackerz. gives *brosten* in York P., Alex., *brusten*, *brustyn*, Townl. M., and *brest* only once in Alex. Dunb. has a wk. form *bristit*, cf. Kaufmann p. 99, who takes the prt. *brist* to be a strong form, but rightly recognises a wk. form in *bristit*, which is probably the same as our *brist* in Clar., only with the full ending -*it*. Murray NED. shows that in the 16th cent. *brast* was often used right throughout for all three forms, but about the end of that cent. *burst* (for all the parts) began to gain the ascendancy. We see here that in Scotl. yet another form, *brist*, was sometimes used for all parts.

$\mathbf{E}'_2$ mut. of $\bar{\mathbf{o}}$

§ 185. rimes with — a) itself. steid : speid, vb. 1. 958 : gleid, sb. 1. 32 : speid, sb. 1. 496, spied 3. 1664. greine : keine 1. 984 : scheine 1. 128 (&c). keine : queine 4. 1786. deimis (3 sg. *dēman*) : seimes (*sēman*) 4. 900. — b) Angl. $\bar{e}$ = WS. $\bar{\imath}\bar{e}$, later $\bar{y}$. greine : seine, ptc. 1. 28 (&c) : fyftine 4. 1074 : steid : neid 2. 1116. queine : seine 3. 1386 (&c) : beseine 1. 670 (&c) : scheine, adj. 1. 628 (&c), schyne 5. 562, quine (= queine) : scheine 2. 540. bleid : neid 1. 988. keine : scine 2. 52. in feire : heire, vb. 4. 666. feill, vb. : steill, sb. 2. 32, 1154. — c) OE. $\bar{e}\bar{o}$. greine : teine (*tēona*) 1. 736, 5. 1178 : seine (inf. and ger.) 2. 732 (&c) : beine (*bēon*) 1. 1352 : beine, 3. sg. 4. 868. steid : ʒeid (*ēode*) 1. 58, 2. 30. meit, vb. : greit (*grēotan*) 3. 1908. sweit : greit 3. 166, 4, 134. keine : seine, inf. 1. 66 : teine 2. 34 : beine 3. sg. 3. 716. weipe : deipe 3. 2138, 4. 2066. keip : creipe 3. 722. queine : beine, 3. sg. 1. 1422 (&c) : beine, ptc. 4. 62 : beine, ind. pl. 4. 794 (&c) : betwine 5. 2552 : seine, inf. 5. 274, 344, quene : beine, inf. 5. 2664. gleid (*glēd*) : ʒeid (*ēode*) 2. 1140. feit (*fēt*, pl. of *fōt*) : greit (*grēotan*) 3. 112. — d) OE. $\bar{e}$ (general OE.). feill, vb. : weill, adv. 2. 266. in feire : heire, adv. 5. 240, — e) ON. $\bar{w}$, see § 244 (e). — f) ON. jū, see § 358 (b). — g) ON. $\bar{e}$. in feire : seire (*sēr*) 5. 770. — h) Angl. $\bar{e}$ = WS. $\bar{w}$ (WGmc. $\bar{a}$). sweit : weite (*wǣt*, NE. *wet*) 3. 778. steid : weid 1. 2 (&c.) : dreid 4. 774, 834 : meid 4. 970 (&c.), steidis : deidis 3. 1106 (&c.) : weidis 4. 860 (&c.). speid. vb. : weid 1. 950 : dreid 2. 1126 (&c.) : deid 3. 1310, speid, sb. : deid 3. 1084. sleip : keipe 1. 1472 (&c.) : weipe 3. 246, sleipit : weipit 3. 926. meit, vb. : streit 3. 1450. gleid (*glēd*) : meid 4. 1034 : dreid 5. 110. in feir : war (opt. *wǣre*) 3. 1482 : war *wǣron*, prt.) 5. 2896. — i) OE. $\bar{w}$, mut. of $\bar{a}$, Gmc. *ai*, see §§ 226 (e), 238 (a), 241 (e). — k) OE. $\bar{e}\bar{a}$ + gutt., see §§ 217 (b), 223 (f). — l) OE. $\breve{e}\cdot$, see § 130 (e). — m) OE. $\bar{\imath}$. greine : syne (*sippan*) 4. 1308. — n) OE. y. in

feir : speir (*spyrian*) 5. 2378. — o) OE. **ea.** met, prt. : ʒet (*geat*) 1. 1058.
— p) OE. e :. met, prt. : set 4. 802. forbled : bed 5. 94. sped : bed 3. 542,
5. 1672. — q) Fr. e, ie. greine : susteine 4. 1058, sustine 1. 752. queine :
susteine 4. 1860, 5. 1468. keine : conteine 2. 294. sweit : secreit 1. 274 :
compleit 2. 360. heid (sb. = heed) : proceid 3. 2216 : exceid 1. 1410. feiris,
sb. pl. : cleiris, vb. 1. 424 : prissonieris 1. 520. ifeir : bachelier 1. 828 : maneir 2. 198, 3. 1204 : cleir 5. 2674. in feir(e) : cleir 2. 116 : cheir(e) 2. 346 (&c.)
: compeir 2. 1908 : maneir(e) 4. 568, 5. 2488 : suppeir 5. 2452. on feir : maneir 1. 1334. ifeire : peir (OFr. *piere*) 5. 2516. feir (adj. = healthy, sound,
OE. (*ge-*)*fēre*, OHG. *gi-fuori*, cf. Bradley) : maneir 2. 406. — r) Fr. i. sweit :
spreit 2. 374 (&c.). deime, vb. : expreime 4. 2240.

§ 186. The oldest form of this vowel was *ǣ*, which maintained its
existence longest in the ONthmb. dial., cf. Sievers §§ 27, 150; it soon coincided, however, in the OE. period with original *ē* and produced a closed
ẹ̄ in all ME. diall., belonging to t. Br.'s class γ.

We have γ : γ rimes in (a), (b), (c), (d), (f), (g), (q), β : γ rimes in
(h), (i), and an α : γ rime in (l).

The shortened form before double cons. is *ĕ*, which rimes with *e*
from other sources, see (o), (p) and some of the others.

§ 187. The rimes in (m) and (r), especially the latter, give evidence
of the transition of *ẹ̄* to *ī* (in the former, we have an example of the survival of the older pronunc. of ī as monophthong, cf. § 432); this change
became general in the 15th cent., but had begun in some diall. at an earlier
date; it was at any rate complete and acknowledged by the grammarians
of the 16th cent. who were anything but innovators, and for whose acknowledged pronunciations a much earlier date may be accepted. Cf. Kluge
PG. 1. 880, Zielke p. 28, Brandl p. 60, Hoofe p. 31, Hattendorf p. 22.

§ 188. The rime in (n) cannot be interpreted in the same way, for
the y in *spyrian* became *e* at an earlier period and then shared the fortunes of this vowel, becoming with it, later on, ī; if it had remained *i* after
its unrounding we should expect to find the diphthong *əi*, *ai* in mod. Sc.;
this rime is more useful to us for the history of the y in *spyrian*, cf. § 538.

§ 189. The mod. Sc. diall. have only ī, or with the recent shortening,
usual in some diall., ĭ. The form produced by older shortening before
conson. groups is *ĕ*.

Angl. ē = WS. ie

§ 190. rimes with — a) itself. scheine : seine, ptc. 2. 1456 (&c.) : beseine 4. 224, 5. 704; scheane : beseine 4. 962. — b) General OE. ē, WGmc. ō.
heire, vb. : heire, adv. 5. 1800. steill, sb. : weill, adv. 2. 1136, 5. 2328. —
c) OE. ō̆, mut. of ō, see § 185 (b). — d) OE. ēo. seine, ptc. : beine (*bēon*)
2. 588 (&c.) : scheine : seine, inf. 1. 1430 (&c.) : beine 3. sg. 4. 16, 5. 1048 :
beine, ind. pl. 5. 1560. — e) OE. ǣ, mut. of ā, see §§ 226 (f), 238 (b). —
f) Angl. ē = WS. ēa before a gutt., see § 223 (d). — g) OE e :. ten : ken
2. 884. — h) OE. eo, see § 326. — i) OE. y-, see § 537 (c). — k) Fr. e, ie.
seine, ptc. : conteine 2. 464, 3. 138. scheine : perteine 1. 834 : conteine 2.
1324. beleiue : greiue, vb. 3. 214 : acheve 3. 508, beleve : greine, sb. 4. 1414.
neid : exceid 4. 302. heir(e), vb. : cheir(e) 1. 1190 : cleir(e) 2. 1882 (&c.) :

maneir 1. 1262 (&c.) : bacheleir 5. 2932 : parqueir (*per quer, cuer*) 2. 746 : conqueir 1. 1306 : peir (L. *parem*) 3. 1032 : circuleir 5. 1632. heiris, 3. sg. : effeiris, 3. sg. 4. 818.

§ 191. This vowel belongs also to t. Br.'s class γ. We have $\gamma : \gamma$ rimes in (a), (b), (c), (d), (f), (k), $\beta : \gamma$ rimes in (e), shortening to $\breve{e}$ in (g). The rimes in (h) and (i) are discussed in the §§ referred to.

The mod. Sc. diall. always have $\bar{\imath}$, or with shortening $\breve{e}$, except that the prt. of the vb. *hear* generally has $\breve{a}$.

General OE. or ON. $\bar{e}$ = WGmc. $\bar{e}$ or $\breve{e}$ (lengthened)

§ 192. rimes with — a) itself. me : the (pron.) 2. 68 : ʒe, 3. 1304 (&c.) heir, adv. : seir (ON. *sēr*) 2. 508. — b) OE. $\bar{e}$, mut. of $\bar{o}$, see § 185 (d). — c) Angl. $\bar{e}$ = WS. $\bar{\imath e}$, see § 190 (b). — d) OE. $\bar{eo}$. me : be 1. 110 (&c.) : se, vb. 2. 216 (&c.), see 2. 456 : three 4. 478 : knie 4. 2648. he : three 1. 610 (&c.) : thie (*þēoh* = thigh) 1. 1000 : fre 2. 132 : kne 2. 592 : be 2. 768 (&c.) : se 3. 1156 (&c.) : trie (*trēo*) 5. 1108. ʒe : se 4. 926 : be 4. 1530, 4. 2838. we : be 4. 2568. heir, adv. : deir(e) (*dēore*) 1. 232 (&c.). seire (ON. *sēr*) : dier (*dēore*) 4. 298. — e) Angl. $\bar{e}$ = WS. $\bar{ea}$ before a gutt., see §§ 217 (c), 223 (e). — f) Angl. $\bar{e}$ = WS. $\bar{æ}$, see § 195 (d). — g) OE. $\bar{æ}$, mut. of $\bar{a}$, see § 226 (d). — h) ON. øy, see § 499 (a). — i) Fr. e. me cuntrie 1. 1386 (&c.) : agre 2. 1686 : pitie 4. 1470. he : cuntrie 1. 1316 (&c.) magnanjmitie 2. 528 : lawtie 2. 556 : meinʒe (*maisnee*) 5. 1242 : mellie 3. 2116 : Spainʒe 4. 2834. heir, adv. : maneir 1. 1506 (&c.) : cheir 2. 586 (&c.) : tabilleir (*tablier*) 3. 1164 : mater 4. 2500 : requyre 4. 706. seir(e) : effeire (vb. *efférir*) 4. 164 : cleire 5. 1618. weill, adv. : reveal 3. 2034, reveill 4. 272 : parentell (OFr. *parentele*) 3. 1416 : parentillie (for *parenteill*, cf. Lyfe of Jos. EETS. 44. *parentycle*, 402) 2. 310 — and many more. — k) Fr. ieu. me : pardie 2. 1038, perdie 5. 1380. he : perdie 4. 1244, 5. 142. — l) Lat. e. ʒe : apersie (for *A per se*; i. e. A by itself, the height of perfection, similar to mod. Engl. *A 1*, cf. Murray N. E. D. under A. 4) 4. 2156. — m) Fr. i. seire : laseure (for *laseire* ?) 4. 456.

§ 193. This, too, belongs to t. Br.'s Class γ. We have $\gamma : \gamma$ rimes in (a), (b), (c), (d), (e), (i), (l), $\beta : \gamma$ rimes in (f), (g). Those in (k) can also be considered as $\gamma : \gamma$ rimes, for the Fr. combination *ieu*, which generally produced ME. *eu*, is always represented by ME. $\bar{e}$ in the word *parde, pardie*, see Sturmfels, Angl. 8. 255. (h) also contains a $\gamma : \gamma$ rime; (m) gives us another proof of the raising of $\bar{e}$ to $\bar{\imath}$.

The mod. sc. diall. always have $\bar{\imath}$.

§ 194. *Weill*, adv., is included here, as it comes from OE. *wēl*, a lengthened form which existed by the side of *wĕl*, cf. Sweet §§ 387, 628. This explains the existence of two forms *węl* and *wĕl* in ME. Cf. Kluge PG. 1. 879, Morsb. p. 18, t. Br. p. 27 & Angl. 1. 542, Buss p. 12, Zielke p. 14. That the adv. only rimes here with β and γ vowels must be due to mere chance, as in Clar. there is no distinction between the three classes α, β and γ, and consequently none between the sb. OE. *wela* and the adv. OE. *wĕl*; both are *weill* (with $\bar{\imath}$); we have already seen that *weill*, sb., rimes with an original γ vowel. Cf. § 132.

Most of the mod. Sc. diall. still have either long (ii) or the half-long (i), instead of Engl. (e), in the adv. *weill*; cf. Murray DSS. p. 145.

Angl. ē = WS. ǣ, WGmc. ā.

§ 195. rimes with — a) itself. war (wǣron) : thair (pār) 3. 1788. — b) OE. ēā. feare : eare 1. 1370. — c) OE. e-, see § 130 (d). — d) General OE. or ON. ū (WGmc. ū). ware (opt.) : heir(e), adv. 2. 394, 4, 278. war (wǣron) : scire (ON. sēr) 5. 926. were (wǣron) : seir 3. 1944. feir : heir, adv. 3. 1752. — e) OE. ē, mut. of ō, see § 185 (h). — f) Angl. ē = WS. īē. ʒeir : neir 3. 24. ware (wǣron) : nar 1. 474. cf. §§ 223, 224. — g) OE. a-. thair(e) : fair(e) (faran) 2. 422 (&c.) : weilfair 2. 608, 3. 1340 : cair 3. 598. — h) OE. ā. thair(e) : sair(e) 3. 402 (&c.) : more 3. 1152. thore : more 3. 80. quhair : sair 3. 738. — i) OE. ǣ : ? see § 80 (d). — k) OE. ǣ + g, see § 94 (f). — l) OE. y-, see § 537 (a). — m) Fr. e, ie. thair : officer 3. 1800. war(e) (wī ron) : cleir 3. 854 (&c.) : persevere 5. 2382 : portar 3. 2228 : supper 5. 410 : apeire 5. 1396. war (opt.) : maneir 5. 1148. — n) Fr. a. thair(e) : declaire 4. 892. haire : sqare (sic) 1. 964. — o) Fr. ai. thair : chyre (= chair) 5. 2800. hearis (= hairs) : peirs (= pairs) 4. 1206. — p) Fr.'ei. thair : impair 1. 444 : faire (Lat. fēria) 3. 962.

§ 196. A glance at the foregoing lists makes it at once apparent that we have here to do with double forms; if the rimes are at all pure, there can be no doubt as to there being two quite different pronunciations to a word which, like were, ware, rimes with OE. ēa, e, ē, on the one hand, and OE. ǣ + g on the other; we have at least two sounds for the vowel, viz. ē < ā and ɩ < ẹ. We cannot avoid this twofold pronunc. as Fick, p. 26, tries to do; the rimes pere : dere and pare : fare cannot contain the same sound; or would Fick maintain that dere and fare both contain the same vowel? Either the poet of the Pearl was a very bad rimer, in which case we can argue little from his rimes, or the adv. there had two distinct forms in his pronunc.

§ 197. The words NE. there, where, were have given rise to much discussion on account of this double pronunc. which they often had apparently in one and the same dial., i. e. in the language of one and the same author, as used in his writings, which need not, however, have correctly reflected one actual spoken dial.

In other texts we find yet a third vowel in these words, viz. ō, which appears also occasionally in the MS. of Clar., see (h). Cf. Brandl, p. 55, &c.

§ 198. The regular development of the vowel ǣ, ē in these words would be a ME. ẹ̄ in the SW. and ę̄ in the other districts. But the effect of an r was to make a vowel open if it was closed, and to keep it open if it was already so, although its regular development would otherwise tend to a closing. As a result of the same effect of the r, in the late OE. period there existed the forms pār, hwār, cf. Morsb. p. 46; this ā would, of course, produce ME. ā later ę̄, in the North, and ME. ǭ in the Midl. & South; hence the three possible forms there, thare, thore, which sometimes all appear in one and the same text; they all appear in Clar., but we have no rimes to prove the o-form, which is not to be expected in a northern text; the few instances of the o-spelling are either due to a Midl. scribe or are merely imitations of Midl. forms on the part of a Northern copyist.

§ 199. Cf. further on these words, Sievers § 321, note 2, Kluge PG. 1. 874, Scholle, p. 14, who with ten Brink, § 49, note 1, derives *ware*, *wǭren* &c., from ON. *váru*. Morsb. p. 46 prefers to explain *ā*, *ǭ*, also in this word through the influence of following *r*, OE. *wǣron* for *wǣron*, rather than from Norse influence. Both are possible, and it may be that both influences cooperated, but for the S. the former alone is probable; cf. Bülbring pp. 58, 59.

§ 200. We will consider separately each of the words which appear in § 195. *Were* (prt. and opt.) rimes in Clar. with *e*- vowels, but these of all three classes, *α*, *β*, and *γ*, and once with OE. *æg*; *fear* rimes with OE. *eā*, *e*-, *ē*, *y*-; *hair* only with previous *ā* and *ai*, which, as we know, coincided in Sc.; similarly *there*, with one exception, in which it rimes with Fr. *e*, see (m); *where* only appears once, in rime with OE. *ā*, and *year* only once, in rime with *neir* (Angl. *nēr*); i. e. *hair* and *where* only have (proved by rime) *ǭ* < *ā*, *fear* and *year*, ı < *ē*, *were* generally ı < *ẹ̄*, but also *ẹ̄* < *ā*, and *there* mostly *ẹ̄* < *ā*, only once ı < *ę̄*. The author, then, used only one fixed pronunc. for each word, except *were* and *there*, in which he occasionally adopted a second pronunc.

In the text we find *thair*, *whair* (sometimes *whar*), and almost without exception *war(e)*, the latter also in rime with a previous *ē*.

The *o* in *thore*, *more*, 3. 80, is evidently not due to the author; the passage is altogether somewhat doubtful, the sense not being clear, and the second line of the couplet lacking a syll. or two.

§ 201. The same variety of forms is to be observed in most ME. and MSc. texts, although some, like *Clar.*, give the preference to one form, and sometimes know *only* one form. Brandl, p. 55, has collected statistics with regard to the words *there*, *where*, *were*; he shows the threefold pronunc. and how, from the middle of the 14th cent. on, first *were* and then *there* gradually assert themselves in the N.; Kölbing says from 1300 on, as the *e*-form is found in *Sir Tr*. Cf. Menze, p. 62: "the *a*-forms were at first characteristic for the N., but the *e*-form makes its appearance early, especially in *þere* [this should be rather *were*]. The *e*-forms were usual in the S.; in the Midl. all three forms, *a*, *e*, *o*, but in the western portion there was a preference for *a*, and *o* was particularly characteristic of the northern portion, especially NE. Midl." But *o* was just as characteristic of the S. E. Midl. as of the N. E.; *Gen. Ex.*, for instance, has mostly *o* in all three words. *a* is also found sometimes in the S., see Bülbring p. 58.

§ 202. Here following an extension of Brandl's statistics is submitted, partly collected from various dissertations and introductions to texts of the EETS., and partly, especially with Sc. texts, from my own examination of such as were accessible; in the latter case there is no claim to completeness, as it was impossible to examine whole texts from beginning to end; but the forms given are certainly found, and, where confirmed by rimes, specimens of these are given.

§ 203. Scotch.

Bruce: *there* and *were* with *ā*, *ẹ̄* and *ę̄* in rime (cf. Skeat. EETS. ed. p. 633, and Buss pp. 501, 503, *where* only *a*, *quhar*, *ayquhar* : *schar*, prt.

2.91 : *bar*, prt. 12. 22 : *thar* 19. 441. — Sc. Leg. *there* and *were* mostly with *a*, sometimes *ę* (in rime, see Buss, l. c.), *where* only with *a*, *wydquhare* : *war* 1/68. — K. Q. *there* and *were* only *e* in rime (Wischmann p. 3); the scribe has *a* and *e* in *there* and *were*, but only *a* in *whare*. — Wall. *there*, *where* and *were* only with *a* (also written *ai*), *thar* : *mar* 1. 62 : *sar* 1. 72 : *war*, prt. 1. 342 : *dispar* 1. 260 : *repayr* 2. 16, &c., *war* : *sar* 8. 394 : *euirmar* 8. 628, *quhar* (in middle of verse). — Gol. *thair*, *quhair*, but *weir* : *sapheir* : *deir* (*dēor*), *were* : *spere* : *bachilere*, and *war* : *bair* (*bær*) : *air* (*ǣr*), *war* : *Cesar*, inside the verse chiefly *a* (Noltemeier, p. 18). — Lanc. *thoore* : *bore* (*bār*, sb.) 628, *thore* 1102, *thare* : *ayre* (= air) 352 : *bare* adj. 1220, *there* : *were* 408; *quhar* 124, *whare* 427; *wer* : *here*, vb. 68, *were* : *here* 1428 : *chere* 1308, 1552 : *sper* 1512, *veir* : *steir*, vb. 818, *ware* : *poware*. This poem shows in other respects strong Engl. influence (see Skeat's introd.), so that we cannot accept the above forms from this alone as being really Scotch; the rimes, prove only *a* for *there*, but *a* and *e* for *were*; the *o* of *thore* may possibly also be due to the author, for we find *hore* (= hair) : *wharfore* 366. — Rat. Rav. has only forms with *a* for all three words : *thare* : *are* (*ǣr*) 1161, *war* : *mare* 1471, *ware* : *mare* 1772 : *movare* 1595, 1599 : *thar* 1661; *quhar* 162; but perhaps *ware* : *movare* may mean an *e*-pronunc. in *were* rather than an *a* in *movare*? — Dunb. has few, if any, rimes with these words, they all appear in the text with *a* or *ai*, and sometimes *there* and *were* with *e*. — Dougl. *there* has only *ā*, written *ai*, *thair* : *fair*, adj. : *Lair* (= Loire?) : *riuair*, 1. 42. 20 : *sair* : *declair* : *wair* (*wǣre*) 1. 54. 25 : *butlair* : *thair* : *hair* 1. 70. 1 : *stair* (= look) 2. 29. 16 : *langair*, comp. 2. 109. 22 and many other similar rimes; *where* also only *a*-vowel, *quhair* : *fayr* (*faran*) : *rair* (= roar, sb.) : *stair* 1. 113. 1 : *sair* 2. 42. 24 : *chair* 2. 48. 6 : *bair*, prt. 2. 61. 10, *quhar* : *keipar* 2. 132. 18; *were* has both *a* and *e* confirmed by rimes, *wair* : *quhair* 2. 46. 18, *war* : *thair* 2. 91. 16, 2. 137. 26 : *familiar* 2. 140. 22, *weir* : *seir* (ON. *sēr*) 2. 208. 16 : *in feir* : *appeir* 1. 52. 16, also written *wer* 1. 8. 3, 1. 19. 20, &c. The rimes with *riuair*, *langair*, *keipar*, prove an $\bar{e} < \bar{a}$ for *there* and *where*; the accompanying rime-words show that the vowel must be *ā* or its outcome *ę̄* or the rimes are imperfect; we have a similar rime in *spair* : *strangeair*, 2. 120. 28. It is better to look upon such rimes as proof that the change $\bar{a} > \bar{e}$ has already taken place, than as evidence that the -*er* denoting the agent in *keipar*, &c., has become -*ar*, for we cannot explain the -*air* in *riuair* (= river) and *langair*, comp., in the same way; in the former the Fr. vowel $\bar{e}$ is retained and the latter has $\bar{e}$ lengthened from $\breve{e}$. — Compl. Sc. *there* with *e*, *where* and *were* only with *a*. — Gau, only *a*, except sometimes *e* in *were*. — Lyndes. (the orthography is by no means uniform, e. g. the Sat. generally has *ai* where Mon. has *a*) *there* only *a*, *thair* : *mair*, Sat. 2242; *where* only *a*, *quhair* : *spair* Sat. 320; *were* chiefly *a* in the Dreme and Sat., sometimes *e* in the Dreme, but in the Mon. and other works *e* is written oftener than *a*, but *ware* : *declare*, Mon. 1. 1274; the *wer* in the inside of the verse might be only due to unstressedness; as far as examined, there is no rime to prove an *e*-vowel. — Roll. C. V. only $\bar{e} < \bar{a}$ in all three words, *thair* : *mair* : *contrair* : *hair* : *cair* 3. 200 : *mair* : *pair* : *Thamar* 3. 576 : *mair* : *declair* : *cair* 3. 447 :

rair : *cair* : *euermair* 4. 403 : *preclair* : *singular* : *dangear* 4. 420, &c.; *war* : *mair* : *Interlinear* : *declair* : *compair* 3. 788 : *mair* : *preclair* : *dangeir* : *snair* 4. 458; where appears as *quhair*. But OE. *ǣr* rimes with *e* and *a* in the same stanza, *eir* : *cleir* : *Thamar* : ʒ*eir* 3. 825. The rime with *dangeir*, must be explained in the same way as those with *riuair*, &c. in *Dougl.* — Satir P. there only with *a* in rime, *thair* : *sair* : *air* : *declair* 4. 73 : *Air* (= Ayr) 23. 43 : *mair* : *compair* : *lair* (= teaching) 24. 55 : *declair* : *Registair* : *spair* 26. 55, there : *mair* 45. 31; where only *a*, *quhair* : *prepair* 42. 308 : *mair* 42. 562, 580 : *spair* 42. 590, *alquhair* : *cair* : *mair* : *spair* 40. 287; *were* only with *a* in rime, *war* (opt.) : *far* 42. 298, written *wer* 31. 95. In the three poems which are of Engl. origin (Nos. 1, 9, 34) we find there : *warre* (bellum) : *Jarre* (= quarrel) 1. 584, and generally written there; where : *appere* 1. 326 : *appear* 9. 276, written *quhair* 34. 5; *were* (opt.) : *clear* 9. 164, 328, *were*, prt. : *declare* 9. 46; i. e. there with previous *ā*-vowel, and *were* with previous *ē* and *ā*. — Winʒet, only *a* in all three words, *thair*, *thairto*, *tharin*, *tharof*, &c., *quhare*, *quhair*, *quair*, *quhairat*, *quhairby*, &c., *war*, *ware*, *var*. — Leslie, only *a*, *thair*, *quhair*, *war*. — Montg. there only with *a* in rime, *thair* : *dispaire* C. 378 : *quhair* C. 758 : *declair* C. 1498 : *ayr* : *chayr* : *rare*, adj. S. 31, but occasionally written there, F. 425, &c.; where only *a* in rime, *vhair* : *dispaire* MP. 24. 14, 44. 6 : *air* : *repair* : *sair* : *dispaire* : *evermair* MP. 25. 7, *quhair* : *air*, sb. C. 238, also written *vher*, S. 29, &c., and *where* F. 269; *were* with both *e* and *a*, *wer*, prt. : *deir* (*dēore*) C. 1277, *war*, prt. : *dar* (= dare) C. 728 : *far* MP. 30. 7 : *start* : *far* : *ar* S. 13, *war* (opt.) : *ar* MP. 12. 15, *ware*, prt. : *rare* : *mare* : *care* S. 49.

§ 204. The result of this examination, limited to the works quoted, is that, with the exception of K. Q. (which shows altogether strong Engl. influence) Bruce and Sc. Leg., there only has the vowel *ā* (or later *ę̄*) proved by rimes, although *e* is written in Lanc., Dunb., Compl. Sc., and Satir. P., and *o* is written in Lanc. alone. We see from this that the *e*-form of there did not advance further than the N. of Engl. (cf. Brandl p. 56) and that there did not go parallel with *were*, in its new form with an *e*-vowel, in Scotl. any more than it did in the N. of Engl. *Where* only appears written with *a* or *ai* in *all* the works quoted, except in those of the Satir. P. which are decidedly English; it is a rare word in rime, but the *ā* (or later *ę̄*) is proved by rime in Bruce, Sc. Leg., Dougl., Lyndes., Montg. and Satir P. *Were* appears with *ā* and *ē* proved by rime in Bruce, Sc. Leg., Gol., Lanc., Dougl. and Montg., only *e* in rime in K. Q., but *a* and *e* in the text. If Barbour and the writers of the Sc. Leg. were free from Engl. influence, then the date of the establishment of the *e*-pronunc. in *were* must be set in the 14th cent., and is then not so very much later than that established by Kölbing for the N. of Engl.; but it is strange that this *e* appears (as far as is yet settled) in no other works, proved by rime, besides K. Q., Gol., Lanc. and Clar. (which all certainly show Engl. influence), till the time of Dougl., i. e. much more than 100 years later than Barbour, and then again is not proved by rime till we come to Montg., nearly another 100 years later. The abnormal *e* in *there* in Bruce and Sc. Leg. has, too, yet to be explained, for in this respect they stand quite alone among genuine Sc. works. We know that Barbour was for some time at Oxford, and often travelled into Engl. to pursue his studies there and at various other places. This might explain his use of the *e*-forms of *there* and *were*, but it would be strange if he only betrayed Engl. influence in these words and not in other ways; in fact, he does so once in the treatment of OE. *ā*, cf. *mor* : *befor* 10. 199, although *more* is generally written *mar* or *mair*. Perhaps a thorough investigation of his rimes would throw more light on the matter.

§ 205. It is not surprising that Clar., whatever date we may have to assign to it, should show, in addition to its other tinges of Engl. influence, the *e*-form of *were*, although it is noticeable that this has by far the preference over the native *a*-form, which it has almost completely displaced, while *where* has still, as far as the rimes testify, no trace of the *e*-form and *there* only once. Clar. stands, then, on a level with Gol., Lanc. (with the exception of the forms of *there*, perhaps), DougL and Lyndes. (Mon.), and shows a marked contrast to Wall., which has only *a* in *were*. This is, then, perhaps a sure reason for not dating the poem much before 1500.

§ 206. The mod. Sc. diall. also show a variety in pronunc., which, however, does not at first sight exactly correspond with the above observations in all particulars. *There* has only an *e*-vowel, both open and closed, or (ii') in D. 33, which may both correctly represent the MSc. form with *ā*, which, we have seen, is the only one proved by rime in pure Sc.; the *ē* would also coincide with the form of rec. sp. *Where* has (ee) in 33, (ee) or (A), (AA) in 34 and 35, (AA) or (a), (aa) in 36 and 37, and (a), (aa) in 38, 39, 40, 41, 42. *Were* has also occasionally *ă*, but also *ĕ*, *ē* and *ĭ*; but Ellis's material is here too scanty, and the word is, owing to its use in unstressed position, liable to too much irregularity for us to derive any definite information. Of the similar words, *hair* and *fear*, *hair* has only an *ē*-vowel, as in rec. sp., and *fear* (i') in 33, (ii) in 35, but (ee) in 37, 38, 39, 41, 42, also (ii') in 39. It is noticeable that an *a*-pronunc. is only found in *were* and *where*, particularly the latter; this may be a preservation of the MSc. form with *ā*, for *ā* would produce in regular development a modern *ē* vowel, or perhaps of more recent origin and due to the preceding *w*, exactly similar to the short *ă* resulting from earlier *ĕ* preceded by *w*, cf. § 179; but the latter seems less likely when we consider the exclusive use of the *a*-form *whare* in MSc., and the firm establishment of *a*-forms especially in the mod. diall. of the extreme N. in contrast to the southern diall., which leads us to conclude that the *ā* is old. It is perhaps better to ascribe to the *w* merely a preserving influence over the *ā*; without this it would be difficult to see why the *ā* should not have been retained in *there* as well. The modern *ē*-forms of *where* are most probably, where found, simply borrowed from rec. sp.; they cannot be MSc. *e*-forms retained unaltered on account of the *r*, for such *e*-forms are not found proved by rime in MSc., and they can scarcely be developed from MSc. *ā*-forms, for then we should expect to find (ii') in D. 33, as we do in *there*, and, besides, *two* genuine native forms of such difference are not likely to be found in one and the same pure dial.

We conclude then as follows:

	MSc.	NSc.	
there	ā ──	ē	both by regular undisturbed
	╲─ (ii') in D. 33	development.
where	ā ──	ā	in Central and North^n Scotl., retained through
	╲		influence of the *w*.
	╲─	ē	in South^n and Central Counties, from rec. sp.

were is too uncertain to tabulate.

§ 207. Let us now look at some of the diall. of Engl. Although this takes us beyond the boundaries of our task, yet the statistics collected may well be inserted here for comparison. The rimes may be found in the dissertations and treatises quoted, or, where no treatise is quoted, in Brandl's list.

Northern.

Horn Ch. (Caro, p. 20, 26), *there* with *a* and *o*, *where* with *a* and *o*, *were* with *a, o* and *e*. — Sir Tr. (Kölbing, pp. 64, 73) *there* with *a* and *e*, *where* only *a*, *were* with *a* and *e*. — Surt. Ps. (Wende, p. 18, Kölbing, p. 73), *there* only *a*, *were* generally *a*, twice *o*. — York P. (Kamann p. 61), *there* with *a, o*, *where* with *a*, *were* with *a, e, o*. — Yw. Gaw., *there* with *a*, once *o*, *where a*, *were a, e*. — Hamp. (Brandl. p. 56, Ulmann, Engl. St. 7. 425) only *a* in all three words. — Octav. (North^n version, Sarrazin p. 36), *there* only *a* in rime, *e* and *o* also written, *were a* and *e* in rime. — Mel. (Dannenberg p. 19), *there* with *a*, once *e*, *where* not in rime, but only *a* written, *were* with *a* and *e* (equally frequent). — Sir. Egl. (Zielke, p. 26), *there* and *where* only *a*, but also written with *e*, *were* with *a*, once *e*, occasionally written also with *o*. — Rol. & Ot. (Dannenberg p. 19) *there* and *were* both with *a* and *e*. — Bone Flor. (Wilda, p. 34) *there* and *were* with *a* and *e*. — Athelstone (Wilda p. 64), *there* with *a*, *were* with *e*. — Thom. Erc., all three words with *a* and *e*. — Townl. M., all three words with *a, o* and *e*. — Thornton, *there* and *were* with *e*. — Sir Perc. (Ellinger, pp. 7, 9, 13, Brandl, p. 55) *there* with *a*, *were* with *a* and *e*, *where* with *a*. — Isumbras, *there* and *were* with *a*.

§ 208. From this we find that *there* is generally found in the N. with an *a*-vowel; *e* is proved by rime in Sir Tr., Rol. & Ot., Bone Flor., Athelst., Thom. Erc. and Townl. M. That *e* is not found in the intervening works is probably due to difference of district; *o* is found established by rime earliest in Horn Ch., which Caro assigns to the border of the Midl. district, perhaps even S. of the boundary line; otherwise it is only found (i. e. confirmed by rime) in York Pl., Yw. Gaw. and Townl. M., also to be placed near the border line.

Where has only *a*, except in Townl. M.

Were is found everywhere with *a*, but generally with *e* as well, from Horn Ch. and Sir. Tr. on, though sometimes the *e* is in the minority; it is found with certain *o* in Horn Ch., Psalter, York P. and Townl. M.; this form is evidently more at home in the southern portion of the northern district, which agrees in many respects with NE. Midl.

Just as *were* extends earlier and farther into the North than *there*, so, on the other hand, *thare* extends earlier and farther into the South than *ware*, cf. Wilda, pp. 30, 54.

§ 209. N. E. Midland.

Cf. here especially Menze, 59, ff., as well as Brandl. Menze's material is not complete, forms which are corroborated by rime (e. g. *þar* in *King Horn*) are sometimes not mentioned by him; in the following, however, where no other authority is mentioned, I chiefly depend upon him.

Orm. (Menze) *there* and *were* only *e*, *where* with *a* and *e*. — Deb. Body and Soul (Menze) *there* with *e*, *a* and *o* (*o* in rime), *where* and *were* only *e*. — Best. (Menze) *there* with *e*, *where o*, *were e* and *o* (*o* in rime). — Hav., all three words with *a*, *e* and *o*; *a* proved in rime for *were*. — Am. (Kölbing, Sir. Tr. p. 73, Am. Amil. p. 27), *there* with *a* (in rime) and *e*, *where* with *e*, *were* with *a*, *e*, *o* (all in rime). — Emare (Wilda, p. 29) *were* with *e* and *o* (in rime), there with *a* and *o* (in rime). — Rob. Brunne (Menze) *there* and *where* with *a*, *e*, *o* (all in rime), *were* with *a* and *o* (in rime), and *e*. — Minot (Scholle p. 14), *there* and *were* with *a* and *e* (in rime), *where* with *e*, once *o*. — Alex. Leg. (Brandl p. 55) *were* with *a* and *e* (in rime). — Rol., *there* and *were* with *a*, *e*, *o* (*a* in rime). (According to Wissmann, Litt. Bl. 1880, 334, this last belongs to N. E. Midl., not to S. W. Midl. as Schleich would have it; Schleich's defence of his assertion, Angl. 4. 309, is not conclusive; Fer. is not a good text to use in argument for Southern dial., for it has mixed forms; Schleich only brings forward rimes from Rol. which prove an *a*-pronunc.) — Erl Tol. (Lüdtke pp. 32. 45), *there* with *a*, *e*, *o* (*a* and *o* in rime), *were* with *a* and *o* (in rime) and once *e* (in rime). — Sir Torr. (Adam p. 12) *there* with *o* (in rime), *were* with *a*, *e*, *o* (in rime). — Ipom. B. (Kirschten pp. 25, 26, Kölbing, Ipom. p. 175) *were* with *e* (in rime).

§ 210. We find, then, that all three forms, *a*, *e* and *o*, are used in all three words in the N. E. Midl. dial. Rob. of Brunne is the earliest with whom all three are found in *there* and *where* proved by rime, and Am. the earliest text showing the same threefold pronunc. in *were*; but *o* is proved for *there* as early as in the Deb. and for *were* in the Best. Beyond Rob. of Brunne *o* is only once proved in rime for *where*, viz. in Minot, so that it does not seem so firmly established in this word as in *were* and *there*.

§ 211. N. W. Midland.

Aunt. Arth., *were* with *a* and *e* (in rime). — Ipom. A. (Kölbing pp. 162, 167) *there* and *were* with *a*, *e* and *o* (all in rime). — The Pearl (Fick p. 25 and Knigge p. 42), *there* and *were* with *a*, *e*, *o* (in rime). — Sir Gaw. (Knigge p. 42), *there* with *a* and *o*, *where* with *a*, *were* with *e* (all in rime).

Here the state of things is much the same as in N. E. Midl., except that, as far as our information goes, we have no proof of *e* or *o* in *where*.

For the further diall. see Menze.

Angl. $\bar{e}$ = WS $\bar{æ}$, WGmc. $\bar{a}$,

§ 212. rimes with — a) itself. weid : dreid 2. 1498. deid : dreid 3. 834 (&c.) : meid 4. 1086. — b) OE. $\bar{w}$, mut. of $\bar{a}$. see § 226 (b). — c) OE. $\overline{ea}$. feare : care 1. 1370. evine (for eve, OE. *ǣfen, ēfen*) : leaue, sb. 3. 102. — d) OE. $\bar{e}$, mut. of $\bar{o}$. see § 185 (h). — e) OE. $\overline{eo}$. α) sleip : diep (for *deip*) 3. 1870. weine, vb. (*wǣnan, wēnan*) : betwine 3. 182. weid : ʒeid 1. 1094. meid : ʒeid 1. 1418. β) adreid : fled 3. 1126. — f) OE. e : adred(e) : wed (inf.) 2. 622, 3. 1874 : wade (for *wed*) 4. 1896. adreid : bed 1. 1068 : wade (for *wed*) 4. 1872. wate (*wēt*) : set 5. 2338. — g) OE. $\bar{æ}$. adred : had, prt. 3. 1456. — h) Fr. or Lat. e. dreid : proceid 4. 1900 : poseid 2. 702. streit : repeit 5. 2910, streits (for *streit*) : repleit·5. 2786. reid (*rǣd*) : remeid 3. 752. — i) Fr. a. blast (*blǣst*) : past. ptc. 4. 1762. wat (*wēt*) : plait (Fr. *plate*) 2. 44.

§ 213. This vowel belongs to t. Br.'s Class β. We have β : β rimes in (a) and (b), β : γ rimes in (d), (e) and (h), and β : α rimes in (c). When shortened before conson. groups, the regular form is $\breve{e}$ for the Midl. and N., and $\breve{a}$ for the SW., cf. Sweet § 675, t. Br. p. 40; we have examples of $\breve{e}$ in (b), (e) adreid : fled, and (g); (the spelling with *ei* in *adreid* is false, as is shown by the alternate spelling with *e* and corroborated by the rimes in (f)). The reason of the difference is that in the SW. the shortening took place before $\bar{æ}$ had become ME. $\bar{ę}$, i. e. $\bar{æ}$ became $\breve{æ}$, which was developed further like any other $\breve{æ}$, while in the Midl. and N. the OE. form was generally already $\bar{ę}$, and therefore the shortened form $\breve{e}$.

We must assume that shortening took place *after* OE. $\bar{æ}$ had become $\bar{ę}$ in the case of general OE. $\bar{æ}$ (β. 2) and also in those cases where an $\breve{e}$ instead of $\breve{a}$ appears for β. 1. in the S. W., unless we are to explain from the influence of outside diall. For Clar., *e* must have been the genuine form of the shortened vowel, and the rime in (g) with $\breve{a}$, if $\breve{a}$ is really meant, is evidence of the mixed dialect of the author; cf. § 91. The other rimes show that *adreid* is also used by the author with a long vowel; it is another word with an unfixed pronunc.

§ 214. The mod. Sc. diall. show a long i for the MSc. unshortened form in most words of this class, the pronunc. generally being uniform throughout, (with the exception that it is sometimes shortened to $\breve{i}$ in those diall. which are addicted to late shortening; this is especially the case in the more northern diall.); so we find ĭ in *read, cheese, speech, deed, needle, sheep, sleep*, which are nowhere found with *e*, and even in *thread*, which in rec. sp. has an *e*-vowel. Forms are found with an *e*-vowel only in *bleat*, (D. 39), *meal* (39) (but in other diall. only an *i*-vowel) and *breath* (in all diall. just as in rec. sp., except that in Sc. it is sometimes long).

The shortened vowel before conson. groups is ĕ, not ă, (except in the word *wat*, = wet, see § 216), e. g. in *read*, prt., Ellis gives (ræd) once in 33, and (rid) in 42, but otherwise only (rɛd).

§ 215. *blast*, see (i). This word generally appears only in this form in the N.; but in Dougl. we have *blist : trist*, 2. 87. 9, i. e. a short ĭ, which is difficult of explanation unless it be from a previous ĕ (?). (In Ayenb. it appears with *e*, the regular development of ǣ in Kt. and Angl.). The form with *a* might be considered to be a south-western form which had asserted itself in other diall.; but this seems an unlikely explanation for the extreme N.; perhaps it would be better to connect with ON. *blāstr* or the corresponding vb. *blāsa*, to blow; this seems better than Sweet's suggestion, HoES. § 675, since we should expect, if the verb *blāwen* influenced the form of the noun, to find *blǭst*, as soon as *blāwen* became *blǭwen*. But it is not even necessary to go to Old Norse, for, just as in OE. there was a form *māst* in the N. by the side of *mǣst*, (cf. Sievers, § 312, note 1), so there seems to have been a form *blāst*, as well as *blǣst*, at any rate we find it in composition, cf. B.-T., where the two forms *blǣst-belg* and *blāst-belg* (= bellows) are given. None of these explanations, however, remove all difficulties; for why did not *blăst*, if this was the early form, develop itself like the exactly similar word *măst* and produce in mod. rec. sp. *blŏst* and in Sc. *blɛ̄st*? We must either assume that OE. *blǣst* first shortened its ǣ to ĕ, and that then this ĕ was later lengthened after becoming ME. ă, just as *fæst* became ME. *făst* and NE. *fāst*, or else perhaps in the N., *blāst* > ME. *blăst* > NE. *blāst*. Although "long vowels are generally kept before *st*" (Sweet § 397), e. g. *gāst, mǣst*, &c., yet this rule is not absolute (see Kluge, PG. 1. 869), for there was often shortening before *st* in the 12th cent. Morsb., p. 20, says this was rare; his citation of mod. Engl. as a proof of this is unsatisfactory, for in many words the long vowel before *st* is certainly of purely modern growth. In this case the shortening may perhaps have been assisted by the co-existent word *blǣst* (of different meaning, = flame, *blǣst* = a blowing), or it may be simply a case of confusion of the two words, *blǣst* eventually ousting *blɛ̄st*; but this assumption is by no means necessary. In any case we must probably assume the form *blăst* at some stage or other, for most of the words containing *ā + s* in rec. sp. are derived from OE. forms containing *æ + s* e. g. fast, mast, hasp, grass, glass, ghastly, = OE. *fæst, mæst, hæspe, græs, glæs, gæstlic*. Moreover the orthography with *a*, not *ai*, in MSc. (cf. *maist* with a long *ai*) as well as the rime in (i), point to shortness of vowel.

There are other cases both of ǣ and ā producing NE. ā before *s*, e. g. ask (= *āscian*), last (= OE. *lɛ̄st, lāst*, for shoe), last, vb. (= *lāstan*); all of them probably contained ĕ at some stage or other of their development; in fact, ǣ can still be heard in some of the mod. diall., and is especially characteristic of the N. ME. had mostly ăsken, not āsken, (Kluge PG. 1. 876); this would be an exactly similar case to blăst > blăst > blāst, unless we have to explain through the form acsian > äcsen > äsken > ǣsk or āsk. In Chauc. we have lǎsten for lǣstan, and yet the later language has lāst (t. Br. § 16. β).

Cf. Fick, Engl. Stud. 8. 503.

§ 216. weite = wet. This word appears in Clar. in no less than three forms; it rimes with OE. ē, ĕ and Fr. a. It is also spelt in different ways in the MS. weite, wate, and wat. The usual ME. form is wēt, the ē, of course, being closed in the non-Westsaxon districts, hence such rimes as weite : sweit in § 212 (d). The shortened form of this ē, that is ĕ, which was quite regular in the compar., was afterwards transferred to the positive and hence the form wet in rec. sp. and the rime wate : set, § 212 (f); the a in wate is due to the scribe, and must be altered to e, wet : set. The a form is especially Scotch, cf. Satir. P., watt : that 48. 39; as we have already seen, there was a tendency in Sc. diall. to change we into wa, a tendency which is reflected in the mod. diall.; wat appears in almost all of them; wıt, the regular development of ME. wēt, appears in D. 20, 21, 22 and 30, 32, i. e. North Midl. and Northern English, but not in Scotch, although wĭt is found in D. 33, 38, 39, 40, and 42. wat seems to be the real Scotch form, it is found in 33, 34, 35, 36, 38 and 39; and one of the scribes was evidently accustomed to this form, for he writes a where the rime certainly proves an ĕ; similarly in other words, e. g. wade (= wed) : adred, see above (f) (still it is possible that this means wad : adrad; cf. § 91). It is noticeable that wet is not found at all in the mod. Sc. diall.; it is therefore all the easier to understand why a Sc. scribe changed wet into wat; the author had evidently allowed himself an Anglicism in writing and riming wĕt. But another explanation of the a in wat is possible; for in (i) we find it riming with an undoubted long ā, in plait; (the orthography wate. with final e, proves nothing alone; it might mean wăt or wāt). We have similar rimes elsewhere, e. g. Dunb. wait : state : lait : debait, 72. 133, where the spelling, ai, proves an ę̄ < ā. There is no doubt that we have here another case of Norse influence, and we must connect with ON. vātr, for the ā is in no way to be explained from OE. ǣ, Angl. ē. So the ă in mod. Sc. wăt may be a shortening of the ā in wāt, though the other explanation of it as a parallelism to wed > wad is just as good. It is strange that the author of Clar. uses all three forms węt, wıt, wĕt, from previous wāt, węt, wĕt.

Other Sc. authors use the form węt or wıt; Bruce, wet, vb. : gret, (inf. = weep) 3. 518, wete, adj. : het (= heat) 11. 612. — K. Q. wete : great (grēat). — Roll. C. V. weit : spreit (= spirit) 1. 36. — Montg. weet : greet, MM. Ps. 6. 35. weit : Margareit MP. 51. 6; also Sir Tr. wete : mete : grete : sket, 732.

Angl. ē = WS. ēa before gutturals.

§ 217. rimes with — a) OE. ēo. eine (ēagan, pl.) : beine, ind. pl. 4. 372 : seine, inf. 2. 1550 : betweine 3. 1594 : teine (teōna) 3. 2268. ey (ēage) : se, inf. 3. 2296 : see, indic. 4. 2060. hee (hēah) : see 1. 70, hie : be 4. 2328 : sie (sēon) 5. 1954, 2992 : thrie 4. 498. — b) OE. ē, mut. of ō. eine : queine 3. 1848. eik(e) : beseike 1. 420 (&c.) : seike 4. 790. — c) General OE. ē. he (hēah) : me 3. 644. — d) OE. or ON. i + g. hie (hēah) : worthie 5. 2402 : joyouslie 5. 1524. ey : eydentlie 2. 1406. — e) ON. øy. he (hēah) : die (døyja) 3. 1098. — f) ON. jū. eik(e) : meik(e) 2. 1552 (&c.). — g) Fr. e. ey : meinʒe 2. 912 : quantitie 3. 1394, eyes (for ey) : bewtie 5. 298, eie : royaltie 5. 1034. hee (hēah) : degree 1. 252 : cuntrie 1. 1242, hie : degrie 5. 1796, 1882 : quantitie 5. 1604 : solemnitie 5. 1630 : royaltie 5. 2004. — h) Fr. i. eeine (ēagan) : Palexine 4. 1196.

§ 218. In OAngl. ēa was smoothed to ē before gutturals, see Sweet § 465; consequently ę̄ is to be found in ME., but it is not confined to Angl. districts, as we might expect, but is met with in all diall. except Kt. (Sweet §§ 677, 679).

Hence the word eke has an ę̄ almost everywhere in ME., though the form with ę̄ from OE. ēac is also found, e. g. Chauc. has both forms (t. Br. § 24 γ, note 3, Kluge PG. 1. 880). In MSc., as may be expected, it only had ę̄ and with the change ę̄ > ĩ became ĩk; see above in (b) and (f).

§ 219. All the rest of the above rimes concern the two words, OE. ēage and hēah, Angl. ēge and hēh. It is well known that in MSc. in these and other words containing OE. ēa, ēo + gutt. the gutt. disappeared without leaving any trace, and the result was a pure vowel ę̄. The loss of the gutt. was not complete at the time Bruce was written, but it was accomplished by the beginning of the 15th cent., cf. Brandl, Th. Erc. p. 59, Buss p. 497, Wischmann p. 6, &c. Buss gives a number of rimes from 15th cent. texts. Clar. has pure Sc. rimes and shows none of the Engl. influence which is so apparent in K. Q. in these words. The rimes in (a), (b), (c), (e), (g), are all proof of previous ę̄, and similar to those given by Buss.

§ 220. Such rimes are, on account of the OAngl. forms with ē and the ME. forms with ę̄ in all diall. except Kt., not generally reckoned amongst the α : γ rimes; and we have further above taken ey, he, eik as γ-words. But we might look upon this class of words as only the first in which the change ę̄ > ę̄ was effected, and consequently also the only ones in which the ę̄ obtained a large extension beyond its original home, the Angl. dial. (in OE. the ē forms were confined to the Angl. dial.).

§ 221. The rimes in (d) are, as explained in § 126, evidence of the change ę̄ > ĩ; so also that in (g) with Fr. i; the final syll. of Palexine cannot have contained an ē, but must have retained its Fr. pronunciation, as in many other cases, in which the ĩ was not changed to a diphthong ǝi, ei.

§ 222. The mod. Sc. diall. have ĩ and ĩn for rec. sp. eye and eyes, and sometimes hĩ for rec. sp. high, e. g. D. 34, (always so in the compound *hīlands* = highlands), sometimes *hei*, *hai*, e. g. in 33, 34 and 37 (this probably due to influence of rec. sp., exc. in D. 33, in which a diphthong generally stands for Central Sc. final *ī*); we also find (heikjh, haikjh) in 33, 41, (hekh) in 34, (hiikh) in 35, 38. and (hĭkh) in 39; *height* appears as (bekht) and (hikht).

§ 223. The word neir (= rec. sp. *near*), nearly always spelt with *ei*; the rime words contain:

a) OE. $\overline{eo}$. — : deir 3. 1140. — b) Angl. $\bar{e}$, WS. $\bar{æ}$ (or ON. $\bar{a}$?) — nar : ware (*wǣre*) 1. 474, n'eir : ʒeir (ʒ$\bar{e}r$, ʒ$\bar{æ}r$) 3. 24. — c) OE. y-. — : speir (*spyrian*) 1. 534, 1258. — d) Angl. $\bar{u}$ = WS. $\bar{\text{ie}}$. — : steir, vb. 2. 1524. — e) ON. $\bar{e}$. — : seir 4. 982. — f) OE. $\bar{e}$, mut. of $\bar{o}$. — : in feire 4. 1232 : feir 3. 406. — g) Fr. e, ie. — : cleir 2. 260, 1662 : suppeir 2. 558 : maneir 2. 1394 (&c.) : mater 3. 476 : cheire 5. 1400.

§ 224. All the rimes prove an $ī < \bar{e}$, except perhaps the first in (b). *Nar* is a form often found in Northern and Sc. texts by the side of *nēr*, e. g. nar : war (adj.) and nere : here, adv. Townl. M.; *nar* : *bar* : *dar* : *far*, Roll. C. V. 1. 516; *nar* : *debar* : *afar* : *dar* Montg. MP. 36. 53; *nar* : *sar*, Satir. P. 39. 160. But the *a* seems mostly to be a short *ă*, and as in *all* the other rimes we find only *nĭr* < *nẹ̄r*, and *wĭr* < *wẹ̄r* is the most usual form for OE. *wāron* with our author, it is probably better to ascribe *nar* and *ware* to the copyist and to change into *neir : weir*, or *were*. It has already been noticed above that the copyist prefers the form *ware* to *were*.

The form *neir* must be derived, of course, from Angl. *nēr* (cf. Laws of Alf.) = WS. *nīer*, *nyr*; can *nar* be explained from *nēar* or *nēarra*? perhaps from the latter through a form *neărra*, with shortening. In the mod. Sc. diall. the pronunc. is generally the same as in rec. sp., with *ī*; but *năr* is found 38 and 39, and also in Engl. in 25 (South Cheshire), *năr* in 31 (N. Lancs.). Jam. Dict. gives *nar* for Scotl. and Yorks., also the compound *nar-side*.

§ 225. **ancist** (= Angl. *anē(h)st*, Northumb. *aneist*, see Sievers § 166, 5.) : *breist*, 3. 1010. This word, or the shorter *neist*, is of frequent occurrence in MSc. texts; e. g. Satir. P. *ncist : breist* 30. 99 (&c.). In mod. Sc. diall. we still find (niist), e. g. in 35, 38, 39, 41, 42, and (nist) in 33, 36.

Æ' (mut. of OE. $\bar{a}$, Gmc. **ai**).

§ 226. 1. Not followed by r or w. — rimes with
(In these lists, forms with a long vowel are given under *α*, those with vowel-shortening under *β*.).

a) itself. *α*) deill (vb.) : heill (*hǣlu*) 3. 810. *β*) led (prt.) : vncled (ptc., acc. to Skeat from ON. *klǣþdi*) 3. 2134. — b) Angl. $\bar{e}$ = W. S. $\bar{æ}$ (Westgmc. $\bar{æ}$). *α*) breid (*brǣdu*) : meid 5. Prol. 4. *β*) led (prt.) : adred 4. 118. — c) OE. $\overline{eā}$. *α*) leid (vb.) : reid (adj. = red) 1. 1128. feid (OE. *fāhð*) : reid, adj. 5. 84, 1190. gleimes, (pl. of OE. *glǣm*) : streamis 4. 1188. *β*) left (ptc.) : bereft 1. 178. — d) OE. $\bar{e}$ (general OE. $\bar{æ}$). (*α*) sea : me 3. 102 : he 3. 1142. deale, deill, sb. : weill, adv. 2. 104, 931. — e) OE. $\bar{e}$ (mut. of $\bar{o}$). (*β*) delt : felt 3. 352. bespred : sped (prt.) 5. 2366. cled (ptc.) : fede (ptc. of *fēdan*) 4. 1670. — f) Angl. ē = WS. īē. (α) cleine : seine, ptc. 2. 982. deill, sb. : steill, sb. 3. 378. — g) OE. ēō. α) meine (vb.) : betweine 1. 298. cleine : beine, ptc. 3. 2356. β) led, ptc. : fred (liberatus) 2. 130. spred : fled 3. 404. — h) OE. ä. mone (sb. from vb. = OE. *mǣnan*? rec. sp. *moan*) : wo-begone 2. 676 : allone 3. 710 : stone 3. 1598 : gone, ptc. 3. 1834. — i) OE. e: . (β) lest (*lǣstan*) : rest, vb. 2. 58 : best 2. 1246 : mirriest 2. 1768 : vnrest 3. 526 : rest, sb. 4. 1904, 5. 2180. les (*lǣssa*, cf. Sievers, § 312; but Grein and B.-T. give *lĕ˘ssa*) : nobilnes 1. 370, 5. 2630 : blythnes 2. 1256 : humbilnes 3. 1600, humblenes 4. 48 : bissines 3. 1852. — k) OE. æ, see § 80 (h). — m) Fr. c. α) leist, least (superl.) : feist 2. 1804 (&c.). teace (for *teache*) : fleich (flechir) 2. 290. sea : cheritic 3. 850 : cuntrie 3. 52. deill, sb. : reveill 3. 2148. β) ment (prt. of *mǣnan*) : intent 4. 2228. les (compar.) : dres 2. 820, 5. 2888 : procos 5. 668 : distres 5. 918. lest (*lǣstan*) : opprest 2. 664. — n) Fr. a. maist : haist 1. 1364. — o) Fr. ei. dcalle, vb. : leill 3. 832. — p) Fr. o. mone, sb. : Palamon 5. 90. — q) ON. ig. sea : trewlie 5. 2746.

For $\bar{æ} + ht$, see § 99 (a).

§ 227. This vowel belongs to ten Brink's Class β. As $\bar{æ}$ is found in all the OE. diall., we should expect it to rime chiefly with an open ẹ̄ in ME., and it does so in the SW.; but just as Orm's $\bar{æ}$ for Gmc. $\bar{æ}$, Goth. $\bar{e}$, soon became ẹ̄ in East Anglia (see Morsb. p. 154), so also did the ẹ̄ from general OE. $\bar{æ}$, mut. of $\bar{a}$, Gmc. *ai*; hence the β : β rimes in (a) and (b), and the β : γ rimes in (d), (f), (g), (m), would be quite in order in any Angl. district. We have also β : α rimes in (c) and (o) and one in (m), *leist, least* : *feist*. The sound we have to understand in most of the above rimes is ı < ẹ̄ (for possible exceptions see § 230).

§ 228. The shortened form before conson. groups is chiefly ĕ, see (a), (b), (c), (e), (g), (i) and (m); but perhaps once ă, in *mad*, see (k); in the other rimes referred to in (k) we can understand an ĕ, cf. §§ 82, 90, 91. Kluge P. G. 1. 876, note 2, explains some of the ĕ-forms through the influence of the ME. $\bar{e}$ in non-shortened forms. Since the ĕ is more frequent in the Midl. and N., as contrasted with the more usual ă of the S., we might be inclined to look upon it as evidence of the different treatment of $\bar{æ}$, and a further proof that this early produced a closed ẹ̄ in the Midl. and N., whose shortened form could not then be ă. If so, then the *a*-forms in Clar. are further borrowings from Engl. In Bruce we find *a* written for *e* in *rad* (*rādde*), *lad* (*lǣdde*). &c., see Buss p. 12. But ĕ-forms are also found in Southern texts as well, (cf. Bülbring p. 108, &c.) and Kluge's explanation, which is that also given by Bülbring and Morsb. p. 154, must be correct as far as the S. is concerned, although the same result may have still been arrived at in another way in the N.

§ 229. The rime in (q), *sea* : *trewlie*, is probably a proof that $\bar{e}$ had already become ı; cf. § 126.

§ 230. The mod. diall. offer many instances here of an *e*-vowel, where rec. sp. has ı, far more than in the case of Angl. $\bar{e}$ = WS. $\bar{a}$. Sometimes the $\bar{e}$-vowel is only found in single diall.; in D. 33 it is only found in *sea*, which, however, has ı in all other diall., and in *breadth*, which has also an *e*-vowel in 39, but ī in 35 and 36. D. 33 agrees very closely with D. 32 (Northumberland), where ī is found throughout, just as an *i*-fracture is found in these two diall. for the *ē*-vowel of the other Sc. diall., which proceeds from MSc. *ā*. An *ī*-vowel is found in all diall. beyond 33 (i. e. as far as notified by Ellis) in *heal*, vb., *heathen*, *deal*, sb., (which certainly generally had closed *ẹ̄* in MSc.), and, in all diall. but 35, in *leave*, vb., *lead*, vb., and *heat*; and further it is occasionally found in *clean* (36), *wheat* (37 and 38, and *ai* in 39), *sweat* (38, 41, 42, and *ai* in 39, where also *teach* has *ai*); while *mean*, vb., has an *e*-vowel in all Sc. diall. The abundance of *e*-forms, which cannot be accounted for by English influence, being contrary to the pronunc. of rec. sp., is very striking, and difficult to be brought into harmony with the evidence of MSc. texts, although traces of such forms are not wanting in MSc., e. g., Satir. P. a greit *daill* moir, 33. 222, (*ai* = *ẹ̄*) and above in § 226 (o), where the spelling *dealle* certainly points to *ẹ̄* for the scribe who wrote it, and perhaps also the rime with *leill* for the author. Perhaps OE. *ǣ* (*β*. 2) should, for some parts of Scotl., be classed with *a*. 3, and *a*. 5 (1), as an exception to the rules given above. If Ellis's lists were less incomplete than they are, and less open to suspicion than they sometimes appear to be, we might be more easily able to get at the true history of this vowel in Scotl.

§ 231. *never*; the vowel only rimes with Fr. *e*. — *never* : *dissauer* (= dissever, separate, *intrans*.) 5. 552.

Probably the *a* in *dissauer* is a scribal error for *e*, and the *ē* from *c* in *never* has been regularly shortened to *ĕ*. (The mod. Sc. diall. have generally an ĭ in *ever*, *never*, just as in *together* — *iver*, *niver*, *togidder*). Or does the *a* perhaps mean a long *ē* in the pronunc. of the scribe? Cf. Satir P. *euer* : *disseaver* 25. 52. Montg. has *ever* : *fever* p. 35.

§ 232. *mone*, sb. = complaint, lament, see (h) and (p), (the latter proves the *o*-pronunc.) is a Southern form and must be derived from a form with OE. *ā*, either a sb. *mān, or a vb. *mānian. Elsewhere we find *ā* or its outcome *ē* in Sc., e. g. Sc. Leg. *mayne*, sb. : *nane*, 24/668, Roll. C. V. *mane* : *ane* : *tane* : *grane* (= groan) : *Montane* 2. 382, but *mone* : *begone* : *stone* : *anone*, 2. 405, *mone* (sb.) : *anone* : *gone* : *fone* : *propone*. The verb *meine*, with different sense = NE. to mean, has the vowel ĭ < *ẹ̄*, see (g) and (m), and is quite regular; it has ĭ everywhere in NSc. But Roll. C. V. seems certainly to have ĭ also in *mene* (= moan, complain) : *serene* : *pertene* : *sene* : *quene* 1. 730, *menit* (= moaned) : *complenit* : *sustenit* : *convenit* : *pertenit* : *vnrefrenit* 1. 819.

§ 233. *maist*, see (n), should properly be included under OE. *ā*, for it must be derived from ONorthmb. *māst*; the form *mǣst* would produce ME. *mẹ̄st*, (which is found in Chauc. &c.) and in MSc. *mẹ̄st*, later *mīst*, but in all early Sc. texts the form is generally *māst*, the forerunner of the *mēst* of all the mod. Sc. diall. exc. D. 33, which has, of course, (*i'*).

§ 234. *deill*. The difference between the sb. with *ẹ̄* and the verb with *ẹ̄*, which Buss observes in the Sc. Leg., we should not expect to find in Clar., yet it might appear to exist, for the sb. only rimes with a *γ*-vowel, whereas the vb., which only appears once in rime, rimes with an *α*-vowel, and that one which generally produces *ẹ̄* in late MSc. and NSc., but from a single appearance of the vb. we cannot form any decided conclusions. In Montg. MP. 2. 12, *deill,* vb. : *weill* adv., it certainly has an $i < \bar{e}$, cf. the corresponding rime-words in the other stanzas, *steill, seill, meill, feill.* Still it is noticeable that the verb is in Clar. once spelt with *ea,* 3. 832, but in 3. 810, it is spelt with *ei,* the symbol for $i < \bar{e}$, and the sb. is also spelt with *ea* in 2. 104. These irregularities of spelling are due to difference of dial. on the part of the scribes; the *ea* is an English orthography, which can scarcely be ascribed to the author; so also in the rime *teache : fleiche.*

§ 235. *feid* is the regular Sc. form for the incorrect Engl. form *feud;* see Skeat, Princ. 1. 206. Its vowel is against Bradley's derivation from MLat. *faida;* it is rather from OE. *fǽhð,* perhaps with Norse side influence on the conson. (Dan. *feide*?)

§ 236. *lest,* vb. The form in rec. sp., *last,* must be explained in the same way as *blast,* cf. § 215, viz. OE. l$\bar{æ}$stan > l$\breve{æ}$stan > l$\breve{u}$st > l$\bar{a}$st; *lest* is especially Sc., and here again we must assume that in the extreme N. $\bar{æ}$ early became $\bar{e}$, or that the shortening did not take place so early as in the S. The rimes prove conclusively the shortness of the vowel; it is a parallel form to the Kentish *blest* for *blast.* The same form is found in Bruce (but not in rime), Gol., Lanc. *lest : fast* 812 (i. e. the author used an Engl. rime, and the scribe altered to *lest* to suit his own pronunc.), Dunb. *lest : best* 24. 15, 30, Dougl. *lest : drest : rest : vnrest* 1. 97. 3, Satir. P. *lest : manifest* 40. 107, 44. 115.

§ 237. *sweit,* sb. = rec. sp. *sweat,* appears once in rime with *beird* 5. 2022, a corrupt orthography which we can almost with certainty alter into *beit,* prt., OE. *beōt,* he beat. The OE. form of the sb. is *swāt,* but it has been influenced by the vb., OE. *swǣtan,* or else we must derive from an alternative OE. form with $\bar{æ}$, mut. of *ā,* **swǣt,* as Ellis does in EEP. 5; hence the long $\bar{e}$, later i, of the North, and the $\breve{e}$, through shortening from $\bar{e}$, of rec. sp.

§ 238. The word *bedeine.*

As usual in northern ME. verse, this word also appears in Clar. The rime-words contain.

a) OE. $\bar{e}$, Angl. $\bar{æ}$ (mut. of $\bar{o}$) — : *queine* 3. 536, 4. 1344, 5. 2490. —
b) Angl. $\bar{e}$ = WS. $\bar{ie}$ — : *seine,* ptc. 3. 12; i. e. its vowel is $i < \bar{e}$.

§ 239. Murray, N. E. D., says it is "of uncertain origin", but "its latter part is almost certainly the early ME. adv. *œne, ene,* OE. *ǣne,* once, at once, in one, together, (cf. the ME. phrases *at ene,* at once, *for ene,* for once); but the *bid-* is difficult of explanation." According to Skeat it = *bi* + *dēn* (= done), with mutation, instead of *dōn;* cf. *mididone* in Alisaundre. The vowel, whether belonging to the α, β, or γ class, unless it be α. 3 or α. 5. (1), would be $\bar{e}$ and then i in late MSc., so that the rimes in Sc. texts can throw no light on its origin, though it is somewhat striking that it almost everywhere rimes with β and γ vowels *only;* we require rimes from Southern texts to decide between β and γ, but the word seems to be strange to the southern dial. For further rimes see Kölbing's glossary to Sir Tr., NED. s. v. *bidene,* and Bruce : *queyn* 5. 144 : *fiftēne*

15. 108, Dunb. *bedene* : *ene* F. 422, Roll. C. V. : *schene* : *sene* : *ene* : *circumvene* 2. 598 : *schene* : *clene* : *Quene* : *ene* 4. 644; Hamp. P. C. : *sene*, ptc. 7968, Sowdone of Bab. : *kene* 2942. &c.

§ 240. The suffix — heid, — head.

The suffix which appears in rec. sp. as -*head*, appears in Clar. only in the form -*heid*, and cannot, of course, be derived from OE. -*hād*, which produced the Chauc. form -*hood*, but either from an alternative mutated form -*hǣd*, -*hĕd*, = OHG -*heit*, as *i*-stem, as Kluge P. G. 1. 874 explains, or from a Low Germ. form, as explained by t. Br., § 55 and Skeat, Princ. 57, 218, 219. The former is preferable, especially as it at the same time accounts for the difference of quality of the $ē$, open in the S., closed in the N.

§ 241. In Clar. it has, with every other $ẹ$, already become ī; the rime-words all contain earlier $ę̄$ from various sources.

a) OE. $\bar{æ}$: abreid (*on brǣdu*) 4. 2334. — b) Angl. $\bar{e}$ = WS. $\bar{æ}$: dreid 1. 244 (&c.) : deid 1. 1260 (&c.) : dread 2. 384, 454 : weid 5. 1756, 1932. — c) OE. $\bar{e}$ (mut. of $\bar{o}$) : speid 1. 404 : gleid (OE. *glēd*) 3. 1554 : steid 4. 1750. — d) OE. $\bar{eo}$: ʒeid 1. 1426, 2. 80. — e) Fr. $\bar{e}$: proceid 1. 272, 2. 72.

All other Sc. texts show similar rimes in abundance.

2. $\bar{æ}$ before r — rimes with

§ 242. a) OE. $\bar{e}$ — leir (*lǣran*) : heir (adv.) 3. 872. — b) OE. æ + g — aire (*ār*) : faire, adj. 5. 746.

The vowel in (b), *aire*, is $ę̄$ from previous $ā$ = an OE. $ā$, which arose out of c before *r*, as in *þēr*, *hwēr*, *þār*, *hwār*, cf. Morsb. p. 46. This change did not take place in all words, e. g. in *lāran*, which accordingly developed quite regularly a ME. $ę̄$, $ẹ̄$, later ī; we have the latter already in Clariodus, as implied by the spelling *ei*.

3. $\bar{æ}$ + w.

§ 243. Only the word OE. *slǣwþ*, which rimes with OE. $\bar{eo}$ + w in *trēowþ*. slewth : trewth 4. 1098. sleuth : trewth 4. 2342.

Engl. *sloth* has been affected in its pronunciation by the corresponding adjective *slow*; the Sc. form *slewth* = (sliuth) is the correct one, OE. $ǣ + w > ę̄ + w, ę̄u > ẹ̄u > ĭu$, just as OE. $\bar{eo} + w > ę̄ + w > ẹ̄u > ĭu$. Of course at the late date of Clar., when all $ẹ̄$'s have become ī, the last stage, ĭu, of the diphthong has already been reached in both combinations OE. $ǣ + w$ and $\bar{eo} + w$, which coincided at a previous stage, when $ę̄u$ became $ẹ̄u$, just as simple $ę̄$ became $ẹ̄$. We find the same rime as above, as early as the K. Q., sleuth : treuth, 144; cf. for a later period, Montg. *sleuth* : *truth*, C. 1560, *sleuth* : *treuth* D. P. 4. 41; Satir P. *sleuth* : *treuth*, 12. 27. Montg. also shows the corruption of the *iu* form through the influence of the adjective, e. g. C. 824 *slowthing*; but C. 556 *slewthing* (= lingering). But the form *sloth* is otherwise almost unknown in MSc.; it does not occur in Dougl. Jam. Dict. gives *sloth* as a verb, by the side of *sleuth*, and quotes for it King James VI; otherwise he gives *sleuth*, sb. and vb., *sleuthful*, (Lyndes. Dreme. 890) *sleuthan*, *sleuthun*, sb. =

a lazy person, and *sleeth* = sloven, sluggard, a form found in Aberdeen, in which district earlier (iu) is now generally represented by (ii).

In *slow* : *slewth*, we have the same difference of vowel as in *broad* : *breadth, whole* : *health*, &c., due to mutation in the sb. on account of the following suffix (= Goth. *-ipa*).

ON. ÆI.

§ 244. rimes with

a) OE. ēā. scate (ON. *sāti*) : great 5. 1526. — b) OE. ǣ, rade : bade 4. 116. — c) OE. ea, a, thrall (*prǣll*) : sall 1. 390 : all 4. 696, 5. 808. — d) OE. e, cled(e) (ptc. *klǣpdi*, Sweet) : bed 3. 918, 1646 (MS. *bedis* for *bed*). — e) OE. ē (shortened), clede : fede (ptc. of *fēdan*) 4. 1670. — f) Fr. ai, seat : retreit, 5. 2082.

§ 245. ON. *ǣ* belongs to t. Br.'s α-class, but like OF. *ai, ei*, it does not produce MSc. *ẹ̄*, later *i*, but instead of this a late MSc. *ę̄* which coincides and rimes with *ę̄* from previous *ā*; cf. § 108. The rimes and spelling in MSc. texts in the word NE. *seat*, ON. *sǣti*, show this plainly; cf. Satir. P. *sait*, 39. 278 : *gait : debait : estait* 43. 63, Montg. *seat : stait : bleat : fleat* (prt. of OE. *flītan*), MP. 3. 78, Winzet, *sait*, 2. 35. 19, *saitis*, 1. 106. 17, and see Jam. Dict. s. v. *sait*.

In Clar. *seat* only appears in two rimes, see (a) and (f), which, however, both agree with the *e*-pronunc. For we have seen in § 280 that *great* was pronounced by the author with *ē* as well as *ī*, and it is also found in the mod. Sc. diall. with *ē*; and *retreit*, in spite of the spelling with *ei*, must have contained an *ē*-vowel, for OFr. *ai* always gives *ē* in late MSc., cf. § 108.

Some rimes between OFr. *ei, ai* and previous *ā* are given in §§ 1 (g, h), 96 (i, k); many other similar rimes are to be found in Clar., e. g. *consait : debait* 3. 1466, *deceave : knaue* 4. 1452. The spelling with *ea* in *seat* and *great* also points to an *ę̄*-pronunc. on the part of the scribe.

In the mod. diall. we find *seat* with an *ē*-vowel in 38 and 41 (Ellis does not give its pronunc. in the others) and the corresponding (*i'*) in 33 (Murray DSS.). All the diall. also show *ē* for Fr. *ei, ai*, in words in which rec. sp. has *ī*, e. g. *deceive, conceit*, &c., exc. 33, which has, as usual, (*i'*); cf. Murray DSS. 145, 146. Bradley gives OE. *sǣte* as the origin of NE. *seat*, but ON. *sǣti* must have been of influence in Scotl., or why should not OE. *ǣ* '(β. 1) have produced MSc. *ę̄* and *ī* here as in other words?

§ 246. Above in (b) we have probably the shortened form *ǎ*, cf. § 59. For the etymology of *rade*, see Brate, p. 53, and Stratm.-Bradl., and cf. Sc. Leg. rade : bad, prt. 17/170 : had 19/300, Bruce (see Skeat's glossary), Dougl. *rad : had* 4. 152. 18, *raddour* = fear, 3. 265. 17, *radour*, 1. 94. 19, Montg. *rad : sad* DP. 6. 25, *rad to reveil* S. 45, Yw. Gaw. *rad : bad*. But the vowel *ě* is also known in the same word; it appears in the text in Clar. in 4. 1417, "Full red scho was that he sould pase hir fro." Jam. Dict. says mod. Sc. of Clydesdale has *red*, I'se *red* = I am afraid; cf. Sc. Leg. *rad : sted* (= placed) 24/676, *red : sted* 24/682, Wedderburn

(Irving, p. 387) *red* : *fred* (= freed, liberatus), Dunb. *redour* = fear, 2. 11.; John Gau has *reid*.

In (e), too, the shortened form of the vowel is *ă*, but in (c) and (f) it is most decidedly *ĕ*. The cause of the difference in form of the shortened vowel is not quite clear; it cannot depend upon the following consonants alone, as *hrǣddr* appears in both forms; perhaps the cause lies in the difference of dial. and of date at which the shortening took place; the words may have been adopted from the Norse at different dates.

ON. EI.

§ 247. rimes with

a) itself. ay : they, thay 1. 318, 660. nay : thay 5. 1106. — b) OE. e + g, see § 134 (c). — c) OE. æ + g, see § 94 (i). — d) Fr. ei. ay : perfay 1. 836 : deray 5. 2272 ; pray, vb. 1. 1522, 3. 2180. nay : perfey 2. 1032. raise : praise 4. 1044, raisit : praisit 4. 1104. they : tornay 2. 730, thay : perfey 4. 1312. — e) Fr. ai. bewaill : assaill 3. 906. thay : delay 3. 1604 : aray 4. 340 : assay 4. 876. — f) Fr. e. thay : livaray 4. 1520.

§ 248. The rimes in (b), (c), (d), (e) are all with the older diphthong *ai* or *ei*, and that in (f) with Fr. *e* is therefore a further proof that the monophthongal form of this diphthong was already *ē*; perhaps the occasional spelling with *ey* may be looked upon as an indication of the same.

The mod. Sc. diall. have almost exclusively an *e*-vowel in all words of this class. The word *aye*, however, appears as a diphthong, only D. 34 has a monophthong (ææ).

§ 249. Words of uncertain etymology.

feir(e), effeir(e), fair(e), fayre. These are the forms of two, or perhaps even more, words used in the sense of *manner, demeanour, behaviour, carriage, comeliness*, &c.; e. g. *with ane knichtlie feir* (: *speir*) 2. 1106, *with awfull feir(e)* (: *speir*) 3. 44 (: *thair*) 5. 1176, *foure fresch wirginis of effeir* (: *beir*, vb.) 2. 872, *smylit, kissit*, &c., *with womanlie effeir* (: *weir*, vb.) 3. 2212, 4. 296, 1. 452, (: *deir*) 3. 1024, (: *cheir*) 3. 2178, 5. 342, (: *chyre* = chair) 1. 164, *the wonderfull beawtie and the fresch effeir* (: *eare*) 1. 336, *to the kirk to go all in effeire* (: *maneir*) 3. 2362, *I wald gone to Queine Meliades with fresche effeire* (: *beire*, vb.) 5. 862, *with sorrowfull effeir* (: *teiris*, for *teir* = tear, sb.) 5. 2524, *This noble Count of manlie effeiris* (: *weiris* = wars) 5. 2984, *with awfull fair* (: *mair* = more) 3. 634, *the manlie faire* (: *maire*) 4. 1046, *with courtes faire* (: *thair*) 4. 2034, *with glaidsume visage and with faire* (: *speir*) 2. 1528 (the sense would also allow this to be taken as = *fæger*, fair, adj., but the rime would then be impossible), *the minstrellis playit with ane mirrie fayre* (: *chyre* = chair) 5. 1530.

§ 250. The rime-words to the forms *feir(e), affeir(e)*, contain OE. *e-, ǣ, ēa, ēo* and Fr. *ie, e, ai*; those to the forms *fair(e), fayre*, contain OE. *e- ā, ē* and Fr. *ai*.

It is at once evident that these forms cannot all be referred to the same origin. Jam. Dict. gives "*fair, feir, feyr* = shew, carriage, gesture = OE. *fær*, (iter) or *feorh* (vultus)" and says "*affer* has the same meaning and source." These two derivations would account for the vowels satisfactorily enough, if we take the form OE. *faru*, instead of *fær*, though not quite so satisfactorily for the meanings, and it is difficult to see where the *af-* in *affer* comes from. Can we not assume an OE. sb. **ge-fēre* or **ge-fēr* = Gmc. **gi-fōri*? cf. OHG. *gi-fuori*, OFris. *fēre*, ON. *fǣri*, OLG. *(gi-)fōri*. This would explain the vowel and the prefix, which latter, however, could be dropped, and so cause confusion with *faru* or *fær*, whence the variation in the rimes. There was the OE. *gefær*, too, and possibly the vb. *effeir* = OFr. *aferir*, to become, beseem, may have been of influence, and a noun been derived from it. Fr. *affaire* has scarcely anything to do with it? Anyhow there seems to have been a confusion of forms, words of different origin, whose meanings had come to be almost synonymous, being interchanged with each other at random. The OE. *fēran*, ME. *fēre* = go, travel, also *behave*, may also have had a share in the development. Small, in his note to Dunb. 26. 36, suggests Icel. *atferð*; so also Skeat in his Glossary to Bruce, s. v. *effer*, says "this difficult word is also spelt *affeir*, probably by confusion with Fr. *affaire*, and probably when the word means 'business', it is merely French. Jam. hesitates about the etymol., but needlessly. It is clearly Icel. *atferð*, conduct, from *at* and *fara*, to go." But this latter is very improbable. In Bruce, *feire*, *affeir*, &c., rime with *deboner*, 1, 361, *debonar* 8, 382, *wer(e)* (*wǣron*) 10. 305 (&c.), *ere* (*ēr*) 7. 30, *maner* 2. 182, *speir* 5. 608; and *far*, in similar meanings ("behaviour, demeanour, appearance, equipment, make, stature, business, array, pomp", Skeat) rimes with *war* (*wāron*) 19. 730, 20. 100, *thar* 16. 46.

§ 251. For similar uses and rimes, cf. Wall. *with manly feyr*, 9. 306, *The quein com in hyr effer* : *wer* (= war) 9. 312; Gol. *with felloune affere* : *were* (= war) : *here* : *bere* 707, *vvith ane fel fair* : *maire* : *saire* : *fair* (*vvith ane fresch fair*) 570, *with ane fell fair* : *schair* (prt.) : *bair*, (prt.) 932; Lanc. *effere* (shew, pomp) 2360, *affere* (= warlike preparation) 985, (= bearing, aspect) 3043, 3334, 3394; (here Skeat says = OFr. *afeire*, *afaire*); Rat. Rav. *effere* (= manner) : *gere* (= gear) 3. 137; Dunb. *discirnyng all thair fassionis and effeiris* : *speiris* : *weiris* = wars, 49. 128, *the pepill so wickit ar of feiris* : *beiris*, 3. sg., 66. 33, *Thay micht weill ken be thair effeiris* : *speiris*, 27. 65, *with sic ane feir* : *mensweir* : *weir* : *beir*, 27. 87, *feir of weir* = accoutrement of war (the same phrase occurs in the Scotch Acts of Parl., James II, 1457, p. 14, c. 78), *Ffrawart wes thair affeir* : *scheir* = OE. *sceran*, 26. 39, *on syde scho lukit wyth ane fremyt fare* : *fair*, adj. : *mare* : *repaire*, 1. 125, *with lusty effeiris*, 3, 49, *all is bot frutlese his effeir*, 3, 401; Satir. P. *with fresche effeir* : *deir* 11. 83; Sir Gaw. *fare* (= behaviour, conduct) : *ware*, adj. 2386.

§ 252. **weir**, sb. = doubt, in the phrases, *but weir(e)* (: *maneire*) 4. 2400, (: *heir*, adv.) 3. 680, *withouttin weir* (: *cheir*) 3. 880, *þis is no weir* (: *maneir*) 1. 1320. With regard to the etymol. of this word, Skeat (Bruce) suggests Icel. *vari* = caution; in Lanc. he gives OE. *wc̄r*, cautious, wary, elsewhere he gives Du. *war*, confusion. Morris, Hamp. P. C., gives OE. *wǣr*, caution. This last would be the most satisfactory, if the form with *ǣ* were found in OE., but our authorities only give us *wǣr*, and both this and ON. or Du. forms with *a* are impossible, for the word rimes in Clar. only with previous *ę̄*, and so in most other texts; e. g. Bruce : *heir*, adv. 9. 637, *neir* 13. 592, 16. 110, 17. 496 : *inqueir*, vb. 4. 222 : ʒer (= year) 13. 730 : *weir (wǣron)* 16. 500 : *fer (haill and fer)* 9. 231; Dunb. *in weir* (doubt) *is* : *reuerteris* (Lat.) 11. 22, *but weir* : *cheir* 25. 70 : *appeir* : *freir* 30. 50 : *perqueir* : *speir* (= ask) 90. 30 : *neir* 36. 1 : *prisoneir* 42. 102, 110; Roll. C. V. : *geir* : *stranger* : *deir* 3. 216, Henryson *but weir* : *heir*, vb. (see Roll. C. V. Introd. p. 18); Hamp. P. C. *were* : *apere*, vb. 2296.

Is it possible anyhow to connect with OE. *werian*, defend?

EA

After *sc'*, *g'*.

§ 253. In ONthmb., after *sc'* and *g'*, an *e* is found inserted before *a*, in most cases just as in WS., cf. Hilmer, p. 9. This *sc* and *g*, produce, in the N. as well as in the S., *sch*, *sh*, and *y* respectively, except, of course, where Norse influence is at work. After *sc*, the *e* merely marks the palatal pronunc. of the *c* (cf. Sievers, § 76, note 5); this *ea*, then, is no diphthong, and we must divide *sce-a* not *sc-ea*. So that the following words really belong to the section on *a*. The development of the *a* in *sce-a* is the same as that of the usual *a*, but the *sce* produces usually *sch* in Sc. orthography.

§ 254. The rimes show no exception to the ordinary treatment of *a*.
1. In open syllable not foll. by *g* — *schame* : *name* 2. 1074, 5, 1142 : *eschame* (vb.) 5. 2038.

The word *skaith* (: *baith*, 2. 496) is probably from ON. *skaða*.
2. Before *g*, *shaw (sceaga)* rimes with OE. $\bar{a} + w$: *snaw* 1. 740 : *raw* (NE. row, sb.) 4. 1770. Cf. §§ 52 ff.

§ 255. But after *g*, the *ea* is of a different character from that of *ea* after *sc*, see Sievers § 76. note 5.; in *gea* we have a real diphthong, as is shown by the later development, which is not that of simple *a*. In Clar. we have only one word in question, OE. *geat* (porta) which rimes with

a) OE. e — ʒet : *sete*, ptc. 1. 570. — b) OE. ēū (shortened) — ʒet : *grit* (magnus) 5. 2470. — c) OE. ē (shortened) — ʒet : *met*, prt. 1. 1058.

The spelling in *grit* is evidently faulty; i. e. for the author's pronunc.; it may have been perhaps correct for the scribe, for the pronunc. with ĭ is still found, e. g. in D. 34; but the author here more probably wrote and pronounced *gret*, which is still to be heard in D. 33.

§ 256. The pronunc., then, was *yĕt* in Clar. For similar rimes cf. Freirs of Berwik (Irving, p. 294) *yet* : *lat* (= let, vb.); Thrie Priests of Peblis (Irving, p. 303) *yet* : *get*; Roll. C. V. ʒet : *fret* : *get* : *set*, 2. 483; Satir. P. *yeatt* : *geatt* (= get) 45. 682, *yeatt* : *sett*, 45. 73, *yeattis* : *debtis* 45. 825; Montg. ʒett : *sett*, MP. 48. 272; Horn Ch. ʒete : *mete* : *sete*.

The form *yet* (= porta) is also found in most of the mod. Sc. diall.; e. g. in 34, 35, 37, 41, (ſæt) in 33, (ȝeet) in 34; the forms with initial *g*, (geet) in 35, (gèt) in 37, (git) in 38, (gīeit) in 39, are not pure dial., but due to the influence of rec. sp. On the other hand *gĕt*, *gĕt*, *gjĕt*, with *g* not *y*, are the regular forms found in the sense of *via*, quite a different word.

§ 257. The *e*-vowel in *yet* (= porta) is a support of what Sievers says. If the *e* in *geat* had merely been a sign of the palatal nature of the *g*, then the *a* would have been treated like any other *a*, (as it is after *sc*, cf. §§ 253, 254) and we should have had the form *yat* in MSc., a form which is not found. But the *ea* was treated like any other diphthong *ea*, and subject to palatal smoothing, i. e. became *ĕ*, *ȝet*, cf. Sievers, § 102.

§ 258. On the other hand the rime above in (b) might be understood as proving a long vowel, for *great* generally rimes in Clar. with a previous long *ē*; but this *ē* had already become *ī*, and, if the vowel is long, we must therefore understand *yīt*, which is scarcely possible, while the form *grĕt* is not unknown.

There is, however, another form found in MSc. as well as ME., viz. *ȝate* with a long *ā*, the forerunner of the *yēt*, still found in dial. e. g. D. 34; cf. Gol. *yate* : *estate*, 181, K. Q. *ȝate* : *vnquestionate*, 125, Freiris of B. (Irving. p. 295) *yet* : *lait* (= late, adj.), Deb. *ȝate* : *late*, 329, Hav. *ȝate* : *late* (*lĕtan*) 6781; Orm. and Townl. M. have both *ȝate* and *gate*. The rime may mean, therefore, *yēt* : *grēt*, but *yĕt* : *grĕt* is more probable.

§ 259. The right explanation of the fluctuation in the form of the initial conson. in this word is given by Sweet, § 748, where he remarks that "Chauc. has *gate* and North. *yate*, thus reversing the usual relation." OE. *geat* and pl. *gatu*, produce regularly ME. *yet* or *yat* and *gāte* respectively; in the S. the latter became fixed; in the N. it assumed by analogy the conson. of the former, and thus produced a mixed form *yate*, which existed and still exists side by side with *yet* in Sc.

§ 260. The explanation of the *g* in *gate* (= porta) from Norse influence can hardly be correct, from the fact that it is specially a Southern form; if due to Norse influence, it would certainly have been most firmly settled in the N. On the other hand, *gate* = road, is especially Northern English and is rightly derived from ON. For the difference between the two words cf. Dunb. *ȝettis* (= portae) 5. 19 (&c.) but *gait* (= via) 5. 29. The latter rimes in Sc. only with *ā*, later *ē*, e. g. Satir. P. *geat* : *esteat* (= estate) 45. 640 (the *ea* is merely Engl. orthography, which in the second half of this particular poem is extensively used for Sc. *ai* = *ē*). *gait* : *Dissait* 33. 298, *gait* : *sait* (= seat) : *debait* ; *estuit* 43. 63.

For *gave*, prt., see § 88, and for *care*, § 1 (c), (d).

§ 261. WS. ea + r + cons. = generally Northmb. ār + cons.

    a) Before a palatal cons. — rimes with

ON. e — marke (*mearcian*. vb.) : sarke 3. 484.

Before a palat. cons. the *ea* was sometimes smoothed to *ĕ* or *ǣ* in ONthmb., see Sweet, § 438. The above being the only rime, we cannot

tell from it alone whether the vowel-sound is *a* or *e*, but as we have
accepted *a* for *sarke* in § 180, we must also accept it for *marke*; cf.
§ 318, &c., where the treatment of *er* + *cons.* and *ar* + *cons.* is fully discussed. In §§ 304 f. instances of the form *merk* in other Sc. texts will
be found.

§ 262. β) Before other consonants. — rimes with

a) OE. e — *geir* (*gearwe*. f. pl.?) : *speir* 1.500, 2.1516 : *weir*, vb.
4.318, 436. — b) OE. eo, see § 302 (b). — c) Fr. a. *eftcrwart* : part. 3.470.

§ 263. The rimes in (b) and (c) will be found discussed below in
§§ 303 ff.

There are no examples in rime of *ear* + voiced cons., unless we
reckon the word *geir*, which is generally derived from OE. *gearwe*. It
has everywhere $\bar{e}$ in ME. and MSc., so also here $\bar{\imath} < \bar{e}$, see above (a).
Sweet, p. 281, explains the $\bar{e}$-vowel from the cognate vb. *gerwan*, prt.
gerede, and the *g* (guttural) from ON. *gǝrvi* or *gervi*. This is certainly
the right explanation of the *g*, for the OE. conson. would produce a ME.
and NE. *y*, as it does in the adj. *yare* from OE. *gearu*, the sing. form of
gearwe; cf. also NE. *yard*, &c. And we cannot simply derive altogether
from ON. *gervi*, on account of the *vi*, and the *we* of the OE. word presents the same difficulty, for from it we should expect the NE. form
yarrow. The derivation from ON. *geirr*, given by Noltemeier p. 30, is
impossible, for ON. *ei* gives a ME. diphthong *ei*, MSc. $\bar{e}$, cf. the pronunc.
they, *their*, &c. Dannenberg, p. 16, gives Swed. *gere* as the derivation.

It seems clear that there has been a confusion of forms in this word.
It would not be the only example (if we derive the vowel from *gearwe*)
of OE. *ear* producing ME. or MSc. $\bar{e}r$, later *ır*; we have only to think of
NE. *beard*, and in ME. we meet with such forms as *erme* (= *earmian*),
fern (also in mod. rec. sp. but with a short $\bar{e}$), *yerd*, &c., (cf. t. Br. § 48,
Morsb. p. 50, Noltemeier p. 23, Zielke. p. 20, Knigge, p. 20, Menze pp. 24,
25, Carstens p. 9). The *e* in these words, where long in ME., is due to
the lengthening in OE. before vowel-like + cons., b̆eard > beard; the
new *ēa* was treated like original *ēa*, and produced ME. $\bar{e}$, later $\bar{e}$, NE. *ı*,
except in *fern*, *earn*, &c., in which, in the ME. period, or at any rate
before $\bar{e}$ became *ı*, shortening again took place. Chauc. has *fĕrn*, *yĕrd*,
bĕrd, cf. Kluge, P. G. 1.866, 880. This $\bar{e}$, found in Midl. and South[n] texts,
arose at quite a different time and in a different way from the $\bar{e}$ in Sc.
airm = arm, &c., see below §§ 310, 317, &c. Zielke localises them in the
SW. and Kt. and says they made their way from these into other diall.
Menze shows that they are met with (though only in particular words) in
E. Midl. (except the Northern and Southern parts of it in which only *a*
is found) and in the whole of W. Midl. Could we, therefore, satisfactorily
account for the disappearance of the *w* (perhaps from the OE. nom. form
gearu, only with the vowel of the oblique cases?) it would be possible
to do without Sweet's explanation from the verbal form; but then the
word would stand alone over against such similar words as OE. *arwe*,
spearwa, *nearu*, *bearwe*, *gearwe*, sg., which produce ME. *arwe*, *sparwe*,
narwe, *barowe*, *ʒarwe*, = NE. arrow, sparrow, narrow, barrow, yarrow.

So Sweet's explanation of the vowel remains the best, unless a Norse word such as Swed. *gere* (?) was the origin.

§ 264. WS. eal + cons.
= Northmb. *āl* + *cons.* (acc. to Sievers § 158), *ăl* + *cons.* (acc. to Hilmer p. 9.)

α) *cal* or *eall* — rimes with

a) itself. fall : wall 1.92 : all 5.1186. all : sall, vb. 1.226 (&c.) : befall 2.620, 3.446 : wall 2.890 : hall 2.1682 (&c.). — b) ON. all. all : call 1.1054 (&c.). hall : call 1.1126. wallit : callit 1.1350, 3.1446. — c) OE. æl. all : small 2.648 (&c.). hall : small 2.1716, 3.1238. — d) ON. ǣll, see § 244 (c). — e) ON. ū + g. faw (feallan) : law (adj. ON. *lāg*) 2.1076. — f) Fr. al or Lat al? all : royall 1.1162 (&c.) : angellicall 2.916 : liberall 2.972 : imperiall 3.988, 4.1114 : speciall 4.592 : universall 4.1976. hall : royall 1.1568 (&c.) : collaterall 2.1630 : triumphall 4.2452. sall : mortall 3.1698. call : royall 1.1044. — g) Fr. ai. all : apparrell 5.1944.

§ 265. The rimes in (f) show that *al* is the regular representative of WS. *eal* in Clar., and herein there is perfect agreement with most ME. and MSc. texts; whether ONthmb. had *āl* or *ăl*, it is plain that in the ME. period the vowel was short. The long vowel of mod. rec. sp. and diall. is of later origin; cf. Köllmann, p. 36. The rimes in (a), (b), (c), (d) are all in accordance with this, that in (g) is not a correct rime, and is due to the unstressedness and consequent uncertainty in pronunc. of the final syll. in *apparrell*; for the scribe, too, it was not a pure rime.

§ 266. In (e) we have the only instance in rime of the vocalisation of *l* after *a*, which is also found in other MSc. texts; the result of this vocalisation was either a diphthong *au*, or else the *l* quite disappeared in *al* and the *u* in the diphthong *au* (with which it rimes), leaving in both a broad open monophthong ą̄ or *ā*, Ellis's (AA) or (aa). Cf. Buss, pp. 509, 510, where a number of examples from Wall. are given. Bruce and the Sc. Leg. have not yet this vocalisation of *l*, but it is proved once by rime in the Troj. War; cf. further Th. Erc. *Fawkirk* (= Falkirk) 360, Dunb. *fawd* (= fold) : *frawd* : *hawd* (= hold) 49.37, Satir. P. *faa* (= fall) : *saw* 45.690, *wawis* (= walls) : *cause* 24.32. Hence the confusion between *al* and *a*, the former being often used where there was originally no *l*, e. g. in K. Q. *walking* = waking, st. 173, Lyndes. Mon. *walk* = wake 4.5551, Roll. C. V. *awalk* 1.672, Montg. *aualk* MP. 43.1. Cf. Murray, DSS. p. 123.

§ 267. Whether the development was *āl* > ą̄ direct, or *āl* > *āu* > ą̄, this last is the well-known characteristic of the mod. Sc. diall. The words *all, hall, fall, wall, call,* &c., are all to be found everywhere without any sign of the *l*, but with Ellis's (AA), (aa) or (ɔɔ). Burns' and other Sc. poems offer numerous examples of this. The form with *l*, when found in dial., is probably borrowed from rec. sp.

§ 268. β) WS. ea before ld (ONthmb. āld) — rimes with

a) itself. behold : tauld 1.966 : told 2.40 : fold, inf. 1.1010 : old : 2.754 : ʒold (prt. WS. ʒeald) 2.896 : ʒold, ptc. 2.1496 : bold 2.1000 : bauld 5.2010 : wold (prt. North. *walde*, WS. *wolde*) 3.1596. behauld : bald, adj. 1.864 : hald, inf. 5.942. behald : fold, inf. 4.306 : cauld, adj. 4.2456.

hald, inf. : wold, prt. 5. 2678. houshold : moniefold 2. 1772 : bold 4. 724. old : bold 1. 1032 : wald, prt. 4. 2366. told : moniefold 4. 1320 : wold, prt. 4. 1518 : hold, ptc. 5. 220 : bold 5. 1310. taulde : hauld, inf. 5. 610. — b) OE. o. ʒold, prt. : gold 1. 450. behold : gold 1. 804 (&c., 10 times in all). bold : gold 4. 1360. told : gold 5. 2440.

§ 269. WS. -*eald*, ONorth. -*āld*, produces in ME. no less than three different forms, -*ald*, -*old*, -*eld*, or four, if Morsb. (p. 154) is right in distinguishing between -*ĕld* and -*ēld*. ME. -*ald* and -*old* both come from the OAngl. form -*āld*; -*ǭld* is the form predominant in the Midl. and S. (where every *ā* became *ǭ*) and is the origin of the form in mod. rec. sp.; -*āld* (spelt also -*auld* in later Northern texts, esp. Scotch) is the Northern form. According to Kölbing (Am. p. 34) and Wilda (p. 13, &c.) -*eld* is peculiar to Kt. and the N.; it is also found in the adjacent districts of the Midl. dial., though not frequent, according to Menze. Morsb., p. 154, says -*ĕld*, the shortness of whose vowel is proved by rime, is a form taken by Chauc. from the S., where *ea* was not lengthened before *ld*, and often became *ĕ*; while -*ēld* is the form known in the N. of Engl., which has only a long vowel, *ē*, mut. of *ā*, having been transferred by analogy from the 2 and 3 sg. pres. indic. into the infin. Forms with *e*, short or long, are, then, liable to be found in all texts, except in the dial. of the S. W. We might also expect to find -*old* encroaching on the Northern territory just in the same measure as *o* from general OE. *ā* replaced the correct Northern form *a* or *ai*; but as a matter of fact the combination -*old* was somewhat slower in forcing its way into the language of Sc. writers. It first appears in the N. of Engl. in the Surt. Ps., i. e. in the 2nd half of the 13th cent. (cf. Zielke, p. 20, Wende, p. 16, Dannenberg, p. 16; the last mentioned shows how far *o* occurs in other Northern texts). It will probably be found that only those Sc. writers who are strongly influenced by Engl., e. g. James I (cf. Wischmann, p. 6), employ the *o*-form, which can only be explained as a direct copying of Engl. models, not as evidence of the spoken language being influenced by a more Southern dial., for -*ald* was the correct Sc. form, as is shown by the mod. Sc. diall., and by its predominance (if not sole existence) in some even of the latest MSc. texts, written *ald* and *auld*, and the complete absence of -*old* from the earlier ones. Bruce has only *a*, e. g. *vald* (prt.) : *hald*, inf. 16. 54, *ald* : *sald*, prt. 19. 178. As far as present materials go, there is no trace of *o* in Sc. writers before James I (behold : gold : cold, hold : wold : rold, &c.); *o* is also found in Gol., *behold* : *gold*, *bold* : *gold* (Noltemeier p. 23) and we have it in Clar., see above (b). Dunb. has *a*, *au* and *o*, according to Kaufmann, p. 50, who, however, only gives one example of *o*, and no rimes at all; Dougl. *a*, *au*, *aw*, cf. *withhald* : *wald*, prt. 2. 26. 2, *cauld* : *hald* 2. 27. 18, *tawld* : *hauld* 2. 41. 8. &c.; also *o*, e. g. *behold* : *mold* : *gold* 1. 69. 12, *mony fold* : *gold* 1. 70. 13, *behold* : *gold*, 1. 89. 7.; Wynt. *bald* : *cald* (= named). In the later texts. such as Satir. P. and Montg., which have on the whole pure Sc., I can find no rimes with *o*, as far as examined; words of this class rime chiefly only with themselves, and only *a* or *au* is written. For a sketch of the treatment of WS. *eald* in the various diall. of Engl. see Menze, p. 23 and cf. t. Br., § 48, Morsb., pp. 49 and 154, Kölbing, Sir Tr.

pp. 62, 69, Am. p. 25, Ipom. pp. 159, 173, Dannenberg, p. 16, Zielke, p. 20, Danker, p. 7, Carstens, p. 8, Köllmann, p. 36.

We have no rimes in Clar. to prove definitely an *a*-pronunc., e. g. with such words as *called*, prt. (cf. *bold* : *ytold* : *old* : *cald*, Am. 1636), and it is difficult to say how far the author is responsible for the spelling with *a*, *au*; perhaps he, like James I, used only *o*-forms, and the scribe here, as in K. Q., is answerable for the *a* and *au*, which are also more frequent inside the verse than *o*, although the latter is not rare. In the absence of rimes of proof, the question must be left unsettled; we only know that the author certainly used *o*-forms. The rimes with *wold*, *wald*, prt. prove nothing, as both forms, with *a* and *o*, are proved by rime in Northern texts.

§ 270. There are two rimes which at first sight might lead us to suspect an *ē*-form; but very slight and probable emendations remove the necessity of interpreting in this way. For the one, see § 173; the other is in Bk. 3. 1. 1890, where the MS. has: "That pitie it had beine for to behold Ane efter vther he in his armes fold And kissit them bot micht no wirdis say", &c. It is evident that *fold* is intended as a prt. and the correct strong form for the pret. of OE. *fealdan*, *fēold*, would be in ME. and MSc. *fęld*, on the analogy of *hęld* from *hēold*. This form is found, too, in ME., e. g. Fer. *felde* : *schelde* (= shield) 841. The question is, whether it is really found anywhere in any Sc. text; if so, the rime here may prove an *e*-pronunc. in the infin. *behold*, which should then be written *beheld*, or *beheild*. But instead of *armes fold* (3 syll.) we can read *arm(e)s did fold* or *can fold*; for the ending *-es*, generally written *-is*, is a very convenient instrument in the hands of the author, who treats it as a full syll. or suppresses it altogether, just as it pleases him, according as it suits the metre or not. We have to make a similar emendation in another case, viz. 5. 2677—8, "And in fyve dayis as Dame Fortoun wold Toward the land lustilie thay hald". All the surrounding verbs are preterites, so it is probable that the verb in the second line of the couplet should also be a pret., and the correct form for this would be *hęld*; if this is so, then *wold* should be *weld*, an impossible form; therefore we must read, "Towárd the lánd thay lústilié did hóld", or *can hóld*, especially as this redeems the metre of the line, which is imperfect as it stands in the MS. Piper's emendation, insertion of *full* before *lustilie*, sets the metre right, but then, if the rime is to be saved, *hald* must be taken as a historic present, in the midst of a lot of preterites; this, it is true, is not impossible with MSc. writers, but we need not accept it, where we are not compelled to do so; some change from the MS. is necessary, and the above emendation removes all difficulties; in either case, the nature of the rime here remains the same.

§ 271. There is no proof, then, of an *ē*-form in Clar.; such are, in fact, rare in Sc., though frequently found in N. Engl. The fact that they do not occur solely in verbal forms of the *hold*-class, is against Morsbach's explanation of the length of the *ē*. Jam. Dict. gives the form *beild*, adj. = bold, quoting from Houlate; it also gives *eild*, as an adj. = old, in Dougl. Virg. (but in Small's edit. this is altered to the noun *eld* = old-age); we also find in Dougl. *eldfader, eldmoderis*. Zielke, p. 20, quotes from Sir Egl. the rime *elde* (eald) : *felde*; Wilda, p. 33, from Bone Flor. *welde* : *behelde* : *schylde* : *belde*, and *welde* : *felde* : *helde* : *belde*. Such preterites as *ȝeld, teld, seld*, &c., quoted by Kölbing, Sir Tr., p. 62, cannot always be explained (as by Dannenberg, p. 16, note) as new-formed preterites from the pres. forms *ȝeld, tell, sell*, &c.; this is satisfactory only when the vowel is short, and is undoubtedly the correct explanation of the forms in the mod. diall. with short $\breve{e}$, see below, § 273. But they are also found with long vowel in Northern ME. texts, e. g. Sir Tr. *teld*, prt. : *feld* : *ȝeld*, inf. : *beheld*, inf. 3252, *teld* : *ȝeld*, prt. : *queld* : *scheld* : *feld* : *biheld* (bih$\bar{e}\bar{o}$ld) &c.; Bone Flor. (Wilda, p. 33) *welde* : *schylde* (for *schelde*) : *selde, welde* : *felde* : *helde* : *belde*. Similarly apparently in the S. E., where according to Morsb. we should expect a short vowel, e. g. Lyb. Disc. (Wilda, p. 13) *telde* : *scheld*, Guy W. (Wilda, p. 51) *teld* : *feld, helde* : *felde* : *yelde*; although here, too, the short vowel is found, to judge from a similar rime in Lyb. Disc., *beld* : *dwellde* : *held*; otherwise we must suppose that in the preterite *dwellde*, the vowel has undergone a secondary lengthening. It seems better, then, to leave the *e* in *-eld* < *-eald* as a kind of "schwebender vokal" (see t. Br., p. 26, and below § 362), for the explanation of *-ĕld* and *-ēld* from different origins does not always suffice. Kölbing, Sir Tr., pp. 69, 70, has shown that all three forms, with *a, o* and *e* are met with in N. Engl. in the middle of the 14th cent. (cf. also Ellinger, p. 12, Zielke, p. 20). Besides Sir Tr., Sir Perc. and Sir Egl. and the works previously quoted, the *e*-form is found in Sir. Torr. (Adam, p. 11), Lyric Poems (Schlüter, p. 16), Ipom. (Kölbing p. 159) and Sir Gaw. (Knigge, p. 19).

§ 272. The form *wield* in rec. sp. is generally derived from OE. *-weldan*; in Kt. and the N., however, OE. *wealdan* might have produced the same form, ME. *wĕlden*, NE. *wĭld*; and perhaps this coincidence of the two verbs assisted the final supremacy of the form *wēld* > *wĭld* instead *wā̆ld* > *wō̆ld*. We have a similar form (in pronunc.) in the *Weald* (in Kent and Sussex); this is certainly a Kentish form and derived from OE. *weald* = Germ. *wald*. In the *Wolds* of Yorks. we have the corresponding Midl. form, *wāld* > *wǫld* > *wōld*. The orthography of *Weald* would point to a ME. *węld*, while that of *wield* would rather indicate a ME. *węld*; so that, if any weight can be laid on this difference, *wield*, if derived from *wealdan*, can only be a Northern form. But still, OE. *-weldan* satisfactorily explains the mod. form.

§ 273. The mod. Sc. diall. have only the broad (ᴀᴀ) sound, or something near it; sometimes the *d* has disappeared, so in *bold, old, cold, fold, told*, which all appear with (ᴀᴀl). Sometimes the *l* has been vocalised and disappeared; so always in *hold*, and occasionally in *old, fold, cold, sold, told* — (hᴀad, aad, fᴀᴀd, kᴀᴀd, sat, taad). The two last mentioned are often found in the forms *selt, telt*, corresponding to the ME. forms mentioned above, new-formed from the pres. *tell, sell*. Forms with *ld* are also given by Ellis, e. g. (ᴀᴀld, bᴀᴀld, kᴀᴀld, fᴀᴀld, sᴀᴀld, taald) but never (hᴀᴀld) only (hᴀᴀd, haad) or (had).

6*

Probably in this combination the *l* disappeared directly, without first producing a diphthong *au*, cf. Satir. P. *calld thame* : *forbade thame* 45. 114.

EA'

§ 274. 1. = Gmc. **au**

α. Not followed by w or gutt. — rimes with
a) itself. heid (*hēafod*) : deid (mortuus) 3. 374 : reid(e), adj. 4. 838 (&c.). heade : reide 4. 536. deid (mors) : breid (panis) 3. 744. — b) OE. *e*-, see § 130 (c). — c) ON. *w̄*, see § 244 (a). great : seate (ON. *sǣti*) 5. 1526. — d) Angl. *ē* = WS. *w̄*, see § 212 (c). — e) OE. *w̄*, mut of *ā*, see § 226 (c). — f) OE. *ā*. clave (prt. *clēofan*) : drave, draue 1. 48, 730. — g) OE. e: dreidles : gentilues 1. 1530 : worthines 2. 778 : nobilnes 5. 1008. saikles : hevines 3. 662, and others. — h) OE. ea:. grit (*grēat*) : ʒet (porta) 5. 2470. bereft : beft (= beaten, ptc.) 3. 732, cf. below § 279. — i) OE. *ī*-. leaue, sb. : give 3. 1014, leave : geiue 4. 146. — k) Fr. e (α-class). eist : feist 5. 606. eare : weir (bellum) 3. 1194. doubtles : maistres 3. 800. — l) Fr. e (γ-class). reid (adj.) : remeid 1. 442, 3. 1590. deid (mortuus) : remeid 4. 122 (&c.). deid, dead (mors) : remeid 3. 1696, 2270. great : repeit 1. 1146, 5. 2568 : quyet 2. 330, grite : repeit 5. 1360. leave, sb. : greiue 1. 878 : mischeve (vb. *meschever*) 1. 1258. eare : cleire 5. 814. — m) OFr. ai. great : treite, vb. 5. 1348. — n) Du. i (?). doubtles : ges, vb. (= MLG. *gissen*, Bradley) 3. 2406.

§ 275. OE. *ēa* belongs to t. Br.'s α-class, but as shown above, in §§ 122 &c., it produces *ẹ̄* in Sc. in most positions, and not only in a special class of words in which the *ea* was followed by *c*, *g* or *h*, and became *ẹ̄* already in the OE. period, for which cf. above §§ 217—225. Hence we have α : γ rimes in (l). There can be no doubt about these rimes, they clearly prove that *ēa* had, at any rate in some words, become *ẹ̄* in Scotl.; the rime-words rime frequently with other recognised γ-vowels.

§ 276. The beginnings of this are apparent in the ONthmb. dial., where *ẹ̄* is found for WS. *ēa* before other consonants than *c*, *g*, *h*, e. g. in *nēd*, *nēten* (pecus), *ēðor* (facilius), &c., (Hilmer, p. 26). And there was much confusion between the symbols *ea* and *eo*; for instance, the following forms are found, with *ēo* for WS. *ēa*: *rēofia* (diripere), *rēof* (spolium), *ēore* (auris), *ēost* (oriens), *ēostre* (Pascha), *ceōpia* (emere), *hēofod* (caput), *lēof* (folium); see Hilmer, p. 31. (The *ēa* form is found as well; it is not to be understood that these words are *only* found with *ēo*). These peculiarities of the ONthmb. dial. are sufficient to explain the *early* existence of *ẹ̄* for OE. *ēa* in the N.; most probably it was *ẹ̄* from the very beginning of the ME. period, at least in some words.

§ 277. With regard to the orthography in Clar., we notice that in these words *ea* is occasionally written, whereas it is rarely, if at all, used for the *ẹ̄* from OE. *ēo*, &c. (Class γ). This difference is probably only due to a scribe, for whom there was an appreciable difference between the two sets of vowels; the author scarcely wrote such imperfect eye-rimes as *leave* : *greiue*, *eare* : *weir* : *cleir*, *great* : *repeit*. But it is very difficult to distinguish between the orthographies of author and scribe;

there is no approach to consistency on the part of the latter, and we do not know, in fact, through how many hands the copying has gone, before arriving at the form of our MS.

§ 278. We have $\alpha : \alpha$ rimes in (a), (b), (c), (k) and (m); those in (c) and (m) have a different meaning, however, from the others, cf. §§ 245, 108; $\alpha : \beta$ rimes in (d) and (e).

The vowel is shortened to $\breve{e}$ in the suffix -*les* (OE. -*lēās*), as in all other diall., see (g), (k). In (n) the vowel is also certainly $\breve{e}$; cf. § 393.

§ 279. Also when shortened in verbal contracted forms the vowel seems to have been $\breve{e}$, not $\breve{a}$, e. g. bereft, see (e) and (h). The rime-word in (h), *beft*, is given by Murray, NED. s. v. beft, as only found in the N. as prt. and ptc.; "it is uncertain whether the pres. would be *beff*, of the same origin as *baff*, sb., or *beft*, = ONorth. *beafta or *beaftia for *behaftian, from *be-* + OE. *haftian*, to clap, strike with the flat of the hand". Jam. Dict. gives pres. *beff* or *baff*, but quotes no examples for this. Cf. Dunb. *beft* prt. : *heft* 26. 40, *beft* 33. 78.

§ 280. The rime-word *ʒet* in (h) also contains $\breve{e}$, cf. §§ 255—7. It seems that the author knew three forms for the word *great*, viz. *grēt*, see (c) and (m), *grĕt*, see (h), and *grĭt*, see (b) and (l), and the scribe yet another, *grĭt*, for he often spells the word so to the detriment of the outward appearance of the rime, e. g. *grite : eit*, *grite : repeit*, *grit : ʒet*. The word is also irregular in the mod. Sc. diall., appearing, as will be seen below, in three different forms, chiefly in the form *grēt*, as in rec. sp., but, strange to say, never as *grĭt*; it seems, therefore, to be an exception to our rules made above, and rather to agree with t. Br.'s rules: i. e. if Ellis EEP. V. is correct.

§ 281. The rimes in (i) are a further proof of the closed nature of the earlier $\bar{e}$, cf. § 120. Here again the rimes were not pure for the scribe.

§ 282. The form *clave*, see (f), with undoubted $\bar{e} < \bar{a}$, cannot be anyhow explained as regularly developed from OE. *clēaf*. It is no exceptional form, for it is found in all Sc. texts and also in Engl.; it is, in fact, not yet entirely extinct in Engl., still retaining an artificial existence from its occurrence in the Bible (Ps. 78. 15). It is a parallel form to *chāse* (cf. t. Br. Chauc. pp. 38, 40), and similar forms may be found of the preterites of one or two other verbs of Class II in ME. The following examples are given by Wackerzapp, pp. 37 &c. — Curs. M., E. *claue : draue*; Curs. M., A., *raf, chas : was, claue : draf, claif : draif, claf : raf*; Metr. Engl. Hom., *raf*; York P. *chaas : grace, raffe*; H. Leg. *raf*; Yw. Gaw. *rafe*; Bruce, *claf : gaf, clave : gave, claff : gaff*, (*clafe : drafe*), *flaw*; Townl. M. *rafe : grave, rofe, clofe : grafe*; Alex. *rofe*; Rel. P. *chose, raue*; Thornt. Rom. *chese : was, rafe*; Sc. Leg. *crape, rafe : strafe : lafe : clafe, grate, rayf, flaw : saw, rawe, clawe*; Gol. *flaw, claif* (also *grat* 1141); Dunb. *claif, raif* (also *crap*, see Kaufmann, p. 101); Lanc. *flaw*; Dougl. *crap : hap, raif : cave, flaw : law*; Lyndes. *raue : graue, raif, flaw : law : raw*. To these we can add — Montg. *crap : mishap : trap*, S. 38, : *lap : wrap : mishap*, S. 47, : *hap*, MP. 4. 41 : *shap : lap*,

MP. 32. 53. From the last it seems that the vowel was later liable to shortening.

§ 283. Similar forms are found in the S. (but not to such an extent as in the N.), with an $\bar{a}$, which, according to t. Br. p. 38, never became $\bar{\varrho}$; the $\bar{o}$-forms, which also appear, are explained by t. Br. as resulting from assimilation to the forms of the prt. plur. and pp.; but is it not possible to explain this $\bar{o}$ as arising out of the $\bar{a}$ which is found so frequently in the N.? (If so, then Bülbring's suggestion, p. 89, that *forbode* in Trev. and Sh. is a Northern form, may be justified). Or, if not, we can explain the $\bar{o}$ as arising independently in the S. similarly to the $\bar{a}$-forms in the N., see § 284. Perhaps, too, we can explain in this way the few $\bar{a}$-forms which appear in the Midl. and S., e. g. *chās*, Chauc., see t. Br. § 38; this is better than changing *chās* into *chēs* (cf. Bülbring, p. 90, and t. Br.'s note thereto); the rarity of the examples with $\bar{a}$, would be, of course, due to the Midl. and South^n tendency to change $\bar{a}$ to $\bar{\varrho}$. There can be no doubt as to the $\bar{a}$ being proved in Southern texts, whether they were regularly developed there as in the N., or simply taken from the N., and a possible explanation of the later o-forms is, that they arose from these $\bar{a}$-forms, perhaps helped by plural forms with o, as t. Br., p. 38, explains for *chose*, from ME. *chǫsen*. The forms with short $\check{a}$ in Kt., *ssat* ($<$ *sceat*), *lhapp*, Ayenb., &c., are different in nature; see Konrath in Herrig's Archiv, 88. 1. p. 58, &c.

§ 284. The $\bar{a}$-forms in the N. were most probably due to the influence of other classes of strong verbs which had $\bar{a}$ in ME. in the pret. sg., viz. Classes I, IV and V, especially Class IV. The strong verbs of Class II were very few in number in ME., as most of those which existed in OE. had either died out, or become weak; at the same time, the few remaining verbs would in the N., in their regular development, have the same vowel $\ddot{e}$ both in pres. and prt. sg., for here $\bar{e}a > \ddot{e}$ and $\bar{e}o > \ddot{e}$; hence we should have the forms, prs. *crẹp*, prt. *crẹp*, *crōpen*, ptc. *crōpen*, *clẹv*, *clẹv*, *clōven*, *clōven*, &c, or, after the plur. prt. had been assimilated to the sg., *clẹv*, *clẹv*, *clẹven* or *clẹv*, *clōven* or *clōv*; &c. These verbs would then stand quite alone in having no distinction between the vowel-sounds of pres. and prt., and it was, therefore, an easy change to adopt for the pret. the vowel of another class, and an *a*-vowel being the sign of the pret. in Classes I, III, IV, V (in three of them long $\bar{a}$), *a* had the most chance of being adopted, especially as in Class IV the vowels corresponded with those of Class II in pres. and pptc.; e. g. *bẹr*, *bār*, *born*; hence *crẹp*, *crẹp*, *crōpen* became *crẹp*, *crāp*, *crōpen*.

That this change should have taken place chiefly, if not only (i. e. in the first instance) in the N., is easily understood; for in the S. there was no coincidence of the vowels of the prs. and prt., prs. *crẹp*, prt. *crẹp*; and that it was an easy matter for $\bar{\varrho}$ to assert itself later in the S., is also easily understood, because the prt. pl. and ptc. had already o, and there was a tendency to make prt. and ptc. alike in other verbs. Bülbring, p. 90, remarks that the forms found in Lay. seem to be formed from analogy with Class IV (Class I in his scheme), but he rejects this explanation and prefers to understand the *a* as being = $\bar{\varrho}$, which is not so satisfactory in the face of undoubted *a*-rimes, and even if this were the right explanation for the S., the numerous Northern forms would still require explanation.

It is possible that in the N. there were other influences at work, e. g. confusion with similar forms from the Norse. This was certainly the case with the verb *rēofan*, which was confused with ON. *rífa*; in ME. the verb has gone completely over to Class I, *rīv*, *rāv*, *rĭven*. Or are we to consider that OE. *rēofan* died out altogether and that the ME. *rive* has nothing whatever to do with it? Against this is the fact that the form *ref* is found for the prt., e. g. in Curs. M.

§ 285. The *a*-forms still exist in Scotl., but chiefly with a short vowel; cf. *grat*, prt. of *grīt*, OE. *grēotan*, e. g. in Banffshire, also *crap* in Gentle Shepherd, v. 1. (Murray DSS. p. 204). Mr. Low gives me the forms *grat* and *crap* for Forfarshire, but says the latter is mostly replaced by the weak form *crepit* (kriipit). See also Jam. Dict. s. v. *greit*, *grat* : *sat*, Border Minst. 2. 120, *grat* : *gat*, Ramsay's Poems 2. 143; also the forms *crap* and *craup* as prt. of *creep*. The verb OE. *cēosan* became generally weak in Sc., *chesit* is the most usual form of the prt.

§ 286. The mod. Sc. diall. are not at all uniform in their representation of OE. *ēa*; from the MSc. rimes we should expect to find *ĩ* in all words; this is so in most of them, but other forms with *ĭ*, *ē*, *ĕ* are found as well, though far less frequent. How far these are pure vernacular forms and how far they are affected by rec. sp. is difficult to say. The *ĭ* can be interpreted in two ways, either as shortened from *ĩ* or as a development from *ĕ*.

ĩ is found in *head* (in 34, 35, 38, 41), *dead* (34, 35, 36, 38, 41), *lead*, plumbum (35, 41), *red* (35, 36, 41), *bread* (35, 38, 41), *deaf* (34, 35, 36), *leaf* (35), *team* (35), *bean* (35, 38), *death* (41).

ĭ is found in *head* (33, 36, 37, 39, 41), *dead* (33, 36, 39), *lead*, plumbum, (33, 39), *red* (33, 34, 35, 36, 37, 39), *bread* (33, 35, 39), *sheaf* (33), *deaf* (33, 36), *leaf* (33), *team* (33), *bean* (33, 39), *cheap* (33), *great* (34), *threat* (33), *death* (33, 37), *heap* (33). It is to be remembered here, however, that many of the vowels marked short by Murray in D. 33, were really medial, and this applies to some of the pronunciations given by Ellis in 34 and 35, so that the (i) of the words in the list just given may correctly reflect perhaps a MSc. *ụ̃*.

ĕ is found in *head* (37, 39), *dead* (39), *lead* = plumbum (38, 39), *red* (37, 38, 39), *bread* (35), *sheaf* (38, 39), *deaf* (37, 38, 39), *leaf* (38, 39), *cheap* (38, 39), *great* (33), *threat* (34, 38, 39); *death* (35, 37, 38, 39), *beat* (34). In D. 38. the *e* is of a very close nature. It will be noticed that the *ĕ* is found chiefly in 37, 38 and 39, and mostly in such words as have *ĕ* in rec. sp. This arouses at once suspicion that Ellis perhaps did not obtain pure dial. here.

ē is found in *head* (36), *bread* (39), *sheaf* (35, 41), *cheap* (35), *great* (33, 35, 39, 40), *threat* (35), *death* (34, 35, 36, 39). This is all the more remarkable as it occurs even in words which in rec. sp. have *ĩ*, e. g. *sheaf*, *cheap*.

β. OE. ēāw = WGmc. āw, auw

§ 287. rimes with

a) OE. ū + w. shaw: know 1. 1298 (&c.), schawin : unknawin 3. 1410.
— b) OE. ū + g. show : throw (OE. *prāg*, sb. = time) 3. 1028, shew (inf.): throw 3. 1346. — c) Lat. au. shawid : laud, sb. 1. 786.

§ 288. OE. *ēaw* appears in ME. in various forms, the variety being partly due to difference of dial., and partly to the difference in development of -*eaw*- (medial) and -*eaw* (final); *ę̄, ā, ęu, au, ǫu* are all found, and at least three of these *eu, au, ou,* are represented in mod. rec. sp., e. g. in *dew, straw, show,* the latter also spelt *shew* from ME. *sheu*). Acc. to t. Br. -*eaw* (final) can produce *ē* or *au,* and -*ēāw*- (medial) *eu, ou* or *au* (see his note to Bülbring, p. 105, and Chauc. pp. 30, 39). The regular development in Engl. is without doubt *ēāw* > ME. *ę̄u,* i. e. *eu* > ME. *ę̄,* as usual under ordinary circumstances; so in the words NE. *dew, few, hew, shrew, thew* and ME. *shew,* i. e. in the majority of words of this class.

§ 289. ME. *ę̄* for OE. *eaw* is explained from the early loss of final *w* (see t. Br. § 44, note). ME. *ā* might be explained in a similar way, if we could only find forms with *āw* instead of *ēāw* in OE., a possibility in which one is at first inclined to believe, as it would not only explain ME. *ā* but also ME. *au* and *ou* more simply than is otherwise possible, and put the forms *straw,* &c., on a level with *knaw* (OE. *cnāwan*) &c. We might perhaps compare the OFris. forms *hāwa, skāwia, dāw,* unless the *āw* here is nothing more than an orthographical variety for *auw,* which is sometimes found in the same words. But such forms are not to be found in ONthmb.; *bleāwa* appears occasionally for *blāwa* (Hilmer p. 33), but as yet we have no evidence of the reverse interchange, *āw* for *ēāw.*

§ 290. But we can explain satisfactorily from internal processes and Norse influence. The only word which is as yet found with *ā* in MSc. (and represented in NSc. correctly by *ē* or *i',* see below, § 296) is the word *straw,* OE. *strēaw*; (the form *fo,* Gen. Ex., see below, makes a previous form **fā* necessary). The *ā*-form is not mentioned by t. Br. as it does not occur in Chauc., but it is well-known in Sc., e. g. Bruce, *stra* : *sa* 3. 320 : *ta* 3. 506, Dunb. *stray, strae* (Kaufmann p. 59), Dougl. *stray* : *way* (see Jam. Dict. s. v. *stra, strae, stray*), Roll. C. V. *strayis* : *fais* : *slayis* : *gais* 4. 391, Satir. P. *strais* : *hais* (= has) 16. 78, Montg. *strais,* MP. 3. 36; (Compl. Sc. has *strey,* which probably means *strę̄*); also in the NMidl., e. g. Hav. *stra* : *ga* (vb.) : *wa,* see Sweet p. 352.

We shall probably be right in ascribing this form *strā* to Norse influence, ON. *strá.* This then ousted the form *strę̄* < *strēaw* and probably forced its way into the forms of the oblique cases, i. e. instead of *strę̄, strę̄wes* came the forms *strā, strāwes,* whence the form *straw,* which must be looked upon as a specially Northern form, if the above be correct.

A similar explanation can be applied to the word *raw* (the only other word in this class with *aw* in rec. sp.), viz. influence of ON. *hrār.*

§ 291. The only other Scotch words I can find with *aw* are *schaw* and *fawely.* The latter is given by Jam. Dict. as an adv. = fewly, few in number, and can also be explained from Norse influence, ON. *fár. fowe, vawe* = few, are also found in Rob. Gl., also *fo* : *wo* in Gen. Ex., *fo* : *to* : *go*, in Rob. Br., *fone*, North. (Sweet, p. 352) and Cooper (1685) gives (foo) as a "barbarous" pronunciation of *few*. Jam. Dict. gives *schrow* for *schrew*, *schrowis* : *plowis*, Maitl. Poems, and the verb *to schro* (= to curse); the *o* is very remarkable here (perhaps for *a* through the imitation of Southern forms again?).

§ 292. *Schaw* is found in all MSc. texts, so also in Clar., see the rimes above, all of which contain only *au*. (The rime in Sc. Leg. *schaw* : *Androw*, 5/151, is remarkable). Sweet, § 680, says "the *e* seems to have been absorbed by the preceding front cons., the length being shifted on to the *a*, our present *show* pointing to *schäwen*, although Ancr. R.'s *schawen* points to short *a*". This is better than Morsb.'s explanation (p. 74), "*eā* > *ā* through influence of *w*". If the latter were correct, we should expect to find *aw* oftener, but the words *hew*, *few*, *dew*, *thew*, never appear with *aw*, even in the N., and *sceawian*, being the only word of this class beginning with *sc*, can very well have had a special development of its own. The *show* of rec. sp. must also be derived from a form *shaw*; the two forms *shaw* and *show* stand in the same relation to one another as *knaw* and *know*, or *blaw* and *blow*; the one is Sc., the other Engl.

§ 293. There is yet another explanation, which, it is true, explains all the other *au* forms as well, without the help of Norse influence, but it is not so simple, although it is possible and can be in part supported by analogous evidence. It is as follows — $e\bar{a}w > \bar{æ}w > \acute{æ}w > \acute{æ}u > \acute{a}u$, and then further $\acute{a}u > \bar{a}u > \bar{\varrho}u$ for the Southern *ow*, or $\acute{a}u > \bar{a}u > \bar{a}$, for MSc. *strā*, &c. For the first step, $\bar{e}\bar{a}w > \bar{æ}w$: Orm mostly writes *æw*, *shæwenn*, *hæwenn*, *fæwe*, &c., and *ǣ* is found for *ea* in ONthmb., e.g. *ǣwia* (manifestare) for WS. *ēawian* (Hilmer, p. 26). For the *ǽw* and *ǎw* stages: there are other traces to be found of *a* or *ǣ* as the shortened form of OE. *ea* (cf. Menze p. 72; Peterb. Chron. has *fæu*) and these have been explained through an older *ǣ* for *ēa*; the words NE. *lather*, *chaffer*, *chapman*, for instance, contain *a* from OE. *ea*; the suffix *-lēās* appears as *-las* as well as *-les* in MSc.; the word *near* appears as *ner* and *nar*; Orm has the forms *drah* and *lafe* for OE. *drēag* and *geleāfa*.

§ 294. An *au* from OE. *ēaw* is therefore not impossible, though it is difficult to see why it is not found in more words than it is; and why, if *schaw* is to be explained in the same way, it is the only word (besides *fowe*, *fo*, for *few*) which appears in Southern Engl. with *ou*. *Schaw* must have an explanation of its own, as given by Sweet, and so probably *straw*, *raw*, and *fawe*, *fowe*, *fo* (from Norse influence) although the latter may have had the development traced above, with a Norse side-influence working in favour of the establishment of the *a*-forms. One thing is particularly worthy of notice, viz. that the SE. shows here again its similarity to the N. (*fo* in Gen. Ex. &c.).

§ 295. The $\bar{e}$, $\bar{a}$ forms, with loss of *w*, in ME., can only be developed from final $\bar{e}\bar{a}w$, if they are of pure native growth. They are never found in verbal forms; this is because the *w* could not, except in the imperat., a comparatively seldom used form, appear in final position, whereas in nouns and adjectives the nom. case, generally the most important, ended, of course, in *w*. But it is difficult to see why t. Br., while recognising *au* as a possible form from final *ëaw*, should not allow *eu* from final as well as medial *ëaw*.

The author of Clar. only knew, as far as the rimes in § 287 show, the form *schaw* for OE. *scëawian*, whether the *au* had already become *ǭ* cannot be decided from the rimes; (the final *u* of the diphthong *au* had disappeared in the second half of the 16th cent. in some parts of Scotl., cf. Satir P. *saa* (= saw, prt.) : *Spaa* 45. 520). The scribes knew also the forms with *eu* and *ou*, *schew*, *schow*, and perhaps the *o* form may also have been known to the author, as in the word *know*, cf. § 55.

§ 296. *Show* is not included in Ellis's lists of the mod. Sc. diall. (it is a rare word in the Sc. vernacular, and, when found, has the pronunc. of rec. sp., according to Mr. Low's information). But *know*, where used, has *ā*, like the words *blow*, *throw*, &c. *Slow* has *ā* in 33, in the other diall. *ō* is given. *Raw* always *ā* or *ǭ* (AA). *Straw* has (i') in 33, and *ē* in most of the other diall. (both the equivalent of ME. *ā*), in 41 it has also *ɩ* and in 42, *ā*, (the latter, the equivalent of MSc. *au*). *Few* has (iu) or (iuu) in 33. 35, 36 and 42, but (iau) in 37, 38, 39, also (īǝu) in 39, (īǝu) in 40, and (ɔ¹u) as well as (iuu) in 33.

2. *ēa* through contraction from a + a, a + o, &c.

§ 297. teiris (for *teir*, = OE. *tēar*) : effeir 5. 2524.

There is no difference in the treatment of this *ēa* and that of *ēa* < Gmc. *au*. For the rime cf. § 250; the vowel is here *ɩ* < *ę̄*.

EO -

§ 298. Only *four* examples. — a) *hevin* and *sevin* rime together, 5. 1928. — b) bent (OE. *beonet*?) : went, 3. 1900 (OE. e). — c) swyre (OE. *sweora*, neck) : desyre, 4. 1776 (Fr. i).

§ 299. Whether the vowel in *hevin*, *sevin*, is short or long in the dial. of Clar. cannot be decided, but the spelling with *e* (not *ei*), indicates shortness of vowel for the scribe. That long *ē* also existed in MSc., just as in ME., is proved by the long *ɩ* still found in some of the mod. diall.; both words appear with *ɩ* in 35, 37 and 41. Forms with *ɩ* and also *ē* are found as well.

§ 300. *bent* is included here, according to the etymology usually given to it, which must remain till a more satisfactory one is found; cf. Murray NE. Dict. It always rimes with short *ĕ* everywhere.

§ 301. *swyre* would perhaps be more correctly placed under *i* or *y*, for the word is found in OE. with *i* or *y* (see Koch, Ztsfdph. V. 38, &c.), which is here lengthened in open syll., but rimes, contrary to the usage of *i* and *y* when lengthened (see below §§ 364 ff.), with Fr. *i*. Similar rimes are found in Dougl. *swire* : *fire* : *desire* : *conspire* 1. 12. 28, Satir P. *swyre* : *myre* : *fyre*, 39. 350; Hav. *swire* : *sire*, 311. The rime in Dougl. *swair* : *euirmair*, 2. 26. 18, is difficult of explanation. As used in Clar. the word means a neck between two hills, or mountain hollow, "the buks go bak them in the swyre"; so also in Bruce "*redis swyre*"

17. 13 (cf. Skeat's note thereto). Jam. Dict. says the word is confined to the S. of Scotl. in secondary senses.

EO:

§ 302. 1. Before r + cons. — rimes with

a) itself. hart (*heorte*) : smart 1. 122, heart : smert 3. 152, hearts : smarts 3. 626. — b) OE. ea = Angl. a (before r + cons.). heart : inwart 2. 242, 1390 : invart 3. 1472 : eftcrwarte 4. 2188. — c) OE. æ (with metathesis). hearts : carts (*cræt*) 3. 1644. — d) OE. or ON. e. heart : start (prt. ON. *sterta*) 1. 160. warke (*weork*) : sarke (OE. *serce* = ON. *serkr*) 2. 1404. — e) Fr. or Lat. e. heart : advert 1. 526 : revert 3. 1534, 4. 2758. smart : expert 5. 1492. sterve : serve 1. 290, 4. 2270 : proterve 1. 1038 : conserve 2. 386. — f) Fr. a. heart : dairt, 1. 168 : dairte 5. 1334 : deart 5. 1038 : part 2. 178 : depairt 1. 1380 : pairt (sb.) 4. 386, 702 : escart (*escarter* = discard) 2. 1500, hart : depairt 1. 1514, 5. 2526.

§ 303. OE. *eo* became ME. *e* through *œ* (Sweet § 658); but before r there was a tendency in some diall. to change *e* to *a*, which according to Sweet (see Brandl, p. 57, Kluge PG. 1. 877) began earliest in the N. and came into full operation in the 15th cent., but traces of it are to be found in the Midl. dial. of the 14th cent., e. g. in Chauc. (see t. Br. § 48. V) and Rob. of Br. (Menze p. 30), though not proved by rime. The statements of Sweet and Brandl concerning the N. are based on rimes in some of the earliest known North[n] specimens of ME. Brandl, l. c., remarks on the frequency of *a* for earlier *e* in the Mss. of Bruce and Townl. M., but can find no rime to prove an *a*-pronunc.; *e* : *a* rimes are, however, to be found, e. g. starnys : tharnys (ON. *parna*, *parnask*, see Stratm.-Bradl. s. v. and Brate, p. 60), hart : quart in Townl. M. (Sweet HoES., pp. 306, 308) and there is at least one such in Bruce, viz. ʒarne (adv. = diligently, OE. *georne*) : farne (ptc. = fared, OE. *faren*) 3. 548; and for a still older date we have charre (vb. formed from sb. = OE. *cerr*) : waire (OE. *wær*, adj.) in Metr. Hom. (Sweet, p. 306), which were written according to Sweet, § 584, early in the 13th cent. (? Is this a mistake for 14th?). Perhaps we should read *ar* for *er* in some of the other rimes in Bruce and the *a* in the texts is not perhaps always due to the copyist; in fact, the change might have been made by the copyist in the contrary direction, if he belonged to another dial. in which *er* had not become *ar*. The rarity of rimes of proof (perhaps the above is the only one which proves *a*) is not to be wondered at so much, seeing that the author seems altogether to have avoided rimes with words ending in vowellike + cons.; we shall see further below that not a single rime in -*ind* is to be found; the proportion of rimes ending in vowel-like + cons. to the total number is very small indeed, only particular combinations seem to be used at all; the same is to be noticed in other early Sc. texts.

§ 304. The spelling with *a* is found in Sc. texts from Bruce on, and in most of them it is apparently corroborated occasionally by rime; e. g. Sc. Leg. ʒarne : barne (= child) 32/82 (and again seven times in Vol. 1) and perhaps in the following — wark : mark (vb. = direct, wend, march) 134/784, *vark* : *merk* 65/204, *bark* (vb.) : *mark*, sb. 188/778, *ware* (= worse) : *skere* (? = scare) 218/36, *merrys* (vb. 3. sg. *merran*) : *skaris* (MS. *sakiris*, prob. = scares?) 226/596. In the rime *hard* (heard) : *ferd* (= fared, behaved, went), which appears so often, the form *ferd* can be derived from OE. *feran* (instead of *faran*) and so is not a good example; some of the other rimes, too, may admit of an e-pronunc., e. g. *merk*, and others are not certain as to meaning. — K. Q. *hart : art* (2. sg. = es) 114. — Wall. *hart : part* 1. 386 : *Eduuart* 11. 850 : *Stwart* 10. 170. — Gol. has no rimes proving *a* according to Noltemeier p. 24; although *a* is generally written in the MS. in the word *hart (heorte)*, yet the rimes rather prove *e* even in this word, and *e* is written in most other words, and occasionally in *hert* itself. The *a* is either due to the pronunc. at the time of printing (as Nolt. says); or else to a more Southern copyist; cf. *mer* (= mar) : *wer* (= worse, often found in Sc. as *war*) : *ner* (= near) : *fer* (= far) 1019. — Lanc. *asstart : depart* 1138, *hart : dart* 1228, *hard* (= NE. heard, ptc.) : *hard* (= OE. *heard*, adj.) 1654, *hart : part* 1796, &c. — Rat. Rav. *hart : efterwart* 2. 18. — Dunb. *bark : clerk : merk : sark*, p. 18, *clerkis : warkis : markis*, sb., p. 81, *far : bar*, sb., p. 169, *far : ar : war*, adj. : *dar* p. 177. — Dougl. *hart : depart*, 2. 217, 6, *marrit* (= marred) : *charrit* (OE. *cerran*) : *skarrit* (= skared) : *misharrit* (OE. mis. + OE. *heorra* or ON. *hiarri*?) 1. 13. 17, *hart : expert : art*, sb. : *ouir brouderit* 1. 21. 22, *outwart : hart* 2. 34. 24, *hart : part* 2. 50. 30, *cowart : hart : apirsmart* 1. 73. 2, &c. Cf. from the 16th cent. Lyndes *expart : art* Sq. M. 1158, Roll. C. V. *Hart : inwart : smart : conuart* (= converted) 1. 180, *hart : reuert : aduert : smart : part* 1. 692; Satir P. *pairt : desert* 35. 9, *clerks : barks*, 8. 45, *departit : harlit* 10. 394, *partis : peruertis : startis : hartis* 12. 50, &c. — Montg. *dairt : heart* C. 164, *clarkis : markis* C. 406, *hard* (= heard, prt.) : *debard* C. 674, *carte : expert : art : harte* M. P. 40. 28; but compare with these, *waird : gaird* MP. 7. 11, *sterv : suerv : deserv* MP. 34. 42, *fearce : peirce : reheirce* MP. 40. 61.

§ 305. Such rimes, then, cannot serve as a date test, until we know more of the history of the several diall.; and what is more, they admit of two interpretations, one the reverse of the other; they may prove that *ar* has become *er* just as well as that *er* has become *ar*; for, as the mod. diall. show, all parts of Scotl. did not go in the same course. It will be as well, therefore, first to look at the mod. diall.

§ 306. There seems to be a sharp distinction between D. 33 and the remaining diall. of Scotl. In D. 33 we have three classes of *er*-words, i. e. of words which in early MSc. contained the vowel *e*. First, we have the sound æ (or a) in the following — native or Norse words, work (a), heart, smart, starve, far, star, hearth, dark, carve, farm, start, darn, bark, farthing, sark, hark; French words, certain, deter, mercy, prefer, nerve, merle (= blackbird), concern, serpent, err, divert, serve, stern. Secondly, in a very few words (of French origin) we have e, arbour, clerk, firm, alert, (these are perhaps not purely developed but possibly influenced by some outside dial.). Thirdly, we have i' (a fracture not very distinct from Ellis's (ii_1) and (ee^1), see EEP. Vol. 5, p. 710 (3), and probably arising from a previous *ẽ*) in pearl, hearse, herb, perch, search, partridge, sergeant, desert, insert, insertion, assert, disconcert, term, terse, verse, pert, exert (i. e. only in words not of native origin). With the exception, then, of a few words with e, the mod. forms are of *two* kinds, either œr or i'r, arising apparently from previous ĕr and ēr.

§ 307. In the same way there are two sets of *ar*-words, i. e. words derived either from the French, and originally certainly containing *ar*, or from OE. *ear*. First, we have a in farce, barrel, warrant, bar, par, marl, bargain (these words are also probably not of genuine dialectal development, but to be explained in some other way, perhaps direct French influence, or more likely from rec. sp., and must, like the second set above, be set aside). Secondly, in the great majority of words we have the regular development e in part, large, charge, carry, army, scarce, garter, arch, garden, dart, merchant, market, Charley, alarm, harmony, parish, narrative, card, art, charter, Martinmas, marry; also in cart, yard, arm, harm, warn, yarn, ward, swarm, fern, sharp, warp, park; but *a* in warm, hard, and *œ* in mark and spark. Most of these pronunciations will be found in Murray's DSS. pp. 144, 145.

§ 308. We have, then, chiefly three different developments to explain. 1. *hert* > *hœrt*, *serv* > *sœrv*; here the e of MSc. was not lengthened and was changed direct to *œ* as explained by Sweet and Brandl, the same as in the N. of Engl.; it is noticeable, however, that the change occurs before **voiced** as well as **voiceless** consonants.

§ 309. 2. *perl* > *pi'rl*, *desert* > *desi'rt*; here the ĕ was lengthened in MSc. to ē, which became i like any other ē (probably in the 16th cent. or earlier); the i', given by Ellis and Murray, is of a different nature from the i' in (*sti'n*) (= stone, OE. *stān*), which comes, through 16th century ē, from early MSc. ā; the glide ' in *pi'rl* is only due to the following *r*. That the mod. (i'r) comes from MSc. ēr, 16th cent. ir, and not direct from ĕr, is shown by occasional spelling with *ei* in later MSc. texts, e. g. Dougl. *peirle*, 1. 22. 6, *peirlis* (= pearls) 4. 84. 14, *seirching*, 1. 25. 22; Compl. Sc. *eirb* (= herb), Satir. P. *reheirs*, 4. 135 (&c.), *peirle*, 7. 71 (&c.), *peirtly* (= pertly) 13. 210 (&c.), *veirs* : *reheirs*, 20. 1, 24. 104, *seirche* 26. 72, *peirtryks* (= partridges) 33. 396, *peirs* (= pierce) 42. 291, *leirning* 28. 49, *leirnit* 42. 66, Montg. *peirce* : *reheirce* MP. 40. 61. We have the same development occasionally in rec. sp., e. g. *pierce, fierce, tierce*.

We might think of another possibility, viz. that every *er* became uniformly *œr* in MSc. in this dial., and that for the mod. *i'r* the development was *er* > *œr* > *ar* > *ār* > *ēr* > *i'r*, for which the fact, that *i'* is also the resulting mod. sound of undoubted MSc. ā, might seem to speak; but then it is difficult to understand why *part, large*, &c., which were in the *ā* stage before *perl*, &c., should since have fallen behind and never reached the last stage *i'*, and the MSc. spelling with *ei* points too clearly the other way; therefore it is better to explain the *i'* in *pi'rl*, *desi'rt*, as above, from ēr which arose direct from ĕr, but before *ā*r had become ēr, otherwise the latter would have gone further together with it. Here again there is no difference between **r + voiced cons.** and **r + voiceless cons.**

§ 310. 3. *part* > *pĕrt*, *arm* > *ĕrm*. Here *ăr* + cons. in words of Fr. origin became *ār* + cons., and this *ā* followed the course of general MSc. *ā* and became *ē*, i. e. produced *ĕr* + cons. which might then in mod. times undergo a shortening to *ĕr* + cons. in some words (or a half-shortening, the vowels given as short by Murray for D. 33 are all really half-long). That the *ē* did not become *i'* as in *sti'n* < *stēn* < *stān* is due perhaps to the later date of the change *ā* > *ē*, or perhaps more likely to the effect of the following *r*, which preserved the new open *ę̄*. That the *r* did not have a similar effect on the *ē* in *perl*, can be explained by the different nature of this *e* (= closed *ẹ̄*). In the same way we find (meer) and (seer) in 33, for *more* and *sore*, not (mi'r) and (si'r); cf. § 57. We might explain the mod. Sc. *ē* in words of Engl. origin, e. g. *arm*, *sharp*, &c., in the same way, ONthmb. *ārm* (see Sievers, § 158) > *ę̄rm*, &c.; but perhaps in some words a different explanation is necessary, and we must set the first appearance of an *e*-vowel at a very early date, and conclude that this *e* was, or soon became, short and remained so till a comparatively late date; for the beginnings of the change to *e* are found in the ONthmb. dial., cf. Sievers, § 150, (3) and Hilmer, pp. 9 and 23, fracture *ea* was there often represented by *ae*, *e* or *eo*. Only in one word, *beard*, is an *ī* found in mod. Sc. diall., which would represent a MSc. *ē*. Is this to be explained from the influence of rec. sp. or in some other way? Cf. Bruce, *berdlass*, 11. 217.

§ 311. Murray's silence with regard to D. 34 seems to imply that it agrees with D. 33 in the pronunc. of these words, and Ellis, in EEP. P^t 5, interprets the silence in this way; his lists give us very little information respecting the words in question. But my friend Mr. David Anderson, M. A., L. L. B., Advocate, of Edinburgh, has very kindly taken the trouble to get the Edinburgh pronunc. as nearly as possible, and I find there is some difference, especially in the first set of words, in which *er* has become *œr* in 33. In the first list he sent me, Mr. Anderson gave me *e* instead of *œ* in *heart*, *smart*, *starve*, *farm*, *start*, and *stern* for *star*, also an *e* in *err*, but left the remaining words of the first set with *œ* unaltered. He further gave an *ē*-vowel in *farce*, *barrel*, *warrant*, and *ĕ* in *bargain*, and also in the following words not included above, *Mark*, *march*, *March*, *parch*, *barge*, *marsh*, *tart*. The words which in D. 33 have *er* for early ME. *ar*, (see § 307, *yard*, &c.), he gave with *er* also in the Edinb. dial., and in addition *mark* and *spark*, which in 33 have *œ*.

It was evident from this that the *ar*-pronunc. is even less extensive in Edinb. than in D. 33; and thinking that perhaps some of the words, in which Mr. Anderson had allowed *œ* to stand, might have been influenced by rec. sp. or some other Sc. dial., I requested him to test the pronunc. once more, which he did "from the mouth of a man who has spent most of his life in Edinb." As result, his revised list gives an *e*-pronunc. (i. e. pure *e*, not the *ə* of rec. sp.) also in *far*, *hearth*, *dark*, *certain*, *mercy*, *nerve*, *concern*, *serpent*, *divert*, *serve*, *warn* (about *warm* and *hearth* he seemed doubtful and gave both pronunciations). He still gave only *ar* in *carve* and *prefer*, and (AA), = rec. sp. *au*, in *hard*. The words with *i'* in D. 33 are pronounced according to him in the same way in Edinb.

We find, then, that this dialect corresponds much more closely with those further North than with Dr. Murray's dial.

§ 312. For the remaining diall. Ellis's lists are very meagre in respect of these words. In the following I take D. 37 and 38 as example, because Ellis gives us some material from these, and I fortunately have the advantage of the oral information kindly given me by my friend Mr. J. Webster Low, B. A., whose home is in Forfarshire, just about the border line between 37 and 38; his rendering of the pronunc. agrees with Ellis's, where the latter gives any, and on the whole seems to belong to D. 38; but in the pronunc. of these words the two diall. go together.

§ 313. First, *er*-words, i. e. with early ME. or Fr. *er*; here the regular development seems to be *only* e; so in *heart, smart, starve, hearth, farm, start, certain, mercy, nerve, concern, serpent, err, divert, serve, clerk, firm, clergy, herb, perch, sergeant,* (not with *ǝǝ* as in rec. sp., but with *e*). But Mr. Low gives *i'* in some words in which D. 33 has *i'*; so in *pearl, hearse, search, desert*, but the *i* is very short. It is difficult to say whether this is a regular development (the *i* is given by Mr. Low only in four French words, against *e* in fifteen), also whether the *i'* is to be explained in the same way as for D. 33. The following contain an *a*, which is probably to be explained from surrounding consonants (-*k* seems to favour *a*) or from Norse influence: — *work* (with *a* in all Sc. diall.), *far* (ON. *fjarr*?), *star* (ON. *stjarna*).

§ 314. Second, *ar*-words (Fr. *ar*, OE. *ear*, &c.); here there is on the whole perfect agreement with Murray's D. 33, in most of the words we have *e*, (but it seems here to be always long, sometimes particularly so, the result of MSc. *ār*), and in a few *a*, just as in D. 33, see above; also *a* in *mark* and *Mark*, but *e* in *march, March, parch, marsh, tart*.

§ 315. As far as Ellis's materials go, *all* the other diall. agree with this, the vowel *a* is only given in *work, far, star, bargain*, which everywhere have an *a* vowel, and once in *starve* in 42 (but *e* in 35. 36. 38. 39) and once in *part* in 35 (but also *ē* in 35. 38. 39). The other words as *heart, farm, serve, certain*, &c., are only given with *e*.

§ 316. Now the question comes, whether we are to suppose that in these diall., in the *er*-words, the modern *er* is the direct continuation of MSc. *er*, i. e. that there has been no change since the MSc. period, or whether here as elsewhere *er* first became *ær, ar*, in MSc., and then between MSc. and NSc. there has been a refronting of the vowel, a return to *er*. Both are possible. On the one hand, *ar* has certainly become *er* in such words as *part*, &c., and may have gone hand in hand with an *ar* from earlier *er*; on the other hand, there may have been a tendency in these diall. both to retain *er* and to change *ar* to *er*, except where some other influence was at work. This is much simpler, and quite in accordance with what Dr. Murray has observed, viz. that the diall. of Central Scotl. represent an older stage of the language than those of the S., which have undergone a much further development, in the same way as the English of New England and also of Ireland is in many respects more antiquated than Engl. rec. sp. He says, p. 82, this "evidence thus agrees with the historical fact that the Lowland tongue has been longer established South of the Forth than elsewhere in the North-east and West of Scotl. It is a curious though well substantiated philological law, that the transplantation of a language into a new region gives a check to its growth, and interrupts for a time its normal rate of development; so that while the same dial. in its original home continues to grow and change, in its new position it remains for a longer or shorter period stationary at the stage at which it was transplanted. .... There are two tendencies observable in the case of a transplanted language. One is that produced by contact with the language which it supersedes, and which always gives something of itself to the new comer; the other is the conservative tendency produced by reaction against the contact which strives to fix and crystallise, as it were, the new tongue in its actual state."

§ 317. Taking this view of the matter we may draw the following scheme of development for the diall. in question (all but 33): —

		16th cent.	19th cent.
early ME. er Fr. er	}	er	ēr
early ME. ar Fr. ar	} ār	ĕ̄r	ĕ̄r

Compare
| early MSc. | ā | ē̜ | ō̜, ī |
| | ē | ī | ī |

For D. 33 we can represent as follows: —

		16th cent.	19th cent.
early ME. er	⟩ ĕr	ær	ær
Fr. er ⟨ ēr		ōr, īr	ī'r
early ME. ar Fr. ar	} ār	ĕ̄r	ĕ̄r

Compare
| early MSc. | ā | ē̜ | i' |
| | ē | ī | ī |

The above is suggested with all diffidence; there are difficulties in the way, however we try to explain. To decide with certainty we require more exact chronological knowledge than we have at present of the dialects of *Middle* Scotch.

§ 318. At any rate the rimes give us here another proof that the author's dial. was not that of D. 33; *heart* and *part* cannot rime there at the present day and they did not do so in the 16th cent.; for having originally contained different sounds and being different to day, it is impossible that they can have coincided at any intermediate period. And this being so, the rimes must be interpreted in accordance with some dial. other than that of D. 33, and therefore it is possible that the rimes between older *e* and *a* prove rather that *a* has become *e* than *vice versâ*, except perhaps in the word *wark* (which may have had already its general mod. pronunc.) and *sarke*, and, if so, then also *mark*, cf. the rimes, warke : sarke, sarke : marke; but this must remain doubtful, the author may have used two pronunciations; *wark* was, however, the regular MSc. form, just as in mod. Sc.; cf. Sc. Leg. *warke* 5/14, Satir. P. *work* : *stark* 5. 113, *vark* : *dark* : *mark* : *vark*, 44. 16, but *clerk* : *werk* 42. 234, 972. The spelling with *a*, *hart*, *smart*, *start*, must then be attributed to a scribe who must have been either from the N. of Engl. or the S. of Scotl.

§ 319. The rimes in (f) are particularly interesting; to the eye they are almost altogether imperfect. According to our supposition the vowel is *e*, probably long, in all the words; it would be so to a man from D. 34 or 38, for instance (*hĕrt* : *pĕrt* for *heart* : *part* would be a perfect rime to-day in 34 or 38), but to a man from D. 33 the sound would be *œr* or *ar* in *hart* and *ēr* in *dairt*, *pairt*, *depairt*, and the spelling in the latter words is quite in accordance with this, for there is no doubt that *ai* means, in the 16th cent., the *ē* which arose out of earlier *ā* which was written *ai*. This is plain not only from rimes with undoubted *ē*, but also from the occasional interchange of *ai* and *e*, and some rimes between *ē* and *ĕ*, written *ai* and *e*. A few examples will suffice, e. g. Dunb. *waist* : *haist*, 32. 30, in another MS. spelt *west* : *hest*, Satir. P. *traist*, adj. : *raist* (= rest), 10. 138, cf. *trest*, vb. : *rest* 17. 183, *gaist* (= guest) : *manifest* 34. 75; in Montg. we find *blait* (= bleat, OE. *blǣtan*), *implaidging* (= pledging), where there is no question of *ai* possibly meaning *ā*; it must have meant *ē* or *ĕ*. We have similar indications in the MS. of Clar., e. g. *dewaist* (= divest) : *rest* 2. 850, *gaist* (= guest) : *possest* 4. 500, and *ay*, which means the same as *ai*, is always written in the word *livaray*, *levaray*, where Fr. *e* cannot have become *ā*.

§ 320. It is then certain that *ai* meant *ē* in the 16th cent. and *air* must have meant *ēr*; and the spelling with *ai* and *e*, and rimes with *e*, give us an interesting proof of the establishment of the *ē*-pronunc., which is found in the mod. diall., in the words which had previously contained *ā*. It is very probable that this was so even earlier then the 16th cent.; cf. Bruce, *herd*, adj. 12. 530, 14. 26, 19. 642, *herd*, adv. 18. 482, *sterkar* (= stronger) 15. 491, Sc. Leg. *gerris* (= makes, usually spelt *gars*) 3/10, *gert* 6/85, Early Sc. Laws (end of 14th cent., in vernacular translation) *pert* (= part), *mercat* (= market) (see DSS. p. 32), Sc. Acts of Parlt (AD. 1424, 1436) *mercat*, *merchande* (see DSS. p. 39). For the 16th cent. the following examples can be given in addition to Clar. — Gol. *merk*, Dunb. (see Kaufmann, p. 51), *ern*, *sperkis*, *berd*, *scherp*, *stervit*, Dougl. *schairpe*, 1. 28. 12, *rewarde* : *lairde* 1. 86. 24, *barn* : *dern* 4. 23. 12, *expert* : *dart* 4. 67. 28, *smert* 4. 70. 16, *sterve* : *deserve* 4. 75. 2. Lyndes. Sat. *rewairds* : *lairds* 1547, *Laird* : *spaird* 2592, *bairds* (= bards) : *Lairds* 2608, *spaird* : *wairde*, vb. 4489, Satir. P. *gaird* : *rewaird* : *Laird* 7. 219, *regaird* : *spaird* (= spare) : *rewaird* 14. 86, *paird* : *divertt* 27. 40, *paird* : *desert* 27. 128, *hairme* 35, 59, *schairpe* 35. 64 (&c.), *hairt* 36. 1 (&c.), *lairge* 36. 59, *gaird* : *prepaird*, 35. 18, *expert* : *hairt* : *mairt* : *paird* 36. 119, *foirwairnd* 41. 62, *forwairns* 45, 5, *baird* : *rewarde* 45. 917, *Berge* (= barge) : *chairge*

46. 3, *cairdit* (= carded) 48. 41, *harme* : *werme* 48. 95, *bergane* (= bargain) 17. 77, *mercat* (= market) 20. 22, *merkis* 45. 223, *perciall* (= partial) 47. 1, *onmerkit* 47. 32, Montg. *harte* : *advert* : *darte*, MP. 47. 16, *heart* : *convert* MM. 22. The following examples show what confusion there was in the use of *er* and *ar* in the words *peril, quarrell*, Sc. Leg. *parele* 5/6, Gol. *beryell* (= beryl) : *quarrell* : *pereill* 1088, Satir. P. *perell* : *querrell* 27. 43, *parrell* 31. 119, *parrell* : *querrell* 38. 88, *parel* : *quarel* 39. 176, *perrell* : *querrell* 43. 200. Hume in his Orthographie &c., AD. 1617, (EETS. 5) gives us later testimony for the sound $\bar{e}$ in *part*; on p. 10, § 2, he proposes *ae* to be written for the sound $\bar{e}$ in *shour of hael*, and in § 4 he writes *paert*.

§ 321. The orthoepists of the 16th cent. give double forms for England with $\bar{a}$ and $\breve{a}$ before *r*-combinations in Fr. words, e. g. *lărge, chărge*, &c., and in the native words *bărn, wărn*, see Kluge, PG. 1. 876, so that the forms *lẹrge, chẹrge, bẹrn, wẹrn*, were perhaps also possible in England, (as Kluge says, $\bar{a}$ was of a very palatal nature all through the 16th cent. in Engl.), unless the authorities referred to were only quoting Sc. forms when they gave the long vowel.

§ 322. It is pretty clear, since *ai* meant $\bar{e}$ for one at least of the scribes, that he pronounced *pērt* (= part), &c., and, like the author probably, also knew nothing of an *a*-pronunc. in the Fr. & Lat. words in § 302 (e) which are spelt with an *e*. The difference in spelling in *pairt* and *expert* is quite intelligible; it is the result of traditional spelling and perhaps of the learning of the scribe; *pairt* had formerly had an $\bar{a}$, but *expert* had always had *e* and there was the existence of the Fr. word to keep him from writing *ai*; perhaps, too, a difference of quantity, *pairt* with $\bar{ẹ}$ and *expert* with $\breve{ẹ}$. Perhaps in *heart* the author had a double pronunc. $\bar{\breve{ẹ}}$, hence the riming with both sets § 302 (e) and (f).

The rimes in (a), (b), (c), (d) all admit of the same interpretation, that the vowel is *e*; although those in (b), (c), (f), might of themselves imply the very reverse, that *er* has become *ar*, yet the evidence of the mod. diall. and the orthographical irregularities together point the other way. Still it is here also uncertain how far the author may have adopted an Engl. pronunc.

§ 323. Kluge, in PG. 1. 875, explains the double forms *mark* : *merk*, *barn* : *bẹrn* from doubleness of origin, OE. *mearc* : ON. *merke*, ON. *barn* : OE. *bearn*. The foregoing paragraphs show that this is unnecessary; if *barn* were only due to Norse influence we should expect to find this form especially in the N., and the case is just the reverse, the $\bar{e}$-forms are the prevalent Sc. forms, and are independent of the character of the cons. following the *r*, so that it is not necessary to assume that OE. *ear* produces *ar* before a voiceless cons. and $\bar{e}r$ before a voiced cons., as we must do with the above explanation of Kluge's.

§ 324. It will be noticed that *heart* is almost always spelt with *ea*, which appears occasionally in other words of this class, e. g. *deart, pearte* (= part) 4. 2579, *search*, &c. This is most likely English orthography, and means probably $\bar{ẹ}$; but why it should be particularly used in this word is not clear; *ea* is written nearly, if not quite, without exception in *Earl*, and *sea* has invariably *ea*; otherwise it is not very much used, the reason being that *ai* represented in Scotl. the open ẹ̄ which was represented in Engl. by *ea*. But there seems to have been altogether an Anglicising tendency on the part of one of the scribes; we notice it in the substitution of -*ght* for -*cht*, *ʒoung* for *ʒing*, *maiden* for *may*, (the latter even to the destruction of the rime). So with *ea*; where used, it must generally have meant *ē*. In the following words it can only have meant the earlier *ā* or the later ẹ̄ : — *heast*, *leave* (= remainder, : *save*, *gave*, &c.), *heave* (= have : *saue*), *bease-dance*, *beace* (: *space*), *recleame* (: *fame*), &c.; and in the following it can only have meant the earlier *ē* (ẹ̄ in Engl.) or the later *ī*. : — *leave* (= permission), *beames*, *heade*, *speache*, *meane*, vb., *leave*, vb., *leaves* (of tree), *streames*, &c. Therefore the general value was ẹ̄, and the alternate spellings prove the same, e. g. *haist*, *heast*, *receave*, *resaue*, *speach*, *speech*, *meane*, *meinit*, *pealʒeoun*, *pailʒeoun*, *leaves*, *leives*, (in two consecutive lines, 5. 286, 287). In one case *ea* represents an older pronunciation for the younger *ei*, i. e. an English or Anglicising scribe had the older pronunc. ẹ̄ in words in which the Sc. diall. already had ī, represented by the alternative spelling *ei*, and in the other a younger pronunc. for the older *a*, *ai* (= *ā*), i. e. the pronunc. of the scribe agrees with that of the author, ẹ̄, but he expresses it by an Engl. orthography, *ea*, instead of Sc. *ai*. When *least* can be written for *lest*, *readie* by the side of *reddie*, *traist* by the side of *trest*, the value of the *ea* can only be an *e*-sound. Thus we see that the orthography is altogether very confused, but we conclude that *ea* before *r* + *cons.* means *e*, and is only the Engl. equivalent of the Sc. *ai*, which is also sometimes replaced by *e*.

§ 325. If the author used the dial. of D. 38 or 34 or of a corresponding district, probably he only knew the sound *er* in all the words we are discussing; but in the text we find no less than *five* different spellings: — the Sc. *ai* in *pairt*, *depairt*, *rewaird*, *airlie*, *bairnis*, *lairg* (= large), *dairt*, *waird* (= weird, fate), *wairn*, &c.; the Engl. *ea* in *heart*, *hearpe*, 2. 446, *pearte* (= part) 4. 2579, *search*, *pearle*, *fearce*, *rehearse* (: *verse*), *dearte*, *heard* (= herd), *peart* (= apert) : *desert* 3. 1004, *beard*; *e* in *herp* (= harp) 2. 352, *hertfullie*, *perke* (= park) 4. 1739, *merchald* (= marshalled) 4. 2436, *smert*, *enermit* (= unarmed) 1. 118, *mervell*, *persoun*, *dwerff* (= dwarf) 1. 478, and in many more words from Fr. in which rec. sp. has *er* (being of such rare occurrence, these *er* forms are perhaps forms written by the author and left unaltered by the scribe); *a* in *hard* (= heard, prt.), *armeine* (= ermine), *start*, *staris* (= stars), *farder*, *hart*, *marmaid*, *wnarmit*, *harberie*, *wark*, *smart*, &c., (here, of course, *a* is meant, which points to a scribe from the S. of Scotl. or some part of Engl.; the change from Fr. *er* to *ar* is found in almost all mod. Engl. diall.); and once *ei* in *peirt* (= pert : *desert*) 9. 2166. This last is one solitary example which can point to the *i'r* of D. 33, for *ei* meant *ī* in the 16th cent., including the chief scribe of our MS., see § 127. There are no more traces of this pronunc. for the scribe, and no rimes at all to prove it for the author, in words of Fr. origin.

7*

§ 326. *eard*, OE. *eorþe*, rimes with OE. *eo* and Angl. $\bar{e}$ = WS. $\bar{\imath}e$.
eard : raird (OE. *reord*, for *reard, Goth. razda) 1. 734.
: steird (prt. of Angl. *stēran*) 3. 366.

This is not included above as the development is here different from that of the other words containing OE. *eor*; the second rime plainly shows that the vowel is $\imath$ from previons $\dot{e}$. In OE. the *eo* was lengthened before *rþ*, hence a ME. $\dot{e}$. In Sc. this $\dot{e}$ remained, but in Engl. it became $\dot{e}$ on account of the *r*, just as in the words *learn*, *earnest*, *earl*, *heard*, hence the spelling with *ea* in rec. sp., cf. Kluge, PG. I. 880. In Engl. the vowel was also shortened. In MSc. texts we often find *eird*, e. g. Henryson, *eird* : *effeird* : *appeired*, Dougl. *eird* : *weird* : *Feird* (= 4th) : *vnleird* (= unlearned) 1. 81. 5, Roll. C. V. *eird* : *leird*, Prol. 78, Montg. *eird* : *appeird*, C. 108: *weird* MP. 46. 32; cf. also the spelling of the rimeword *steird*. But the last scribes seem to have pronounced it with open $\dot{e}$, for which they used the Engl. symbol *ea* (it is generally *eard* in the text, but sometimes also *erd*, 1. 497, 503, &c.); but in the other rime-word *raird*, for the same sound, one of the scribes has used the Sc. *ai*, though elsewhere we find *rearde*, 4. 1039, *reard*, 5. 2030, *reardit* (prt. = resounded) 4. 1660, 5. 2322. This latter word generally has $\dot{e}$ or $\imath$ in MSc. and is often spelt with *ei*, so Gol. *reirdit*, Montg. *reird*, vb, S. 12, "Can thunder reird the higher for a horne?"; Orm has also *rę̄rd*. The rimes must be altered to *eird* : *reird* : *steird*, cf. Dunb. *reird* : *eird*, 27. 85. The above rimes are also proof of the change from *rþ* to *rd*, which is so frequent in Sc. texts.

The mod. diall. agree generally with the form used by the author of Clar. rather than with that used by the scribes and represented in other texts by *erd*; they nearly all have (jerd), commencing with a consonantal *i* or *y*, the development being probably thus, MSc. $\dot{e}rd$ > $\imath rd$ > $i'rd$ > *ierd* > *jerd*, with shifting of the accent from the *i* to the following parasitic *e*, which thus became the bearer of the syll., while *i* was changed from sonant to consonant. This form or a similar one is given by Ellis in 35, 38, 39, and, with the same initial sound, but *th* at the end, in 33 and 36. In D. 35, 36, 39, *ĕrth* is also found, and in 42 *ērt*.

§ 327. *starne* : *decerne* 2. 902, *star* : *Lucifer* 2. 1398.

Starne and *star* owe their spelling with *a* certainly to the scribes, the vowel was in both cases *e* for the author. Cf. for the first form the *sterrne* of Orm (Brate, p. 58, derives it from the unfractured form of ON. *stjarna*); and further in Bruce, *stern* 4. 127, *sternis* 4. 711, Dunb., *sternis* 2. 3, *stern* 1. 52, Dougl. *leidsterne* : *eterne* 2. 17. 26 : *decerne* 2. 64. 26, Gau, *sterne* 67. 8, Wisd. Sol. *sternis* 812, Hamp. P. C. *sterne*, Destr. Troy, *sterne* 1057, 1498. We find the same spelling *starne* in the text in 5. 2076, cf. Montg. *starnis* : *harnis* (= brains) C. 227.

The form (starn, stærn) is given by Ellis only in D. 33, (for which œr instead of *er* is characteristic) and in 42, (which shows irregularities in many ways); we find (stAAr) in 35, and (star) in 38 and 39 but there is no trace of *ster* or *stern*. Is the *a* in *far* and *star*, *starn*, due to a later second Norse influence after the *e* was fractured to *ja*, or merely to be explained from rec. sp.? The text shows elsewhere *staris* 4. 1104, *lodstar*

4. 1202, *star* 1. 22, but we have *sterre*, *sterres* in K. Q. st. 1 and 99, and in Dunb. *ster* : *desuper* 10. 3.

§ 328. *schorte* rimes only with words containing Fr. o —
schort : report 1. 1556 : disport 2. 568 (&c.) : sport 2. 630, 5. 1506 : support 3. 50 : sorte 3. 1044, schorte : report 3. 1232.

The *e* in OE. *sceort* merely marked the palatal nature of the *c*, hence *sce > sch*, and the *o* remains and rimes perfectly regularly.

§ 329. 2. Before l + cons. — rimes with
OE. i — silke : ilke 3. 960

silc is found in OE. already as well as *seolc*, cf. Koch, Ztsfdph. 5. 38, and at the same time ON. *silki* may have been of influence in fixing the *i*, cf. t. Br. p. 36; the adj. *silcen* may also have helped.

The word is not given by Ellis in his lists, but the similar word *milk* is found with an *e*-vowel in 33, 35, 36, 38, 39, 42, probably a recent development of *i* on account of the following *l*.

EO'

§ 330. = (1) Gmc. eu, (2) contraction from $\breve{e}$, $\breve{i}$, $\breve{y}$, with following *a* or *u*, through dropping of intermediate *h* or *j*. Both kinds of *eü* are treated alike.

1. Not followed by w, g or h. — rimes with

a) itself. thrie : be 1. 1294, 4. 2320 : sie (*sēon*) 5. 1420. be : see 1. 1016, 1544 : se 2. 378, 3. 604 : sie 3. 1786 (&c.) : kne 3. 148 : glie 5. 804. knie : sie (*seon*) 5. 1072 : se 4. 40, kne : se 3. 2242. scho, (pron.) : be 4. 828 (&c.) : sie 5. 1726 : knie 5. 1438, schoe : see 4. 2068 : be 5. 1450. betweine : beine (inf.) 4. 2230, 5. 1236 : beine, ptc., 4. 2234, 5. 1064 : seine, inf. 4. 2390, betwine : seine, inf., 3. 1916. — b) OE. $\bar{eo}$ + gutt, see § 346 (a). — c) General OE. or ON. $\bar{e}$, see § 192 (d). — d) OE. $\bar{e}$ = Angl. $\bar{oe}$, mut. of $\bar{o}$, see § 185 (c). — e) Angl. $\bar{e}$ = WS. $\bar{ie}$, see § 190 (d). — f) OE. $\bar{oe}$, mut. of $\bar{a}$, see §§ 226 (g), 241 (d). — g) Angl. $\bar{e}$ = WS. $\bar{oe}$, see § 212 (e). — h) Angl. $\bar{u}$ + gutt. = WS. $\bar{ea}$ + gutt., see §§ 217 (a), 223 (a), 225. — i) OE. $\bar{u}$. scho, (pron.) : wo 3. 2264. — k) OE. $\bar{o}$. scho : do (inf.) 3. 826 : to 3. 1018. — l) OE. or ON. $\breve{e}$. quheill (*hweöl < *hweohol*) : weill (sb. *wela*) 3. 524, see § 132. beheld (prt.) : feild 1. 216 (&c.), see § 172. — fell, prt. : tell 3. 564 (&c.) : dwell 3. 2284. — m) ON. jū. seik (adj. *sēoc*) : meike 3. 1542. — n) ON. øy, see § 499 (b). — o) ON. ig. be : womanlie 5. 504. — p) Fr. e. thre : degree 1. 364 : mellie 1. 502 : contrie 2. 2, thrie : dignitee 4. 2518. deir(e) : cleire 1. 24 (&c.) : altare (OFr. *alter*, see Behrens Franz. St. 5. 83, not from OE. *altar*) 4. 2410 : spheire 5. 2230. ʒeid : proceid 2. 80. scho (pron.) : pitie 3. 836 : adversitie 3. 2058 : degrie 4. 2556 : countrie 5. 566. kne : humilitie 1. 1536. see, se, sie : cuntrie 1. 116 (&c.), contrie 1. 862 : weritie 4. 404 : bewtie 3. 772 : destanie 4. 2092, and many more. be : pitie 3. 136 (&c.) and many more. — q) Fr. ie, later e. betwine : contine 2. 554. siene (inf.) : contine 5. 2062. beine, inf. : conteine 3. 2434 : perteine 5. 1002, beine, ptc. : susteine 3. 2106. beine, ind. sg. : conteine 2. 1510, beine, ind. pl. : susteine 1. 438. fleice (*flēos*) : Greice 5. 74.

deir (e), adj. : inquire 1. 1454 : coller 1. 1564 : colleir 4. 2010 : maneir (e) 1. 138 (&c.) : cheir 1. 1366, 3. 614 : inteir 4. 2650 : require 2. 1684 : requyre 4. 2080 : cleire 4. 1992, 2738. deir (sb. *deor*) : cheire 5. 1194. — r) Fr. ei. thrie : monie 4. 492. se, sie : monie 4. 1334, 5. 2496. — s) Fr. ieu. be ; perdie 5. 16, 1504. — t) Fr. i. be : supplie, suplie, 3. 1370, 120.

§ 331. This belongs to t. Br.'s γ-class of e-vowels, which produced ρ everywhere in ME.; in our text it has, like every other earlier $\bar{e}$, the value $\bar{\imath}$, cf. the rimes with ON. *ig* and Fr. *i* in (o) and (t), see §§ 125, 126. We have $\gamma : \gamma$ rimes in (a), (b), (c), (d), (e), (m), (n), (p), (q), (s), $\beta : \gamma$ rimes in (f) and (g). Those in (h) can be reckoned $\alpha : \gamma$ rimes, cf. § 220; in (l), *quheill* : *weill*, we have certainly an $\alpha : \gamma$ rime; those in (r) are only apparently so, for we find *mone* (: the) as early as the 14th cent., which Behrens, PG. 1. 822, explains by exchange or assimilation of suffix. $\bar{eo}$ before *r* is treated in the same way as in other positions, cf. the word *deir* above.

§ 332. The words *knie*, *trie*, *glie*, are, of course, derived from the OE. nominatives *cnēō*, *trēō*, *glēō*, or Nthmb. *trē*, &c. (cf. Sievers, § 250, 2 and 247, note 3); the *w* of the inflected forms (gen. *trēowes*, *cnēōwes*, *glēōwes*) has left no trace here, as, for example, in Roll. C. V. *glew* (= glee) : *vntrew*, Prol. 31 : *blew* (= blue) : *trew* : *hew* (= hue, sb.) 1. 90 : *persew* : *new* : *rew* 1. 243 : *few* : *trew* : *persew* 3. 97, Lyndes. *glew* : *knew*, Sq. M. 1040. This form for *glee* is also found in Engl. texts, e. g. Rob. Br., Gen. Ex., Hav., Metr. Hom., Map.; Dougl. has the verb *glew* (to make merry) : *trew* : *hew* : *rew* 1. 106. 4, but *gleis* (sb. pl.) : *greis* : *treis* : *seis* : *tapestries* 1. 2. 3. The mod. diall. show $\bar{\imath}$ in these words almost uniformly throughout, (except in D. 33, where (ei) is generally found for final $\bar{\imath}$ of the remaining diall.).

§ 333. The shortened form of $\bar{eo}$ is found in rime in the prt. *fell*, see above in (l) and in *fled*, see (f) and (g) (although the rime-word is spelt *adreid*, the vowel is short, cf. § 213), and even in *fred* see § 226 (g), where in rec. sp. we have the long vowel $\bar{\imath} < \bar{\rho}$; perhaps the latter is a new formation, for shortening should be the rule, and *free* and *flee* ought to be treated alike.

The case of *fred* for *freed*, shows that the form *fled* can be explained as a weak prt. of *flee*, just as well as from a conjectured OE. *flēdan*, to flow; cf. Zupitza, Litt. Bl. 1885, 610. Is not the difference of meaning alone a rather formidable difficulty for the latter derivation? Just as *fred* stands over against the *frēōde* of Laȝ., so *fled* against *flēōde* or *flēde*.

In *beheld* the vowel is not shortened, as is shown by the rime with *feild*, cf. § 172, or else the rime is imperfect; it was so apparently to the scribe; cf. *biheeld*, Langl.

§ 334. *greit*. In 3. 112, "bristing out of greit", there may be an error, *of* for *to*; cf. 3. 166, "brist out to greit", or it may be a lawful construction, for which analoga can be found, where *of* apparently precedes the infin. and where in mod. Engl. we should use *to*, e. g. More, Utopia (p. 124, Arber's edit.) we find, "yf any thing ..... should chance of offend and myslyke them". Or *greit* may be a noun, cf. *grēte* in C. M. 189 (from

ON. *grēti*, according to Bradley) and Aunt. Arth. XXV, and Mir. Pl. 150. This is unlikely if Bradley's etymol. is correct, for ON. *œ* generally produces an open *ę* in Sc., which never becomes *i*, cf. § 245. But we can compare Goth. *grēts*, sb. = weeping; the corresponding Angl. form for this, if there was one, would contain *ē*, which would produce MSc. *ę̄* and *i*.

§ 335. The verb is very common in MSc. and is still found in dial., being quite common in the N. of Engl. and in Scotl. Gregor gives *greet*, (pronounce *grīt*), *grat*, *grutten*, as the conjugational forms of the vb. in his Banffshire Glossary. It is also found in Spenser, Shep. Cal. April, l. 1. *greete* : *sweete*. The form of the pres. could be derived from OE. *grǣtan*, *grētan* or *greōtan*, (the latter alone is given by Sievers, Ags. Gram.). The cognate languages show corresponding forms only to the former; Goth. *grētan*, ON. *grāta*, MHG. *grāʒan*. But the other forms, *grat*, *grutten*, in mod. diall., which are confirmed by MSc. forms (quotations are given by Jam. Dict. s. v. *greit*, e. g. we find grat : sat, &c., cf. § 285), especially the ptc. form, are rather to be derived from the other form OE. *greōtan*, of the 2nd Ablautsreihe. In either case the pret. would be irregular, both *grēt* and *grēat* would produce MSc. *grę̄t*, NSc. *grīt* and thus coincide with the pres., but we have shown above how *a* has arisen in the preterites of other verbs of the 2nd Ablautsreihe, and the *u* of the ptc. *grutten* is more easily explained from this class than from the redupl. form *grǣtan*. For this reason the word is included here under *ēo*, contrary to the etymol. usually given to it. BT. gives *grǣtan*, *grētan*, prt. *grēt*, *grēton*, ptc. *grētēn*; *grēten*, with 9 references to passages in which it is used, and *greōtan*, *grēat*, *gruton*, *groten*, with only 2 references; but it would seem either that the latter was the more usual form in the N., or that it eventually gained the upper hand, or else it is a case of complete transfer into another class. The same dial. (Banffshire) conjugates in a similar way *loup* (= leap, OE. *hleapan* or ON. *hlaupa*?), *lap*, *luppen*; this is a clear case of transfer; Dunb. has *lap*, prt., and Dougl. *lap* : *gap* : *hap* 1. 63. 28. The form *greōtan* would be Goth. *griutan; OSax. *griotan* is found. The verb is not found at all in the S. of Engl. (Bülbring, p. 108).

§ 336. scho. In our MS. only *scho* or *schoe* is written, although the majority of the rimes prove the form *sche*; there are only three rimes to prove an *o*-pronunc., one of these being with *wo*, which contains a Southern *ō* for Sc. *ā*, see § 330, (i) and (k). This *scho* is the regular N. Engl. and Sc. form for Midl. *she*, and it seems that the author here with three exceptions entirely gave up his native pronunc. while the scribes always substituted the Northern *scho* for the author's *sche* or *she*. The consistency of the spelling *scho* is a remarkable contrast to the variety which is found in other words.

§ 337. The form has always been a puzzle to those attempting an explanation. Morsbach, p. 121, says *sēo* in stressed position gives *sē* in ME. and in unstressed position *sho*, and through contamination of the two forms arose the *she* of rec. sp. But if this be correct, why do we not find the form *sē* in ME. texts? and why in Northern texts often only *scho* in both stressed and unstressed position? Kluge, PG. 1. 902, suggests the possibility of Norse influence, OIcel. *sjā*; but where is the Northern Engl. and Sc. form with *ā* which would be the correct representative of *sjā*? It is better to derive from *scó* with stress-shifting, (which we are also compelled to accept in other cases), and explain as Morsbach does his "unstressed form" and Sweet the $\chi ho < heo$, viz. thus *séo* > *seó* > *sjo*, written *scho*.

§ 338. But why this development should be confined to the N. is difficult of explanation. Perhaps Murray's assumption (DSS. p. 126) of Celtic influence ($s > sh$ before *e*) is hardly necessary, it does not account for the loss of *e* and also requires the acceptance of stress-shifting, and with the latter alone the *sh* would arise without any help at all from Celtic influence. The difficulty seems increased by the fact that in nearly all the mod. diall. of Sc. as represented in Ellis's lists, we find *shī* as in rec. sp. (*ei* of course in D. 33); in D. 36 a closed $\bar{e}$ is found by the side of *ī*, of which it is merely a variation; we find *ī* in 34. 35. 36. 38. 39. 40. But we do find the correct representative of MSc. *shō*, viz. (shəə), in D. 41 and 42, where OE. and MSc. *ō* has become (əə) generally. Of these diall. (the Orkneys and Shetland Isles), Ellis says, p. 788, "the present language is English, taught by Lowlanders, chiefly from the N. Lowland districts, to Norwegians. It is therefore an acquired tongue, and has not lasted long enough to be a true dialect". But it can give us older forms which have become obsolete on the mainland, and perhaps it is not altogether obsolete there, for the *shī* of D. 39 and 40 can also represent MSc. *shō*, since in this dial. earlier *ō* has generally become *ī*, e. g. *rīf*, *stīl*, *brīm* = rec. sp. *roof, stool, broom* (cf. § 462).

§ 339. But the question arises, what has become of the *shō*-form in the remaining diall.? for in none of the others further S. than D. 39 and 40 has *ō* regularly become *ī*, and yet *she* always appears with *ī*. In Engl. we find forms equivalent to ME. *shō*, with *u* or *o*, only in S. Yorks., Lancs. and Derbyshire, D. 22, 24, 26, and part of 31. In other diall. we find *ī* or *ei*. But *shō* was the regular MSc. form, also of the Central Counties, and of the N. of Engl. as well, as will be seen from the material given below, collected from various texts. The only explanation seems to be in the Anglicising influence, which, probably proceeding from the capital, Edinburgh, introduced the Southern form *shē* or *shī*. and drove out the proper native form as far as the extreme N. of Scotl., where it survives in D. 39. 40, 41, 42, and a considerable distance southwards into England, where it enjoys a still more limited existence in the districts mentioned. This Anglicising influence is evident in many MSc. texts, as is naturally to be expected, and would seem, from the evidence of the mod. diall., not to have been confined to the literary language, unless the disappearance of *sho* is only of more recent date. Many MSc. texts show both forms *scho* and *sche*, but there are few which have such a preference for the *ē*-form as Clar. and in none is the *o*-form altogether absent except K. Q. The fact that the scribes often write *o* where the authors must have written *e*, shows that the new pronunciation proceeded from the higher classes, poets, courtiers, &c.

§ 340. Bruce has always *scho* (with one exception, *sche*, 13. 635), once proved by rime, *scho* : to 4. 760. In Sc. Leg. *scho* is always written, as yet I have noticed no case of it in rime. K. Q. has only *sche* (not in rime); Wall., always *scho* (not in rime); Gol., not found, according to Noltemeier; Lanc. *scho* once in l. 1169, but usually *sche* or *she*, in rime *sche* : *see* 2798, *shee* : *free* 2390, *sche* : *fre* 2298; Dunb. *scho*, rarely *sche* (Kaufmann, p. 81), both forms in rime, *sche* : *do* : *to*, p. 161, *sche* : *degre* p. 218, in the Freiris of B. (attrib. to Dunb.) *scho* : *to*, l. 434; Dougl. *scho* and *sche* both in text and rime, but *sche* predominating in both, *scho* : *ado* 2. 13. 12 : *ado* : *lo* 1. 70. 20 : *se* : *bewtie* : *ee* 1. 19. 5, *sche* : *kne* 2. 40. 2 : *Phenicie* 2. 41. 10 : *be* 2. 43. 8 : *hie* (= high) 2. 50. 6 : *se* (= sea) 2. 57. 22, &c.; Compl. Sc., *sche* and *scho* (author probably from the Southern Counties — Murray, Introd.); Lyndes. mostly *scho*, *sho* in text, but *sche* : *Heresie*, Kittie's Conf. 20; Roll. C. V., *scho* always written (not in rime); Satir P. only *sho*, *scho*, : *ado* : *to* 12. 142 : *Cro* : *to* : *do* 24, 71 : *to* 30. 96; Winzet *sche* and *scho*; Montg. *scho* : to C. 174, 294, *sho* : *do* MP. 30. 33.

§ 341. Northern England — Sir Tr., only *sche*, once in rime, : *fre* : *me* : *be* : *se* 237 (*hye*, 101, is another form altogether due to the Southern scribe, Kölbing, p. 78); this appearance of *sche* in such an early text is further support for the suggestion of the southern portion of N. Engl. as the home of the author; Kölbing, p. 77, excludes Yorks. — Horn Ch. *scho* : *do* (Caro, p. 22). — Thom. of Castelf. always *scho*, : *do* : *unto*, (Perrin, p. 23). — York Pl., *sho*, *she*, *scho*, *sche*, (Kamann, p. 45). — Hamp. *sco*, *sho*. — Octav. (North^n version) *scho* in Linc. MS., *sche*, *she* in Camb. Ms. (not in rime); the South^n version has *sche* : *cyte* : *be* : *þre*, 509. — Sir Egl. generally *sche*, four times *scho* (Zielke, p. 44). — Thom. Erc. *scho* in T, *she* in other Mss. — Sir Perc. *scho*.

§ 342. It seems, then, that *sche*, *she*, came into use in Sc. poetry in the course of the 15th cent., but only in those writers who are in other respects not free from Engl. influence. In writers of pure Sc. it is unknown even to the end of the Sc. literary period, e. g. Montg. But since that time it has naturalised itself in most of the diall. The author of Clar. is in this respect almost as anglicised as James I and the author of Lanc. In Northern Engl. Sir. Tr. stands alone in having *she* at such an early date. This form is found, however, in many texts of the 14th cent., but rimes of proof are still wanting for this cent. and also the next.

§ 343. OE. *ēode* only appears with ɪ < ę, not with ō, cf. Dougl. *ʒoid* : *woid* (= mad) 2. 113. 18, but *ʒeid* (not in rime), 2. 93. 21.

§ 344. breist, OE. *brēost*, has not shortened its vowel as in rec. sp.; the mod. Sc. diall. have all *brĭst* or *brīst* (in D. 33 Ellis gives *brĕst* as well), and the MSc. Mss. have generally *ei* (= ɪ), e. g. Lyndes. *breistis* : *preists*, Sat. 1063, *breist* : *neist* : *preist* Sat. 538, and so nearly everywhere. Chauc. has both long and short vowel, *brẹst* and *brĕst*.

§ 345. seik, rec. sp. *sick*, has a long vowel, as usual in Msc., see § 330 (m); the mod. diall., however, have ɪ according to Ellis; the shortening has taken place since the 16th cent. We also find *seik* in the text, 4. 62.

§ 346. 2. ēog, ēoh — rimes with

a) OE. ēo (without gutt.). drie (drēogan) : see, inf. 1. 1482. theis (pl. of þeoh) : treis (arbores) 3. 1070. — b) OE. ē. thie (þeoh) : he, (pron.) 1. 1000.

§ 347. These words contain ī from ę̄, as usual in Sc., where the gutt. disappeared altogether, and the vowel ę̄ (it was ē already in the OE. period in Angl.) remained unaffected by it, hence no diphthong in these and similar words, nor a long ī (i. e. in early MSc.) as in Midl. and Southⁿ ME. (Cf. Brandl, Th. Erc., pp. 59, 60, Buss p. 497); ēog > ę̄g > ų̄ > ī (late MSc.), in just the same way as eā + gutt. produced MSc. ę̄ and then ī. In the case of þeoh, the h was lost in OE. already in the inflected forms, cf. fēoh, fēos, hence we find in ME., even in Southern texts, thee, &c., without a trace of the gutt., e. g. Owl & N., þeo : beo, Rob. Br. þe : be, see Sweet, p. 359.

Such forms are frequent in Sc. texts. The mod. diall. show perfect agreement, we find the forms thī (= thigh), flī (= fly), lī (= lie) in all diall.; thigh is given by Ellis once with ai, in D. 39; this is, of course, not pure dial.

Clar. betrays here no anglicising influence.

§ 348. To Buss's examples we can add — Dougl. dre : adversitie 2. 57. 16, theis (= thighs) : kneis 2. 157. 2, hie (= high) : see 2. 40. 32 : thrie 2. 27. 4 : sey (= sea) : eye : me 1. 42. 3, de : ee 2. 27. 16, ee : bewtie : se : scho, 1. 19. 11, leis (3 sg. lēogan) : fleis, 3 sg. : seis (maria) : seis (videt), &c. — Lyndes. eine (= eyes) : meine Sat. 492, theis : kneis, Suppl. 83 and Sq. M. 1348, &c. — Roll. C. V., hie : destinie : mollifie : sle (= sly) 2. 400, &c. — Montg. sie (seāh) : trie, C. 319, ee : thrie, S. 41, ee : see : dee : be, S. 591, &c. — Rosw. hie : be, A. 130, hie : me 528, 602.

§ 349. 3. ēow = Gmc. iuj, iw, — rimes with

a) itself — new : hew (hēow) 1. 170 (&c.) : schew, (prt. *scēow, see § 357) 2. 516 : knew (cnēow) 4. 1398. treuth : rewth 5. 1096. rew (hrēowan) : knew 3. 2026. hew : knew 2. 710, 4. 996 : schew, prt., 3. 1470 : trew, (adj. trēowe) 3. 228, 4. 230. drew (OE. was drōg, but cf. § 355) : threw 2. 1526 : flew (OE. was flēah, but cf. § 355), 3. 856. — b) OE. ū. ʒow (pron.) : how 3. 830. — c) OE. ū + w. ʒow : trow (trūwian) 2. 552. — d) OE. w̄ + w. trewth : slewth (OE. slǣwþ, NE. sloth) 4. 1098, sleuth 4. 2342. — e) Fr. u. ʒow : avow 4. 820. ʒouris : collouris (= colours) 4. 2016 : honouris 5. 2422 : amouris 4. 1508. — f) Fr. ü. schew, prt. : wertew 3. 298 : salew (saluer) 2. 532. trew, adj. : wertew (MS. wertew & bewtie for bewtie & wertew) 3. 1424. knew : vertwe 1. 1150. — g) Fr. eu, ieu. new : persew 2. 1010 : blew, adj. 4. 1178 (&c). trew, adj. : persew 4. 488, 5. 1260. knew : persew 1. 910, 3. 1078 : adew (a dieu) 1. 926 : blew, adj. 2. 1438. hew, sb. : blew 4. 1004 (&c.) : pursew 1. 36. schew, prt. : persew 4. 1142 (&c.). drew (for OE. drōg, see below) : Pardew 5. 2396. — h) ? schew, prt. : eschew 1. 880, see § 357.

§ 350. The regular development of OE. eow is eow > ǭw > ę̄u̯ > iu̯, which later became iu; we have iu or iū (prob. the former) in the above words, not only in new, hew, schew, knew, flew, but also in trew, *treuth, rew, threw, drew*; for though it will be seen below that after *r* the *iu* only remains to-day in D. 33, while in the other diall. we find *ū* as in rec. sp., *drū* (= drew), &c., so that we might imagine perhaps the spelling *ew* to be only due to the copyist, still we do not know *when* the *i* disappeared in the central diall., and on the analogy of the orthography in other words, we should expect *ow* to appear occasionally in the MS., if the author had used it, as he would have done, had he pronounced with *u* instead of *iu*; so that it is perhaps safer to suppose that *iu* still existed after *r* in his pronunc. Although we might be allowed to accept *iū* : *ū* rimes, yet as *all* the rime-words contain certainly *iu*, we must accept *iu* in the above mentioned words as well. Cf. Montg. MP. 17, where all of the following words rime with *perseu — sleu, greu, bleu, aneu* (= enough), *deu* (= due), *reu, kneu, fleu, dreu, threu, sheu*, (prt.).

§ 351. There is another possible development of *ēōw*, viz. to *ŏu*, which remained *ou* in medial and became *ū* in final position, according to t. Br., p. 39. Our rimes only show this in *ʒow*, see (b) and (e), and, with transference of the *u*-final by analogy into the medial position, in *ʒouris*, see (e), as explained by t. Br. l. c. In *ʒow* the *i* of *iu* has become conson. and the *u* alone is bearer of the syll., hence the rime with *ū* not *iu*.

§ 352. In accordance with this, the verb *trow*, generally derived from OE. *trēōwian*, is, on account of its riming with OE. *ū*, to be derived, in this form, from OE. *trūwian*, and will be found below under *ū* in § 535. As remarked in the preceding paragraph, we cannot here assume that *triu* has become *trū*, witness the adj. *trew*, only spelt with *ew* (not *ow*) and riming with *iu* not *u*. The spelling *ow* may mean *ū* as well as *ou*, and must mean *ū* alone for our author, if he wrote it. Skeat accepts *ū* as the value of *ow* and *ew* even as early as Barbour's Bruce (EETS. 29, p. 638), also Buss, p. 499, for Sc. Leg., and the words *now, how*, have still the long vowel *ū* (not diphthong) in most of the Sc. diall. Sir Tr. has *trowe now* : *Peticru* : *ynouʒ* : *how*; if *ow* here meant the diphthong *ou*, the change from *ū* to *ou* in *how, now* is to be dated very early indeed. Similar rimes are in Lyndes., *trow* : *now* : *ʒow*, Sat. 471, : *how* 734 : *now* 852, Satir. P. *trow* : *how* : *pow* (= pull) : *now* 16. 1.

The pronunc., then, of the vb. *trow* was *trū*.

§ 353. The scribe as well as the author observed a difference between the vb., which he writes *trow*, and the adj., written *trew*. Similarly in Satir. P. *trow*, vb. (cf. § 352) but *trew* : *few* 16. 24 : *grew* : *rew*, vb. : *anew* (= afresh) 16. 29 : *anew* (= enough) 16. 66. To-day *triu* is spoken for the adj. in D. 33, but *trū* in all the other diall. except 41, where a solitary instance of *triu* is given by Ellis. If *trow* contained the diphthong *ou* for the scribe, probably the rime-word *now* did too, which would point to D. 33 or the N. of Engl. where *you, how, now* are all pronounced with a diphthong, while in all other diall. of Scotl. they have *ū*.

ʒow and *ʒouris*, which had *ū* in the pronunc. of the author, may possibly have had *ou* in that of the scribe, as at the present day in D. 33 &c. For different explanations of these forms see t. Br. p. 39, note 2, Sweet § 685, Morsbach p. 74.

§ 354. The following is the only material given by Ellis for the mod. diall. — *you* has (əu) in 33, (uu) in all the other diall., also (uu) in 32 (Northumbld.), but (óu) in some of the diall. of N. Engl.; *true*, (iuu) in 33 and 41, also in 32 and nearly all diall. of the N. and N. Midl., (nu) in all other diall. of Sc.; *truth* is very varied in pronunc., (əu) in 33, (óu) in 39, (əu) in 40, (y) or (yy) in 34, 35, (ə) or (əə) in 35, 36, 42, (iuu) in 33, 41, also in 32 and most of the diall. of N. Engl. and N. Midl., (u) or (nu) in 38 and part of 32; *trow* is only once given, with (óu), in 33; *brew* has (iuu) in 33, (uu) in 35, 38, 39, 42, also (ii) in 39; *rue* (əu) in 33; *chew* (óu) in 33, 39, (áu) in 35, 36, 38, 42, also (AA) and (aa) in 39; *four* (óu) in 33, 39, 41, (áu) in 35, 38, (oo) in 33; *forty* only (o) or (oo).

Here again the evidence, as far as it goes, tends to show that the dial. of the author was not that of D. 33.

§ 355. *drew* and *flew* are included here, for, although the OE. forms were *drōg* and *flēag*, the forms which arose regularly from these were replaced by others formed on the analogy of *threw*, *blew*, &c., cf. Bülbring, pp. 92 and 99. The vowel-sound is (iu), cf. Montg. flew : anew (= enough) C. 800, dreu : fleu : perseu, &c., MP. 17. 1.

§ 356. *eschew*, see (h), has had different etymologies given to it. Skeat in his Princ. gives Fr. *eschuer*, in his Dict. and his edit. of Lanc. Fr. *eschever*; Bradley in his edit. of Stratmann and Skeat in his edit. of Bruce give Fr. *eschiver*. Perhaps there was here a mixture of two Fr. forms, and possibly further also of a native word, the ME. *schēowen* = avoid, see Stratm.-Bradl., cognate with M. L. G. *schūwen*, which is connected with OE. *scēoh*, adj. and NE. *skew* (by Skeat derived direct from MDu.). At any rate there are two forms in MSc., sometimes both used in one and the same text, one with *iu* the other with *ēv* or *iv*; cf. Bruce, *cscheve* 18. 532, *eschevit* 20. 454, *eschewe* 12. 473, 15. 349, *eschewit* 11. 535, 16. 207; Sc. Leg. *eschewe : leife* (= permission) 29/1022, *eschew : nov* (= now) 68/428, *eschewe : leyfe* 96/322; Wall. *eschew : inew* 9. 812; Lanc. *eschef : beleif* 2732 : *pref* (= prove) 3475; Rat. Rav. *enschew* (for *eschew* according to Lumby) : *wertew* 1147; Craft of Doyng, *eschef* 153, *eschewyng* 18; Dunb. *eschewit : bespewit* 27. 80, *eschew* (construed with *fra*) : *slew : new* 33. 9, *escheve : greve : leve* (sb. = departure) 81. 42; Dongl. *escheuit : releuit : engreuit : brewit* (= briefed, written) 1. 31. 16, *escheuet* (= escaped, departed) : *aggreuit* &c. 1. 79. 4; Satir. P. *eschew : persew : slew : brew* 5. 68; Montg. *eschew : trew* C. 1298, *esheud : breud* (= brewed) : *outspeud : indeud* (= indued) S. 24.

§ 357. *schew*, prt., a new-formed pret. on the analogy of *knew*, &c.; the verb was originally weak, as in NE. *showed*. We find the same form in other Sc. texts, e. g. Wall. *schew : drew* 11. 92; Dunb. *schew* 3. 252; Montg. *shewe : trew*, C. 1016, *sheu : perseu* MP. 17. 55, *sheu : heu : bleu* 35. 57, *furthsheu : kneu : sleu : ouirthreu : treu : heu : feu : adeu*, 27. 5.

The passage referred to in § 349 (h), is not quite correctly rendered in the MS.: "His father is displeasit, and in schew Dangeris þairin quhilk he micht nocht eschew", but a slight emendation (change *in* to *him*) renders it intelligible.

ON. JU'

§ 358. rimes with

a) OE. ēo. meike (ON. *mjūk*) : seik (*scoc*) 3. 1542. — b) OE. ē, mut. of ō. meike : scike, vb. 4. 612. — c) Angl. ē = WS. ēa before a *gutt.* meike : eik(e) 2. 1552 (&c.).

In ME. *mẹke*, there was a substitution of *ẹ̣*, the representative of OE. *ēo*, for the corresponding ON. *jū*, which, of course, then rimed with *ẹ̣* from all other sources. Cf. Zupitza, AnzfdA. 2, 7.

I

§ 359. Short ĭ is usually represented by *i*, sometimes, but only seldom, by *y*, e. g. *ryssine* 1. 1177, *sympleness* 1. 223. In ME. texts it was often the custom to use *y* for ĭ immediately before or after *m* or *n* for the sake of distinctness, (see t. Br., § 9), but in Clar. this is quite exceptional; instead of it we sometimes meet with *j*, which serves the same purpose, especially in the suffix *-jng*; and at the beginning of a word we sometimes find a capital *I* when *m* or *n* follows, e. g. *Innis*. The absence of *y* in this use is due to the fact that it is almost exclusively used, at any rate in medial position, for earlier long ī, which has become the diphthong *ei*, *əi*, see below §§ 432 ff. There is no example of *u* for OE. *i*, and only a few of *e, mekill* (also *mikill*), *wemen* &c.

I-

§ 360. 1. **Not followed by c or g** (for which see §§ 410, 411) — rimes with

a) **itself.** leiue (= live) : giue 4. 154, 2632 : geiue 4. 2386. — b) OE. ēa. geiue : leave (OE. *lēaf* = permission) 4. 146, giue : leaue 3. 1014. — c) OE. e, WS. ie after palatal. wite (*witan*, vb.) : ʒit (= yet, OE. *get, giet*) 1. 1348. — d) OFr. ie, AFr. e. leive : grive, vb. 1. 306.

§ 361. (The two vowels *i* and *u* are so similar in their treatment, and the history of the one throws so much light on that of the other, that we shall find it advisable to discuss them together, hence *u-* is treated in advance with *i-* in the following §§). It is generally stated that the vowels *i-* and *u-* are not "subject to new-lengthening in ME.", Sweet §§ 623, 647, cf. Kluge in P. G., Morsbach, p. 21, 181, &c. But this has raised doubts in the minds of some who, like t. Br., have been unable to see why these two vowels should be exceptions to the general rule of ME. lengthening in open syll. Morsb., p. 21, seeks an explanation in the fact that in the pronunc. of these vowels the angle of the jaw is smaller than in the case of the other vowels; but it is difficult to see why this should be any hindrance to the lengthening. ten Brink in ZtsfdA. 19, N. F. 7, 212, Angl. 1. 512, &c. and Chauc. §§ 3, 35, 36, 37, finds refuge in a "schwebender vokal", which he assumes, in order to explain the occasional rimes with long vowels in Chauc. This expression, however, has met with much disfavour, and although the existence of such a vowel-quantity, situated mid-way between long and short, is by no means impossible, (we possess such a one at the present day in words in which the vowel is followed by a liquid or voiced cons., e. g. *live, bill*, where the vowel quantity is not quite the same as in *sit, sip*, and according to Ellis every so-called short vowel in Scotch is half-long in comparison with Engl.), still the expression in this sense as used by t. Br. is perhaps not to be defended.

§ 362. The custom of an author such as Chauc. sometimes riming a word with a long vowel, sometimes with a short, is to be taken rather as evidence of a two-fold pronunc., *both* long *and* short; in fact, that he here, as often in respect to the quality of vowels, had also two strings to his bow with regard to the quantity, and that these two different forms came from different diall., not resulted from his own normal pronunc. intermediate between short and long; in this sense we can defend the term "schwebender vokal".

§ 363. The whole difficulty seems to lie in the fact that up to the present two important matters have been somewhat overlooked in the discussion of this question, (1) the exact nature of the OE. *i̯* and *ŭ*, and (2) the difference of development in different diall.

§ 364. OE. *i* was not = (i), high-front-narrow, but = (i), high-front-wide, a sound approaching *e* in character; cf. Ellis, p. 105, "the Engl. sound (*i*) lies between (i) and (e)", (the latter = mid-front-wide), i. e. it approaches (*e*) in so far, that being a wide vowel, the size of the sound-passage was larger than for (i) and nearer that for (*e*); and just as *i̯* rimes with *ĕ* in closed syllable, see below, so we should expect that this sound lengthened would rime with *ẹ̄*, (from which it would not much differ), instead of with ī, and it actually does so in Clar. and many other Sc. texts, cf. (b) and (d) above. Cf. Ellis, EEP. 1. 271, 272, who compares similar pronunciations of the present day and mistakes arising therefrom; see also Ellis, p. 106, "the true long sound of (*i*) is not an acknowledged sound in our language, though in frequent use among such singers as refuse to say happ*ee*, st*ee*l, *ee*l, when they have to lengthen happ*y*, st*i*ll, *i*ll".

For this value (*i*) and its rimes in closed and open syll. cf. further Morsb. p. 33, Wackerzapp, p. 30, &c., Buss, p. 504, Schleich, Angl. 4. 308, Zupitza, Guy, p. XIV, Brandl, p. 60, and AnzfdA. 13. 97 ff., Ullmann, p. 13, Zielke, p. 15, Sarrazin, Octav., p. 173, Kölbing, Ipom., p. 173, Dannenberg, p. 14, Noltemeier, p. 14, Fick, p. 14, Zietsch, p. 75, Lloyd, pp. 166, 183 &c.

§ 365. Similarly OE. *u* was not pure (u), high-back-narrow-round, but (*u*), high-back-wide-round, a sound approaching (o), mid-back-wide-r., in character, cf. Ellis, V. p. 823, so that we can say of this (*u*) that it lies between (u) and (o); from it the mod. Engl. (ə) in *but* is more easily explained than from pure (u). It is sometimes represented by *u̯*, just as (*i*) is represented often by *i̯*. We are naturally led to expect that this sound, when lengthened, should, on the parallel of *i̯*, rime with *ọ̄* (from which it would not much differ), instead of with *ū*, and it actually does so in Clar. and many other Sc. texts, cf. §§ 377, 500. The true long sound of (*u*) or *u̯* is frequently used in singing *foot* or *pull* to a long note, (fuut, puul); we then distinctly hear the difference from (fuut, puul). It is often also found before r, where it is particularly liable to become (oo); an Englishman's pronunc. of the German word *Uhr* generally sounds like *Ohr* to a German ear, and is really (oor), and the common pronunc. of *poor* as *pore*, (poor) instead of (puur), is well known.

It should be noticed that Sweet in his HoES. assigns the pure values (i) and (u) to OE. *i* and *u*.

§ 366. The lengthened sound of (*i*), or *i̯*, changed, then, as we consider, from (ii), *ī* to (ee), *ē̜*, or in accordance with the tendency of long vowels to narrowing, noticed by Sweet, § 53, became (ee), *ē̜*, after which it followed the same fortunes as ordinary *ē̜*, producing NE. ĭ, not the diphthong (əi) or (ai), which are the modern representatives of ME. ī. Similarly, the lengthened sound of (*u*), *u̯*, changed from (uu), *ū̜* to (oo), *ō̜*, or, with narrowing, (oo), *ō̜*, and then followed the same fortunes as ordinary *ō̜*, which produces, where undisturbed by other influences, NE. *ū*, (uu) and NSc. (əə) or (yy), not (au), or (əu) the representatives of ME. *ū* in rec. sp., nor (uu), the mod. Sc. equivalent of MSc. (uu). It is this fact, that the lengthened forms were not ME. ĭ and ŭ, coupled with the rarity of examples in which the long vowel is still found in rec. sp. (various external causes having tended to prevent it) that has misled people to assert that *i* and *u* were not liable to lengthening in open syllable.

§ 367. First let us consider the development of *i*- in rec. sp. If we examine the word-list in Sweet's HoES., we find that in many cases the lengthening has been prevented by an *l*, *n*, *r* or *y* in the following syll. (Sweet's "back-shortening"), e. g. in *fiddle*, *flicker*, *withy*, *risen*, or by syncope, e. g. *church*, *cir(i)ce*. In some, the short ĭ may be due to inflected forms in which the *i* was not in open syll., as *shin*, *sinew*; in others Sweet might have given another OE. form, as *tillan* instead of *tīlian* (he does give *swillan* as a by-form of *swīlian*). In others, again, a form with vowel-length exists in dial.; for instance, *sieve* has a long vowel, ĭ, in D. 31, 32, 33, 34, i. e. in the N. of Engl. and South and Mid Lowland, in which districts the short vowel, sĭv, is altogether absent, and once Ellis gives sĭv in the S. of Engl. in D. 4. By the side of *wit* we have *weet*, an archaic form frequently used in the time of Elizabeth and James I, e. g. Spenser, F. Q. : feet, 1. 3. 6. In other words, again, analogy or differentiation may have been at work. But in five words, mod. rec. sp. has ĭ, the representative of ME. *ē*, viz. *weevil*, *beetle* (unless this is to be derived from OE. *bētl*, see B-T.) *beaker*, *these*, *week*. In the first three mentioned we might perhaps have rather expected a short vowel, on account of the following *l* and *r*, but we have similar cases of the absence of back-shortening, e. g. *cradel*, *navel*, which have a long vowel in rec. sp. (cf. however the dialect forms bĭtl, nævl, for instance, in Somersethire, see Elworthy).

§ 368. The dialectal forms, as sĭv, and the forms in rec. sp. *weevil*, *beetle*, *beaker*, *these*, *week*, are due, then, to ME. forms with *ī* or *ē̜*, and this long vowel was possible in all words containing OE. *i*-, at any rate in some diall. of ME., but in rec. sp. either there has been a return to ĭ in all but the five words mentioned, or else the lengthening in the ME. dial. of rec. sp. was limited to these five, or they are merely forms which have crept into rec. sp. from an outside dial. (northern?). (In the words *live* and *give* the vowel can have been shortened through the influence of the forms *lived*, *given*, &c., in which the short vowel is quite in order). That this lengthening existed in ME. is confirmed by a number of rimes in which words that now have ĭ in rec. sp., must then have had a long vowel in the respective diall. in which the rimes are found, and the mod. dialectal forms are a further support.

§ 369. Completer lists than Ellis's would probably contain many more dialectal forms with ī; (the Somersetshire dial., Elworthy, p. 47, has *līv* for *live*, but this is not an example on which much weight can be laid, for there is a tendency in this dial. to turn every ĭ to ī, in closed as well as open syll.). Ellis's general list unfortunately only includes (besides those words in which *g* or *w* follows the *i*), *week*, *sieve*, *ivy*, *her*, *these*, *get*. Of these *get* is of Norse origin (*git*, also due to northern influence on account of the initial *g*, instead of *y*, is much commoner-in dial., *get* is found chiefly in the N.); *these*, *sieve*, *week* have already been mentioned above; *her* shows no irregularity in the treatment of *i* before *r* when short, it is found, however, riming with long *ē* in some ME. texts, e. g. Chauc., *here* : *swere*, which proves a long vowel, and, what is more, even an *open* $\bar{e}$, on account of the following *r*; and *ivy* does not properly belong here, for it is OE. *īfig*, or *ĭfig* (see Morsbach, p. 181, Mayhew § 811), it has the diphthong *ai*, *əi* or *oi* in all the mod. diall., except in the Midland, where, on account of the following *y*, it has been regularly shortened to (ivi).

The form *gī* for *give*, common to almost all diall., Engl. and Scotch, is also more easily explained from a form *gīv*, i. e. early NE., the ME. would be *gĕv*; but a complete chronology of the word would make this clear; if our explanation is correct, we should, of course, not expect to find *gī* before *ē* became ī. Still this is not absolutely necessary, for we can derive *gīs* from *gifis*, 3. sg., just as *lūs* comes from *lufis*, loves, and then from *gīs*, by analogy, *gī*. Ellis gives the forms *gin* in D. 34 and 39, and (gjiiyn) = giving, in 39; also (leevin) = living, in 39; Murray, DSS., p. 140, gives *leeves* = (liivz), as the mod. pronunc. of *lives* in 33.

§ 370. Now for the ME. and MSc. rimes in evidence. In Clar. we have rimes with OE. *ēa* and Fr. *ie*. The rime-words *leave* and *grieve* rime otherwise in Clar. only with words containing a long vowel, viz. previous $\bar{e}$, and have kept their vowel-length till the present day in rec. sp. and all diall.; therefore we must conclude that *live* and *give* were pronounced by the author of Clar. with a long word, viz. ī. The orthography with *ei*, *leive*, *geiue*, implies of itself an *i* for the scribe. Fick, who also notices this tendency to lengthening in the Pearl, ("OE. *i* has become long *ē* in a few cases") gives an ill-chosen example, *forgete* : *grete* (OE. $\overline{ea}$) : *retrete*, for in *forget* we have Norse influence again; the original vowel was *e*, not *i*. He says "OE. *i* had in common with every OE. short vowel the tendency to lengthening in open syll.", and then apparently gives it the value ī, (i. e. ME. ī = NE. *əi*, *ai*), which is certainly wrong. He brings forward examples of rimes with long ī, e. g. *per-īne* : *lȳne* (OE. ī) : *vȳne* (OE. ī), but his explanation of this rime seems very questionable.

Such rimes we must consider, in spite of their comparative frequency, imperfect in quality, rather than suppose that ī has become ī, for which we find no trace in the mod. diall.; the apparent exception (sâi) and (sàil) for *sieve* in D. 21 and 22, Lancs. and Derby, may perhaps be a different word; Ellis gives (sâi) as being used in a special sense, = a sieve for milk.

Menze, too, p. 36, speaks of "a tendency to lengthening in open syll., even if the rimes give us no certain proof". t. Br., Chauc., p. 25, gives as examples of his schwebender vokal in open syll. from Gen. Ex. *liuen*, inf. : *bilewen (bi-lǣfan)*, *dede*, prt. : *stede*, sb. : *childhede*, *deden* : *steden*, &c. Brate, AnzfdA. 13. 97, gives among his list of *i* : *e* rimes some in which *i* in open syll. rimes with *ē*; these seem to be confined to the N. and N. Midl.

§ 371. Here follow a few more examples from Sc. and N. Engl. — Wall., *geyff* : *leyff* (sb. = departure) 1. 448, *gyff* : *myscheyff* : *leiff*, sb. : *preiff* (prove) 2. 206, *giff* : *scheyff* (= escheve, escape) 3. 263, *weite* (? = *witan*, to know, or ask ?) : *heit* (= heat) 5. 346, *leyff* (= live) : *preffe* (= prove) 5. 630, *leiff* (= live) : *raleiff* 10. 724; Gol. *geif* : *encheif* (= achieve) 1063, *leif* (= live) : *cheif* (vb. "for chance þat may cheif") 1193; Lanc. *lewis* (= lives, 3. sg.) : *prewis* (= proves) 1210, *geif* : *leiv* (= departure) 1718, *if* (= give) : *relief*, vb., 1740, *lewyt* (= lived) : *prewit* (= proved) 2174, *lef* : *eschef* (= achieve) 2514 : *rapref* (= reprove) 3230; Dunb. *leif* (= live) : *mischeif* 69. 19; Dougl. *speitis* (= spits, sb.) 2. 229. 19. Lyndes. *forgeue* : *leue*, sb., Sq. M. 337, *geif* : *leif* (= permission) Sat. 460; Davidson (Irving, p. 402) *lewis*, 3. sg. : *neuis* (= fists); Maitland (Irving, p. 410) *geif* : *sleif* (sleeve) : *neif* (fist); Satir P. *geif* : *leif* : *mischeif* : *preif* (= prove) 40. 135, *lewis* : *neuis* (= fists) 42. 428, *geif* : *greif*, vb., 42. 834, *give* : *neife* 45. 450, *leivis*, 3. sg. : *theivis*, *teill* (vb. OE. *tilian*) : *Commonweill* 33. 372, *speit* (sb. OE. *spitu*) : *sweit* : *meit*, adj., 33. 998; Montg. *leiv* : *bereiv* MP. 21. 1, *leive* : *grieve* MP. 14. 16, *give* : *prieve* : *relieve* : *deiv* (= deafen) MP. 33. 42, *givis* : *bereivis* 35. 80. — Hamp. (Ullmann, p. 13) *ȝeue* : *greue*, *lyue* : *greue*, *gyfe* : *belyefe*, &c.; Sege Mel. *weite (witan)* : *mete*, vb. : *grete*, vb. : *mete*, adj., 120. Many more such could be given, cf. Heuser p. 17, Carstens, p. 12, &c. *Give* and *live* are of most frequent occurrence; a long *ē* is found even in the S. in *ȝēve*, numerous examples of which are given by Bülbring, Gesch. des Abl., who derives from a non-WS. form.

§ 372. For further examples of ī : ī rimes, cf. Bruce, *tharin* : *vyne (wīn)* 15. 93, *within* : *tyne* 1. 107, Sc. Leg. *begyne* : *lentrine* 144/120, *Ine* : *virgine* 150/651, (cf. *vergine* : *lyne*, 2/57); Troj. W. *vith-Ine* : *tyne* 2. 235, *witht-Inne* : *syne* 2. 647. — Sir Tr. *inne* : *sinne* : *pine* : *mine* (pron.) 2669; Sir Egl. (Zielke, p. 15) *wete (witan)* : *tyte*; Th. Erc. *blyn* : *syen (sīþþan)* 8; Mass Book, *dryue*, ptc. : *beliue*, 84. 28. — Gen. Ex. *hire*, (pron.) : *kire (cȳre)* 1694 : *shire* (vb. subj. pres.) 2036, *writen*, ptc. : *wliten* (OE. *wlīte*); this word *wliten* rimes also with *eten*, inf., 2290; Launfal (Münster, p. 19) *þeryn* : *wyn (wīn)*, *here* (pron.) : *sere* (Fr. sire); Lyric P. (Schlüter, p. 19) *ywis* : *his* : *unwis* (OE. *wīs*) : *ys* (= is), *is* : *rys* (OE. *hrīs*) : *wys (wīs)* : *pris* : *bys* : *his*, *yn* : *wyn (wīn)*; Partenay (Hattendorf, p. 23) *therin* : *Melusine*, *yn* : *fyne*. Menze, p. 65, gives a number of such rimes from the EMidl. dial.

§ 373. Contrary to the observations made above as to modern dialectal $\bar{\imath}$ for rec. sp. $\check{\imath}$, in one word just the very reverse is to observed, viz. *week*; here the form *wĭk*, with short vowel, preponderates in all the diall.; *wĭk* is found occasionally in the S., and a little more frequently in the N.

§ 374. There is a Sc. form *gleit* for rec. sp. *glitter*, which perhaps belongs here, if we derive from ON. *glita*. It appears only in rime with $\bar{e}$; in Clar. *when balmie liquore dois on leavis gleit* : *sweit*, 5. Prol. 2.; Dougl. *gletis* : *streitis*, 2. 88. 16, *gleit* : *spreit* (= spirit) : *sweit* : *fleit*, vb., 1. 33. 18; Montg. *all is not gold that gleits* : *freits* (= superstitions, omens) C. 1288, : *weitis* (*nor water all that weitis*) MP. 5. 42.

§ 375. Now let us look at OE. *u-* (exclusive of $u + g$, which had a development of its own). Here again back-shortening has sometimes taken place, e. g. in *honey*, *thunder*, *butter*, *ruddy*, *slumber*, *numb*, *summer*, *cuttle*, = OE. *hunig*, *þunor*, *butere*, *rudig*, ME. *slumeren*, OE. *genumen*, *sumor*, *cudele*; in the latter there was also the external influence of Du. *kuttelvisch*. Or there has been syncope, as in *monk*, *wont* = OE. *munuc*, *gewunod*. Perhaps inflected forms have given the decision in *crumb*, *shun*, *stun*, = OE. *cruma*, *scunian*, *stunian*. In the remaining instances, with the exception of *nut*, OE. *hnutu*, the spelling in rec. sp. points to a possibility of ME. $\bar{o}$, *door*, *love*, *above*, *son*, *come*, *wood*, and the mod. pronun. is perfectly compatible with it too, for with these words we can compare *floor*, *glove*, *done*, *gum*, *good*, which are exactly similar in pronunc. to the above in mod. Engl. and all have an $\bar{o}$ in OE., *flōr*, *glōf*, *gedōn*, *gōma*, *gōd*, which in some of them becomes a short vowel in mod. rec. sp.

§ 376. And further, as in the case of *i*, the diall. often show forms with a long vowel, and this generally corresponds to the vowel which represents OE. $\bar{o}$ in the several diall. But here the N. does not give the preponderance of evidence, for the short vowel of rec. sp. is extensively found there, and the S. offers some examples of long vowel.

One word, *above*, is found almost everywhere with long vowel, in the forms (abəən, abuun, abiиn, abiún); although the vowel-length might in this case be explained by the loss of intervocal *f*, still it is noticeable that the resulting long vowel is in every instance the same as that resulting from OE. $\bar{o}$, and, moreover, we find the long vowel in forms in which the *f* has not disappeared, e. g. (abuuv) in D. 18, (aboov) and (abuuv) in 19. The forms with *n* are not confined to the N. (although they are the only ones found in Sc. and the N. of Engl.), we find (abuun) in D. 5, 20, 22, 24, and (ʋbee) in 10, (ʋbyy) in 11, without any final cons.; here again with the vowel corresponding to OE. $\bar{o}$. *love* has in Sc. nearly always a short vowel (ɜ) or (ə), but (oo) is found in 41, (y₁) in 42, and pret. (luud) in 41; in Engl. we find (luuv) in 20 and 24, and, what is particularly interesting, (liиv) in 30, where there is no doubt of the origin of the (iиv) being a former $\bar{o}$, cf. below, § 463. The word *door* it is not necessary

THE MIDDLE-SCOTCH ROMANCE CLARIODUS. 115

to derive from OE. *dor*; it agrees with *floor* in rec. sp. and in very many
of the diall. we find forms with (uu) or (uuʋ, ûʋ) or similar sounds, in
most cases agreeing with *floor*, which has the same sounds; where $\bar{o}$ is
represented by (iiʋ) or (iu), D. 30 and 31, there *door* appears with (iiʋ)
or (iu); the $\bar{o}$ of rec. sp. and some of the diall. is, of course, the effect
of the following *r*, and this is the form usually found in Sc. diall., but
D. 33 has (dər), which is probably a development from early MSc. *dōr*,
late MSc. *dŏr*. *come* and *son* generally have (ᴀ) in Sc., but *son* has also
(o) in 38, (ɵ) and (eé) in 39, (i) in 40 and 41, some of which sounds may
be from MSc. $\breve{o} < \bar{o}$, and we have traces of $\bar{o}$ in 32, with (oh); *come* has
also (oh) in D. 5, and (nu) in 1, 12, 20. *wood* is only given by Ellis with
short vowel in Sc., but this short vowel is (y) in 39, and (i) in 42, otherwise (ᴀ); in Engl. we generally find (u) as in rec. sp., but D. 5 has (uud),
and D. 10 (əə₁d), corresponding to (stəə₁d) = stood. This authorises us
to agree with Kölbing and Wülcker with regard to the rime *rode* : *wode*,
in WL, VIII. 13, Lyric Songs in MS. Harl. 2253, who quite correctly consider *rode* as = OE. *rōd*; Böddeker and Schlüter object to this on account
of the rime and derive from OE. *rudu* (see Schlüter, p. 21 and note).

We see, then, that the diall. give decided proof of ME. $\bar{o}$ in some
cases and strong traces of it in others.

§ 377. But we have not only the mod. diall. to depend upon; ME.
and MSc. rimes give us a valuable confirmation of the lengthening of *u*
in open syll. Those in Clar. will be found below in § 500; we find
rimes with OE. $\bar{o}$, Fr. *ü* and *o*. The spelling, too, with *ui* is evidence of
vowel-length (= $\bar{o}$) in the pronunc. of the scribes. The following may
be added as a few examples from Sc. and N. Engl. texts: — Bruce,
schonand = shunning, 5. 201, *aboue, aboun, abovin, abovyn, abowyne, sone*
(= son) : *wone* (= wont); no rime of proof, but the orthography, as will
be seen below, is of some value as evidence; the verb *come* appears as
com, *come*, *cum*, *cume*. — Sc. Leg. *wone* (= dwell) : *mowne* (= moon)
12/578, *sone* (*sunu*) : *alsone* (*sōna*) 23/618, *abone* : *done* 168/556. — Wynt.
cum : *Rwme* 6. 3. 77. — Wall. *abuff* : *ramuff, remuif* (= remove) 1. 68,
nome (ptc. *genumen*) : *come*, prt., 1. 124, *abuffe* : *luff* : *pruff* (= prove) :
behuff 2. 224, *luff* : *appruff*, *lufe* : *apprufe* 3. 346. *dur* (door) : *cur* (Fr.
cure) 4. 234, *off buffe*, *abufe* : *pruff* 5. 230, *luffe* : *pruff* 5. 636, *luff* : *ramuff*
5. 716, *dur* : *flur* 5. 1112, *luff* : *pruff* : *abuff* : *ruff* (= rest) 6. 60. (NB. *u*
is generally the representative of OE. $\bar{o}$ in Wall.). — Gol. *dure* (*duru*) :
sture (*stōr*) 110, *gome* (OE. *guma*) 525 (&c.). — Dunb. *abone* : *redoun* :
toun (= tune) 81. 20 : *done* : *Scone* : *vndone* 2. 276 : *sone* 30. 8. — Dougl.
aboue : *remoue* : *Loue* : *behuif* 1. 101. 7. Roll. C. V. *abufe* : *vnrufe* (=
unrest) 2. 446. — Satir. P. *luif* : *muif* 26. 11, *abone* : *sone* 31. 53, *abone*
yame : *tone yame* 31. 134, *sone* (*sunu*) : *done* 33. 64, *abone* : *done* : *sone*
(*sōna*) : *none* (= noon) 39. 63, *abone* : *tone* : *sone* : *done* 39. 313, &c., &c. —
Montg. *abune* : *tune* C. 100, (but *aboue* : *Loue*, C. 105), *abone* : *tone* :
sone : *mone* : *done* MP. 3. 14 : *tone* (= tune, vb.) S. 44. 14 (cf. *tune* : *sune*
= OE. *sōna*, 44. 1) : *soon* MP. 48. 95, *luve* : *commuve* : *abuve* : *ruve* (vb.
= rest) MP. 52. 14 : *pruve* C. 1593, *love* : *prove* : *remove* : *rove* : *above* :
behove : *glove* MP. 6. 7 &c. — Surt. Ps. *come* : *dome* 24. 9. — Curs. M.

8*

come : *dom* 23055. — Metr. Hom. *cum* : *dom* 25. 5 : *kingdom* 96. 3, *com* : *gone* 95. 17 : *gom* 127. 12. — Horstm. Leg. (N. Engl.) *com* : *dom* 28. 106. — Hamp. *come* : *wysdom(e)* PC. 144, 149 : *dom* 263, *loues* : *proues* 4ᵇ 42, *loue* : *behoue* 5ᵇ 6 : *reproue* 21ᵃ 29, *dore* : *flore* 24ᵇ 1. — Scge Mel. *sone* (*sunu*) : *done* : *mone* : *konne* 303, *gones* (*gumas*) : *stones* 1288. — Bened. *cum* : *dom* 519, 1311 : *dome* 1899. — Sir Egl. *sone* (*sunu*) : *done* 1265. — Sir Perc. *wonne* : *sonne* (*sunu*) : *donne* 165, *wonne* : *sonne* : *bygone* 349, *wonne* : *sonne* : *donne* : *nône* 580, *wodde* (*wudu*) : *stode* : *fode* 180, *wodde* : ȝ*ode* : *gude* 193, *mone* (OE. *mune*, opt.) : *sone* : *done* 567. — Sir Torr. *dore* (*duru*) : *before* 367, *son* : *Aragon* 765, *com* : *kyngdome* 1762, *sonne* (*sunu*) : *done* 1801.

Such examples could easily be multiplied; more will be found given by Fick, pp. 16, 17, and Menze, p. 40, who, with some others who have written on Northern and Midl. diall., have noticed this lengthening and recognised the *o*-quality of the lengthened vowel; most of the above quotations (with the exception of the Sc.) are collected from their treatises, from Wackerzapp and the following: Wende, p. 17, Ullmann, p. 14, Dannenberg, p. 17, Zielke, p. 17, Ellinger, p. 11, Adam, p. 12, Schlüter, p. 21, Hattendorf, p. 25. We see from these that the lengthening is not confined to the N., but also appears in Midl. texts.

§ 378. Further evidence is given by the orthography and also by the grammarians of the 16th and following centuries. From Sweet, HoES., I collect the following : — *dore*, Lay., North. (i. e. Northern Engl.), Wicl. and Chauc., pron. with (oo, uu) Gill, (*door*) Lediard, Buch., Sher.; *loov* Cheke, (uu) Smith; *son* with (o) Bullokar; *honey* with (o) Buch.; *thoner*, Ps., Town l. M.; *sonien* (= scunian) Lay., *schones* Ps.; *stonien* (= stunian); *wont* with (o) Buch., (cf. the usual pronunc. in rec. sp.); *nhote* (OE. hnutu) Ay., *o* Prompt.; *wo(o)de*, Chauc., *woode*, Tindal.

§ 379. In the course of the preceding §§ we have occasionally hinted at the second consideration, the neglect of which has led to erroneous statements. The long vowel is not found to the same extent in all diall.; as far as our present materials go, it would seem that it is of far more frequent occurrence in the N. than in the S., but the question requires further investigation before this can be settled; fuller examination of the mod. diall. would probably make this more clear. At any rate the lengthening is certainly to be accepted for the N., both of *i*- and *u*-.

§ 380. In the face of the above evidence it is impossible to agree with Morsbach (p. 181). His first statement against t. Br.'s theory is "that OE. *i* and *u* in open accented syll. appear neither in ME. nor in NE. as a lengthened vowel or diphthong". It is true, as shown above, that there is no trace of a diphthongal pronunc., but the vowels are lengthened both in ME. and in NE., and more in dial. than in rec sp. The number of words in rec. sp. with long vowel is but small (the number of words with OE. *i*- and *u*- in which there is no disturbing influence is altogether small), five with OE. *i*-, or *six* if we include *weet*, and perhaps only one, viz. *door*, with OE. *u*-. Of the former, three have a *w* before the vowel;

if these were the only examples, it would be tempting to seek an explanation in the *w*, as Morsb. does; but would not its influence tend rather to produce *wu* instead of *we*? (the forms *wuke*, *wouk*, &c., are found). And M. himself says it is only in *open* syll. that this *e* is found (p. 64); *wi* remains *wi* in closed syll. And there still remain the words *beaker*, *these* and perhaps *beetle* to be explained, and the dialect forms with ı̃, as *siv*. Morsbach's by-forms *weke*, *wevel*, *wete*, are quite in keeping with what has been said above, the *e* represents that vowel $\bar{\imath}$ lengthened, nearly, if not quite, = lengthened *e*, as he says, and hence the NE. form ı̃ instead of *ai*, as he correctly observes.

§ 381. M.'s second argument, (p. 182), from the use of *o* for *u* is just as much a support for the long vowel as it is against t. Br.'s theory. He shows that *o* represents a changed *u*-sound, (i. e. the development from OE. y, (*u*), which was not very different from *o*), in closed syll. as well as open, and in proximity to all kinds of consonants. But because there is no difference in the representation it does not follow that the vowel must be in all cases short; it does away with t. Br.'s argument in his § 37, the *o* cannot be taken as a mark of a "schwebender vokal", but it may be either short or long, not exclusively the one or the other. M. shows clearly that the origin of the *o* for *u* is not to be sought in orthographical but in phonetical considerations; it was not originally used for the sake of distinction from accompanying conss., but in order to express the changed sound-value of older *u*; *u* is often written in proximity to *m*, *n*, &c., and M. shows in another place (p. 35) that there was no necessity for using *o* instead of *u* in proximity to *w*, and in many cases there is no question at all of the surrounding conss. being confused with an *u*. Still, because *u* in open syll. is only found before *n*, *m*, *v* (according to Morsb., who rejects the word *door* from this class and seems to have forgotten *wood*), he allows the preference for *o* here to be due to this striving after clearness in writing. But, even supposing this were the reason for *o* being preferred to *u*, what grounds are there for not supposing that in each case the *o* may have represented that lengthened $\bar{u}$-sound, which was not very different from $\bar{o}$, just as it certainly did in *wode*? Perhaps it may have been different in different diall., and the later return to *u* in the orthography and the pronunc. of mod. rec. sp. may be due to some dial. which did not lengthen; or there may have been actually a return to vowel-shortness in one and the same dial. Differences of dial. *must* be borne in mind in investigating this question.

§ 382. M.'s third argument, from the rimes in Chauc., seems very wide of the mark. Rimes between ı̃-, *ŭ*- and ı̃, *ū* are, as we have shown, not the ones to be at all expected, and where they appear (examples of ı̃ : ı̃ rimes have been given in § 372), they are to be considered as imperfect either in quantity or in quality. The rime *site* (*sittan*) : *wite* (*witan*) is no difficulty; it merely shows that *i* in open syll. may rime as a short vowel as well as long; in Clar. we have one example of the short vowel, *wite* : ʒ*it*, see § 360 (c), cf. Wall. *wit* : *sit*, 7. 1160; or we might even explain *site* in the same way as we do *live*, from inflected forms, *sitest*, *siteð*; in this case the two words *site* and *wite* are exactly similar and the rime proves nothing.

§ 383. The rarity of rimes in Chauc. to prove a long vowel is due, as we think, to the position of his dial. Had he written in a more northern dial., they would have been as numerous as they are in northern texts. M. makes mention of the frequent rimes in the N. between OE. $\check{u}$ on the one hand and OE. $\bar{o}$ and Fr. $\bar{o}$ on the other, but prefers to consider them incorrect in quantity and approximately good in quality. Considering the frequency with which they appear, this is too much to assume, and we must undoubtedly consider them good both in quality and in quantity.

§ 384. Another argument of M.'s against vowel-length is "the circumstance that ME. Mss. have no instances of reduplicated vowels as a sign of length". But Clar. and other Sc. texts have, if not reduplicated vowels, the spelling with *ei*, and *ui*, which amounts to the same thing, and in later ME. texts a final *e* is found as a sign of length.

§ 385. The single occurrence of an accent on the *u* in *lúfian* in the marginal notes to the Nthmb. Gospels, (see Bouterwek, p. 258, l. 1) is perhaps not altogether without meaning and may be evidence of the early date of the lengthening.

§ 386. As result, we have, then, the following parallel development of OE. *i* and *u* in open syll., as far as they are regularly developed: —

OE. i = (*i*) > ME. $\bar{\imath}$, $\bar{e}$ > NE. $\bar{\imath}$ — e. g. *these*.
u = (*u*) > $\bar{u}$, $\bar{o}$ > $\bar{u}$, $\check{u}$ (*ü*) — e. g. *wood*.

for Scotl. as follows: —

OE. i   > early MSc. $\bar{e}$, late MSc. $\bar{\imath}$ > NSc. $\bar{\imath}$
u   > $\bar{o}$ >   (*əə*), &c., see § 462.

Before *r* probably $\bar{o}$ and $\bar{e}$ became $\bar{o}$ and $\bar{e}$, cf. *door* and *here* : *swere* in Chauc.

It may be, however, that in some Engl. diall. the lengthening never took place at all.

I:

§ 387. 1. Not followed by nd, ht, g, c — rimes with

a) itself. thing : bring 1. 1092, 3. 174 : sing 1. 1186. I-wis : thus (for *this*) 1. 218, 2. 1920 : blis(e) 2. 1378, 5. 988 : this 3. 1190. will : still 1. 334 (&c.). wine (vb. = win) : begyne 3. 790, win : begine 5. 2926. is : blis, bliss 4. 2596, 2860. gift : schift (OE. *scift*, = trick) 5. 2168 — and numberless others, esp. between *sing*, *bring*, *thing*, &c. and verbal nouns and partic. forms in *-ing*. — b) OE. y (later i), see §§ 540 (a), 544 (b). — c) OE. e. still : fell 1. 980. flynt : hint (OE. *hentan*) 2. 1138. — d) ON. e. will, vb. : dwell 3. 2440. — e) ON. $\bar{y}$ (shortened) see § 550 (c). — f) Fr. or Lat. i. thing : bening 1. 210 (&c.) : resing (= resign) 4. 1480. bring : being (for *bening*) 1. 162 : cousingne 2. 1704 : bening (MS. bricht) 2. 1832. sing : bening 2. 1880. it : promit (sb., influenced by Lat. *promitto*) 5. 188. wist : resist 3. 294. thring : cousigne 3. 388. will : volateill

5. 2244. — g) Fr. ci. bring : ringe (regnare) 4. 2384. *ring* is the usual Sc. form of this word. — h) Fr. u. this (?) : Clariodus. thus (= this) : Clariodus 3. 1674. — i) Fr. -ble. thairtill : Constabill 5. 2002. (This rime might be included among the imperfect, but such rimes are very common with poor versifiers, when a final syll., usually unaccented, to suit the emergency acquires the accent.)

§ 388. The rimes in (c) and (d) are instances of the quite common association of *i* and *e* in ME. texts. They are not to be considered altogether imperfect, for the *i* and the *e* were not pure (i) and (e), but, as stated above, *i* represented a more open sound than strict (i), approaching to *e* (in fact, it had in OE. the same value, see EEP. V, 823, II, 510, 525, 573, and where it has not suffered lengthening it has remained the same sound (*i*) from OE. times down to the present day), and *e* was often in ME. a more closed sound than strict *e*, approaching to *i*. So the rimes might be perfect with a sound intermediate between *i* and *e*, which t. Br., § 7, and others represent by the symbols $i̯$, $i̦$, i^e, &c., = Ellis's (i), cf. above § 364, where references to other treatises are given. This $i̯$ is also common to the Northern and Sc. diall., as it is to all others, as Brandl has already shown, and the *i* : *e* rimes cannot be explained away by the assumption of different original forms, as Buss attempts to do with those occurring in the Sc. Leg. In *still* : *fell* we can find no authority for *stell* instead of *still*, nor for *fill* instead of *fell*. They are either imperfect rimes, which in the abundance of examples in all diall. would be very remarkable, or to be considered as perfect with the pronunc. $i̯$, or perhaps as Brandl, AnzfdA. 13. 102, designates them, "half-pure".

§ 389. The mod. Sc. diall. do not throw much light on the matter. On the one hand OE. *i* has become *e* in closed syll. in (med'l) = middle, (geld) = to gild, (steqk) = stink, (sweqk) = swink, (ren) = run, (thres'l) = thistle, (set) = sit, (te¹mʊr) = timber, (shre¹qk) = shrink, (fe¹qər) = finger, (en) = in, (theq) = thing, (hem) = him, (lc¹p) = lip, (kwek) = quick, (tel) = till, (fe¹lk) = which, (wel) = will, (ge¹f) = if, (c¹z)d) = is it, (shɛp) = ship, (kest) = chest; (in many of the foregoing the *i*-form exists by the side of the *e*-form). On the other hand, OE. *e* has become *i* or $i̯$ in (strik) = stretch, (biz'm) = besom, (binsh, bintj) = bench, (drintj) = drench, (wintj) = wench, (linth) = length, (strinth) = strength, (rist) = rest, (twinty) = twenty; (here, too, there are often two forms given by Ellis, *i* and *e*, by the side of each other). It will be noticed that the two sounds interchange chiefly before *n*, *m* and *l*.

§ 390. Zielke, p. 15, says *e* becomes *i* in proximity to palatals and dentals in all ME. diall., and that this is very extensive in the mod. diall. of the Midl. and S.; cf. Franz, Engl. Stud. 12. 210, and, for the 16th Cent., Panning, Dialektisches Englisch in Elizabethanischen Dramen, p. 32. Brandl, AnzfdA., 13. 102, says *i* is lowered to *e* especially before *s*, *n*, *r*, *l*, followed by a conson., and in somewhat less degree before single dentals, *n*, *r* and *v*. It seems, then, that there were two tendencies, one by which *i* could become *e*, and another by which *e* could become *i*, so that both were liable to become $i̯$, the half-way sound between them, thus rendering rimes between them possible, and that this sound might then become *e* in mod. diall. or remain *i*. The laws, if any, by which this was settled, have yet to be found out; at any rate a following palatal was, as the above examples show, decisive for the *i*-sound.

§ 391. ʒeing, ʒing. This is not from WS. *geong*, but from the ONthmb. form *ging* which existed by the side of the regular *giung*, *gung* (see Sievers § 157, Sweet § 430, Hilmer p. 18), just as *gind* stood for WS. *geond*. The rime words contain

a) OE. **i**, ʒoung : thing 2. 1542 : abasing 1. 54 : fighting 1. 82 : biding 4. 350 : commoning 4. 1700 : sojorning 5. 2854,

ʒing : king 1. 806 (&c.) : distelling, ptc. 4. 1792 : commoning 5. 526 : beholding 5. 1814,

ʒeing : king 2. 1626 (&c.) : luging (= lodging) 3. 410 : clothing 4. 968 : sing 3. 1252 (&c.) : thing 3. 1264.

b) Fr. **i**, ʒoung : bening 1. 180.

ʒing, or ʒeing, is the usual MSc. form, but it has disappeared in the mod. diall., all of which have the same pronunc. as in rec. sp. with (ᴣq). The scribe in many instances has substituted the other form (English) ʒoung, but not so often in rime as in the text; there was here some attempt at retaining good eye-rimes, notwithstanding that to the ear of the scribe they were imperfect.

§ 392. *kist* must be derived from ON. *kista* and not from Angl. *cest* = WS. *ciest*, as is shown by the *k* in place of *ch*; the vowel, too, is then explained directly, without a raising from *e* to *i*. Murray's dial., D. 33, still has *kist* for *chest*, see DSS., pp. 121, 122.

§ 393. *ges* = NE. guess, is generally derived from one of the cognates, MLG. *gissen*, MDu. *ghissen*, Dan. *gisse*, Swed. *gissa* (see Stratm.-Bradl.), but it is strange that in all dialects the vowel is *e*; the word must come from some form (OE. or other dial.?) with *e*-vowel. Clar. has *ges* : *riches* 3. 804 : *doutles* 3. 2406.

§ 394. *this* and *thus* are often interchanged in the MS., cf. § 387 (h), where *this* rimes with *Clariodus*. In other texts we find the same confusion between the two words; e. g. *this* is written for *thus* in Sc. Leg. 26/853, Dunb. 42. 82., Roll. C. V. 2. 562.

§ 395. 2. Before **nd** — rimes only with itself.
fynd : behind 2. 1062, finde : binde 3. 1668.
lynde (OE. *lind*, lime-tree) : behinde 4. 1772.

§ 396. These rimes alone give us no positive evidence as to the quantity of the vowel, but the negative evidence is very important; for whereas there are otherwise rimes in abundance between OE. *i* and *y*, before all kinds of consonant-groups, it is before *nd* alone that the two vowels are kept distinct, which points to a difference of development in this position. This is further supported and confirmed by the evidence of the orthography and of the mod. diall. The occasional spelling with *y* might imply length, cf. § 359; but the *y* is very rare, in the above six examples it occurs only twice, and in the middle of the verse we generally find *i*, *blindit* 3. 237, *windo* 2. 1309, *to-blindit* 3. 1796, *windis* 3. 1957, *wind* 3. 1965, &c. On the other hand OE. *y* before *nd* is *always* represented in Clar. by *y*, inside the verse we always find *mynd*, never *mind*.

§ 397. The mod. Sc. diall. show the same difference, as will be seen from the following, summarised from EEP. 5: — OE. *blind* appears as (blend) 33 (i), (ble¹n'd) 33 (ii), (blin) 35, (bli₁₁nd) 38, (ble¹n) 39; OE. *rind* as (rɛin'd) 33 (ii), (rɛnd) 38; OE. *wind* as (wɛnd) 33 (i), 36, (wɛn) 33 (ii), (wi₁₁nd) 38, (we¹n, win, wyn) 39, (wind) 42; OE. *bindan* as (bend) 33 (i), (be¹n'd) 33 (ii), (bin) 35, (bi₁₁nd) 38, (be¹n) 39; OE. *findan* as (fend) 33 (i), 37, (fe¹n'd) 33 (ii), (find) 34, 37, 42, (fən) 35, (fin) 35, 36, (fi₁₁nd) 38, (fe¹n, fen) 39, (fin') 42; OE. *grindan* as (grend) 33 (i), (gre¹n'd) 33 (ii), (grɛn) 35, (gri₁₁nd) 38, (gre¹n) 39, (grind) 42; OE. *windan* as (wɛn'd) 33 (ii), (wɛn, win, wáind) 35, (wóind) 38, (win) 39, (wind) 42; OE. *hind* as (hent) 33 (i), (hidmʊst, hinmʊst) 42; OE. *behindan* as (a-hént) 33 (i), (ʊhent) 41. But OE. *gecynd* appears as (kɛin'd) 33 (ii), (kin) 35, (kéind) 36, 38, (kjáin) 39, (ká¹ind) 41, kindness = (kennys) 34; and OE. *mynd* as (mɛin'd) 33 (ii), (mɛin, mɛin) 35, (móind) 36, 38, (máin, móind, móin) 39, (má¹ind) 41. That is, for OE. *i* we have a short vowel, but for OE. *y* the diphthong which regularly represents ME. *i*. The few discrepancies in the above must be due to false information on the part of Ellis's authorities, or to the diall. having been subject to disturbing influences.

§ 398. Further, it will be seen below that OE. *y* before *nd* rimes with *i* in words of Fr. origin, in which the vowel certainly was long, and which at the present day contain the diphthong *ai*, *ei*, &c., in the mod. Sc. diall. So that we may look upon it as certain that the dial. of our author had a short vowel in *find*, *bind*, *lind*, *behind*, but a long vowel or diphthong (probably the latter) in *mind* and *kind*, and that the dial. of the chief scribe was in this respect exactly similar.

§ 399. It will be noticed from § 397 that in the Mid and North Lowland diall. more often than not the *d* is dropped after *n*. This is also reflected in Clar. in the rimes of OE. *y* with Fr. *i*, cf. § 542 (b). For -*ind* there is no evidence in this particular, but we shall probably not be wrong in allowing the mod. diall. here to lead us to the assumption that the words *find*, *bind*, had also lost, or were losing, their *d* in the author's dial. This is, in fact, one of the special characteristics of the Middle Period of Lowl. Sc., when the Mid Lowl. variety of the Edinburgh division had the upper hand as the language of the court and the literary world; it is, according to Murray (DSS. 28, 53, 121) due to Celtic influence, and has its analogy in the dial. of Barony Forth in Ireland, where *loane* stands for *land*, &c.; also in SW. Engl., cf. Elworthy, Dial. of W. Somerset. Some of the rimes which have been reckoned among the assonances, such as n : nd, ng : nd, are rather to be considered as correct in Sc. texts, (final -*ng* was also liable to drop its *g*). Perhaps this throws some light on an obscure passage in K. Q. st. 107, in which we obtain a better sense by taking *bynd and* as written, and *mynes* as = *myndes*, and translate —

with others to bind and to discern their minds (i. e. to tell whether your lady is favourably disposed towards you), that belongs not to me to perform alone (independent of other deities).

§ 400. The other MSc. writers, with the exception of those who are undoubtedly affected by Southern influence, observe on the whole the same difference between OE. *ind* and *ynd*. It is striking how seldom the words in question appear in rime in some authors; this is probably due to this very difference in pronunc., which made the Sc. poet's range of rimes much more limited than of a writer in a Southern dial. Bruce has no rimes at all with these words, which is very strange considering the length of the work, over 13,500 lines. In the Sc. Leg. they are rare, but generally regular; an examination of over 17,000 lines (Prologue and Nos. 1 to 26, vol. 1 of Horstmann's edit.), gave as result *seven* rimes with $i:i$, viz. 23/626, 70/552, 77/366, 85/22, 171/78, 173/192, 195/236 (*eleven* if we count four assonances, *fynd : mornynge* 164/266, *bynd : kinge* 165/384, *bynde : thrynde = thrynge*, according to Horstmann, 6/86, *fynd : lowynge* 170/686), one with $i:e$, viz. *fynd : kend* 191/984, three with $y:y$, viz. 110/220, 148/470, 152/822, one assonance with OE. *ig* : Fr. *i*, *nynte : Ynde* 86/4, only one rime with $i:y$, *fynd : kynd* 153/890, and one with $y:e$, *mynd : wend* 128/276. The Troj. War fragments have four $i:y$ rimes, *fynde : kynde* 1.78, 514, 564, *wynde : kynde* 1.458, one with $i:i$, and one with $y:y$. Can the fact of these rimes occurring at all in the Sc. Leg. and Troj. W. be used as a further piece of evidence in support of Buss's arguments against the authorship of Barbour?

In Wall. these rimes are also scarce, but perfectly regular, $y:y$ five times and $i:i$ only once, although the poem has no less than 11,853 lines. Gol. has *bynde : wynd* 440, and *kynde : fynd : lynd : bynd* 125. Lanc. (3486 lines) has nine rimes with $i:y$, ll. 19, 197, 503, 868, 1244, 1426, 1910, 1984, 2008, one with $i:i$, 1606, and one with $y:y$, 1864. Rat. Rav. (2750 lines) has four rimes with $i:i$, seven with $y:y$, one with $i:y$, *fynd : kynd*, 1.1780, and five in which the word *friend* rimes with OE. *y*, *kinde* 2. 332, *vnkind* 2. 388, 3. 128, *mankynd* 3. 54, *vnkend* (for *vnkind*) 3. 216. It must be remembered that in this word *friend* the short vowel is only of recent date; formerly it had, like *fiend*, a long vowel and in the mod. Sc. diall. we still find *frīnd*, *frīn*, but not with diphthong *fraind*, the *ī* comes from a MSc. *ę̆* (not *ī*), and it is from ME. *frĕnd* that the mod. Engl. *frĕnd* is to be explained. So the last mentioned rimes are impure in quality unless the OE. plur. *friend, frȳnd* produced ME. or MSc. *frīnd*; at any rate they do not break the rule that OE. *ynd* has a *long* vowel in MSc.

Dunb. is perfectly regular, only the word *Ynd* (proper name = India) always rimes with long vowel, with *mynd, kynd, strynd*. With regard to this word we must remember that proper names are often irregular. Perhaps the length of vowel is due to the nature of the French vowel? *Ynde* appears in many other texts with a long vowel. Dougl. has $i:i$ 28 times, $y:y$ 33 times, OE. i : Fr. i once, *wind : Ind* 3. 64. 6, OE. y : Fr. i 3 times, *mynd : fynd* = refined 3. 60. 20, *kynd : Inde* 3. 201. 24, *mynd : defynd* 2. 252. 12, and *i : y* only three times, *rynd : kynd* 3. 78. 18, *myndis : wyndis*, 3. sg., 3. 262. 32, *mynd : rynd* 4. 52. 8. Lyndes. (altogether over 18000 lines) has *i : i* 12 times, *y : y* 8 times, *y* : Fr. *i* 5 times, (*mynde* : *Ynde* 3 times, *kynde* : *Ynde*, and *mynde* : *inclynde*), OE. *y* : OE. *ī* once, *mynd* : *pynd*, ptc., and twice we find the triple rime *kyndis* : *Hyndis* : *strandis*, Mon. 5022, Dreme 824; here there is evidently laxity of rime in *strandis* and perhaps also in the other two words. Roll. C. V. (3982 lines) has *y : y* 3 times, *i : i* once, no rimes with *i : y*. The Satir P. give an interesting confirmation of the difference between OE. *ind* and *ynd* in pure Sc. These poems are of a late date (1565—1584), and from their nature, being intended for the people at large and not for an educated class of readers, were likely to be more popular in language and preserve local peculiarities of pronunc. Some of them have very poor rimes, being full of assonances, but the vowels rime for the most part correctly and it is striking that the two classes of words, with one exception (p. 170, *unkynde, mynde, strynde, rynde*) never rime with each other in those poems which are of Sc. origin, but in three of them, Nos. 1, 9 and 34, which the editor in his preface, p. XII, says are undoubtedly of Engl. origin, such rimes are found, e. g. *finde : mynde* 1. 28, *wynde : mynde* 1. 40, 100, *blinde : assynde : mynde* 1. 350, *myndes : finde* 1. 608, *mind : find* 9. 34, *kynd : find* 34. 25, *mynd : find* 34. 67. In the others, genuine Scotch, we meet with such rimes and assonances as the following: — *cryme : kynde : mynde : Ingyne* p. 34, *mynde : pynde* p. 86, *minds : pynis* p. 133, *mynd : strynd* p. 162, *kynd : freind* p. 231, *kynd : Inclynde* p. 245, *kynd : Inclynd : mynd : defynd* p. 256, *find : sin : win : burne* (for *brin*) p. 35, and many others with *i : i* or *y : y*, but only the one single instance mentioned above of *i : y*. With Montg., one of the latest poets of the Sc. literary period, it is only to be expected that Southern influence should be shown to some extent, and in addition to this with his elaborate system of riming, not only at the end of the lines, but often three times in the middle of the line, it was but natural that he was sometimes at a loss for a suitable rime-word, and often strained a point or two to bring in words which did not make the best of rimes. So we find the rimes: — *kynd : fynd* p. 31, *behind : pind* (= tortured) p. 85, *strynd : kynd : hynd* (= deer) : *mynd* p. 155, *Hyndis : kyndis : tyndis* (= horns) p. 193. Otherwise we find 13 rimes with *i : i*, 5 with *y : y*, and the following in which OE. *y* rimes with OE. *ī* or Fr. *i*: — *kind : mind : pinde* (= tortured) : *inginde* p. 64, *Ind : mynd : kynd : pynd* p. 119, *pynit : unkind : mind* p. 133, *mynd : pynd* p. 147, *mynd : defynd : kynd* p. 169, *mynd : enclynd : pynd : kynd* p. 203, *inclynd : kynd : mynd : pynd* p. 218.

It is noticeable that amongst the exceptions the words *rind*, and *hind* appear oftenest with the unexpected long vowel, cf. also *Tayis Bank* (Irving. p. 206) *mynd : kynd : rynd : hynd*, but (p. 207) *wynd : wodbynd : lynd : fynd*; and these words are given by Ellis 1. 290, as having the same sound in NSc. as *mind* and *kind*, viz. the diphthong *ei* or *əi*.

§ 401. In N. Engl. we do not find this difference observed. Sir Tr. has *kinde : finde* 141, 1364, *kinde : tinde : finde : linde* 511, *kinde : finde : binde : Ynde* 2894; in the first 10,000 lines of Curs. M. we find *i : i* 14 times, *y* : *y* twice, *i* : *y* 13 times and, of these latter, *four* are only found in the Trin. MS. C.; in the first 6,000 lines of the North[n] Leg. we find *i* : *i* three times, *y* : *y* 8 times, *i* : *y* 4 times (12/90, 74/690, 77/16, 85/400) and *Ynde* rimes with *kynde* and *fynde* once each, 20/20, 21/108; Yw. Gaw. has *find* : *kynde* 957, 1035, 1051; Mass B. has also *i* : *y* rimes in MS. C. (Northern dial.); Relig. P. *mynde* : *strynde* : *kynde* : *fynde* p. 85, *kynde* : *mynde* : *blynde* : *fynde* p. 87.

N. W. Midl. — Sir Gaw. *wynde* : *kynde* p. 11, St. Werburge (Chester) has *y* : *y* 14 times, *y* : *i* 19 times.

NEMidl. Desp. Body and S.: *kinde* : *minde* : *binde* : *blinde* 361, Am. *kinde* : *Ynde* : *finde* 760, *minde* : *bihinde* : *finde* 2193, Ipom. *mankynde* : *fynde* 503.

§ 402. It appears, then, that in Scotl. the distinction between -*ind* and -*ynd* is always observed except in the poems which bear strong evidence of Southern influence, (from the end of the 16th cent. on very little really pure Scotch poetry is to be found), while in the N. and Midl. the rule is not so strictly observed, and further South there is no distinction at all. Such rimes, then, as the above may perhaps be used, with restrictions, as a test for localising the dial. of Northern ME. texts. At any rate, in all future investigations attention must be paid to these rimes; up to the present all dissertations have simply taken for granted that lengthening has taken place before -*nd*, without separating words with OE. -*ind* from those with OE. -*ynd*.

§ 403. Fick's reasoning, p. 20, requires some modification in the light of the above facts. He assumes for the N. W. Midl. district that in the ME. period there was lengthening before -*nd*, and that in the NE. period there has been a return to the short vowel, for, as he observes, the dial. there show no lengthening of *i* in *ind* as a rule. (The Engl. diall. of the N. all show the same difference between OE. -*ind* and -*ynd*, as the Scotch; *bĭnd*, *fĭnd*, &c., are found with short vowel as far S. as Lincolnshire on the East Side, and as S. Lancs. on the West, but *mind* and *kind* have everywhere a diphthong). But Fick's only example contains OE. *y*, not *i*, *kynde* : *schynde*, and the mod. diall. do show lengthening for *ynd*; so that his theory falls to the ground and the truth probably is, that -*ind* was *ĭnd* in the N. W. as well as in Scotl. right through the ME. period, and has never been altered in pure dial., while OE. *ynd* became -*īnd* there as everywhere else, for which Fick's rime is satisfactory evidence. But, as shown by the examples given above, the ME. texts of the N. and N. Midl. diall. did not always correctly reflect pure dial., or else the treatment of these words gives us a criterion for localising the texts more exactly, -*ĭnd* being proof of a more Northern locality.

§ 404. Kluge, PG. 1. 866, sets *bĭndan*, *blĭnd*, *fĭndan*, *grĭndan*, *wĭnd*, *gecȳnd*, as general OE., with long vowel, and says this lengthening must have been completed at the latest by the 10th cent.; but he also says, "the chronology of these lengthenings (before certain conson.-groups) is very complicated", and again, "not all vowels are to the same degree liable to lengthening" and "*nd, ng* lengthen, as it seems, 'only in a few diall'." He brings forward as evidence of the lengthening the frequent use of accents in OE. texts, such as the Blickling Homilies, &c.; and stress is also laid upon the importance of these accents by Sievers § 124, and Sweet, § 395. The latter says, "the accuracy of the mss. differs greatly", § 379. Sievers says, "the different texts vary very considerably in the matter of the lengthenings, but there are the rule in Lind. and Rushw.".

§ 405. Matters would be very simple for us, if we could show that there was no lengthening of *ĭ* before *nd* in ONthmb. But this seems difficult to decide until the whole question of the meaning of the accents in OE. mss. has been satisfactorily cleared up, although the evidence we have at present leads us to assume that there was lengthening of *i* as well as of other vowels before *nd*. In the ONthmb. glosses of the Gospels, (Skeat's edition), there are instances in which an accent is placed over the *i* in *ind*, viz. *uínde* (vento) Matt. 11. 7, *gebínde* 12. 29, *wínd* (ventus) 14. 30; *blínd* Joh. 9. 24, *ofblíndade* (excaecavit) 12. 40; *wudu bínde* Mk. 1. 6, *blínd* 10, 46; *blínd* Luke 18. 35.

§ 406 How are these accents to be interpreted? The accents are, it is true, not used with much regularity; in some chapters they are hardly found at all; in others it seems to have occurred to the scribe to pay particular attention to them and he puts them in very profusely; and in others he seems to have been careful only to mark certain particular words, as *ríc, tíd, éc*, which appear very frequently with an accent. Sometimes a word is accented once and appears again in close proximity without an accent; in Joh. 12, where we find *blínd* once, there are twelve cases of *blind* or its inflected forms or compounds without accent in the same chapter. But on the whole the accents appear on vowels which must have been long, as we learn from comparative grammar and the later development of the words in English; where they appear on vowels that can only have been short, Sweet, § 381, explains them partly as "the result of pure carelessness", and it is in many cases possible that "the accent was meant for the preceding syllable" or the following one. In the case of *índ* it might be considered that the accent was used to distinguish the stroke of the *i* from those of the following *n*. This would appear more probable if we could find examples of an *i* similarly accented in words in which the vowel could only have been short. These failing, and an accent being found on other vowels before *nd*, e. g. *infánd*, Matt. 12. 44, *ge-ónduorde* 12. 48, *hónd* 12. 49, *énde* 13. 40, &c., &c., in which such an explanation would not apply, we must probably accept vowel-length in *índ* as well as in *ánd, énd, índ, únd*.

§ 407. We must not forget the possibility that the accents in the Nthmb. Gospels may be due to a Midl. or Southern revising scribe. If they are not, and if it should finally be proved that there *was* lengthening before *nd* in ONthmb., we then have the further questions, when did the shortening take place in the N. of Engl., why only in the N. and why only in the case of certain vowels? A possible solution may be found in Norse influence, viz. the adoption in place of the vernacular *fínd, blínd*,

&c., of the very similar Norse forms *fĭnd*, *blĭnd*, &c., just as *yive* and *foryit* were replaced by *give* and *forget*. Cf. Kluge, PG. 1.791, "Im allgemeinen scheint sich der mischungsprozess so vollzogen zu haben, dass skand. worte neben den urverwandten engl. platz nehmen und diese dann schliesslich ganz verdrängen.".

Brate, p. 8, prefers other causes than Scand. influence to explain the absence of lengthening in certain words in Orm.; but none of these, though evidently correct for Orm., give a satisfactory explanation of these Sc. forms, which do not appear in isolated instances, for, as shown above, all words with original *-ind*, whether the syll. be unstressed, followed by shortening syll., liable to influence by analogy, or not, show vowel-shortness.

§ 408. Ellis, in EEP. 1. 276 ff. and 290, misses the point altogether, for he does not separate original *-ind* from *-ynd*, but simply classes them together (as has generally been done by all others) and thereby introduces matter which is no support to his arguments. From the fact that *bĭnd*, *blind*, *find*, &c., still have a short ĭ in the N. of Engl. we cannot argue that in Chauc.'s language they had a short ĭ too, and that therefore the words which rime with them in Chauc., as *mind*, *kind*, could not possibly contain a diphthong; they probably did not, but the words *bind*, &c., give no argument to prove this; the dial. of Cumb. cannot prove anything for Chauc.'s dial. (Although Ellis does not use these words directly as arguments, he does so indirectly, speaking of them as "analogies" with *mind*, *kind*, *Ind*). Again, on p. 276, he argues similarly, that *kind* was pronounced with a short *i*, from rimes with *Ind*. But, as we have seen above, this word seems generally to have had a long vowel, and, as Ellis says, still has to-day in poetry. He looks upon this as an irregularity due to eye-rimes, and says that, as *India* has a short vowel, *Ind* must too. But this is not convincing; *Ind* and *India* can stand in the same relation to one another as *chĭld* and *chĭldren*. That "the nasal pronunc. in French is not indicated in the numerous words beginning with *in-*" is also no proof; in most of them the *in-* is a mere prefix which did not originally bear the stress; and beyond these there is no instance of Fr. *ind* or *in* before a voiced conson. which would make lengthening possible, so that analogous cases are wanting. In one word we have *int*, viz. *pint*, and here the *i* has been lengthened and diphthonged even before a voiceless cons. We may probably, therefore, look upon (əind) as the regular pronunc. of *Ind*, which, either through the rare use of the form or through the influence of *India*, has been gradually lost, except where it survives in poetry, and this form is regularly developed from the ME. form with ĭ. Whether this is to be explained from the nasality of the French vowel, or is due to some other cause, the fact that it did not coincide with the sound in *bind*, *find*, &c., at any rate points to a difference in quality of Fr. *-ind* from native *-ind*. The correct interpretation of the rimes given by Ellis, p. 276, as appearing in Chauc., such as *kynde* : *Inde*, *fynde* : *kynde* : *mynde* : *Inde* : *bynde* : *lind*, is rather that the vowel in *find*, *bind*, *lind* was lengthened in Chauc.'s dial. and could thus rime with that in *kind*, *mind*, *Ind*, which was long in all diall.

§ 409. In Ellis's D. 1., the dial. of the Baronies of Forth and Bargy, in which, at the time the materials were collected from which Ellis's lists were made, ME. ī was still kept pure and not diphthonged to ǝi, we also find ī in the words *kind*, *wind*, &c., i. e. both OE. *ind* and *ynd* had the long vowel.

§ 410. 3. i + c

In the pronoun 1 pers., the *i* was originally short, ĭc, but it appears already in OE. as īc, with long ī, cf. Sievers, § 332, and after this ī, the c became vocalised and absorbed, producing ME. ī, without guttural. The rime words contain

a) OE. or ON. i + g. I : ly (vb.) 1. 1086 : ladie 2. 282, 4. 1746 : worthy 4. 1354, and many adverbs in *-ly*, *-lie*, cf. § 413. — b) OE. e + g. see § 164 (I : say). — c) Fr. i. I : victorie 1. 198 : melancholie 1. 1030 : adulterie 2. 302 : cry 4. 1466 : genealogie 2. 308 : companie 2. 964 : chevalrie 4. 1434.

For the pronunc. of this Fr. *i* in unstressed syll. cf. § 415.

§ 411. 4. i + g — rimes with

a) OE. ī. ly (vb.) : by (OE. *bī*) 1. 1160, 2. 1310; lyis (3. sg.) : wayis (for *wise*, cf. § 441) 3. 434, 4. 652 : syis (*sīþas*) 2. 370. — b) OE. i + e, see § 410 (a). — c) Fr. i. nyne (*nigon*) : defyne 5. 102 : cristallyne 5. 2184. ly (vb.) : companie 3. 1060. — d) Fr. ei, see § 164 (by : perfay).

For *ig* in unstressed syll. see §§ 413, 414.

§ 412. It is evident that here, as everywhere else, OE. i + g has become ī through vocalisation of the gutt. and absorption in the preceding vowel, in the same way as *i + c*, see § 410. The mod. Sc. diall. show invariably the diphthong *ai*, *ei* or *ǝi*, with no trace of the gutt. and this diphthong had probably been formed already in the dial. of our author, cf. § 432 &c.; hence we read *ei* or *ai* in all of the above rimes.

§ 413. The adverbial ending -ly or -lie.

This is to be derived from ON. *-ligr*, *-liga*, cf. t. Br. § 53. The OE. *-līce* produced ME. *-liche*, *-leche*, which is abundantly found in Southern texts.

The rime words contain (only a few of the numerous examples are given)

a) OE. ī. quhy : tenderlie 2. 504, why : lustillie 4. 1922. by : aluterly 2. 910 (&c.). — b) OE. i + g. ly (*licgan*) : delyverly 1. 56. and numberless rimes with the ending OE. *-ig*, as worthie : glaidly 4. 520, ladie : greattumlie 2. 1622 (&c.), &c. — c) OE. ĭ + e. I : perpetualy 1. 1118 (&c.). ferlie (*fǣrlīc*, Angl. *fērlīc*) : oppinlie 2. 780. — d) OE. ēo, see § 330 (o). — e) OE. ēāg, ēāh, Angl. ēg, ēh, see § 217 (d). — f) OE. æ + g, see § 164. — g) OE. æ, see § 226 (q). — h) Fr. i. cry : suddentlie 3. 1662 (&c.) : fellounlie 1. 1256 : petiously 1. 98, 476. allay (= *ally*) : truely 1. 410. victorie : only 1. 240 — and numberless others. — i) Fr. ei, see § 164. — k) Fr. e. bewtie : heartfullie 3. 674, pitie : cruellie 3. 1514, cuntrie : glaidlie 4. 390, degrie : fullie 5. 780. — l) ? Guy : worthilie 1. 1080.

§ 414. OE. ig in the adjectival ending *-ie* (usually unstressed) has exactly similar rimes, with Fr. *i* and also with OE. ēāg, eah, &c., Fr. e.

§ 415. We have evidently to do with two pronunciations here. On the one hand we have rimes with OE. $\bar{\text{i}}$, $\breve{\text{i}}$c, which only produced a diphthong, *ei* or *ai*, and on the other hand with $\bar{ea}$, $\bar{e}$ + gutt., $\bar{eo}$ and Fr. *e*, which produced an $\bar{\text{i}}$ ont of previous $\bar{\text{e}}$; these two sets of rimes are irreconcilable without the assumption of two different sounds; and further, we have rimes with Fr. *i*, which resembles OE. *ig* in likewise producing two pronunciations, according as it appears in stressed or unstressed syll. Usually, in the words in question, the suffix -*lie* or -*ie* was, of course, unstressed and the vowel $\bar{\text{i}}$ was consequently not subject to the diphthonging, hence the numerous rimes with previous $\bar{\text{e}}$, which prove for the latter that the change $\bar{e} > \bar{\text{i}}$ had already taken place. But when in rime, or for the sake of emphasis perhaps, they became stressed, then they underwent the usual diphthonging, cf. the mod. occasional pronunc. of *sure-lý* in dial., with (əi). Gill distinctly admitted the double pronunc. of the adverbial ending -*ly*, cf. Kluge PG. 1. 898, and below § 445;. and Murray, DSS., p. 136, shows that the same doubleness exists in the mod. diall., the adv. suffix *ly*, usually = (li), is "sometimes purposely accented and made (lai), trew-lȳ = (trəu-lai)."

§ 416. Words in -ight, -icht, -yght, -ycht

The vowel, spelt *i* or *y*, has in these words various origins: —

1. OE. ie, i < eo = Gmc. i, ë; knight, right, bright, wight (sb. = person), sight, plight, fight, wight (= weight). — 2. OE. i < ea (Nthmb. æ); night, might (sb. and vb.). — 3. OE. i = Lat. i; dight. — 4. OE. eo (with later palatisation) = Gmc. $\bar{\text{i}}$; light (adj. and adv.). — 5. OE. $\bar{\text{i}}$; alight, vb. — 6. OE. $\bar{ie}$, Angl. ë, mut. of $\bar{eo}$, $\bar{ea}$; light, (vb.), height. — 7. OE. $\bar{eo}$ (with later palatisation) = Gmc. iu; light, sb. — 8. OE. y, mut. of u; flight. — 9. ONthmb. e in redupl. pret.; hight (= was called, heht). — 10. ON. ü; sleight (*slǽgþ*). — 11. ON. $\bar{\text{i}}$; wight (adj., ON. *vīgt*, neut. of *vīgr*).

§ 417. In Clar. these words rime promiscuously with one another, but with no others, except in the isolated case of *plicht* : *quhyte* (OE. *hwīt*) 5. 910. This is clear evidence that the gutt. was pronounced, as is usual in all other MSc. works, and as it still is to the present day in all Sc. diall. There is now no trace of the gutt. in the S. of Engl., where it finally disappeared early in the 17th cent. or at the close of the 16th, cf. Sweet, p. 260; its absence is first admitted by Butler (1633); for the evidence of the other early mod. Engl. phonetic authorities see Sweet, p. 259 ff., Ellis, EEP. Pt. 3, and Kluge, PG. 1. 849. It was certainly in existence in some parts of Engl. in the 16th cent. and t. Br., § 121, is probably right in assuming it to exist in Chauc.'s pronunc. and not yet to have become silent as Morsbach p. 101 would have it. Traditional as opposed to phonetic spelling was hardly so far established at such an early date, and according to Morsbach's examples the gutt. was generally written. But in the N. it disappeared much later than in the S. and in Scotl. not at all; all the authorities have universally recognised it as a peculiarity of Northerners, the septentrionales (Wallis), and the rime *plicht* : *quhyte* is another instance of Southern influence, or is to be considered as a piece of careless riming or faulty copying of the scribe, as Sarrazin, Octav., p. 37, suggests for similar rimes, *fyȝt* : *smyte*, and *streyght* (= OFr. *estreit*) : *ryght* : *myght*; Fick gives *tyȝt* (OE. *tiht*) : *quit* (OE. *hwīt*) : *crysolyt*. The word *plight* seems in other diall. to have been one of the first words to drop the gutt.; cf. t. Br. Chauc. § 121 *plīt* : *appetīt*, Hattendorf, p. 24 : *disherite* : *dispite* : *cite* : *delite* : *white* : *write* : *site*, Zielke, p. 38 *tyȝt* : *quit* (*hwīt*) : *plyt* : *crysolite*, *plyȝt* : *delyt*; cf. also K. Q. *plyte* : *a lyte* 53, Dougl. *plite* : *indite* : *write* : *site* : *quhite*, 1. 36. 22, but on the other hand *plycht* : *flicht* : *micht* : *vnrycht* 1. 94. 5.

§ 418. It is unnecessary to give a full list of the rimes in Clar. The word of most frequent occurrence is *knicht*, *knight*, which rimes with almost every one of the other words in the list in § 416. It is perhaps worth noticing that in this and other words the spelling *-ght* seems to be preferred to *-cht* in the 4th and 5th Books; *knicht* appears 64 times in rime, in Bk. I 23 times, II 27, III 14, *knight* appears 54 times in rime, in Bk. I twice, Bk. II twice, III once, IV 27 times, V 22 times. With the words *bright*, *wight*, *night*, *might* it is exactly similar. The only word which decidedly prefers *c* is *dicht*, *c* 15 times, *g* twice. In Books IV and V *knight* is *only* written with *g*, and mostly with a capital K, whereas in Bk. I it is usually written with small *k*; but in this respect II and III agree with IV and V. This probably shows that in a previous copy of the existing MS. (which is the work of *one* hand) two hands at least must have been at work.

As a rule there is a striving apparent here to make good eye-rimes, and we generally find *-icht* : *-icht* and *-ight* : *-ight*; but there are exceptions to this, especially with particular words, e. g. *height*, which very seldom has *c*.

§ 419. *ycht* and *yght* are very rare; *ei* only appears in *height*, *heicht*, *weight* and twice in *leicht*. This preponderance of *i* points to vowel-shortness, and the mod. Sc. diall. prove the same, they mostly have a short vowel, *ĕ* or *ĭ*, and always the guttural, Ellis's (kjh).

§ 420. Worthy of notice is the rime *weight* (pondus) : *fight* 4. 290, where the author must have written an *i* or *y* instead of the *ei* in *weight*. Here we have the *regular* development of OE. *wiht*, instead of the *weight* of rec. sp. which is either due to the influence of the verb *weigh*, or to be derived from the Norse; in the mod. Sc. diall. the word generally has the same vowel as *might*, *right*, *night*, *sight*. It is strange that here, where we should expect Norse influence to be strongest, MSc. and NSc. show a regular development from the OE. form, and this may perhaps incline us to accept the influence of the verb *weigh* as the more likely explanation of the noun *weight* in rec. sp., as is also suggested by the similar spelling; cf. Sweet, p. 303, Morsbach, p. 69.

§ 421. Other words which only appear *once* in rime are *height*, prt. = was called (: *wight*, adj. 5. 1654) and *slicht* (: *knigt*, 3. 420). The latter rime gives us the only instance of *-gt* for *-ght* or *-cht*.

§ 422. The verbal noun in -ing.

The suffix is found in the OE. period in the form -ing, as well as -ung, therefore it is included here under Y. The rime-words contain

a) OE. i. cunyng : thing 2. 474 : bring 5. 1116 : ringe 4. 2600. walkeing : sing 1. 1400, and numberless others, also numerous self-rimes as ludging : cherising 4. 1166. — b) OE. y — numerous rimes with *king*. — c) Fr. i. fein3eing : benigne 1. 536. having : bening 2. 788. tydings : florings 2. 1330. (The word *tiding* is of Norse origin, but appears in the late OE. period already as *tidung*, Chro. F. 995, having adopted the Engl. suffix of the verbal noun, instead of the -*inde* of ON. *tiðinde*. The regular ME. form is therefore *tiding*, and the Sc. form *tydand* is due to Norse influence, with mere substitution of the Sc. suffix -*and*.) fain3eing : cousing 1. 1526. imbracing : bening 4. 398. cumjng : bening 4. 2200. loving : conding 5. 2140. crounjng : dinge (dignus) 4. 2406. — d) Fr. ei, only in the word *reign* which appears as *rigne* and *ringne*, for *ring*, the usual form in all Sc. works, and rimes with thinking 3. 222, cumjng 3. 1818.

§ 423. The Present Participle in -ing — rimes with

a) Verbal noun in -ing (the following lists are complete) — 3aiking : fighting 1. 1066. ryding : meitting 2. 200 : morning 3. 2. sitting : tyding 2. 450. distelling : speiking 3. 230 : depairting 5. 2522. leving : regrating 3. 1986. desyring : weiping 3. 2062. inclyning : tyding 3. 2292. schyning : justing 5. 1974. advysing : justing 5. 2092. — b) OE. -ing in nominal stems. thing : asking 1. 248 : pertinjng 1. 1142 : dwelling 3. 1426, 4. 1914 : distelling 3. 1490 : changing 3. 1922 : inclyning 5. 1244. bring : cunjng 2. 708 : lying 3. 2004. 3ing : distelling 4. 1972. king (OE. *y*, later *i*) : standing 2. 1680 : haistining 3. 458 : willing 3. 2418 : tending 4. 282.

§ 424. With the exception that there are no rimes with Fr. i, (probably mere chance), the above are exactly similar to the rimes of the verbal noun in § 422. The form in -*ing*, instead of Sc. -*and*, is one of the Southernisms adopted by the author of *Clar.*, and many other Sc. authors who were influenced by Chauc. and the Engl. poets. In Clar. it has to a large extent supplanted the genuine Sc. partic. in -*and* as will be seen from the following statistics : —

-*ing* appears in rime   25 times (Bk. I—3 times, II—4, III—11, IV—3, V—4),
-*and*   „   14 „ („ 1 „ „ 1, „ 3, „ 7, „ 2),
-*ing* appears in the text 508 „ („ 84 „ „ 111, „ 101, „ 121, „ 91),
-*and*   „   78 „ („ 18 „ „ 23, „ 16, „ 14, „ 7).

From the above are excluded *comjng*, which appears 11 times for *cumin*, perf. ptc.; and *vnwitting*, which is written twice for *vnwittin*, perf. ptc., vnwitting of ony wight, vnwitting of the King Clariodus. In the phrase "with tearis distelling", I take *distelling* to be intrans., = dropping, flowing, and therefore look upon it as a ptc. and include it in the above. Also in "fra day being", 3. 1035, I take *being* to be a ptc.

§ 425. Although the suffix -*and* is fairly on the way to be ousted by -*ing* (the scribes use it even much less than the author) still it is by no means lifeless; it is, in fact, sometimes used where we find in general

Engl. and also in Sc. a form in -*ing*, e. g. *tydandis* 2. 482, *tydand* : *land* 3. 6, 4. 10, cf. § 422; there are also many words derived from French present participles in -*ant* which are spelt with -*and*. It may be that these latter forms are to be explained from a general tendency to change final *t*, after a vowel-like, to *d*, as in *rugend* 1. 67, and the pret. *ordand(e)* (instead of *ordanit*) : *land* 1. 700 : *stand* 2. 1338 : *Commande* 4. 346 : *Ingland* 5. 46. Or it may be that the Fr. words were felt as pres. participles, as in most cases there was a corresponding verb also in use, and that then they acquired the ending -*and*, even in those cases where no corresponding verb existed in Engl., as *valiand*. We also find -*and* for Fr. -*ain*, e. g. *chalmerlands* 5. 1419; cf. also *mundand* = mundane 3. 115.

§ 426. Perhaps these last imply that the *d* in -*and* has disappeared in pronunc. and consequently often a meaningless *d* was tacked on to a word ending in *n*. And so it is possible that *cumand* 4. 2331 is also falsely written, like *cuming*, instead of *cumin*, the perf. ptc., MS. "day cumand was anone". -*ing* is used for Fr. -*ine* in *femening* : *inclyne*, 5. 340, evidently due only to the scribe, as the rime shows; -*ing* may have actually existed in the dialect of the latter, (cf. DSS. p. 135, and the mod. dialectal use of -*ing*, as in *garding*, *curting*, *heaving* = garden, curtain, heaven), or the *g* may be meaningless, *ng* having become -*n*. Cf. Dunb. doctring (= doctrine) : spending, &c., 41. 7, garding = garden, 3. 16, Montg. burding = burden, C. 329.

§ 427. The correct Sc. forms were -*and* for the pres. ptc. and -*ing* for the verbal noun. When Sc. poets copied Southernisms they, in this as well as in other respects, produced a confused mixture of forms which was quite artificial and did not exist in any actual dial., as is shown by Skeat, introd. to K. Q. pp. 15 and 34. So here we find the -*ing* or -*and* of the pres. ptc., the -*ing* of the verbal noun, and the -*in* of the perf. ptc. all confused with each other: but there is no case of -*ing* being used for the Chaucerian -*en* of the plur. indic. as in K. Q. Perhaps it is used for the Southern -*en* of the infin. in telling : king 1. 896, "quhen thay hard telling".

§ 428. Here follows a list of the words which have -*and* for Fr. -*ant* (where the form is confirmed by rimes, the rime-words and references are given) : —

valiand (4 times), (: fand 4. 1696 : hand 3. 1222), waliand (4 times), (: fand 2. 1022 : Northumberland 4. 2084), valʒeand (1) (: wnderstand 3. 1226), vailʒeand (2) (: Esturland 3. 1414), wailʒeand (2), plesand (8), pleasand (4) (: hand 5. 1898), pleisand (2) (: command 5. 898 : land 5. 2414), plesandlie (3), servand (3) (: Ingland 4. 232), seruand (1), servandis (3), avenand (2) (: diamand 1. 362 : diamant 5. 2447), aveinand (1) (: land 4. 1548), merchand (3), merchandis (2), marchandis (2), triumphand (3) (: band 4. 2762), triomphand (3) (: hand 5. 1572, 2178 : land 5. 2696), triumphandlie (1), Pursephand (1) (: fand 4. 34), Livetenand (1) (: land 5. 2556), Luiftenand (1) (: strand 5. 2868), cunand (= covenant) (1), briggandis? (1), thimphand? (1). Twice we find -*ond* in diamond.

emerand 5. 1788 is probably the result of exchange of suffix, cf. emerant, Dunb. Gold. T. 39.

For similar appearances cf. Zupitza, Guy p. 12, where many rimes between voice-conss. and breath-conss. are given. Z. infers from these that the poet was apt to pronounce final voice-conss. as breath-conss., but the reverse is probably the case at any rate for these words in *-ant*, *-and*; the final disappearance of the cons. is in this way better explained.

§ 429. Pres Partic. in *-and*

inclynand : band 1. 820 : Ingland 2. 436 : strand 3. 944, inclynande : handis (for *hand*) 4. 2412; dissaveand : hand 3. 1680, birnand : land 3. 1442 : hand 4. 1556, comonand : Ingland 4. 412, aboundand : fand 4. 748, desyrand : Ingland 4. 1916, abydand : fand 4. 2168, lyand : hand 5. 1302, livand : Irland 5. 2778, commonand : land 4. 744.

Ī

§ 430. OE. $i + g$ is included here, as the g became vocalised and absorbed in the i, in the same way as in $ī + g$, thus producing a simple long $ī$. Words in which an intervocal cons. has been dropped are also included with the rest, e. g. syis (OE. *sīþas*), syne (*sīþþan*).

There is no trace of any change effected upon an $ī$ by a preceding w.

(For *wyse* or *wayis*, sb., see §§ 440, 441, and for $ī$ in final syllables *ine-*, *-ite*, &c., see §§ 443—6.)

§ 431. The rime-words contain

a) OE. or ON. ī. lyve, sb. : scryve (vb. OE. *scrīfan*) 1. 236 : belyve 4. 206, 1256 : fyve 3. 648. lyfe, sb. : belyve 1. 1374 (&c.) : wyfe 1. 1462 (&c.) : knyfe (ON. *knīfr*) 2. 262 (&c.) : dryve 4. 2090. wyd(e) : syd (*sīde*) 1. 90 : synde (for *syde*) 5. 278 : abyde 4. 2026 : glyd (*glīdan*) 3. 1344. blyth : sweith (*swīþe*) 1. 1154 (&c.) : alswyth 2. 476 : alsweith 2. 656 (&c.). wyne (*wīn*) : syne (*sīþþan*) 4. 922, and many more. — b) OE. i + g, see §§ 411 (a), 413 (a). — c) OE. or ON. ȳ, see § 550 (b). — d) OE. i + h, see § 417 (plicht : quhyte). — e) OE. æ + g, see § 164. — f) OE. ē, mut. of ō, see § 155 (m). — g) Fr. i. ryde : devyde 1. 470 : cryit 3. 1854. quhy : fellonie 2. 158 : espy 3. 720. belyve, belyne : aryve, arryve 3. 34 (&c.). hy (sb. = haste, from vb. *hīgian*?) : melancholie 3. 472 : companie 2. 952 (&c.). syne (*sīþþan*) : declyne 1. 320 : discipleine 3. 868 : fyne, vb. 3. 1398 : defyne 3. 2316 : fyne, adj. 4. 338 : inclyne 4. 378 (&c.) : lyne 4. 2792. syse (*sīþas*) : compryse 4. 598 : impryse, sb. 4. 710 : pryse, sb. 4. 1988. ryce (OE. *hrīs*) : paradice 4. 1652. wyse, adj. : praise (read *pryse* as in 1. 344, cf. § 441) 5. 2158. ferlie (*færlīc*, Angl. *fērlīc*) : chevalrie 2. 1056. quhyt(e) : indyt(e) 1. 1200 (&c.) : delyt(e) 2. 368 (&c.) : perfyte 3. 1300, 5. 276, and many more. — h) Fr. ei, see § 164.

§ 432. The diphthongisation of $ī$ began in the South soon after 1400; see Kluge, P. G. 1. 872, Sarrazin, Octav. p. 37 and Litt. Bl. 5. 270, Luick Angl. 14, pp. 280, 285, Münster p. 29. If the rime in Octav. is to be interpreted in the way Sarrazin suggests, the date of the change must be set even earlier for the N. of Engl. This would only be in accordance with other observations that have been made with regard to the N., which in many respects went ahead of the S. in its sound-changes, so that Sarrazin's alternative suggestion, that the rime in question may be only due to the scribe, is perhaps unnecessary. In Scotl. the change may have taken place just as early or even earlier than in the N. of Engl.; but the question of date for Scotl. must yet remain open. Still we may at all events with comparative certainty consider the change complete by the time Clar. was written. Similar rimes to those on which Sarrazin bases his conclusions for the early date will be found in § 164, which we have taken as a possible indication of the diphthongal pronunc. of the ī if we allow the author to have occasionally employed an antiquated pronunc. in such words as *faire*, &c. We have a similar case of the retention of an older pronunc., viz. of ī as monophthong, in *syne* : *greine*, cf. § 187.

§ 433. But we have another indication perhaps of the diphthongal pronunc. in the orthography. As has already been mentioned in § 359, we notice that almost always *y* is written for OE. ī and ȳ and extremely rarely to represent the short vowel. Cannot this be taken as a sign that the copyist at least felt that there was a difference in *quality* between the short and the long sound, and that he attempted to express this phonetic difference by the employment of different symbols? The few exceptions in which *i* is used for the long sound may perhaps be due to a scribe who used an older or an Engl. orthography, possibly, though not probably, even to the author himself.

§ 434. There are other works, especially Sc., which show this same difference, but it is not observed strictly till the 16th cent., although a striving after a distinction is observable before this. Skeat, in his rime-index to Bruce, says *y* denotes long ī, but *i* is also written and there is no sharp distinction, although *y* may perhaps be more frequent. The same applies to K. Q. and the Sc. Leg. The following appear to make no difference, using *y* and *i* indiscriminately both for the long and the short sound: — Wall., Lanc., Rat. Rav., Dougl., Compl. Sc., Gau, Roll. C. V. In Dunb.'s poems OE. ī and ȳ are represented both by *i* and *y*, so also OE. ī, although *y* is preferred (Kaufmann p. 56), while OE. ȳ is *only* represented by *y*. In Gol. it is the same as in Dunb. In some texts the long sound is further often represented by *yi*, so in Roll. C. V., occasionally in Dunb., Dougl. and other Sc. poets. With regard to Lyndes. there is some variety; in the Mon. *y* and *i* are not distinguished, the suffixes *-yt*, *-yng*, &c., appear; but in the Sat. *y* is pretty consistently used only for the long sound, *-yt*, *-yng*, &c., are rarely or never found, for them *-it*, *-ing*, &c., are used; but still *y* does appear for short ī in some words, e. g. *nycht*, *mys*; perhaps this is the usual use of *y* in proximity to *m*, *n*, &c., for the sake of distinctness. Wynʒet has, according to Hewitson, in his introd., p. 96, "no definite rule to guide him in spelling. ..... The letters *y* and *i* were freely interchanged, the *y* apparently being also pronounced (*sic*) *yi*". This does not seem to be altogether correct; there appears to be a difference in the principles of spelling between the earlier and the latter portions of the work; at the beginning both *i* and *y* are used for i̯, the latter especially with *m* and *n*, while for the long sound mostly *y* is used except in French words which may have been pronounced with (ii) instead of a diphthong; in the latter portions only *i* is written for the short vowel, even with *m* and *n* (and we then see the difference between *mynd*, *kynd*, with *y*, and *bind*, *find*, &c., with *i*). Lesl. has generally *i* for the short and *y* for the long sound, except in *mycht*, *rycht*, &c. In the Satir. P. and Montg. we find the same rule as in Clar.; *y* is written with great regularity for the long sound and *i* for the short; the end-syllables *-ing* and *-it* of the participles, which in older writers are so frequently written as *-yng* and *-yt*, are so no longer.

Of course the usual restrictions apply to the above mentioned works in which *i* and *y* vary, viz. *y* is preferred by many in proximity to *m* and *n* and finally. Perhaps a closer examination of some of these would show that, with these restrictions, *y* is more often used than *i* for the long sound, as in Bruce and Dunb.

§ 435. Outside of Scotl. the same attempt at a distinction is sometimes found. In many works OE. *ī* and *ȳ* are represented by *y* consistently, while there is some variability in the representation of the short vowel. We also find *ey* used sometimes to express the diphthong, cf. Sarrazin, Litt. Bl. 5. 271 (feyre, meynde, feynde). In some it is noticeable that OE. *ȳ* is particularly represented by *y*, while OE. *ī* is not so uniformly so represented, as if the unrounding of the *y* were not complete and there were still a difference between OE. *ī* and *ȳ*, but the rimes generally show that such an interpretation is not correct; so in the York P.

§ 436. We conclude, then, that the diphthonging was of comparatively early date in Scotl. Of course the change was gradual and we cannot expect to find overwhelming evidence of the beginnings of such changes, which are probably to be dated long in advance of the time when they are regularly reflected by the orthography. We accept, therefore, a diphthong both for the time of the MS. and the date of the composition.

The mod. diall. all have a diphthong for OE. *ī*.

§ 437. Noltemeier, p. 22, argues from the rime *wy* : *quently* in Gol. that the pure ī-sound was preserved in contrast to NE. with its diphthong; but in this way we could prove that such words as *cry*, *espy*, *sky*, *why*, &c., had still pure ī at the time of Spens. and Shakesp., which we know was not the case, see Ellis, pp. 869, 959, 969. We must rather argue the other way, as above in § 415, that the rime-words in *-ly*, (which was usually unaccented), when the final syll. was stressed in rime, could and did have a diphthongal pronunc., as distinctly recognised by Gill. Ellis proves this double pronunc., unstressed (i), stressed (əi), in the rimes of Spens. and Shakesp. and also in those of Moore and Tennyson, cf. Ellis, p. 933, Kluge, P. G. 1. 898.

§ 438. Zielke, p. 28, says that ī has remained ī, undiphthonged, especially in the N., to the present day. He relies for this statement on Ellis 1. 291; but the examples given here are chiefly such as allow the mod. ī to be explained in other ways, e. g. *high*, *die*, *fly*, &c. The ī in the *child* of Devonshire and *high* = (hii) of Scotl. are of two very different origins. In the former it is a ME. i which has been retained, in the latter it is a ME. ē which has been regularly developed into i. ME. i produces in NSc. always a diphthong. The word *nighest* has the same form *nist* in Sc. and in Dev.; but in Dev. it = a ME. form *nist* from *nighest* through vocalisation of the gutt., and in Sc. it is from a MSc. form *nēst* = ONthmb. *nēsta*, cf. Sievers, § 166, 5 and § 313, note.

§ 439. In 5. 2712 there is an apparently false rime, due perhaps to a misunderstanding of the scribe. The passage as written in the MS. runs thus: —

    The king Clariodus and his companie
    In schipis enterit hes and suddanlie
    They drew vp saillis and over the waves schare
    They glyd anone alse swift as onie fyre
    And day and night thay sojorne not nor rest

The scribe perhaps understood *share*, prt. of *sheer*, to cut, OE. *sceran*, *scær*; so apparently also Piper, who puts a full-stop at *schare*. But the word is really an adj. = OE. *scir*, bright, shining, cf. Dougl. in the schyre air, 2. 192. 10, schire : desyre 2. 152. 8; K. Q. schire : fyre, 76. Jam. Dict. gives the word as still in use in Scotl. in sense of *clear, bright*, and *clear, transparent*, "clear liquor we call shire".

The following line above, then, contains the predicate to which the adverbial phrase *over the waves* belongs, so that there should be no stop at *schyre*, for which *schare* is written. The mingling of pret. and hist. pres. in one sentence need cause no offence; it is not unusual, and is, in fact, very common in Sc. poetry; the following verb, too, *sojorne*, is a present. Mod. rec. sp. has an adj. *sheer*, with (ii), which is derived from ON. *skǣr*, Sweet, p. 341; this would, on the analogy of *seat*, ON. *sǣti*, give in late MSc. and NSc. an ẹ, so that, if we can get over the difficulty of the *sch* for ON. *sk*, (perhaps there was a confusion of different forms) it is possible that the scribe understood the word correctly as an adj., but inserted another word, *schare*, (sheer), with the same meaning.

§ 440. **wyse, wayis, &c.**

    α) *wayis* (OE. *wegas*) also spelt *wayes*, 2. 428 (&c.), *wayse* 5. 26, ways 4. 2246, 2522, rimes with words containing

a) OE. ī — : ryse 3. 1778 (&c.) : wyse, adj. 3. 2018 : sayis (= sīþas) 3. 2314 (&c.). — b) OE. i + g — : lyis (3 sg. *licgan*) 1. 490 (&c.) : ladies 5. 236, 2628. — c) OE. ā ? — : raise (OE. *rās*) 4. 2478. — d) Fr. i - : cervice 3. 1498, 5. 1772, service 3. 1950 (&c.) : gyse 1. 1390 (&c.) : devyse 1. 938 (&c.) : interpryse 4. 842, 5. 948 : advyse 4. 2356, 1. 132 : parradice 5. 376 : Galice 5. 480, 2482 : dispyse 5. 1144 : Meliades 3. 418 (&c.) : gentrice 5. 224. — e) Fr. ei or i ? — : praise 1. 1542 : pryse 5. 3008. — f) ? — : Gandaleyis 5. 2722.

    β) *wyse*, once *vyse* (3. 2220) = OE. *wīse*, rimes with words containing

a) OE. ī — : syse (*sīþas*) 3. 2220 : hyis (3. sg. *hīgian*) 2. 440. — b) Fr. 1 — : devyse 1. 422 (&c.) : Meliades 1. 634 (&c.) : coccatrice 2. 278 : advyse 3. 60 : gyse 3. 1242, 4. 248 : **suppryse** 4. 634.

§ 441. Here it is pretty evident that the author only used the word *wyse* = OE. *wīse*; for the one rime with *ā* is probably only due to the scribe who changed a historic pres. *ryse* into a pret. *raise*, and the rimes in (α. e) are also more probably evidence of previous ī than *ā*, for although the meaning *praise* suits the passages best, the forms *praise* and *pryse* are often interchanged, in fact *pryse, prize*, is used in the sense of praise very frequently in ME. and MSc., it is so even as late as Shakesp. But the scribe was more familiar with the form *wayis*, and often put this in, in spite of the rimes and even when a singular word is necessary, e. g. on this wayis, 1. 1541 (&c.), on sike ane vayes 4. 2639; cf. Wall. in this wayis : dayis (= days), S. 530, (here the author uses the form *wayis*, and as a singular). This substitution of *wayis* for *wyse* led the scribe occasionally to alter the rime-word in the same manner, e. g. *wayis* : *sayis* 3. 2314 (&c.), the latter word being generally spelt *syse* or *syis*; and so in the rime *wayis* : *raise*, he probably found before him *wyse* : *ryse*, and first altered *wyse* into *wayis* and then for the sake of the rime *ryse* into *raise*, to which there was a special inducement in the circumstance that a pret. seemed more suitable than a pres., the surrounding verbs being preterites. He acted similarly in his substitution of *praise* for the author's *pryse*, e. g. *praise* : *suffais* for *pryse* : *suffyse*. In the rimes above in (α. e) the scribe in one case has left *pryse*, in the other has changed it to *praise*.

The rime in Satir. P. 35. 75, *gyse* : *alwyse* (for *always*) shows how completely identical the two forms *wyse* and *wayis* had become.

§ 442. *belyth* appears twice in rime, Thay drest them to the mariag belyth : blyth 1. 664, In land of Calice enterit is belyth : sweith (OE. *swīþe*), 1. 940. In the latter, the meaning *blithe* might suit the passage, as a few lines further on we read, "the fresch Clariodus ... gladlie could him speid", But to suit the metre a dissyllable is necessary and in the former passage the word requires a different meaning from *blyth*, with which it stands in rime. Perhaps it is written for *belyve*, which the author may have written, but a scribe misunderstood, or spelt differently in order to improve the rime. Such an assonance between *þ* and *v* is exceptional in Clar., but we have one in *kyth* : *belyue* 5. 1248, and we have similar ones elsewhere, e. g. Sc. Leg. swith : belyfe 5/32, Freiris of B. belyve : blyth 262, Rosw. blyth : belyve 4, Am. (see Kölbing, p. 21) bliþe : þryue : lyue : fyue. These rimes make it probable that we should alter in Clar. to *belyve*. Or was there another word *belythe* = altogether, in company, and connected with ME. *lið*, sb. = ON. *lið*, order, assembly? Cf. Laȝ. a leoðe, 5307 (in a body?), Langl. in oon liþ, B. 16. 181. Or perhaps more probably connected with ME. *lïþ*, (= ON. *lȳðr*?), a doublet of ME. *leod* = OE. *lēod*, people, race, cf. Sir Tr. liþe, (pl.) : swiþe : bliþe : kiþe, 1640, Hav. lithe, 2515, D. Arth. lithes, 994.

§ 443. Final syllables -ite, -ine, -ive, -ice, &c.

Ellis, EEP., p. 272 &c., uses the present pronunc. of the majority of words containing these syllables, as he does that of those containing -*ly*, to prove that in Chauc.'s time a diphthongal pronunc. of long ī was impossible. In this conclusion he was probably right for Chaucer; but he goes further and says it would be "difficult to suppose that, at a time when the (ai) or (ei) or (əi) pronunc. of long *i* was common, as at the close of the 15th and begining of the 16th cent., it should have been deliberately rejected from these words and replaced by (*i*) when the accent was thrown back permanently. But we know that such words had (*i*) in the 16th cent. and that this sound has continued to the present day. For my own part I cannot force myself to suppose that *i* in the last syllable of the following words ever had any other sound but (ii, i, *ii, i*)". Then he gives a list including such words as *servyse, justise, merite, sangwyn, opposit, superlatif, ypocrite, famyne, doctrine,* &c.

§ 444. But it is perhaps not quite so certain that the (əi) pronunc. could not exist as well in some words. It is true that the majority of such words have no diphthong in rec. sp. in their final syll. at the present day. But anyone familiar with the London dial. will at once acknowledge the frequent pronunc. of *opposite* with a diphthong (əi) or (ai); so also in *favorite* we sometimes hear (əi). In many similar words in which the last syll. has retained the stress, or acquired a secondary stress, or which have, in the case of dissyllables, "level-stress", mod. rec. sp. has the diphthong, e. g. *appetite, satellite, paradise, porcupine, Serpentine, parasite, Palestine, mesmerise, Gentile, divine, revive,* &c.; in others the pronunc. varies, e. g. several words in *-ile*, as *futile, servile,* in *-ine*, as *iodine, columbine*, in *-ive* as *endive*. How are these to be explained? At first one might be inclined to look upon the diphthong as an artificial pronunc. according to the spelling, many of the words being such as are not in popular use, and are therefore first learnt through the eye. But the word *opposite*, with (əi), at any rate, is found amongst such classes in London and elsewhere as render this explanation unlikely. It seems much more satisfactory to accept a possible double pronunc. in popular language, from that point on when the diphthonging of *i* began, according as the final syll. was stressed or not, and to look upon the usage of poets in employing both forms according to the exigencies of rime as resulting partly from this occasional twofold pronunc. of vernacular growth and not altogether as being an artificial poetical licence, as Ellis explains; the (əi) forms were distinctly admitted by Gill and used by him even in prose.

§ 445. These words are exactly similar to the words ending in *-ly, -y*, cf. § 415, which certainly have two pronunciations in Clar. Concerning these Ellis says, p. 281, that Gill does not represent an old pronunc. but only a poetical licence, and "there seems no reason to suppose that this termination *-ly* ever had, in natural speech, the sound of (ləi)". But on p. 855 we find in Gill's transcription of the Psalms, i. e. in prose (tryyləi, oonləi, syyrləi, ckselensəi), and p. 851, Spenser, (infaməi) &c., where the (əi) was not necessitated by any exigencies of rime and metre, and cannot therefore be considered a poetical licence. Gill also gives the forms (mizerəi, konstansəi, destinəi).

§ 446. Of course we cannot explain anything like all the rimes, which prove a diphthong, from popular pronunc.; beyond the adverbs in *-ly*, and nouns in *-y*, it was only a limited number of such words that found their way into popular speech at all, and that could therefore acquire a double pronunc. of vernacular growth; but many of those which have now the (əi) pronunc. are words which have probably long been established in the vernacular, e. g. *delight, Serpentine, opposite* (in dial.) *appetite,* &c., and to this the diphthong is probably due.

The assumption of two pronunciations of natural growth gives us an explanation not only of the use of such syllables in rime, but also of the occasional dialectal or the half obsolete pronunc. sometimes heard from the lips of aged people, of the unsettled pronunc. in many words and of the undoubted diphthong in rec. sp. in many others, as *appetite,* &c., which do not agree in this respect with the majority. It seems difficult to have to assume so extensive a slavery to orthography as would explain all these anomalies.

§ 447. If we allow, as we almost certainly must, a general diphthongal pronunc. of long i for the time when Clar. was written, we must also allow it for the final syllables in the following words in rime, (cf. § 431) — *apitite, fellonie, multiplied, matutine, melancholie, exultive, superlative, discipleine, chevalrie, paradice, exyle, delyte, inclyne, companie,* or consider the rimes faulty. In many the diphthong is doubtless only artificial. Ellis's lists do not contain sufficient material to give us any exact rules about the mod. diall. We find the following words in his lists with i or $\bar{i}$ (not the diphthong) — D. 33, (cf. also DSS., p. 146) *polite, oblige, type, chastise, advertise, baptise, civilise, invite,* D. 38. *delight,* D. 39. *obliged, idolised, practise, advertise, exercise, martyrising, invited,* D. 41. *admire.* It appears, therefore, that the diphthong in these words is not so frequent in Scotl. as in Engl. and that consequently the above rimes may have been for a Sc. poet even more artificial than for an Engl. one, and are perhaps a further sign of the poet's imitation of Engl. models, or borrowing from Engl. rec. sp., if the pronunc. of the words just mentioned agrees with the dial. to which he belonged. Ellis gives no suitable words in the dial. of D. 34, which would probably be nearest to that of Clar. Many words which were used in the poetical works of the MSc. period never got a hold on the spoken language and would probably not now exist among natives speaking true dial. But the very fact of their being introduced into the language of poetry at a time when the political and literary relations between France and Scotl. were so intimate would make it a priori probable that the *i* should have its French pronunc., especially in D. 34, and it is noticeable that some words in the above rime-list are spelt with *i* and not *y*, e. g. *paradice, exultive, superlative,* &c., and occasionally *ei* is written, e. g. *discipleine,* so that the rimes are not correct for the *eye*. The *ei* is doubtless due to a Sc. scribe who pronounced with i; the forms with *i* can be of similar origin, or may be merely instances of Engl. spelling. We have already seen that the author also occasionally rimed Fr. *i* with earlier $\bar{e}$, so that he evidently used both pronunciations in these words, with (ii) and (əi) or (ei); but from the evidence of the rimes the latter was the usual pronunc.; whether this was altogether artificial and contrary to his native dial. or not, cannot be settled till the mod. diall. are more fully investigated.

§ 448. Note. One or two of Ellis's arguments in the passages referred to seem to rest on a faulty understanding of mod. dialectal forms. One of his chief arguments is the rime *mercy* : *sey* (= saw), see EEP., p. 279, in connection with which he quotes the mod. dial. form (sii) in "I see him do it yesterday"; but surely this must be due to a ME. form *sē*. ME. *sī* would give NE. (səi) or (sai), which, as he says, does not exist. We should have to look upon *mercy* : *sey* as another $\bar{\imath}$: $\bar{e}$ rime, if we explain by the mod. Engl dial. *sī*. Similarly, on p. 284, the words with double pronunc. in the mod. diall., as *die* = (dəi) and (dii), must have had in ME. and MSc. the two pronunciations *dī* and *dē*. NSc. *dī* cannot prove a MSc. *dī*, but rather *dē*, which is abundantly proved by rimes; we cannot base any argument for a ME. *dī* on a mod. form *dī*.

O -

§ 449. rimes with

a) itself. befor(e) : þairfor 1. 1158, thairfore 4. 1228. beforne (*beforan*) : sworne 1. 618 : borne 1. 1038. schore (OE. *score* = litus) : whairfore 3. 1946. — b) OE. o: — borne : þorne 3. 628. — c) OE. ō, see § 458 (b). — d) OE. ā, see § 56 (d). — e) Fr. o. before : restore 3. 522, 5. 1222. — f) Lat. o. before : decore 5. 968, 2966, decoire 5. 1718. — g) ? before : Amandour 4. 866.

§ 450. OE. *o* in open syll. was lengthened in ME. and MSc. Most of the above rimes are proof of this; perhaps even those in (a) and (b) in which a vowel has fallen out between *r* and *n*, OE. *beforan, boren*, &c., for it is better to consider these, too, perhaps, and also the rime-word *borne*, as containing a long vowel, or at least half-long, since in Murray's dial., D. 33, the *o* in *born, torn, shorn, storm, corn, horn*, &c., has been treated in exactly the same way as that in *hope, sole, fore*, &c., viz. it appears as (u'). Ellis's material for the other diall. is too meagre and of two mixed a character to allow us to make any rules. *open* appears with (oo, ee, aa), *hope* with (oo, åu, óu, áu, u), *foal* with (o, oo, o). It is difficult to see from this what the regular development is. The rime in (g) is perhaps evidence of the commencement of a raising process towards (u).

It is noticeable that OE. *beforan* appears in two forms, with and without *n*.

O:

§ 451. 1. Before 1 + cons. — rimes with

a) OE. ā̆ld = WS. eald, see § 268 (b).

The *o* which was lengthened before *ld* already in the OE. period, see Kluge PG. 1. 866, remains unchanged. *gold* is the only word appearing in rime; this has in the mod. Sc. diall. (uu) in 33, 35, 36, (oo) in 33, (óu) in 34 and 39 with loss of *l*, in 39 and 41 with *l* retained, (åu) with *l* in 36, without *l* in 35. Thus a difference is made between this late OE. *ō* and early OE. *ō̆*, cf. below; it seems to go together with the new-long *ō* from OE. *o* in open syll., unless the abnormal development is due to the following *l. mould* is found with (ə), the correct representative of OE. ō, in D. 42, otherwise it has (ú, AA, àu, óu).

The rimes with ǭ from OE. *ā* are, as shown in § 269, not Sc., but imitations of Engl.

§ 452. 2. Before r + cons. — rimes with
a) OE. o. thorne : borne. morrow : borrow 1. 22 : sorow 2. 852. —
b) Fr. o. horse : forse, force 1. 52 (&c.). lord : record(e) 2. 2230 (&c.). horne : vnicorne 4. 2458. lordis : accordis 5. 378. — c) Fr. u. word : bourd (= jest, OFr. *burde*) 2. 1200.

§ 453. With the exception of *morrow, borrow, sorrow* and perhaps *word*, the vowel is probably half-long; if it were really long we should expect to find *oi* sometimes written. The rime in (c) is one example of the tendency, often observed, to change *o* to *u* before r + cons. and it also seems to prove the new-lengthening before *rd*, if the *ou* has any meaning.

word generally appears with (ɑ) in almost all the mod. Sc. diall.; this correctly reflects MSc. *ŭ*, so that if there was formerly ever a lengthening, wŏrd > wōrd > wūrd or wŏrd > wŭrd > wūrd, there has been a return to vowel-shortness or half-length in NSc. as in rec. sp. We have the same rime as above, *word* : *bourd*, in Satir. P. 33. 176.

§ 454. o + ht — rimes with
a) OE. ā + ht, see § 58. — b) OE. ō + ht, see § 494 (b). — For these words cf. §§ 59—71.

§ 455. Here we must include the word *flaucht* 3. 638, "hir spirit than was all on flaucht" (: nocht), for, in spite of the spelling with *au*, the rime-word *nocht* and the spelling and rimes in other texts plainly show that the vowel must have been *o*. The meaning of the word is flutter, perturbation, and perhaps Jamieson's suggested derivation from OE. *flogettan* = fluctuare, is the most plausible one. J. quotes Dougl. Venus al on flocht : thocht, on flocht is : thochtis; Burel's Pilg. Feir pat my hairt in sic a flocht; Baillie's Lett. "all the city was in a flought. He also gives quotations for the form *flaught*, but none in rime. Cf. further Dunb. this fals warld is ay on flocht : thocht : socht 24. 1, thair hairtis wer baith on flocht : socht : brocht (Small's note quotes from Henryson, For I am verray affeirit and on flocht" and says *flocht* or *flicht* is still in use. Jam. Dict. gives *aflight* or *in a flight* as synonymous, cf. Dunb. This warld evir dois flicht and wary, 26. 6); Freiris of B. flocht : thocht 430; Roll. C. V. flocht : nocht : brocht : thocht : docht 2. 611.

This word has nothing to do with *fireflaught*, nor with *flaught* in *wind-flaught* (= driven with the wind), e. g. Dougl. 4. 133, (: ourraucht), in which the vowel was originally *a*.

§ 456. Before other consonants — rimes with
a) ON. o. oft : aloft 2. 1328. — b) OE. ō (shortened), see § 458 (b), (c). — c) OE. ā, see § 43 (e).

The vowel *ŏ* remains unchanged; the mod. diall. generally show *ŏ*.

§ 457. *haw* : *tow* 3. 1956, He seames to be na balleist in the haw He sall weill hald ane anker or ane tow. The former line is somewhat obscure, but perhaps *haw* is for *how* = hollow, hold of a ship, OE. *hol*. Jam. Dict. gives *how* = hollow place, OE. *hol*. Cf. Bruce, howis (= holes) 17. 344, Wall. in the holl, var. into the how (= hold) 9. 122, Montg. how (sb. = hollow) : row : mow : know (= knoll) : ʒow (= ewe) : dow (OE. *dugan*) : pow : tow F. 74, houis : bouis (= bows, arcūs) MP. 32. 33.

The word *tow* = rope, is OE. *tow*, and if the above explanation of *haw* is correct, the rime proves the vocalisation of *l* in the word *hol*.

O'

§ 458. 1. **Not followed by ht or g** — rimes with

a) itself. looke (*lōcian*) : tuike (prt. of *taka*) 1. 144, luike : tuike 3. 448 (&c.), louike : tuike 4. 428. tuike : cuike (*cōc*) 3. 1972 : quoke (strong prt. to wk. vb. OE. *cwacian*, cf. Plattdeutsch *jog* for H. G. *jagte*, Reuter) 5. 1534. schoke : awoke 1. 96. gud : blude 1. 1416, 2. 1188 : wood 3. 390 : bluid 3. 1228 : flude 3. 1334, 1962, gude : stude 1. 1392, 4. 332, guide : stude 1. 568. blude : stude 3. 1880 : wod 1. 68, wode 2. 36, bluid(e) : wood(e) 1. 1002, 972, bloode : woode 3. 1100, 1116. stude : fluide 1. 1402 : wode 5. 2340, stuide : wode 5. 1174. fude (*fōda*) : rude (*rōd*) 3. 766. soune (*sōna*) : doŭne, ptc. 1. 380 (&c.) : noŭne (*nōn*) 4. 264. schoune (= shoes) : doune (ptc. *gedōn*) 3. 878. to : adoe 1. 508 (&c.) : doe 3. 464 (&c.) : do 4. 2618. brother : vther 3. 1782, 1840 : other 3. 1538. — b) OE. ŏ. soft : oft 2. 580. behovit : hovit (= hovered; according to Skeat, ME. *hoven* from OE. *hof*, sb., Bradl. derives from MDu. and MLG. *hoven*) 2. 1150. schuike : smoke (*smoca*) 5. 2018. — c) ON. ŏ. soft : loft 2. 1420 (&c.), wnsoft (MS. *wnfost*) : on loft 1. 728. — d) OE. u. soine (*sōna*) : aboŭe 1. 158, soune : aboŭe 1. 506. — e) OE. ēo, see § 330 (k). — f) OE. ā, see §§ 39 (c), 43 (f). — g) OE. or ON. ă-, see § 22 (c). — h) OE. œ-, see § 77 (b). — i) OE. ū, see § 530 (g). — k) OE. u + g, see § 505 (b). — l) Fr. eu. fure (prt. *fōr* from *faran*) : demure (according to Skeat and Behrens from Central French *demeur*) 5. 212. — m) Fr. iii. rute (*rōt*) : suite 5. 1940. — n) Fr. ii. soune : disjune 2. 866, 4. 934 : oportune 5. 1720 : Neptune 5. 2880. doune (*gedōn*) : oportune 4. 1510, 2496, opportoune 4. 2378. behuifis : excuse 4. 2506, behuise, 3. sg. : excuse 1. 1356, behuise (? = sb. "say on for your behuise"; or is it the impers. vb. constructed with *your*? or an error for "you behuise"?) : excuse 4. 2226. dois, 3. sg. : refuse 4. 1526. stude : pulcritude 4. 576, 976. bluid : pulcritude 3. 2436, blood : conclude 3. 1750. gud : conclude 1. 1202, 3. 1636 : denud 3. 116. wod : conclude 5. 2320. leuike (= look, sb.) : duike 5. 2042. fuire (*fōr*, prt.) : figure 5. 2948. — o) Fr. o. soune : toune (*ton*) 2. 1520.

§ 459. OE. ō was a closed ǭ and remained so in ME. till it, during the course of the 16th cent., became ū, which, however, did not become fixed till the 17th cent., since which time it has remained unchanged, cf. the ū in *food, soon*, &c. This is the usual statement of the development of OE. ō, but it is only correct for the Engl. of rec. sp., and the mistakes sometimes made with regard to this vowel are due to an insufficient observance of the difference of diall. Hence it is sometimes asserted that the change $ō > ū$ took place in the 15th cent. or even earlier, cf. Klnge, PG. 1. 884, Büddeker, p. 353, Hoofe, p. 27. This is not true for the S. of Engl. and requires some modification for the N., cf. Brandl, p. 61, Zielke, pp. 28, 29, Fick, pp. 29, 30, Wischmann, p. 7, &c. This theory is based on the occurrence of rimes between OE. $ō$ and Fr. $ü$ and the spelling with u, e. g. *gud*, *buk*, in Hamp., (there is no trace of it in Sir. Tr., $ō$ only rimes with itself or OE. $ā$ and is never represented by u, see Kölbing, p. 65). The more correct interpretation of this, however, is given by Brandl, Zielke, Fick, Wischmann, and Sweet § 693; but these do not all entirely agree, and perhaps we should make some difference between the N. of Engl. and Scotl., thus having at least three distinct districts.

§ 460. In rec. sp. OE. $ō$ and Fr. $ü$ (or $üi$) have never coincided, except under particular circumstances, cf. *food* with *conclude*, *boot* with *fruit*, but on the other hand *food* with *multitude*, *goose* with *use*, *moor* with *cure*, &c.; i. e. there is coincidence only after r and l, and perhaps occasionally after s (cf. *suit*). Nor has there been any coincidence with AFr. u (= OFr. o) except in the case of words which have been re-borrowed at a later period, generally with the Parisian ou (= $ū$), cf. *boot* with *devout* (but *route*), *spoon* with *renown*, &c. In the S. W. we have a partial coincidence between OE. $ō$ and Fr. $ü$ and AFr. u, and, strange to say, in almost the same forms as in Scotl., $(ə_2ə_2)$ and (y_1y_1), cf. Elworthy, dial. of W. Somerset, p. 51, and Ellis EEP., the lists for Devonshire, D. 11, in Vol. 5.

§ 461. In N. Engl. and Scotl. the mod. diall. are perfectly in harmony with Northern ME. and MSc. rimes, for OE. $ō$ and Fr. $ü$ coincide as a rule everywhere (as far as Ellis's lists go), but the forms are very different in Yorks. and Scotl., and it is but natural to suppose that the differentiation is not of recent date and that the rimes between OE. $ō$ and Fr. $ü$ perhaps do not indicate the same pronunc. in Hamp. as they do in Bruce, especially as it is possible perhaps that the Fr. words with $ü$ found their way into Central Scotch at a different date and in a different form from that in which they were received into Southern and Northern Engl.; at any rate they probably soon developed in a somewhat different direction in Sc. Ellis's lists being so meagre with regard to words of Fr. origin, it is difficult to draw any definite conclusions; and the agreement between OE. $ō$ and Fr. $ü$ might be considered to be in some diall. only partial and therefore misleading; but the agreement of the few examples given and the strong evidence of all MSc. texts render this improbable. A full and careful examination of all the mod. diall. is necessary before the vexed question of the development of OE. $ō$ and Fr. $ü$ can be finally settled. Perhaps no other vowels show such a variety in their representation in the mod. diall. as these do.

§ 462. We will first look at Scotland. OE. $ō$ has become (of course subject to some exceptions) (ə, əə) in D. 33, (y), sometimes (ə), in 34, (əə) or (yy) in 35, (y) or (i) in 36, (y, yy) sometimes (i, ii) in 37, (ə, y, i, ɜ) but chiefly (ə) in 38, chiefly (ii) in 39, (i) or (yy) in 40, (əə) in 41, (əə) in 42. Ellis's lists leave us almost altogether in the lurch with regard to Fr $ü$, except in D. 33 and 39, where, however, there is perfect agreement —

(əə) in 33, except in final position and before vowels, in which cases we have (əu) or (ɑu) — (ii) in 39. From Mr. Low's kind information I find there is the same agreement in 38, in the form (ə, əə). The few examples given by Ellis in the other diall. are also mostly in agreement; so that we may probably consider it as settled that OE. $\bar{o}$ and Fr. $ü$ have in Scotl. everywhere shared the same fortunes, and that in all MSc. diall. they must have coincided in value.

§ 463. In the N. Engl. diall. OE. $\bar{o}$ appears in a variety of forms, (iu, iiʏ, yu, u) in 32, (uu, iu, iʏ) &c. in 31, chiefly (iiʏ) in 30, (ɑu, œu, iu) in 26, (œu, u) in 25, (uu, ui, uui, uuʏ) in 24, and variations of (u, uu) in 20, 21, 22, 23; i. e. we may consider the difference from rec. sp. to be confined to the counties Northumb., Dur., Cumb., Westm. and Yorks., which all show a combination with i as first element, which agrees with the (ii) of 39 (Aberd. and Banffs.) rather than with South^n and Central Scotch; while the other diall. of the N. and Midl. show some variation of (uu) and thus agree with rec. sp. There is, in the Northern counties mentioned, on the whole, perfect agreement with Fr. $ü$, just as in Scotl. The question is, has the (iiʏ) of Yorks. arisen in the same way as the (ii) of Aberd.? and is the (əə) of the Southern Counties of Scotl. the result of the same MSc. or ME. representative of one or both of these sounds?

§ 464. One thing is certain, that neither OE. $\bar{o}$ nor Fr. $ü$ ever became $\bar{u}$ under ordinary circumstances in N. Engl. or in Sc., for there is nowhere in the mod. diall. a coincidence with OE. $\bar{u}$; this latter has remained $\bar{u}$ to the present day in the *whole* of Sc. and most of the N. of Engl. The rimes between Fr. $ü$ and OE. $\bar{u}$ or Fr. u which are found in some MSc. and North^n ME. texts must find some special explanation (analogy or transference?). According to the examples given by Behrens, Frz. St. 5. 118, they seem to be chiefly peculiar to words in which the vowel is followed by r or n, and here exchange of suffix may play a large part.

§ 465. In the Sc. Leg. and Troj. W. there are also rimes between Fr. $ü$ and OE. $\bar{u}$ in final position, e. g. *now* : *vertu*, &c., see Buss p. 500. These are at first sight very striking, but Fr. $ü$ in final position and before vowels seems to have had a different development from that which it had before conss., (cf. Nicol. Trans. Philol. Soc. 1877, Appendix III, vi); it has produced (əu) in 33 and (iu) in the others. Can these rimes be evidence of the change ü $>$ i̯u̯ $>$ i̯ú having already taken place at such an early date? This seems to be the only explanation, since OE. $\bar{u}$ has never changed and $i\bar{u}$: $\bar{u}$ is a possible rime. Or else the $ü$ had become here $\bar{u}$ altogether, without any initial glide; but if so, this was not the normal development, and was perhaps limited to particular diall. Further, the (iiʏ) of Yorks. and the sounds in other N. Engl. and Sc. diall. admit of no satisfactory explanation from a ME. or MSc. $\bar{u}$, and we may safely dismiss as thoroughly impossible the $\bar{o} > \bar{u}$ theory for these districts.

§ 466. The normal value of the common North^n ME. and MSc. vowel arising from OE. $\bar{o}$ and Fr. $ü$ has not yet been fixed, and it is a difficult matter to do so. Possibly it was different in different diall., and the neglect of this possibility has led to the conflicting theories with regard to it. We have to account for the following modern sounds (iu, iiʏ, ǝǝ, yy, ii). All but (ǝǝ) are easily explainable in one category, and perhaps also (ǝǝ) as well, though at first sight this seems doubtful.

§ 467. For the latter the explanations of Fick, Sweet, Brandl, Nicol and Murray are very plausible and probably not far from the mark. Fick's first suggestion, p. 30, is impossible; the two sounds after once coinciding cannot have separated again, and the contradiction which he notices in Ellis's statements is explained by an examination of the latter's lists in P^t V of EEP. The (yy) referred to by Ellis on p. 298 of P^t I, as given by Murray in Fr. words, is not found in Murray's own dial., as we have seen above, but *is* found in other diall., in which also OE. $\bar{o}$ has become (yy). Fick then gives, p. 31, a better explanation (following Nicol and Murray), which applies for this particular dial., D. 33, viz.

OE. $\bar{o}$ (mid-back-narrow-round) } > MSc. ui (= mid-mixed-n.-r.) >
Fr. $ü$ (high-mixed-narrow-round) } NSc. (ǝǝ) (mid-front-narrow-round)

i. e. OE. $\bar{o}$ was half-fronted while Fr. $ü$ was half-lowered, and the common resulting vowel afterwards further fronted. Brandl, p. 61, also favours a similar explanation, valuing the MSc. vowel as "œ or œu" (meaning probably the latter for final, the former for medial position), and herein agrees with Sweet § 693, "in North. $\bar{o}$ was fronted to mid-front-narrow-round, Fr. high-front-n.-r. being levelled under the same sound".

i. e. OE. $\bar{o}$ (mid-back-n.-r.) } > MSc. and NSc. (ǝǝ) (mid-front-n.-r.)
Fr. $ü$ (high-front-n.-r.) }

In this case we assume that the mod. sound was already reached in the MSc. period, through OE. $\bar{o}$ being completely fronted, while Fr. $ü$ = (yy) was simply half-lowered.

§ 468. The following is also possible, viz. that OE. $\bar{o}$ was both fronted and raised from mid-back-n.-r. to high-front-n.-r., and so coincided with Fr. $ü$, and that then this (yy) in some diall. remained, in others was unrounded and became (ii), high-front-n., and perhaps in others was half-lowered only to (ǝǝ), mid-front-n.-r., and in others produced a diphthong, (iu), by a gliding from the i-position into the u-position, instead of forming them both simultaneously. (With this we might compare the pronunc. of Germ. $ü$ as (ii) in some diall., as (ǝǝ) in others, and as (iu) in the mouth of an Englishman first learning German.) This would explain all the various mod. sounds from one uniform MSc. sound; but still it is not without its difficulties. And perhaps there may have been, as suggested already, a difference in the form in which Fr. $ü$ was received into the different diall.

§ 469. Fick's scheme differs from the others in that he assumes Fr. $ü$ to have been high-mixed instead of high-front, in which he follows Müller (Kopenhagen) and Ellis; Holthaus, p. 92, also holds the same view. Behrens does not allow this, and Sturmfels, p. 568, says that according to most scholars the sound was $ü$, (yy), from the earliest times. Starting from a high-mixed instead of a high-front vowel we should not have to alter the second of the above schemes very much; it would necessitate some contradictions in the direction of change, but we seem not to be able to avoid that in any case, and similar reversions of processes are not unknown.

§ 470. We accordingly arrive at the indefinite result that the MSc. sound may have been a high-mixed, high-front, mid-mixed, or mid-front vowel, and that it may have been more than one of these, according to dial.

Menze's and Knigge's rejection of Brandl's statement is due to their failing to take difference of dial. into consideration; what they say may be correct for the diall. they specially treat, but, because it does not suit them, it does not follow that Brandl is wrong with regard to the dial. of which he writes.

§ 471. The evidence of the 16th cent. grammarians must be considered in connection with the above, though we must still bear in mind that they may also have had different diall. in consideration, when they made their statements concerning Sc. pronunc.

Salesbury (1547): "The sound of *u* in French, or *ü* with two pricks over the heade in Duch [i. e. German] or the Scottish pronunciation of *u* alludeth somewhat nere vnto the sound of it in Welshe, thoughe yet none of them all, doeth so exactly (as I thynk) expresse it, as the Hebraick Kubuts doeth. For the Welsh *u* is none other thing, but a meane sounde betwyxte *u* and *y* beyng Latin vowels."

§ 472. Hart (1551) in his "former treatise" (see Ellis, p. 796): "The other abuse of the u, is that we sound yt as the Skottes and French men doo, in theis wordes gud and fust: Wheras most communely we our selves (which the Grekes, Latines, the vulgar Italiens, and Germaines with others doo alwais) kepe his true sound: as in theis wordes, but, unto, and further. Yf you marke well his uzurped sound in gud and fust (and others of the Skottish and french abuse) you shal find the sound of the diphthong iu, keping both the i and u, in their proper vertu, both in sound and voel, as afore is said we ought : sounding yt in that voice wherefore we now abuse to write, you. What difference find you betwixt the sound of you, and u in gud and fust?" &c.

§ 473. Hart (in his specimen of phonetic writing as transcribed into palaeograph by Ellis, pp. 801, 802, according to the latter's interpretation of Hart's own symbols; it is possible that where Ellis reads (yy) we should understand (in) with Holthaus, but this is also uncertain, cf. below): p. 801, "Nou third·li for dhe Span·iard, ʜi abyyz·eth dhe *i*, and *u*, in kon·sonants as ui- and the Frensh du, and dhe *u*, oft·n, in dhe Frensh and Skót·ish sound." p. 802, "And nou last ov aul, dhe Frensh, uidh th- abyys ov dhe *u*, in dhe skót·ish leik sound of dhe *iu* diphthoq, ʜuitsh, nor Ital·ian nor Dutsh did ev·er giv tu *u*, &c."

§ 474. Smith (1568), see Ellis p. 166: "Y vel *v* Graecum aut Gallicum, quod per se apud nos taxum arborem [i. e. Engl. *yew*] significat, taxus *v* .... Quod genus pronunciationis nos à Gallis accepisse arguit, quód rarius quidem nos Angli in pronuntiando hac utimur litera. Scoti autem qui Gallica lingua suam veteram quasi obliterarant, et qui trans Trentam fluvium habitant, vicinioresque sunt Scotis, frequentissimè,

adeo ut quod nos per V Romanum sonamus (u), illi libenter proferunt per
v Graecum aut Gallicum (yy); nam et hic sonus tam Gallis est peculiaris,
ut omnia fere Romane scripta per *u* et [probably a misprint for ut?] *v*
proferunt, vt pro Dominus (Dominyys) et Jesvs (Jes·yys), intantum ut quae
brevia sint natura, vt illud macrum *v* exprimant melius, sua pronunciatione
longa faciunt. Hunc sonum Anglosaxones, de quibus postea mentionem
faciemus, per y̆ exprimebant, ut verus Anglosaxonice τρy̆. Angli (huur)
meretrix, (kuuk) coquus, (gund) bonum, (bluud) sanguis, (huud) cucullus,
(fluud) fluvius, (buuk) liber, (tuuk) cepit; Scoti (hyyr, kyyk, gyyd, blyyd,
hyyd, flyyd, byyk, tyyk)". And again, "*O* rotundo ore et robustiùs quam
priores effertur, *u* angustiore, caetera similis τῷ o. Sed *v* compressis pro-
pemodum labris, multò exilius tenuiusque resonat quàm *o* aut *u* (boot)
scapha, buut, (byyt) Scoticâ pronunciatione, *ocrea*". And again in his
Greek Pronunciation: "*v* Graecum Scoti et Borei Angli tum exprimunt
cùm taurum sonant, & pro *bul*, dicunt exiliter contractioribus labiis sono
suppresso & quasi praefocato inter *i* and *u bŭl*". [Ellis is, of course,
responsible for the palaeograph in brackets].

§ 475. Hart (1569), see Ellis, p. 167: "Now to come to the *u*. I
sayde the French, Spanish, and Brutes [i. e. Welsh], I may adde the Scottish,
doe abuse it with vs in sounde, and for consonant, except the Brutes as
is sayd: the French doe never sound it right, but vsurpe ou, for it, the
Spanyard doth often vse it right as we doe, but often also abuse it with
vs; [Holthaus somewhat alters the construction by printing a comma here
instead of a semicolon] the French and the Scottish in the sounde of a
Diphthong: which keeping the vowels in their due sounds, commeth of i
and u, (or verie neare it) is made and put togither vnder one breath,
confounding the soundes of i, and u, togither: which you may perceyue
in shaping thereof, if you take away the inner part of the tongue, from
the upper teeth or Gummes, then shall you sound the u right, or in
sounding the French and Scottish u, holding still your tongue to the
vpper teeth or gums, and opening your lippes somewhat, you shall perceyue the right sounde of *i*".

§ 476. Baret (1573), Ellis, p. 168: "And as for the sound of V
consonant [a misprint for *vowel*] whether it be sounded more sharply as
in the spelling *blue* or more grossly like *oo*, as we sound *Booke*, it were
long here to discusse. Some therefore think that this sharpe Scottish V
is rather a diphthong than a vowell, being compounded of our English *e*
and *u*, as indeed we may partly perceyue in pronouncing it, our tongue
at the beginning lying flat in our mouth, and at the ende rising up with
the lips also therewithall somewhat more drawen togither".

§ 477. Holyband (1609), (Ellis, p. 228, note, Sweet § 870), in his
"French Litleton", a handbook for learning French: "Where you must
take paine to pronounce our, v, otherwise then in English: for we do
thinke that when Englishmen do profer, v, they say, you: and for, q, we
suppose they say, kiou: but we sound, v, without any helpe of the tongue,
ioyning the lips as if you would whistle; and after the manner that the
Scots do sound Gud".

§ 478. Hume, a Scotchman who spent 16 years in England, (he was educated at Dunbar and St. Andrews and was afterwards Headmaster of the High School in Edinburgh, and later in similar positions at Prestonpans and Dunbar), in his treatise "of the orthographie and Congrnitie of the Britan Tongue", EETS 5, ed. Wheatley, which was probably written in or soon after the year 1617, speaking of the "Latine vouales", § 18 (p. 10 Wheatley), says: "u, the south pronounces quhen the syllab beginnes or endes at it, as eu, teu for tu, and eunum meunus for unum munus, quhilk because it is a diphthong sound, and because they themselfes, quhen a consonant followes it, pronunce it other wayes, I hoep I sal not need argumentes to prove it wrang, and not a pure voual". Again, in his chap. "of the Britan vouales" § 9, (p. 11 Wheatley): "U, the last of this rank, the south, as I have said in the latin sound of it, pronounces eu, we ou, both, in my simple judgement, wrang, for these be diphthong soundes, and the sound of a voual sould be simple. If I sould judge, the frensh sound is neerest the voual sound as we pronunce it in mule and muse".

§ 479. From the above we derive at once one certain result; four of the six independent witnesses are agreed that Sc. *u* and Fr. *u* were pronounced alike, viz. Salesbury, Hart, Smith and Holyband. That they do not mean by Sc. *u* the same as OE. *u* is shown by the express mention of the word *gud* by Hart, Holyband and Smith; the latter of whom gives a number of other examples all containing OE. $\bar{o}$; and besides, OE. *u* never could have been identical with Fr. *ü*, as it has remained *ū* unchanged in Scotl. from OE. down to the present day. We thus find that not only had OE. $\bar{o}$ and OFr. *ü* coincided, but that in the 16th cent. the pronunc. was exactly the same as the French of that time gave to their vowel *u*; and from the phonetic descriptions of the sound given both by Englishmen and Frenchmen (e. g. Holyband in "Gentil-homme Bourbonnois") we are led to conclude that it was the same as that of Fr. *ü* of the present day, viz. high-front-narrow-round. The Scotchman Hume also identifies the Fr. pronunc. of *u* with that of *mule* and *muse* in Sc.

§ 480. Holthaus endeavours to use the above evidence in all cases as proof of a diphthongal pronunc. (iu), while Ellis everywhere finds support for a pronunc. as (yy). This latter must undoubtedly be right for the four mentioned, Sb., Ht., Sm. and Holyb., in their references to Sc. Hart's statements are, it is true, difficult to reconcile with each other, but, because he in one place gives a correct definition of a diphthong, there is no reason to hold with Holthaus that he never misused the word. Are any of those early orthoepists totally free from inconsistencies? And as others most certainly "abused" the term diphthong, we are not unjustified in supposing that Hart sometimes did the same. And he may have been led to it by his very explanation of the sound; he distinctly says it "commeth of *i* and *u* (or verie neare it) is made and put togither under one breath"; this must mean that it was a simple sound, but, so to speak, made of the running together of two sounds, which be therefore considers a reason for calling it a diphthong. We can quite understand an Englishman of the present day so analysing the sound of Fr. *ü*; in fact, many a one, whose phonetic knowledge does not go very far, will be found to assert that the sound is a diphthong; in order to reproduce a sound foreign to him he has to think of two vowels known to him. Ellis and Sweet are therefore probably right in disregarding this little ambiguity, for, without doing so, we must find Hart's statements irreconcilable. Either it is untrue that the sounds in Sc. *gud* and Fr. *fust* are one and the same (and that they are is abundantly proved by the other authorities) or the sound in *fust* is a diphthong (iu), (for which there is no corroboration), or else Hart contradicts himself, with regard to the use of the term diphthong (and for this confusion we have parallel instances).

§ 481. But perhaps there is another possible explanation of the inconsistency. Baret also seems to imply a diphthongal pronunc.; we might, of course, suppose this, too, to be the result of inexact appreciation, or incorrect description, as Ellis does; but can we not suppose that Baret was thinking of another dial., not that of Central Sc., but one in which (iu) was really pronounced? We find it to-day in N. Engl. and it may then have existed perhaps in some of the Sc. diall , or Baret may have confused N. Engl. with Sc. And Hart may in the same way have been at one time thinking of Central Sc. (yy), at another of the (iu) of some other dial. Hart is in any case open to the charge of inaccuracy, e. g. when he implies that the sound of *u* in Fr. *fust* is = *you*. Or are we to reckon with the possibility that he employed some dial. of Engl. other than that of rec. sp., in which *you* was pronounced with (yy), e. g. Devonshire, where it is so pronounced at the present day? It is a pity that the works of these grammarians are not published in full, and that we have not full particulars of their personal history. If our best phoneticians of to-day vary in their representation of the sounds of rec. sp., is it not much more likely that those of the 16th cent. should occasionally do the same, especially as the dialectal differences must have been then much more strongly marked in educated men than they are now? It is, of course, a priori probable that in speaking of Sc. pronunc. these grammarians should have had in mind Central Sc., that of the shores of the Forth, "the centre of political and ecclesiastical government, of the education as well as the commerce of the kingdom", but the differences of Sc. diall. have not as yet been sufficiently taken into consideration, and some of the authorities may have referred to other diall.

§ 482. Further, the following suggestion concerning the (yy) of Central Sc. may be allowed. It is perhaps not a perfectly regularly developed form, but due to contamination with French during the 15th and 16th centuries, the time of the "weill keipit ancient alliance, Maid betuix Scotland and the realme of france" (Lyndesay). The two vowels OE. *ō* and Fr. *ü* were pronounced alike in Central Sc. as well as in the other diall.; but the pronunc. of native development may have differed from the *ü* of French as spoken in France, though not perhaps to a great extent, and then, during the time of the close intimacy with France, when there was such a large influx of Fr. words, (which, of course, would be introduced in their native form), the older vowel, whatever it may have been, was perhaps assimilated to Fr. *ü*; i. e. the vowel in the older Fr. words, which had

10

perhaps modified its $\ddot{u}$ sound so as to coincide with the sound developed from OE. $\bar{o}$, now returned to its original pronunc. (i. e. if we assume that Fr. $\ddot{u}$ was always pronounced $\ddot{u}$) and took with it its ally, the descendant of OE. $\bar{o}$. This perhaps may explain the double forms met with in the surrounding diall., (əə) being the older one of native growth, and (yy) being the half-artificial one, which was distributed from the Edinburgh district and partly displaced the other. And in this way we can more easily understand the common (əə) of the Southern Counties and Forfarshire. Moreover, Smith's words "Gallica lingua suam veterem quasi obliterarant", see § 474, directly imply that the Scotch had corrupted their own native pronunc. with a French pronunc.

On this theory we must reject altogether the general MSc. and N. Engl. (yy) suggested in § 468, and the mid-mixed-narrow-round vowel would then perhaps find most favour for Scotland. Still, the (y_1) of Devonshire by the side of the $(ə_2ə_2)$ of West Somerset shows that the (yy) of 34 may also have been of native growth. But the other suggestion is worth consideration.

§ 483. There still remain to be explained — (1) the agreement between N. Engl. and Sc. in 16th cent., if the authorities are right in stating that both have (yy), which may be open to doubt, although this sound might have been regularly developed in N. Engl. as it has been in Devonshire, while the Central Sc. (yy) was of external origin as suggested above — (2) the similar (iɐ) of Yorks. and (ii) of Banffs. The former, (iɐ), must be from 16th cent. (yy); is the latter, (ii), from a similarly developed (yy) or from the (əə) of the neighbouring districts, or from the same (yy) as existed in Central Sc. of the 16th cent.? The last is improbable on account of the (əə) of the intervening districts.

§ 484. The foregoing §§ give us few certain results; an attempt has merely been made to show, from the materials at hand, what varieties of forms we have to deal with, and what considerations are to be observed in order to arrive at a satisfactory solution of the various problems. One thing is certain, the pronunc. of OE. $\bar{o}$ und Fr. $\ddot{u}$ in Central Sc. (and that is what concerns us more particularly) in the 16th cent. was (yy). Salesbury's date, 1547, is, as we suppose, not so very much later than that of Clar., und we may therefore assume that the author's pronunc. of the vowels in question was also (yy) or something very near it.

§ 485. Now, as to the rimes themselves in Clar., although they are as varied as the orthography, still we notice that most of them fall into two classes, (a) and (n) in § 458, i. e. self-rimes and rimes with Fr. $\ddot{u}$, of which enough has already been said. From the rimes referred to in (f) we clearly see that the author also occasionally made use of an older pronunc. with $\bar{o}$, but this can scarcely have been a known pronunc. in pure Sc., as we have to set the change from $\bar{o}$ to $\ddot{o}$ at an early date; we must see here again a borrowing from Engl. The pronunc. of *to* : *so*, *soune* : *gone* in pure Sc. would have been $t\bar{u}$: $s\ddot{o}$, $s\ddot{u}n$: $g\bar{o}n$, impossible rimes. For an exactly similar rime cf. K. Q., *mone* : *stone*, st. 72 (OE. *mōna* : *stān*), also above § 22 (c).

§ 486. We notice also an $\bar{o}$ instead of $\bar{u}$ in the rime *schuike* : *smoke*, see (b); the *ui* must be due to a scribe, cf. the rime *schoke* : *awoke* in (a). Kluge, P. G. 1. 884, has called attention to the fact of this $\bar{o}$ being found instead of u, and proved by the grammarians of the 16th cent., e. g. Bullokar and Gill, and by rimes and spelling in Spenser. It seems to occur especially when the vowel is followed by *k*, particularly in preterites, e. g. *tooke*, *awooke*, *shooke*, *quooke*, but also in the pres. *looke*. Fick, p. 14, also quotes *mote* (OE. *mot*?) : *fote* (OE. *fōt*); (the form *swọ̄r* mentioned by Kluge, is somewhat different, it corresponds to the North^u form *sware*). Cf. Ellis pp. 863, 864, where we find the rime *strooke* : *smooke* : *looke* : *shooke*, Spens. F. Q. 5. 11. 22; this warrants us in assuming that our author borrowed his rime from an Engl. poet who rimed similarly to Spens.

§ 487. The rime *behovit* : *hovit* in (b) is also evidence of *o*-pronunc. in the former word, cf. the pronunc. in rec. sp. *behōv* and *behūv*. We see the regular Sc. form of *behoves* in (a), $\ddot{u}$ (with loss of *f* also). The rimes with *soft* in (b) and (c) merely show the shortening of the vowel.

§ 488. With regard to the spelling, we find *o*, *oo*, *oe*, *u*, *ui* and *ou*, and once each *oui*, *eui* and *oi* (*louike*, *leuike*, *soine*). Of these, *u* and *ui* are the most frequent, and represent genuine Sc. orthography; *o*, *oo* and *oe* are Engl. spellings. *ou* is only found before *n*, and that both in words of Engl. and of Fr. origin; the one case of *oi*, too, is in *soine*, OE. *sōna*, which otherwise only appears with *ou*. This must mean a pronunc. as (uu), (OE. $\bar{u}$ is nearly always represented by *ou*), but there is no trace of this in the mod. Sc. diall. and we must ascribe this spelling to a copyist in whose dial. OE. $\bar{o}$ and Fr. $\ddot{u}$ became $\bar{u}$ before *n*. We find the same spelling in Bruce, and also a similar spelling for OE. *sōna*, fortoune : soyne; cf. Gol. soune : houne (= delay) : broune, adj. : doune (= down) 8 !", Dunb. sonn : tonn 25. 25, Rosw. soon : down 578, 644 : renown 634, Hamp. fortone : sone, see Brandl p. 61 and Menze p. 68, who states that *ou* appears in later ME. texts of the EMidl. dial., especially before nasals. Noltemeier, p. 19, assigns one value, viz. $\bar{u}$, to *all* of the following, *u*, *eu*, *ew*, *ou* and *o*, even the *o* in *broght*!

§ 489. The rimes in (d), *soine*, *soune* : *aboûe*, at first sight seem to imply the same $\bar{u}$-sound, but in the mod. diall. *soon* always appears regularly with (əə, yy, ii, &c.) and OE. *abufan* has everywhere the same vowel as *soon*; cf. §§ 376 and 502.

§ 490. The rimes referred to in (e), with *scho*, pronoun, are virtually self-rimes, for in OE. *sēō* only the *o* has remained as bearer of the syll., cf. § 337. As usual, only *o* is written in final position, but the pronunc. was the same as in medial position, for the mod. diall. show the regular forms (*təə*, *tyy*, *tii*, *shəə*, *shyy*, *shii*, &c.).

§ 491. For the rimes referred to in (h) cf. §§ 78, 79. Most of the mod. diall. have *ither* for rec. sp. *other* (the *i* is easily explained by shortening from (yy) or (ii)) but D. 33 has (ə) and 36 (e), so also in *mother*; a further proof perhaps that the dial. of Clar. is not that of the Southern counties. Very likely the author wrote *i* in other rimes, *brither* : *ither*, &c., which the scribes altered to *brother* : *other*, &c. Cf. Satir. P. mother :

consider 5. 104, brother : togidder 42. 848, &c., Rosw. other : together
280, Burns, mither, ither, anither, thegither in Poor Maillie.

§ 492. If we can judge from the spelling, the rimes in (i) prove no
irregularity in the development of $\bar{o}$, but rather in that of $\bar{u}$, cf. below,
§ 533.

The rimes in (l) and (m) belong to the same category as those in (n),
as Fr. *eu* and *üi* undergo the same development in Engl. as Fr. *ü*, i. e. in
medial position, see Behrens, P. G. 1. 826. The rime in (o) belongs here
too, for *toune*, rec. sp. *tune*, is altogether irregular; it seems to have received in Engl. the *ü*-vowel instead of AFr. *u* = Central Fr. *o*; see Sturmfels, Angl. 9, p. 556.

§ 493. With regard to the mod. diall. of North Scotl., we have seen
above that in D. 41 and 42 (the Orkneys and Shetlands) we have (əə),
while in D. 39 (Aberd., Banffs., &c.) we find (ii), and further South, in D. 38,
(əə) again.

Ellis EEP. V, p. 788, speaking of the language of the islands, says,
"the present language is English, taught by Lowlanders chiefly from North
Lowl. (i. e. D. 37. 38. 39) to Norwegians". Until the end of last cent.
Norse was spoken; Ellis recounts the death in 1810 of a man who spoke
"Norn", i. e. Norse. We must either suppose that the English was derived
from the more southern parts of N. Lowl., D. 37 and 38, where (əə) is still
spoken, or, if it came from D. 39, which is more probable, the mod. (ii)
of that district must be of quite recent growth, and we must understand
the matter thus: OE. $\bar{o}$ became (əə) in D. 39 as in the other diall. and
remained so nearly up to 1800, and in this stage it got transferred to the
islands, where it, as usual with transplanted languages, remained stationary
in this form, while on the mainland it proceeded further and by the processes of raising and unrounding became (ii) in 39, and by raising alone
(yy) in 40.

§ 494. 2. $\bar{o}$ + ht — rimes with

a) itself. thocht (sb.) : besought 1. 882, brocht : besonght 4. 294 :
soght 4. 468. — b) OE. ŏht. thocht, sb. : wrocht 4. 1464. — c) OE. $\bar{a}$ + ht
see § 58.

These words are discussed above in §§ 59—71. The $\bar{o}$ in *-ōht* was
shortened already in the OE. period, cf. Kluge, PG. 1. 868, and Sweet
§ 403, &c., and the *oχt* seems to have remained in Sc. till the present day.
The *ou* and the *g* of the MS. are Anglicisms.

§ 495. 3. $\bar{o}$ + g — rimes with

a) OE. $\bar{u}$. swoun(e), (sb. from OE. *geswōgen*, ptc.) : adoun(e) (*of-
dūne*) 1. 504, 912, doun 3. 372, swone (vb.) : toune (*tūn*) 3. 754. — b) Fr. u.
swoun, sb. : renoune 3. 2090.

The vowel in *swoun* is plainly $\bar{u}$ (as the spelling suggests), due
doubtless, like the $\bar{u}$ of mod. Engl. *woo*, OE. *wōgian*, to the influence of
the preceding *w*.

For *drew*, prt., OE. *drōg*, see §§ 349, 355.

§ 496. *ho*, vb. and sb., generally in the meanings *stop, cease, delay*,
&c., only rimes in Clar. with $\bar{o}$ < OE. $\bar{a}$, see § 39. It has been connected

with OE. *hoga* or *hogu*, and *hogian*, cf. Laȝ. prt. hoȝede, Rob. Glouc., howe, O. and N. hoȝe; cf. also ME. *hō-li*, adv. = ON. *hōgliga* (Bradl.) see Hamp., Ps. 39. 24, and *hūlines*, sb. = tardiness, Hamp., Ps. 39. 24. But could not the verb perhaps be from OE. *hōn*, used in a similar sense to Goth. *hāhan*, to hang, leave in doubt, which has been connected with Lat. *cunctari*? For this the occurrence of a form *hōn*, &c., in MSc., apparently the same word (it has at any rate the same meaning), seems to speak; e. g. Sc. Leg. howne : alsone (*sōna*) 7/196 : done 39/590, hone : sone 32/228; Bruce, forouten hoyne : soyne 14. 182; Wynt. hwne : dwne (= done) 2880, Rat. Rav. hwn (= delay, difficulty) 1160, hwn : done 312, Dunb. hune : sone (= soon), Roll. C. V. hone : done : tone : none : throne 4. 629; Yw. Gaw. hone : undone. From the vb., of course, a sb. could easily be formed. For other instances of the form *ho*, cf. Bruce ho (sb.) : to 20. 429, Wall. hoo (sb.) : go : mo : woo : fro 2. 265, Dougl. ho (= cease, *indic.*) : tho (pron.) : tho (adv.) : go : wo 1. 39. 23. Perhaps there was here a mingling and confusion of two words, OE. *hogian* and *hōn*, and perhaps even a third, the interj. *ho*!, unless this be originally derived from one of the former (Bradl. derives it from ON. *hō*). With Hamp.'s *hōli* and *hūlines*, cf. Montg. hulie (= slowly, gently) C. 396, huly C. 1278.

ON. Œ⁴

§ 497. 1. slœ̄gr — rimes with

Fr. e — slee : cuntrie 2. 1358. This word, like *die*, see § 499, falls into the same class as OE. *ēage*, *hēah*, &c.; the gutt. is absorbed and a long *ę̄*, later *ī*, is the result in Sc., in contrast to the *ī* in ME., later diphthong, mod. Engl. (əi); see Buss, p. 497 &c.

§ 498. 2. slœ̄gþ — rimes with

OE. iht — slicht : knigt 3. 420. This word, by the substitution of ME. *ę̄* for ON. *ǣ* (as in the adj. above) became *slę̄gþ* and so was of necessity bound to follow the same fortunes as native Angl. *hę̄hþu*, which in the N. soon developed *ēgþ* into *iχt* and fell thus into one class with *cneht*, *cniht*, *neaht*, *niht*, &c. Cf. §§ 416 ff.

ON. ƏY

§ 499. døyja, generally spelt *die* — the vowel rimes with —

a) OE. *ē* : me 1. 256, 3. 1748. — b) OE. *ēo* : be 1. 1278 : se 3. 362, 612. — c) OE. *ēah*, Angl. *ēh* : he (*hēah*) 3. 1098. — d) Fr. e : prosperitie 4. 2670, 5. 2810.

The vowel is *ī* from previous *ę̄*. Cf. the preceding remarks on *slee*. All the mod. diall. have (dii) except D. 33 in which (ei) is always found in final position where the other diall. have (ii). (dii) is also found in Nthmbld.

U -

§ 500. 1. **Not followed by g** — rimes with

a) itself. aboue : loue 2. 238 (&c.). — b) OE. u : owercum (inf.) : dumb (OE. *dumb*) 1. 284. sone (OE. *sunu*) : begune (ptc.) 2. 1706, 3. 266. soune (*sunu*) : tonne (? OE. tunne) 5. 100. — c) OE. ō. aboŭe (for *aboune*) : soune (*sōna*) 1. 506 : soine 1. 158. — d) OE. ū. owercum (ptc.) : allone 3. 780. come (ptc.) : home 3. 822. — e) Fr. o = ME. ǭ. luif(e) : repruife 1. 266, reproufe 1. 296, love : remove 3. 698, louit : movit 3. 2174, luifit : movit 1. 264. — f) Fr. o = ME. ǭ. abouue (for *aboune*, OE. *abufan*) : throne 2. 1346. — g) Fr. ü. doure (*duru*) : sure (OFr. *se-ür*) 2. 576, dore : pure 3. 764. spuris (OE. *spura*, *spora*) : injuris 5. 1234. — h) Fr. e. come (pres. or prt.? the surrounding verbs are pret.) : postrum (Fr. *posterne*) 5. 1406. — i) ? aboue : rove (sb. = rest) 5. 1606. loue, vb. : vnrove (= unrest) 1. 1384.

§ 501. The question of the lengthening of OE. *u*- has been fully discussed above in §§ 361—385, where *i* and *u* are treated together. The rimes especially of weight in this question are those above in (c), (d), (e), (f), (g). Carstens, p. 26, derives *above* from an OE. form *ābūfan*, and then gives just the reverse interpretation to such a rime as *aboue* : *loue*, from which he argues that the long *ū* of *ābūfan* has been shortened. We take the vowel *u*- to have been lengthened first to *ǭ* and then, like original *ō*, to have become *ō̄* or *ū̄*, here probably the latter, where pure Sc. is meant; but we must accept *ō* in some of the rimes, for the author in his Anglicising tendencies produces a mishmash neither Sc. nor English. We see, for instance, in (d), that the new-long vowel rimes with Southern Engl. *ǭ* < OE. *ā*, and in (f) with *ǭ* from Fr. *o*, (for the *o* in *throne* is different in character from that in *move*, *prove*, &c., which is (əə) or (yy) in Sc. just the same as ME. *ǭ* < OE. *ō*, cf. the difference in pronunc. in rec. sp.). This is the result of the author's copying a standard poetical spelling which was strange to him. Pure Sc. would be (kəm) or (kəəm, kyym) : (heem) : (throon). It will be noticed that one of the rimes in (d) is also inexact with regard to the conson. For similar rimes of the verb *come* (inf.), see § 377, where we find that the *u*- of *cuman* often rimes with ME. *ō*.

The author, besides the genuine Sc. and Engl. pronunciations with a long vowel, uses yet another sometimes, for the vowel is evidently short in *owercum* and *sone*, *soune*, in (b).

§ 502. The form *abone* or *aboune* for *above* was apparently unknown to the chief scribe, who wrote *aboŭe* and *abouue* to the detriment of the rime; perhaps the latter is merely a mispelling for *aboune*; without the curl over the *u* there would be no difference between the two, but the curl is distinctly written in *aboŭe*. In § 376 the forms of this word in mod. Sc. have been given. It is noticeable that the form with *n* is also found in the extreme S., and that the diall. of Dev. and W. Som. with their (əən) and (yyn) agree here too with those of Southern and Central Scotl.; it is remarkable how many points of coincidence there are in these two distant districts.

§ 503. The rime in (h) is probably the result of an arbitrary change of the suffix in *postrum* from OFr. *postérne*, similar to the change in *guthrone* 5. 990 from *guiterne*, cf. § 43 (i).

§ 504. *rove* = rest, "Etheriall foullis in the air might mak na rove", and *vnrove*, = unrest, "That this regioun hes brocht from sik vnrove", see (h). The former word is not infrequently found, in different forms, in Sc. texts; it rimes generally with *ō*, or the vowel resulting from the lengthening of *u*-. But its etymol. has not yet been settled. Jam. Dict. (Donaldson's supplement) gives *roif, rove, ruve, rufe, ruff,* = break, pause, cessation, hence repose, quiet, peace, and connects with Icel. *rjúfa* to break, pause, interrupt; from which he derives the sb. *rof*, a breach, opening, interruption, and hence the meaning repose, quiet, peace. But this is open to question; the word appears in Sc. always in the latter sense; also the vb. *rufe*, only in the sense of to *pause, cease, rest*. The form *unrufe*, = unrest, Jam. connects with Germ. *unruhe* (!). Donaldson cites from Alex. Scott, rufe (vb.) : lufe (sb.) : mufe, vb., roif, sb. : proif, vb. : remoif, vb. : aboif : behoif. Cf. further Wall. ruff, sb. : luff, sb. : pruff, vb. : abuff, 6. 6⁰, Gol. vnrufe 499, Roll. C. V. vnrufe : abufe 2. 446, Montg. ruve, vb. : commuve : abuve : luve, sb. MP. 52. 14, rove, sb. : love MP. 6. 20, 15. 26, 20. 13.

§ 505. 2. Followed by g — rimes with
a) OE. ū. ȝouth : south (*sū/*) 4. 750. — b) OE. ū. ȝouth : suith (*sō/*) 4. 228.

§ 506. We must derive *ȝouth* from the Angl. form (*ȝ*)*iuguþ*, cf. Sweet § 359, Sievers §§ 74, 157, t. Br. § 33, *ð*. The *g* is vocalised and absorbed in the preceding *ū*, thus producing long *ū*; hence the rime in (a). That in (b) must be incorrect for Sc., probably an Engl. rime. Sweet, § 829, says the preservation of *ū* in *youth* and *uncouth* in rec. sp. is anomalous; perhaps these are Sc. or N. Engl. forms which have found their way into rec. sp.?

U:

§ 507. 1. Before nn — rimes with
a) itself. sune (*sunne*) : run (ptc.) 5. 3022, sone : wine (for *wune*, OE. *gewunnen*, ptc. "to be wine") 2. 970 : begune (ptc.) 2. 1612, soune : woune (ptc.) 5. 1970. wone (ptc.) : tune (OE. *tunne*) 5. 1694. — b) OE. u-, see § 500 (b).

§ 508. The vowel is everywhere short; the occasional spellings with *ou*, e. g. *soune, woune*, might suggest length, but these are either scribal errors (it is true, the curve is sometimes written over the *u*, but we have so many other cases of faulty copying that we might well assume it here) or else the *ou* is to be explained, as by Morsb. p. 184, from the frequent interchange of *o* and *ou* in words both of Engl. and Romance origin (the final *e* is of no consequence). We take the vowel to be, as Morsb., Fick and others explain, not (*u*), *ʮ*, but the mid-back-narrow-round (*o*), the connecting link between (*u*) and the mod. (ǝ), which latter is generally found in NSc. in *sun, won*, &c., just as in rec. sp.; possibly even this last stage (ǝ), mid-back-narrow may already have been reached.

§ 509. 2. Before nd — rimes with
a) itself. wonder : asunder 3. 368, in sunder 4. 1030, wounder : sunder 5. 2310. sound, adj. : wound, sb. 3. 986, woundis (for *wound*) 5. 1510, wounde, sb. : stound 4. 2118. — b) Fr. u. grund : redound 1. 732 (&c.) : round 5. 2284, ground : redound 5. 2030. sound, adj. : round 1. 1502. stound : abound 2. 1508. wounde, sb. : abound 2. 1870. houndis : soundis 4. 1660. asunder : founder 2. 1008.

§ 510. The above rimes, looked at from the standpoint of rec. sp., appear to imply that the vowel *u* in both sets of words has been lengthened before *nd* to *ū*, (which is regularly represented in Clar. by *ou*, as usual in MSc., cf. the lists in § 530) corresponding to ME. *ū* and to the (ᴁu) of rec. sp., except perhaps in the words in which -*er* follows, where we should generally expect to find a short vowel, although we notice that here too there is some uncertainty in the spelling, both *o*, *u* and *ou* being used, e. g. *wonder, asunder, wounder*, and this last would, of course, imply *ū*. In the other words the almost consistent spelling with *ou* shows that the vowel was long in all of them for the chief scribe. The *u* in *grund* may be an original spelling left unaltered, or merely due to careless writing.

§ 511. But the mod. diall. and comparison with other MSc. texts render it doubtful whether they were all pronounced alike by the author and whether the vowel sound in the words in (a) was not different from that of those in (b). According to Ellis's lists there is some variety in the pronunc. of words containing OE. -*und* in the mod. Sc. diall., but *ground*, sb., *ground*, ptc., *found*, ptc., *wound*, ptc., appear everywhere with (ᴇ), and also *pound* except in D. 42, which has (au); *wound*, sb., has always, and *sound*, adj. nearly always (uu) or (u), the latter has a diphthong only in D. 33; *hound* is more variable, it has (ᴁ) and (u) in 33, (ᴁ) also in 39, (au) in 35 and 36, and (ou) in 37. By (u) probably the half-long vowel is meant, it is not to be classed with (ᴁ) as if it were of the same origin; earlier *ū* is nearly always (ᴁ) in mod. Sc. In no single dial. is there one consistent pronunc. with (ᴁ) or (uu) in all the words. We find, however, that two words are given with (uu) or (u) alone, never (ᴁ), viz. *wound*, sb., and *sound*, adj. It would therefore seem that, with these two exceptions, the regular pronunc. is (ᴁ), and the (ᴁu) or (au), where found, must be borrowed from rec. sp., and not of natural growth in Scotl.

§ 512. With regard to words containing OFr. *un*, mod. Fr. *on*, followed by *d*, the evidence of Ellis's lists is, as far as it goes, perfectly uniform, viz. that the mod. pronunc. has only (u) or (un). We find (un) in *to bound, to found*, in 33, *expound* in 39, *sound*, sb. in 42, and (u) in *round* in 37 and 39.

§ 513. There is, then, apparently a sharp distinction between the two sets of words; just as the words which in rec. sp. contain (ᴁind) are divided into two sets in Sc., (ind) and (ᴁind), cf. §§ 396 ff., so also the words which in rec. sp. contain (ᴁund), spelt *ound*, are divided into two sets, (ᴁnd) and (uund), in Sc. (It must be borne in mind that in all cases the *d* is liable to be dropped, cf. § 399; in some it is, in fact, unjustified in Engl., being a so-called excrescent *d*, e. g. *sound*, sb., *bound* = OE.

gebūn). We will call the former class, with (ānd), (α), and the latter, with (nund), (β). To (α) belong all words which in OE. had *-und*, e. g. *grund, stund, pund, fundian* (= to go), the participles *bunden, funden, grunden, wunden*, &c., except the words *wund* and *gesund*, which belong to (β), as also all words containing OFr. *un*, mod. Fr. *on*, e. g. rec. sp. *round, to found, to bound, abound, redound, sound* (with excrescent *d*), &c., and words which earlier had an *ū* from other sources, e. g. *bound* (= OE. *gebūn*); also such words as *crowned, drowned*, &c., belong to (β). The cause of the unexpected *ū* in *wound* may lie in the preceding *w*, (the lengthening would be prevented in *wunden*, ptc., by the analogy of *funden, bunden*, &c., and in *wundor*, by the following *r*), but in *sound*, adj., the reason is less clear.

§ 514. In the Northern counties of Engl. it is very much the same. Class (β) has (un), sometimes (ou, au), but class (α) has (u) or (u₀), which is very different from the Sc. (u), half-shortened from (uu) and corresponds regularly to Sc. (ā), e. g. N. Engl. (up) = Sc. (āp); so that the distinction between the two classes is here just as sharp. *Wound* and *sound*, adj., always have the long vowel (uu) or its local representative; otherwise class (α) has the same vowel as in *under, wonder, up*, &c.

§ 515. It seems, then, that, just as in the case of the words containing OE. *ind*, in the N., there was at first a lengthening and then a return to vowel-shortness, probably through a Norse side-influence; i. e. that in Nthmb. English a native form *grūnd*, on coming into contact with a Norse form *grŭnd*, gave up its vowel-length. The observance of the same distinction between the two classes of words in N. Engl. makes it improbable that the oldest form of English in the S. of Scotl. was different from that of N. Engl. which is reflected in the Nthmb. Gospels, and these give, as in the case of *ind*, certain evidence of vowel-length both through accents and spelling with double *u*, e. g. *hinduelle* (centesimum) Matt. 13. 8; *hūnd* (centum) Joh. 18. 12, 21. 8, *púnda* 19. 39, *suundor* 7. 18, *suunder* 8. 6; *suundorlice*, Mk. 13, 3; *grúnd*, Luke 14. 29; also *fif hūnd*, with straight stroke over the *u*, Luke 7. 41, with which compare *fif huñd*, Luke 9. 14, where perhaps the stroke is meant for the *u* instead of the *n*.

§ 516. Whatever be the correct explanation of the short vowel, the mod. diall. would lead us to expect no rimes at all between words of the two classes (α) and (β) in pure Sc. We must therefore conclude that the author of Clar. did not write pure Sc. in these words, (for the rimes in § 509 (b) are too many for us to look upon them as merely careless riming); that is, his language had in respect of these words deviated further away from the vernacular and adapted itself more to Engl. forms that it had in words containing OE. *ind*, in which, as we have seen, it was more conservative (unless it be mere chance that he has no rimes between OE. *ind* and *ynd*).

§ 517. We find that many other MSc. texts show the same corruption, especially those which in other respects are strongly tinged by Engl. influence.

In the following, α : β rimes are given, where found, at the end of each list: — Sc. Leg. (α) *bundyne* : *fundyne* 19/288, (&c), *fundyne* : *flungyne* 19/346, *hundreth* (for *hunder*) : *wondyre* 111/258, *grownd* : *stovnd* 139/124, *stond* (OE. *stund*) : *fond* (*fundian*), *grond* : *fond* (= go) 155/1062, *wondir* : *vndir* 12/536, *grond* : *stownd* 209/434 ; (β) *fond* (= to found) : *ronde* 111/314 ; α : β, *grownd* : *rond* (= round) 164/264. Bruce, (α) *stound* : *ground* 10. 501 (&c.) ; cf. *pund* 18. 285, 521, *hund* 6. 469, *hwnd* 6. 491, *grund* 20. 324, *grundyn* 12. 520, *fundyn* 1. 322. Troj. W. (α) *founde* : *grounde* 1934, (β) *woundede* : *soundede* 2942, *renownede* : *drownede* 1744. Wall. (α) *ground*, sb. : *bound*, ptc. 6. 202, 11. 1112, *into sowndyr* : *owndir* (= under) 6. 578, *ground* : *found*, ptc. 8. 594, 10. 648, *bwn* (= bound, ptc.) : *fwn* (= found, ptc.), var. *bundin* : *fundin* 9. 664, *bund* : *fund*, var. *bundin* : *fundin* 11. 948, *foun* (= found, ptc.) : *woun* (= won, ptc.) 9. 1498, 10. 960 ; (β) *wound*, sb. : *found*, inf. 3. 204, (&c.), *sound*, adj. : *found*, inf. 5. 464, 9. 58, *wnsound* : *abound* 8. 788, *sound*, adj. : *round* 9. 1922, 10. 280, *wound*, sb. : *abound* 8. 226 : *confound* 8. 732 ; α : β, *stound* : *wound*, sb. 6. 734, 9. 1306. Gol. has *grund* 8. 1026, *fundyne* 16, *fundin* 392 (&c.), *vnbundin* 1040, in which the *u* implies a short vowel for the scribe, but the rimes are all α : β rimes, *found* (*fundian*) : *vnsound* : *grund* : *stound* 642, *wound*, sb. : *found*, inf. : *round* : *ground* 888, *stound* : *found*, inf. 933. Lanc. (α) *founde* : *ybownd* 502 ; (β) *sonde*, adj. : *vound*, sb. 106, *sownis* (= sounds, sb.) : *clariounis* 772, *sown*, sb. : *bown* (OE. *gebūn*) 1036 ; many α : β rimes, e. g. *found*, ptc. : *wounde*, sb. 272, *founde*, ptc. : *expounde* 1150, *ground* : *wounde*, sb. 1192, *founde*, ptc. : *lwond* (= wounded) 246, &c. Dunb. (α) *hunder* : *wnder* 50. 23, *vnder* : *in sounder* 81. 114, *vndir* : *hundir* : *wundir* : *asundir* 8. 39, and perhaps *found*, ptc. : *pound* : *jocound* (if last is derived direct from Lat.) 81. 75 ; (β) *sound*, sb. : *drownd* 2. 160, *soun*, sb. : *toun* 25. 22, *woundit* : *refound it* : *soundit* : *confoundit* 38. 31, *cround* : *renownd* 48. 154, *wounde* (sb.) : *sounde*, adj. 90. 17, *soun*, sb. : *crown* 6. 32 ; α : β, *habound* : *wound* : *stound* : *sound*, adj. 9. 159, *stound* : *drownd* : *round* : *wound*, sb. 72. 103. Dougl. is very irregular, and has mostly mixed, α : β rimes in Pal. of Hon. and King H.; in his Virg. they are also found, although the majority seem to be regular here — *aboundit* : *roundit* (= whispered) : *resoundit* : *ygroundit* 1. 10. 14, *hunder* : *founder* : *wonder* : *vnder* : *thunder* 1. 12. 20, *sound*, sb. : *ground* : *found* : *abound* 1. 16. 6, *confoundit* : *foundit* : *igroundit* : *resoundit* 1. 21. 7, *stound*, sb. : *ground* : *confound* : *wound*, sb. 1. 58. 25, *ground* : *sound*, sb. : *redound* : *wound*, sb. 1. 96. 23, *ground* : *sound*, adj. 2. 127. 26, *ground* : *rebound* 2. 155. 4, *wound* : *resound* : *found*, ptc. 2. 166. 19, &c. Lyndes. (α) Mon. *woundir* : *in schounder* 3859, 5499, *hounder* (= 100) : *wounder* 4027, *ground* : *found*, ptc. 4188, Sat. *hunder* : *wonder* 917, 2120 ; (β) Mon. *sounde*, sb. : *redounde* 187, *confounde* : *drounde* 1922, Sat. *bounds*, sb. : *wounds*, sb. 991, *sound*, adj. : *dround* 2097, *found*, vb. : *abound* 2969, *abunds* : *founds*, vb. 2971 ; α : β, Mon. *grounde* : *sounde*, adj. 764, *grounde* : *founde*, inf. 1700, *bound*, ptc. : *confound* 4111, *wound* : *stound* 3174, Sat. *bounds*, sb. : *punds* 2850, *bounds* ; *pounds* 2959, *pound* : *abound* 3191. Roll. C. V. mostly α : β rimes, e. g. *grund* : *found* : *round* : *sound*, adj. 1. 140, *stound* : *found*, inf. : *wound*, sb. : *ground* : *confound* 1. 648, *found* : *ground* :

abound : *Mappamond* 2. 126, *stound* : *ground* : *abound* : *facound* : *confound* 2. 415, *vererund* : *bound*, sb. : *resound* : *redound* : *confound* 3. 332, *ground* : *stound* : *wound* : *confound* 4. 354, &c. Satir P. (*α*) *ground* : *found* 35. 76, *thunder* : *in Schunder* 32. 120, *hunder* : *vnder* 43. 27, *pundis* (for *pund*) : *bund*, ptc. 45. 803, *fund him* : *jucundum* 45. 118; (*β*) *woundit* : *confoundit* 17. 104, *bound* (*gebūn*) : *toun* 45. 879, *boun* : *toun* 45. 1073; *α* : *β*, *found*, ptc. : *abound* 7. 196, *stound* : *renoun* : *abound* : *resound* 17. 168, *fund*, ptc. : *wound*, sb. 27. 56, *wondre* : *fondre*, vb. 29. 2, *bound* : *redound* : *found*, ptc. : *ground* 36. 143.   Montg. (*α*) *grund* : *fund* C. 122 (&c.), *thundring* : *wondring* C. 235, *thunder* : *vnder* : *wonder* M. P. 40. 54; (*β*) *round* : *profound* C. 84, *abound* : *sound*, sb. C. 90, *woundis* : *boundis*, sb. C. 266, *roundlie* : *soundlie* C. 1441, *rounds* : *sounds* : *bounds* : *confounds*, S. 2, *round* : *profound* : *abound* : *sound* S. 56, *sound* : *profound* MP. 40. 46, &c.; *α* : *β*, *stound* : *profound* MP. 40. 33, *stounds* (vb. = smarts, aches) : *wounds*, sb. C. 741.

§ 518. As some of the above mentioned works were only partially examined, the *α* : *β* rimes may perhaps be somewhat more numerous than appears here. None of them appear to be free from them except Bruce and Troj. W., but it will be noticed that *stound* is of most frequent occurrence among the *α* : *β* rimes, so that perhaps it should like *sound* (OE. *gesund*) be reckoned to the *β*-class for some of the texts; as the word is not given by Ellis in his lists, we have no evidence from the mod. diall. to assist us; but if we make this allowance, then Wall., Dunb. and Montg. are also free from exceptions, which is a strong argument for placing *stound* in the *β*-class; these poets are on the whole so free from Anglicisms, that it would be astonishing if they here showed exceptions. The number of exceptions in the Satir. P. is very striking, seeing that in the treatment of OE. *ind* and *ynd* they are so consistent; we must look upon this as proof that, like the author of Clar., the authors of some of them had from some cause or other a more Anglicised pronunc. in this class of words; the mod. diall. show, too, as we have seen, less conservatism than in the case of *ind*, although it is uncertain how far the irregular forms are of native growth and how far due to Engl. influence. The Satir. P. require an exact examination and separation according to date and dial., for they are by different authors whose language will probably be found to vary in many respects.

§ 519. As in the Ms. of Clar., so with most of the other texts, it is very seldom that the orthography attempts to make a difference between the two classes of words, (*a*) and (*β*). This is intelligible when the rimes also show no difference, or when the texts have been copied at a later date by a scribe whose orthography was confused, as in the case of Bruce and Wall., both copied by the same scribe, John Ramsay, in 1488 and 1489. Only Dunb. and Montg. make an apparent distinction, the latter especially is very exact in using *u* always for the short vowel; an examination of merely the orthography of his poems would probably be very instructive.

§ 520. Other rimes, besides those given above, from Sc. and N. Engl. texts will be found given by Wackerzapp (the ptc. forms of verbs of

Class III); but his lists are often misleading, for he has included the form *boun* or *bound* (= ready, prepared, OE. *gebūn*), which he has falsely understood to be from OE. *bunden*, ptc. of *bindan*; so that some of the apparent α : β rimes are not really so.

§ 521. It will be seen there that some of the earlier N. Engl. texts are free from α : β rimes with the ptc. forms, OE. *bunden*, *funden*, &c., e. g. Curs. M. has none; such seem to appear first in York P. But a special investigation is necessary to establish the date at which they first appear in N. Engl.

§ 522. The words of Engl. origin, in which an -*er* follows, only have a short vowel in the mod. diall. Ellis gives *under* with (ɜ) in 33, 35 and 38, and (œ) in 42, *wonder* with (ɜ) in 33, (y) in 37, (i) in 41. In N. Engl. it is similar. It is uncertain whether the rime *asunder* : *founder* means that the author pronounced *asunder* with a long *ū*, or *founder* with a short vowel, or whether it is a case of bad riming. The latter is, however, less likely, as similar rimes are found in Dougl. and Satir P., see above. If any weight can be laid upon the spelling *wounder*, perhaps we have to understand a long vowel in all these words as well; if so, some other explanation than Engl. influence must be found.

§ 523. 3. Before ng — rimes with
a) itself. toung : soung, ptc. 5. 370. — b) Fr. u. tonge : impunge (vb. OFr. *impugner*) 4. 2504.

§ 524. The spelling in (a) would seem to point to vowel-length, *ū*, for one of the scribes; whether it was so for the author cannot be decided from the rimes, but *tongue* appears in all the mod. Sc. diall. with short vowel (ɜ), and in N. Engl. and N. Midl. it generally has (*u*) or (*u̯*), so that if *ou* correctly represented the pronunc. of any district of that period, shortening must have taken place since then. Most probably the *ou* means a short *ŭ* as in *young*. In pure Sc. texts the vowel was altogether short; Montg. always has *u*, e. g. tung : sprung : sung : hung, S. 10. In Bellenden (Irving, p. 319) we find the same rime as in (b), toung : impugn.

§ 525. 4. Before mb — rimes with
a) OE. u - dumbe : owercum 1. 284, see § 501. — b) Fr. u. dumbe : Colune (? for *Columbe*) 2. 1670.

§ 526. The vowel is probably short, — (*o*), or (ɜ). Montg. has *u*, not *ou*, e. g. dum : cum, C. 822, and we know that *cum* may have a short vowel in MSc. as it has in NSc. The *b* is already silent, cf. Dunb. dum : sum (= some) : cum 15. 26.

§ 527. 5. Before ll — rimes with
OE. y — full : dull (OE. *dyll*, cf. § 549) 2. 1648, 4. 1472.

In mod. Sc. *dull* appears everywhere with (ɜ), *full* has (ɜ) in 33, 36, 38, 39, but also (uu) or (u) in 35, 36, 38, 39, 42, with vocalisation of the *ll*, 33 has also (fɜu) and 39 has also (fol). The author of Clar. probably pronounced (*o*) or (ɜ) in both words.

§ 528. 6. Before rn — rimes with
Fr. u — murne : returne 3. 658.

No evidence to show whether the vowel is long or short; the spelling suggests a short vowel for the scribe. Ellis does not give *mourn*, but

Murray says it and *turn* have (ɑ) in his dial., cf. DSS. 148, 149, and Ellis gives *turn* with (ɑ) in 35 and 39, but (oo) in 41. We shall probably be right in assigning (o) or (ɑ) to the pronunc. of the author in both words. Montg. shows no sign of lengthening before *rn*, we always find *u*, e. g. turne : burne MP. 12. 8, murne S. 4. 11, murning : turning MP. 39. 27; cf. Dougl. Saturne : turne : soiurne : murne : spurne 1. 29. 28, Lyndes. murnit : turnit, Mon. 4005, Satir. P. murne : burne 13. 150, murnee : turne 15. 32, murne : returne : burne : turne 30. 32, &c.

§ 529. 7. Before other conss. — rimes with
a) OE. *ū*, see § 530 (f). — b) Fr. u. thus : Clariodus 1. 208 (&c. passim) : perrellous 2. 1764 : noyous 4. 472. this (MS. for *thus*) : famous 4. 2514 : Clariodus 1. 286, 5. 238.

The vowel probably = (o) or (ɑ). In almost all words containing OE. *u*:, which have not yet been mentioned, the regular sound in NSc. is (ɑ), as in rec. sp.

U‘

§ 530. 1. Not followed by w — rimes with
a) itself. boun(e) (OE. *(ge)-būn*, see Brate, p. 37) : toun 2. 1292, 3. 1628. doun(e) : toun 3. 1460 (&c.). about(e) : out 3. 1548, 4. 2126 : lout (OE. *lūtan*) 5. 2162. loud : clud 1. 726 : cherude (vb. but not from OE. *scrȳdan*, but from the sb. *schrūd* = OE. *scrūd*) 1. 776 : schroud (sb. "syne to the scharpe assay of knightlic schroud", = OE. *scrūd*?) 5. 2006, cf. *ischerowdit*, ptc. 5. 2065. aloud : scheroud (sb. = OE. *scrūd*) 2. 1676. clude (sb.) : scherond, vb. 5. 3024. — b) OE. ū + w, see § 535 (a). — c) OE. ŭ + g, see § 505 (a). — d) OE. ōō + w, see §§ 349 (b), 351. — e) OE. ū + g, see § 495 (a). — f) OE. ŭ. ws : thus 1. 262. hous : thus 3. 782, 2388. — g) OE. ō. bruike (*brūcan*) : forsuike, prt. 4. 2778 : buike (*bōc*) 5. 1700. — h) Fr. u. about : stout 1. 76 : rout 1. 1388 (&c.), rowt 1. 572 : doubt 2. 1028 (&c.). out : doubt 3. 394, 4. 2094 : stout 4. 2460 : rout 5. 2194. without : dout 4. 1322 : stout(e) 5. 1964, 1992. ouris (NE. ours) : valouris 4. 694. boure : houre. 2. 572 : honoure 5. 1714, nichbour : Amandur 2. 1036. bouris : garitouris 3. 290. hous(e) : laborus 2. 720 : joyous 3. 892, 2346 : pretious 5. 896. ws : chevalrus 1. 1264 : Clariodus 2. 466, 5. 794. now : wow (= vow) 2. 402 : awow 3. 1706. doun(e) : sermoune 2. 142 : renoune 2. 1058 (&c.) : fassioune 4. 112, 2180 and many more. adoun : renoune 2. 750 : pardoune 4. 1474 and others. toun(e) : renoune 4. 1662 (&c) : sojorne 3. 862 (&c.) : sound 3. 354 (&c.) : prissoun 4. 684, and many more. — i) Fr. ü. schoure : measoure 4. 1482, cf. Behrens PG. 1. 821 and Frz. St. V. 2. 118, and t. Br. § 75.

§ 531. OE. *ū* has remained the same sound unchanged in Sc. right down to the present day. All the mod. diall. of Scotl. show (uu), or occasionally (u), which may be half-long, in all regularly developed words; there are only a few, generally easily explained, forms with shortened vowel, none with the diphthong (əu) or (ɑu), except in D. 33, of which dial. it is characteristic that it always has (ɑu) for the final (uu) of the other diall., e. g. in *cow*, *now*, &c., so that in this respect this one dial.

agrees with rec. sp.; cf. Murray, DSS., pp. 117, 148, &c. This being so we cannot well suppose that there was ever any diphthong in MSc.; the sound must have been $\bar{u}$ all along, and the almost consistent spelling with *ou* in the extreme N. for pure $\bar{u}$ is a strong argument against Holthaus and others, who argue from the orthography alone that the diphthonging of $\bar{u}$ took place as early as the 14th cent.

§ 532. The rimes above in (a), (b), (c), (d), (e) and (h) are all proofs of an $\bar{u}$ pronunc. The first in (f) shows the usual shortening of $\bar{u}$ in OE. *ūs*, but the second, *hous* : *thus*, is somewhat striking, and most probably to be considered as a faulty rime, for there is no evidence of any shortening of the vowel in OE. *hūs* in any dial. Menze quotes the rime *hus* : *us* from Gen, Ex., but here the vowel in *us* is probably still long, as he suggests, or else the rime is like ours, faulty.

§ 533. The rimes in (g) are difficult of explanation if *bruike* is to be derived from OE. *brūcan*; the *ui* of the Ms. and the rimes seem to point to an older $\bar{o}$; perhaps we have to do with another verb as suggested by Bülbring, p. 90, who calls attention to the form *broke* in Laʒ. and Sir Fer., in the latter of which it rimes with OE. $\bar{a}$. The weak form *brukien*, in Laʒ. explains satisfactorily according to our theory that OE. *u* in open syll. produces ME. $\bar{\varrho}$ and MSc. $\ddot{o}$. We cannot explain from *brūcan*, unless we imagine that shortening took place before the *c*, as in *sūcan* and other verbs, and that then the new $\breve{u}$ was lengthened again in the same way as OE. $\bar{u}$-. Cf. the mod. form of rec. sp. *brook*, also Montg. brook : forsook : look MP. 8. 40.

§ 534. Perhaps the spelling with *u* in *clud*, rec. sp. *cloud*, indicates a short vowel (o) or (ɑ) in the pronunc. of the scribe, for to-day *cloud* is pronounced with (ɑ) in D. 33; cf. Murray, DSS., p. 148, col. 2.

§ 535. 2. $\bar{u}$ + w — rimes with

a) OE. $\bar{u}$. trow (*trūwian*) : now 3. 218. — b) OE. ēōw. trow : ʒow 2. 552. As shown above in §§ 351, 352, we cannot derive the vb. *trow* from OE. *trēowian*, on account of these rimes, which both prove an $\bar{u}$-pronunc.; the bearer of the syll. in ʒow is only $\bar{u}$, ʒ-ow = i-$\bar{u}$. The *w* of *trūwian* has been vocalised and absorbed in the preceding $\bar{u}$.

§ 536. Of uncertain origin. *goune*, NE. *gown* : donn (OE. $\bar{u}$) 2. 1688. The vowel is, of course, $\bar{u}$. *shout*, ("Etymol. unknown", Skeat) rimes only with Fr. *u*, : stout 3. 400 : rout(e) 3. 1064, 1072, and also contains the pure vowel $\bar{u}$.

Y -

§ 537. Besides OE. *cyning*, for which see § 540, we only have the word OE. *spyrian*, to track, inquire, ask; which rimes with words containing a) Angl. $\bar{e}$ = WS. $\bar{\text{ie}}$ — speir : feir (*timor*) 5. 1212. — b) Angl. $\bar{e}$ = WS. $\bar{\text{eu}}$ — speir : neir 1. 534, 1238. — c) Angl. $\bar{e}$ = WS. $\bar{\text{ie}}$ — speir : heir, vb. 1. 1248. — d) OE. $\bar{e}$, mut. of $\bar{o}$ — speir : in feir 5. 2378. — e) OE. $\breve{e}$ — speiris, 3. sg. : murthereris 4. 108. — f) Fr. ie, e — speir(e) : maneir(e) 3. 1378 (&c.), speirit : requyrit 4. 392, 5. 502.

§ 538. This word is in the ME. and NE. periods peculiar to Scotl., where it was perhaps saved from extinction by the existence of the Norse vb. *spyrja*. In Clar. it only rimes with previous *ę*, which has become *ī*, and gives us further support to our observations respecting the treatment of OE. *i-*, cf. above §§ 361 ff.; for the *y* was, as usual, unrounded to *i* in the N., and then underwent the usual lengthening in open syll. in the same way as *ī-*, i. e. it became *ī* and *ę̄*; for the *i* < *y* was also an *į* or (*i*), as shown by the frequent rimes with *ĕ* in closed syll., of which examples will be found below, and which Brandl has shown to be found in all diall. (AnzfdA. 13. 97 ff). The form MSc. spẹ̄r, late MSc. and NSc. *spīr*, can be set by the side of rec. sp. *evil* = OE. *yfel*, ME. *ęvil*, (formerly considered to be a specially Kentish form) which shows the same lengthening in open syll. For a similar rime, cf. Montg. speirit : retyrit, C. 604, (the vowel in *retyrit* is the Fr. *ī*, undiphthonged; the rime does not prove that *y* has been lengthened direct to *ī*, but to *ē* and then *ī*, cf. reteirs : ʒeers S. 2); so in other MSc. texts.

§ 539. There is another verb exactly similar to this in its OE. form, viz. *styrian*, = rec. sp. stir, with short vowel (< ME. *stĭr*, Orm. *stirenn*) and mod. Sc. *stĭr*, with long vowel (< MSc. *stẹ̄r*). Here we see the same difference between N. and S. in the treatment of *i-* or *y-* as in the two forms ME. gĭv, MSc. gẹ̄v, gīv. Stir does not occur in rime in Clar., if it did we should expect to find it riming, in the form *stīr*, with previous *ę̄* (cf. the form *steiring* = stirring, 3. 717, with *ei* = ī), as it does in other Sc. texts, e. g. Sc. Leg. stere : appere 11/476, Dougl. steiris : deiris : heiris : eiris : leiris 1. 16. 8, Roll. C. V. steird : leird 2. 157, Rob. Semple (Irving, p. 438) steir : neir : weir (= war) : feir (= comrade), Francis Semple (Irving p. 580) steer : geer, sb.; also in Wynt., Lyndes, &c., and as sb., Rosw. steer : Oliver 660, *on stere* or *asteer* in Dougl., &c., see Jam. Dict. Chauc. has also *stēren*, with an open *ę̄* according to t. Br. § 24, β.

Ellis gives the form (stiir) in D. 39 and 41, which corresponds to (spiir) = ask, found in many, if not all, the Sc. diall.; both are common in Scott's works.

§ 540. OE. cyning. This word became *cing* in the OE. period, and presents in the ME. period the same form, spelt with *y* or *i*, in all diall., Engl. and Sc. The rime-words in Clar. contain

a) OE. ĭ — king : thing 1. 106 (&c. passim) : ring (OE. ring) 1. 360 : sing 2. 1752. Also numerous rimes with verbal nouns and participles in *-ing*. — b) ONthmb. ĭ = WS. eo — : ʒing 1. 804 (&c.), ʒeing 2. 1626 (&c.). — c) Fr. ĭ — : bening(e) 2. 756 (&c.) : resinge (= resign) 4. 2376 : conding 5. 2392 : ding (dignus) 5. 592 and others. — d) Fr. ei — : ringne (= reign) 1. 398.

These rimes are all perfectly regular.

§ 541. The mod. Engl. words *breach* and *beadle* have been derived from OE. *bryce* (Sweet, p. 327, where *e* in ME. is explained as being Kentish or due to the influence of *brecan*) and OE. *bydel* (= OHG. *butil*, see Menze, p. 46). If these derivations are correct, the two words stand parallel to the word *evil* in rec. sp. and to (spiir) and (stiir) in Sc. Skeat (Princ. 2. 92) derives them from OFr. *breche* and *bedel*; but this is not necessary, for the OE. *bryce* and *bydel* would produce exactly the same forms as these in ME., at any rate in Northern ME.

Y:

§ 542. 1. Before nd — rimes with

a) itself. mynd(e) : unkynde 2. 284, 4. 1422 : kynd 2. 398 (&c.). — b) Fr. i. myndis : declynis 4. 1118, kyndis (for *kynd*) : ingyne 5. 790.

§ 543. These rimes have been fully discussed in §§ 396 ff. The two rimes in (b) prove the lengthening of the vowel-sound, which, as shown above, has already become (əi) or (ei) from previous (ii). The consistent spelling with *y*, not *i*, is to be noticed; also the loss of final *d* after *n*, see (b).

§ 544. 2. Before other conss. — rimes with

a) itself. list : kist (prt. *kyssan*) 2. 206. — b) OE. i. fulfill : till 1. 104 (&c.) : will 1. 1102 (&c.) : still 4. 2264. hill : still 4. 1608, 5. 2182. thrist (by metathesis from OE. *þyrst*) : wist 1. 1498 : kist (ON. *kista*, = WS. *ciest, cyst*) 5. 1842. thine (*þynne*) : within 2. 1484 : skine (ON. *skinn*) 3. 728 : in 4. 1048. forthinke (*for-þyncan*) : drinke 3. 1614. kis, vb. : blise 2. 1256. wis (vb. OE. *wyscan*) : blise 5. 2708. lift (sb. *lyft*) : gift 4. 780. beclipis, 3. sg. : schipis 5. 2512. — c) OE. e. stint (*styntan*) : hint (*hentan*) 1. 94, hinte, prt. 3. 494 : vent (= went) 5. 1120. list : best 1. 640 (&c.). — d) OE u. dull (OE. *dyll, see below) : full 2. 1648, 4. 1472. — e) Fr. i. list : resist 1. 866. — f) Fr. e. list : oprest 3. 1502.

§ 545. The rimes with *i* show the usual unrounding of OE. *y*. This began already in the OE. period, especially after *c*, (*cining*) and before palatals (*hige*) and before *n*, *l* + *palatal* (*ðincean, filiȝan*), see Sievers § 31, note. The rimes with *e* are a further support of Brandl's evidence, AnzfdA. 13. 97 ff., and similar to the i : e rimes above in § 387, &c. There are only two words which in Clar. rime with *e*, viz. *stint* and *list*. With regard to the former we might conclude that the *e* of the rime-words *hint* and *went* had been raised to *i* rather than that the *i* (resulting from *y*) in *stint* had been lowered to *e*, as there is a tendency in many of the mod. diall. to change *e* + *n* + *cons.* to *i* + *n* + *cons.*; but there is also the opposite tendency to change *i* to *e*, as shown above in § 389, and although *hint* is the usual Sc. form for OE. *hentan*, (cf. Dunb. hynting = seizing 2. 8, hint : stynt 33. 88), we almost invariably find *e* and not *i* in *went*; so also in *best*, the rime-word of *list*, cf. Dunb. list : rest, 20. 1. Therefore Brandl's explanation seems to be the right one, viz. that *y* or *i* is lowered to or towards *e*.

§ 546. This becomes more probable when we consider how many words containing OE. *y* are found to-day with *e* in the Sc. diall., e. g. Ellis gives *gelt* (guilt), *hel* (hill), *ferst* (first), *den* (din), *medge* (midge), *breg* (bridge), *reg* (ridge), *sen* (sin), *pet* (pit), *ded* (did), *beznes* (business), *letl* (little), *berth* (birth), *felt* (filled), *kjest* (kissed).

§ 547. This shows that in Scotl., too, *y* is more affected than *i* by this tendency to lowering, as remarked by Brandl, l. c. p. 100. The few examples in Clar. are quite in keeping with his statement (p. 102) that the change occurs principally before s, n, r and l followed by a cons.; but the mod. diall. show an extension in this respect, e. g. *medge, breg, reg* (OE. *mycg, brycg, hrycg*). As B. further remarks we have to do with a variable pronunc., which is not consistently treated in any dial.; sometimes one form gains the upper hand, sometimes the other, so that we can make no hard and fast rule, and it is quite possible that the author of Clar. made use of double forms here again. But it would seem that in general the tendency $i > e$, especially $y > e$, is stronger than $e > i$, and finds its parallel in the change $u > o$ which is also everywhere liable to take place; in fact, there is a general tendency to lower *high* vowels in English.

§ 548. It should be noticed that, although y rimes with e, we do not find e written for y in closed syll., but only i. The scribes, then, did not know the e-pronunc. On this $y : e$ question cf. further Morsb., p. 41, who also remarks on the fact that in the London documents investigated by him e appears for y especially before n, ll, (l), and r, and accounts for this in the same way as Brandl, viz. by the special character of these conss., before which it was easier for i to assume a more obscure form. Cf. further Menze, p. 45 ff. for the EMidl. dial.

[§ 549. dull. Napier has lately, in the Academy, May 7, 1892, p. 447, suggested OE. **dyll.* (= **dulja-*) for the etymol. of *dull*, on the analogy of cluster = OE. *clyster*, bundle = OE. *byndele*, thrust = ON. *prȳsta* &c. This is much better than the hitherto accepted etymol. OE. *dol*. It remains to be seen whether the mod. Sc. diall. bear this out for the N. Generally we find Y̆ or ĕ for OE. ў̆, but Ellis's lists give almost no examples of the words which have in rec. sp. an $u = $ (ɜ) for OE. *y*, *bundle, cluster*, &c., so that we cannot tell, without further evidence, whether (ɜ), which is found in almost all Sc. diall. in *dull*, can be looked upon as a correct NSc. representative of OE. *y*. But we have some evidence which points this way, for besides e and i, we find (ɜ) occasionally for OE. *y* even where rec. sp. has another sound; this is especially the case before r, e. g. in *worm, wort* in 33, *work*, vb. in 35, 36, *birth, mirth* in 35, *first* in 34, 35, 39, 42; but also occasionally before other conss. e. g. in *midge* in 41, *listen* in 42, *little* in 34, 39, *busy* in 36, and everywhere in *muckle*, OE. *mycel*, which may, then, perhaps be explained in the same way as the Engl. (ɜ) in *bundle*, &c. In agreement with rec. sp. we find (ɜ) in *comely* in 33 and *stump* in 39. The sound (ɜ) is in mod. Sc. generally equivalent to MSc. *u*, so that, if it correctly represents OE. *y*, this probably passed into *u* in MSc.; this makes the rime *dull : full* quite in order.

But perhaps there were sometimes parallel forms in ONthmb., with *u* instead of *y*?

Y⁽

§ 550. rimes with

a) itself. lyte (*lȳt*) : syte (ON. *sȳti*) 4. 1376. — b) OE. or ON. ī. kyth (OE. *cȳpan*) : sweith 1. 532 : alsuith 2. 990 : alsweith 4. 38 : belyue 5. 1248. alyt(e) (OE. *lyt*) : quhyte (*hwīt*) 1. 814 : myt (*mīte*) 2. 1168, litt :

wyt (= blame) 2.312, a lyte : tyte (ON. *titt*) 4.1136. hyde (vb. *hȳdan*) : besyde 3.718 : wyde 3.2080. pryde : ryd, inf. 5.2296. bryde : syde 5.1754. tyne (ON. *tȳna*, = lose) : myne (*mīn*) 3.1578. fyre : schare (for *schyre* = OE. *scīr*, see § 439) 5.2712. — c) OE. **ī**. thrist (vb. ON. *þrȳsta*, NE. thrust) : wist 2.1568, thrust : wist 3.2096. — d) OE. **ĕ**. thrist : brist, ptc. 5.2026, brist, prt. 5.2336, see § 184. — e) Fr. **i**. sky (ON. *skȳ*) : cry 1.738, 2.1544 : harmonie 4.1610, skyis (for *sky*) : chevalrie 5.1256. fyre : desyre 1.38 (&c.) : ire 1.968 (&c.) : seir (Fr. *sire*?) 3.1960 : atyre, attyre 4.1056, 5.1724, fyrit : conspyrit 2.1808, fire : desyre 1.946. alite (*lȳt*) : indyte 2.1872, alyte : quite 3.736 : perfyte 4.2830.

§ 551. OE. $\bar{y}$ is, as usual, like $\breve{y}$, unrounded, and therefore rimes quite regularly with previous **ī**, and has with it the pronunc. (əi) or (ei). If shortened before double conss., it rimes with **ĭ**, as above in (c), or with **ĕ**, see (d) and compare §§ 545—548.

§ 552. *lyte, alyt*, &c., also found in Chauc., cf. Ellis, p. 276. The rimes in Clar. all prove length of vowel, (Cf. Dunb. lyte : endyte : quhite : wryte : perfyte 1.71) and this form without final *l* is to be derived from OE. *lȳt*, see Sievers § 319. Sievers also gives *lȳtel* with long vowel, BT. gives only *lytel, lyt*, without any mark of quantity. Ellis's lists give no trace of the monosyllabic form in the mod. diall. where we should expect to find (ləit) or (lait). Ellis, 1.290, says that in the S. of Scotl. *little* is often (lɛitl), especially as a proper name. The form (liitl), often spelt *leetle*, which is occasionally heard, is probably an emphatic form developed out of (litl), not a preservation of ME. *lītl*, for *leetle* is not confined to the diall. which preserve ME. **ī**. In the regular course of development the effect of the *l* in the final syll. would tend to shorten the preceding vowel. In Clar. we find *litill* inside the verse.

§ 553. *thrist* = rec. sp. *thrust*. This is the form to be expected and generally found in the N. The Kt. form would be *threst*, and this is also found in Ayenb. and in Chauc.; the S. W. form would be *thrüst*, which produces mod. Engl. thrust, with (ɜ), in the same way as Southwestern ME. *müche* produces NE. *much* with (ɜ).

§ 554. **List of irregular rimes.**

1.40. *feild : behald*, see § 173. — 1.614. *bricht : meike*. Piper's emendation, *eike* for *bricht*, is probably right. — 1.648. *sende*, ptc. : *goŭe*; the curl over the *u* is wrong, the scribe probably meant *gone*, which he wrote instead of *wend*. — 1.1144 *chirurgiane : se*, So come to him ane great chirurgiane Be the Kings ordinance his hurts for to se. Omit *for* and change *se* to *saine* or *sane*, with P. — 2.106. *raid : remeid*; It was me tauld or this quhair þat I raid Thairfor forʒet it sen þair is no remeid. The meaning is rather obscure; *raid* cannot be OE. *rād*, prt., if the rime is pure; perhaps for *reid* = guess : *remeid* has everywhere else **ī** < **ē**, and is scarcely likely to have had its original *ē*-pronunc. here. — 2.164. *call : deife*; evidently corrupt passage. — 2.426. *diamont : illuminat*; The quhilke bricht was and illuminat. P. reads *illuminand*. — 2.1142. *rap : brake*; assonance? — 2.1196. *prissoun : penance*; P. changes *prissoun* to *firmance*. — 2.1232. *anone : went*, ptc.; read *gone* with P. — 2.1636. *me-*

lodie : *instruments*, P. reads *minstrellie*. — 2.1840. *cheir* : *war*, He said Madame forsuith my commoun war For scho hes oft me feistit for this. Evidently corrupt passage. — 2. 1894. *glaidnes* : *Cousingne*; P. reads *glaidening* for *glaidnes*. — 3. 278. *convoyit* : *barrent*; P. reads *barrnet*, but the mistake is probably rather in the other word: "baith burges and barrent" is probably correct, cf. Gol. banrentis, 5, 1274, 1335, &c. — 3. 370. *bluid* : *bold*; read *wod* with P. — 3. 758. *rebuike* : *fute* (OE. fōt); P. reads *rebute* for *rebuike*. — 3.1214. *harnes* (O. Fr. harneis) : *armis*, pl.; assonance? The 2nd line is faulty in metre. — 3. 1496. *dayes* : *perfay*, P. reads *day*, MS. thir mony dayes. — 3.1932. *lyfe*, sb. : *drave*, As day begouth the night away drave; P. reads As day begouth *and* night away *did drive*; perhaps better, As day begouth the night away *to drive*. — 4. 496. *anone* : *fro*; P. reads *also* for *anone*; the 1st line is too short, MS. And gart be gevine to them anone. — 4. 580. *bline* (OE. *blinnan* = cease) : *meine*. told him all the maner and the meine. Perhaps for "all the maner maire and min(e)" (= less), cf. Gol. þe mare and þe myn : kyn : in : begin 1159, Sc. Leg. mare and myne : þare-In 209/416. — 4. 1500. *dansit* : *France*; read *dance* with P. — 4. 1540. *keiping* : *go*; P. reads *ging* for *go*, but there is no other example of *ging* = go, infin.; it would be better to alter *keiping*, for it makes the line a syll. too long; a monosyllable such as *ho* would put all right; or else read in 2nd line, And bad hir to hir Ladie it to bring. — 4. 2086. *thike* (OE. *þicce*) : *wicht*, adj.; P. reads *dicht* for *thike*. — 4. 2140. *humbillness* : *confidence*. — 5. 176. *also* : *went*; read *go* with P. — 5. 382. *greine* : *cleathing*; *greine* seems to have arisen through the two following rime-words *Queine*, *scheine*; perhaps we should read ʒing, tender flouris ʒing (: cleathing), or perhaps there is a more extensive corruption, and P.'s punctuation should be altered, viz. a full-stop at *cleathing*; then the following line would refer to Meliades who is frequently compared to a *lily*, &c. — 5. 394. *lyke* : *quhyte*; the hevinlie rose with liquor new Pouderit in morrow with cristall dropis lyke The reid in equal junxit with the quhyte. *lyke* is unintelligible; perhaps for *light* if this word be allowed to rime like *plicht* : *quhyte*, 5. 910 (?), see § 417. — 5. 446. *dance* : *leising*; P. changes *leising* to *neance* (?). — 5. 588. *faire* : *cleir*; read *preclair* for *full cleir* (Lat. praeclarus). — 5. 600. *aray* : *taray*; P. reads *turnay* for *fresch taray* which arose through confusion with *fresch aray* in the 1st line. — 5. 892. *might* : *gift*, And said thay had not seine so rich ane *gift*; read *sight*. — 5. 928. *age* : *craigis*; corrupt passage. P. reads *I engage* in 2nd line. — 5. 1246. *knight* : *heart*; read *might* with P. — 5. 1532. *againe* : *hande*. Cf. 5. 2190 and 2396. — 5. 1594. *snow* : *flew*, All kynd of fleuris in the hall thay *flew*; P. reads *flow*, perhaps better *throw*. — 5. 1680. *armes* (brachia) : *armis* (arma); A "rührender reim". — 5. 1870. *veluote* : *bewate*; Hes hir dispuilʒeit of hir goune veluote And put on hir ane rosey of dew bewate. An obscure passage, but the rime may be correct, if *bewate* = *wetted*, ptc. of ME. *biwēten*, and *velvet* be derived from AFr. *veluet*, see Skeat, Princ. 1. 296, note; Bradl. gives Ital. *velluto*. — 5. 1918. *cumin*, ptc. : *windin*. Perhaps only the ptc. endings rime here; but *windin* is suspicious. — 5. 1962. *him* : *wine* (inf. OE. *winnan*); assonance. — 5. 2064. *seine* : *declyne*; *seine* is

evidently a repetition of *seine* in the previous line; P. reads *fine* =
— 5. 2190. *Brisland* : *certaine*; read *Brislaine*, cf. below 5. 2396 and
above. — 5. 2196. *knight* : *ring*; read *king* for *knight* with P. —
blaun : *auld*; P. reads *bauld* for *blaun*. — 5. 2396. *twa* : *Brisland*;
twaine for *Brislaine*; cf. 5. 2190 and 1532. — 5. 2466. *wayis* : *cheir*;
maneir for *wayis* with P. — 5. 2716. *draweit* : *aryvit*; perhaps for *d*
a wk. prt. to *dryve*? or should we read *dryves* : *aryves*? — 5. 2876. *re.*
: *mase*, Blyth was the King to heir of his rehearse Vp gois the illis
preisit in the mase Of all the schipis of King Clariodus. *rehearse* = tory,
message, but what is *mase*? and how is the rime to be explained? Si 'ar
rimes are found in Satir. P. reheirs, vb. : grace : Hercules : allace : ce
: Greice 4. 135, Wall. reherss : press 10. 86.

Most of the above are certainly the result of careful or wilful a
ations on the part of the scribes. Only a few assonances are perhaps ie
to the author.

www.ingramcontent.com/pod-product-compliance
Lightning Source LLC
Chambersburg PA
CBHW031451160426
43195CB00010BB/941